TURBULENT TIMES, TRANSFORMATIONAL POSSIBILITIES?

Gender and Politics Today and Tomorrow

Turbulent Times, Transformational Possibilities?

Gender and Politics Today and Tomorrow

EDITED BY FIONA MacDONALD AND
ALEXANDRA DOBROWOLSKY

UNIVERSITY OF TORONTO PRESS
Toronto Buffalo London

© University of Toronto Press 2020
Toronto Buffalo London
utorontopress.com
Printed in the U.S.A.

ISBN 978-1-4875-8833-5 (cloth)   ISBN 978-1-4875-8834-2 (EPUB)
ISBN 978-1-4875-8832-8 (paper)   ISBN 978-1-4875-8835-9 (PDF)

Library and Archives Canada Cataloguing in Publication

Title: Turbulent times, transformational possibilities? Gender and politics today and tomorrow / edited by Fiona MacDonald and Alexandra Dobrowolsky.
Names: MacDonald, Fiona, 1976– editor. | Dobrowolsky, Alexandra Z. (Alexandra Zorianna), 1964– editor.
Description: Includes bibliographical references and index.
Identifiers: Canadiana (print) 20200190636 | Canadiana (ebook) 20200190679 | ISBN 9781487588328 (paper) | ISBN 9781487588335 (cloth) | ISBN 9781487588342 (EPUB) | ISBN 9781487588359 (PDF)
Subjects: LCSH: Feminism—Political aspects—Canada.
Classification: LCC HQ1236.5.C2 T87 2020 | DDC 305.420971—dc23

University of Toronto Press acknowledges the financial assistance to its publishing program of the Canada Council for the Arts and the Ontario Arts Council, an agency of the Government of Ontario.

Canada Council   Conseil des Arts
for the Arts   du Canada

ONTARIO ARTS COUNCIL
CONSEIL DES ARTS DE L'ONTARIO
an Ontario government agency
un organisme du gouvernement de l'Ontario

Funded by the   Financé par le
Government   gouvernement
of Canada   du Canada

Contents

Acknowledgements

We cannot thank our contributors enough for their profound insights and inspiring research. We are extremely grateful for their prompt, patient and enthusiastic responses to our multiple requests, even when our "asks" involved very tight turnaround times! It was truly a pleasure to work with this phenomenal group of scholars. We remain in awe of their work. We would also like to express our immense gratitude to our initial UTP editor, Mat Buntin, who showed incredible enthusiasm and support in the early stages of this project (during the manuscript conception and realization stages), as well as to Marilyn McCormack and Christine Robertson, who shepherded us through the final stages of the publication process, along with the multiple, careful copy editors involved. We are indebted to University of the Fraser Valley Research Assistant Raveena Walia for her wonderful formatting wizardry; to Tracy Morrison in the UFV Research Office, who always goes above and beyond; and to Michelle Bona, a graduate student in the Masters in Gender and Women's Studies program at Saint Mary's University. Michelle was hired on a SMUWorks grant, and her multiple efforts included the early proofreading, feedback, and formatting of the first complete version of our manuscript. Overall, we have both been stimulated and motivated by our students. Indeed, it is their questions and contributions that spurred the genesis of this gender and politics volume.

Fiona would like thank her family, friends, and colleagues for their support and enthusiasm for this collection. This collection has been a passion project and the motivation has been sustained by the hard work of her students and

colleagues (you know who you are!), who are equally committed to transforming the discipline.

Alexandra would like to thank her family and her partner, Richard Devlin,
for their constant care and the multiple facets of their support. She also credits
her dog, Marta, for making sure she spends at least some time away from the
computer screen. Alexandra dedicates this book to the memory of her mother,
who experienced the most turbulent times imaginable and yet remained positive in the face of devastating forms of adversity. Her diligence and determination ensured transformational opportunities for her three daughters (Roma,
Sonia, and Alexandra) as well as for her four grandchildren (Kalina, Emma,
Alexa, and Ben) and two great-granddaughters (Kalea and Brooklyn). Halyna
Dobrowolsky passed away on May 17, 2019.

Introduction: Transforming and Transformational Gender Politics in Turbulent Times

Fiona MacDonald and Alexandra Dobrowolsky

> "There is no such thing as a single-issue struggle because we do not live single-issue lives."
>
> —Audre Lorde, 1982

A snapshot from 2019: In an online photograph of a rally in Vancouver, one of numerous demonstrations across the country in support of pipeline protestors in northwestern British Columbia (BC), we see Tilly Innes from St'at'imic Nation in a stance reflecting both determination and defiance, raising a drum overhead and leading a cheering group of Indigenous and non-Indigenous women and men.[1]

Meanwhile, on the east coast, a classroom in Halifax is filled past capacity with diverse university students, faculty, and community members. They are listening attentively to Professor Sherry Pictou, a Mi'kmaq woman, previously Chief of Bear River (L'sitkuk) First Nation and former co-chair of the World Forum of Fisher People, who evocatively explains the nature and effects of Indigenous women's struggles with patriarchy, paternalism, and settler colonialism. Dr. Pictou also acknowledges the anti-pipeline solidarity protests taking place from Halifax to Vancouver. She views them as another example of Indigenous resistance and resurgence, and ends her talk optimistically, noting that this turbulence is an indication of transformational times for Indigenous women and men.

A snapshot from 2018: Canada's prime minister Justin Trudeau hosts an international meeting of seven world leaders in Charlevoix, Quebec and dubs it a groundbreaking "Feminist G7." He also renames what was not so long ago a decidedly beleaguered Status of Women Canada agency and upgrades it to the Department of Women and Gender Equality.

Meanwhile, a report is prepared for Ontario Premier Doug Ford's Conservative government's Education Ministry. The report, dated July 25, 2018, deals with anticipated "blowback" from efforts to follow through on a Conservative party election promise to repeal the previous Liberal government's more expansive and inclusive sex-ed curriculum reforms, put in place in 2015. Ontario's Conservative government had considered "suspending sex ed entirely," but then weighed the option of rescinding mandatory learning on consent, sexting, homophobia, sexual orientation, gender identity, and gender expression. However, the drafters of this report, written for Education Minister Lisa Thompson, warned that "utilizing the curriculum last taught in 2014, with 1998 sexual health learning expectations, could be perceived by the public as outdated and not serving the needs of today's students" (quoted in Gibson 2019, n.p.).

A snapshot from 2017: The inaugural Women's March on Washington, held on January 21, is recorded as the largest single-day demonstration in US history. It also inspires sister marches around the globe in locations ranging from Antarctica to Zimbabwe (Chenoweth and Pressman 2017). In Canada, Women's Marches occurred across the country, including an estimated 50,000 marchers in Toronto, 5,000 in Calgary, 300 in Whitehorse, and a notable 15 marchers in the village of Sandy Cove, Nova Scotia, population 65 (Enloe 2017; MacMillan 2017). Marchers carried signs with various protest slogans including "Women's Rights are Human Rights," "If you Build a Wall My Generation Will Knock it Down," "Dissent Is Patriotic," "I'm with Her," and "When You're Accustomed to Privilege, Equality Feels like Oppression" (Beck 2017).

Meanwhile, the Women's March's original January 2017 platform is criticized for failing to include disability as a social justice issue and for not taking into account the march's overall inaccessibility (Bone 2017).

A snapshot from 2016: The first survey on sexual misconduct in the Canadian Armed Forces is conducted by Statistics Canada. The results: four out of five members of the military acknowledge "seeing, hearing or experiencing inappropriate sexual or discriminatory behaviour" in their workplace over the last year, with one in four women in the forces and one in three in the reserves experiencing sexual assault (Cotter 2016).

Meanwhile, at Concordia University in Montreal, Dr. Kimberley Manning and her research team begin university and community consultations to launch a groundbreaking Feminist University initiative. The goal is to develop "an institution where feminism, inclusivity and diversity are built into every aspect of the curriculum and the administration" (Stewart 2017).

A snapshot from 2015: Black Lives Matter (BLM) is described as the civil rights movement for the twenty-first century. While BLM stems from the racist indifference to African American men being shot and killed by police, queer Black women are at the forefront of BLM, and it grows to become a global movement with calls to action from Accra to Sydney and from London and Toronto to Palestine and Paris.

Meanwhile, the newly elected Liberal government of Canada announces it will launch an official inquiry into the estimated 1,200 Indigenous women and girls who have been murdered or have gone missing in Canada in the last 30 years. In making the announcement to an Assembly of First Nations special chiefs gathering in Gatineau, Quebec, Prime Minister Justin Trudeau promises a "total renewal" of the country's relationship with its Indigenous Peoples (Murphy 2015).

A snapshot from 2014: The Canadian Broadcasting Corporation fires media personality and high-profile radio show host Jian Ghomeshi after allegations of sexual assault become public. The voices of a few women grow to over 20 who allege that Ghomeshi engaged in sexual acts that included nonconsensual biting, choking, and punching.

Meanwhile, a tsunami of social media discussions ensues. Early in the process, the leader of Canada's Green Party, Elizabeth May, tweets her support of Ghomeshi, and Judy Rebick, the former president of what was once Canada's leading feminist organization, the National Action Committee on the Status of Women, re-posts a comment in praise of Ghomeshi's talent on her website, but then the tweet is retracted and the post is promptly removed as more details come to light (Sparks 2014).

For those of us studying gender politics across Canada, in the United States, or elsewhere in the world, this selection of snapshots across a five-year period highlights how, in many ways and on many levels, gender and intersecting identities are at the centre of contemporary politics.[2] These snapshots also convey that there are very different ways of learning about and transmitting gendered politics. What is more, they illustrate both the "turbulent times" we live in and some possible transformational opportunities.

There is no denying that we are living in a period of challenge and change. Wendy Brown depicts our contemporary context as one of "intensified inequality, crass commodification and commerce, ever-growing corporate influence in government, economic havoc and instability" (2015, 30). Catherine Dauvergne paints another picture of the intensity and urgency of our "current terrible moment" when she describes how "refugee camps have become a permanent feature of the global landscape ... and powerful regimes have continued to invent new and horrifying ways to infringe the human rights of their citizens" (2016, x). From species extinction to climate extremes and fierce weather events, it is also plain to see that we have reached an environmental tipping point.

Yet this turbulence may also mark a turning point, as history tells us that in times of crisis and struggle opportunities can arise and be seized and shaped. For example, contemporary feminism has increasingly been characterized by "diversity, fragmentation, and a series of internal contestations" (Budgeon 2011, 1). In the recent past, this was taken as a sign of feminism's weakness and imminent demise. However, today the discourses and practices of *feminisms* are much more pervasive. Contested features that were a cause for concern for some, or were deployed as divide and conquer tactics by others, can also be viewed as feminisms' core strengths, with significant strategic potential.

The multiplicity of feminisms also helps to explain how we presently witness the contradictions of, on the one hand, prevalent mainstreaming of feminism and, on the other, its continued mischaracterization and marginalization, particularly as it intersects with other power dynamics. For example, gender mainstreaming can have the intent of transforming gender inequalities but in effect, by focusing on gains for white, able-bodied, privileged women, it may reflect and reinforce other inequalities.

What is also evident is that gender relations are very much in flux. As Shelley Budgeon explains, this is

> due in part to advancements achieved by women; societal changes brought about by the restructuring of economies; increased cultural diversity; the proliferation and the expansion of information technologies; the dynamics of globalization and the rise of global capitalism; crises of environmental degradation; diversifying sexualities and intimate practices; changing demographics; and declining economic vitality. (2011, 1)

Because this volume focuses on gender politics in this time of turbulence and transformational possibility, some clarification of what we mean by gender, politics, and power—and what they entail—will be useful.

Gender is a criterion for differentiation. It is a "primary cultural frame for organizing social relations" (Ridgeway 2018, 10). This cultural construction is also a "powerful ideological device, which produces, reproduces, and legitimates" (West and Zimmerman 2018, 8). Sex has been a way of classifying women and men based on "socially agreed upon biological criteria," whereas gender "is the activity of managing situated conduct in light of normative conceptions of attitudes and activities appropriate for one's sex category," and as a result "gender activities emerge from and bolster claims to membership in a sex category" (3). But today, sex and gender can be viewed as far less distinct ways of defining self and other. Both can be based on shifting constructions and shared, culturally specific, stereotypes.

These stereotypes inform what we perceive, as well as what we envision. For example, social cognition research shows that "we automatically and nearly instantly sex categorize ... We do this not just in person but also over the Internet ... [or] as we examine a person's résumé ... [and] think about the kind of person we would like to hire," and this "initial framing ... never quite disappears from our understanding of them or ourselves in relation to them. Thus, we frame and are framed by gender literally before we know it" (Ridgeway 2018, 11).

Gender is also very much about power. Heteropatriarchal gender premises translate into discriminatory practices when women are, for instance, presumed to be more emotional and irrational or dependent and passive than men, whereas men are positively characterized as being more rational, independent, and political or are negatively depicted as hypermasculine and violent. Variations in sexualities and gender relations have also often been marked as deviant and/or problematically undermining of heteronorms. And so, in the past and at present, taken-for-granted assumptions as well as disciplinary actions and reactions are used to oppress and maintain gender inequalities. What is more, these gender inequalities are also often imbued with others, including racial inequalities, and in this way gender frames intersect with other forms of oppression that serve to further stratify and marginalize. As one example, a dichotomous gender order that defines and circumscribes "men" and "women" is typically the cause of transphobic discrimination and violence, which is also compounded by racialization, classism, and ableism.

Politics comes into play precisely because gender constructs, both real and imagined, are about power, and interact with both institutional and non-institutional arenas. In this volume, politics and power are broadly conceived. Politics encompasses the institutional political, or the "formal," "conventional," or "big P" politics of parliaments and political parties, which can also include the police, military, media conglomerates, and the courts. At the same time, however, the "non-institutional" political realm is also critical, and it takes into account the very broad—sometimes described as "informal" or "small p," and often unconventional and contentious—politics of collective actors outside of the state, in civil society. This can include the politics that take place on the street, on the web, and in the bedroom.

The chapters in this volume also attest to the fact that the institutional and non-institutional political are not mutually exclusive. In fact, they typically involve institutions, ideas, and identities that are very much interrelated. This volume explores the gendered politics that take place both within the state and outside it, as well as how the two are interconnected. For example, social media can spark gendered and racialized politics that can affect and mobilize individuals, families, and movements as well as politicians, parties, and governing practices. In different ways, the various chapters discuss how these gendered politics also relate to and involve public spaces, markets, families, bodies, and the land. As a result, this volume resists setting up an institutional/non-institutional "either/or" dichotomy, which would reflect the problematic binary thinking discussed below, and instead departs from and promotes more "both/and" and "in-between" perspectives.

Power, like politics, is a highly contested concept—that is, an idea that is interpreted differently by many observers. In this collection, power encompasses "power over," as in relations of oppression and domination, and is understood to be structural. For example, racism is about more than individual prejudices and involves deep and long-standing practices of institutionalized racism. The fact that Canadian prisons are disproportionately filled with Indigenous people, and that racialized men are particularly targeted for "driving while Black" or "flying while Arab," are cases in point. To be sure, these dynamics intersect with others; for example, jails are filled with people who are not only racialized, but also gendered, poor, and often disabled. Contributors to this volume consider the ramifications of various axes of oppression, including ableism, capitalism, heteropatriarchy, racism, settler colonialism, sexism, sizeism, and transphobia, among other forms of cross-cutting oppressive practices.

Power manifests through institutions but also through ideas and discourses. It is wielded by the usual political suspects (e.g., politicians, judges, and corporate leaders), but it can also be utilized by less conventional political actors (e.g., social movements). Here it is also important to acknowledge that power can play out due to both actions and inactions and can involve both decision and "nondecision" making (Bachrach and Baratz 1962). It can also involve unconscious ideologies, the "manufacturing of consent" (Herman and Chomsky 2002), and unseen and unrecognized, omnipresent and pervasive manifestations of power (Foucault 1988).

However, the contributors to this collection also recognize the influence and impact of "power to"; that is, collective actors' emancipatory efforts and struggles to effect social, political, economic, and cultural change. They illustrate not only how and why multiple, interconnected power systems are at play but also how and why individuals and groups exercise their agency and seize and shape political opportunities, even in contexts of constraint, and in so doing challenge dominant, complex, and intersecting power relations. A few contributors also point to "alterNative" understandings (Ladner 2003) of power in relation to a much more expansive and interdependent ecological context. In these ways, although the authors are diverse, deal with a wide array of subject matter, and draw on different theories and methods, they share complementary, critical, and alternative perspectives that reflect a commitment to anti-oppression politics and intersectional approaches (see Nath, Tungohan, and Gaucher 2018).

Within various activist and academic circles, intersectionality has become an important lens through which to uncover, analyse, and respond to questions of injustice, especially for those working on issues of gender and politics. While intersectionality is also a contested concept, there appears to be an emerging consensus on its general meaning and significance. As Patricia Hill Collins and Sirma Bilge state, the "complexity" of "human experiences" lies at the centre of all intersectional analysis and activities (2016, 2).

As a theoretical framework, intersectionality is grounded in the premise that our lives are shaped by many different events and conditions. Given these complexities, it follows that we cannot identify or analyse our experiences by examining only one aspect of our lives. Instead, as Nath, Tungohan, and Gaucher explain, we need approaches that uncover how the many different elements of the world we live in impact us in diverse yet mutually reinforcing ways. This kind of intersectional lens allows us to fully consider how inter-locking power structures and intersecting forms of discrimination work in tandem to create injustice (2018, 620).

The growing recognition and application of intersectional analysis are best understood in the context of the activist work that inspired its devel-opment. Intersectional analysis is rooted in the insights of women of colour who found their experiences and needs glaringly absent from many social movements actively engaged in pursuing social change. The ideas present in contemporary approaches to intersectionality can be traced to the nineteenth-century activisms of African American women, including Maria Stewart and Sojourner Truth, and the various global activisms of the 1960s and 1970s (Hancock 2016).

In the late 1980s and early 1990s, intersectionality, as articulated by leading scholars Kimberlé Crenshaw and Patricia Hill Collins, became an important academic approach in law, gender, and anti-oppression research. In her highly influential article "Mapping the Margins: Intersectionality, Identity Politics, and Violence against Women of Color," Crenshaw argues:

> Among the most troubling political consequences of the failure of antiracist and feminist discourses to address the intersections of race and gender is the fact that, to the extent they can forward the inter-est of "people of color" and "women," respectively, one analysis often implicitly denies the validity of the other. The failure of feminism to interrogate race means that the resistance strategies of feminism will often replicate and reinforce the subordination of people of color, and the failure of antiracism to interrogate patriarchy means that antiracism will frequently reproduce the subordination of women. These mutual elisions present a particularly difficult political dilemma for women of color. (1991, 1252)

Crenshaw's experience in both Black and feminist activist circles was instru-mental in the development of her intersectional approach. She found that her experiences were not represented in either of these social movements; and as a result, both of these activist movements reinforced rather than challenged her marginal position. For Crenshaw, the only way to build meaningful move-ments for change was to ground said movements in intersectionality and, in so doing, to represent the different intersections of privilege and oppression experienced by group members.

This intersectional approach is also well represented in Indigenous women's scholarship and activism. Patricia Monture-Angus explains:

> I am not just woman. I am a Mohawk woman. It is not solely my gender through which I first experience the world, it is my culture (and/or race) that precedes my gender. Actually, if I am an object of some form of discrimination, it is very difficult for me to separate what happens to me because of my gender and what happens to me because of my race and culture. My world is not experienced in a linear and compartmentalized way. I experience the world simultaneously as Mohawk and as woman. It seems I cannot repeat this message too many times. To artificially separate my gender from my race and culture forces me to deny the way in which I experience the world. Such denial has devastating effects on Aboriginal constructions of reality. (quoted in Hancock 2016, n.p.; see also Monture-Angus 1995, 177–78)

Contemporary Indigenous feminists thus seek to "shed light on Indigenous women's experiences of heteropatriarchal and colonial oppression" and take up the various intersecting forms of oppression they face by not only resisting but also "revisiting and renewing relationships" (Starblanket 2017, 21, 37).

The fusion of different power structures and discriminatory practices is central to an intersectional approach. Hancock (2016) aptly observes that intersectionality is often interpreted to mean that we should understand the self or "identity" as made up of discrete or separate parts, because when we consider the idea of two or more things "intersecting" we often imagine a kind of Venn diagram with distinct circles that overlap in some areas and remain separate in others. The picture we get from this imagery suggests that each aspect of the self (e.g., gender or race) exists both inside and outside of the intersection. Yet, Hancock explains, this interpretation misrepresents the fuller theory of intersectionality and can result in its misapplication. Intersectionality, she argues, is *not* a framework for disaggregating identity but is rather an approach that reveals the interconnections that exist between and within identities: "In other words, there are no *nonintersecting* areas in the diagram" (n.p.).

Engaging with relationality as a key concept for intersectional analyses can help guard against the dangers of disaggregating identity. Conceptualizing intersectionality as a lens that uncovers and examines interconnections both within the self and between the self and others has been central for intersectionality as theory and praxis throughout its development, and yet this often remains an underexplored aspect. As May asserts, much feminist scholarship and praxis that claim to be "intersectional" often upholds binary-oriented either/or thinking and essentialist approaches to both identity and politics (2015, ix).

Thinking relationally encourages analyses of the in-between rather than either/or binary thinking. Hill Collins and Bilge maintain that "the focus on relationality shifts from analysing what distinguishes entities, for example, the differences between race and gender, to examining their interconnections. This shift in perspective opens up intellectual and political possibilities" (2016, 27–28). From an intersectional standpoint, both individuals and groups are understood as internally heterogeneous. This perspective emphasizes the heterogeneity of all agents and seeks out the complex intersectional relations of power that constrain and enable particular agents in particular contexts, with the goal of revealing and encouraging coalition building. As discussed below, this collection is, in many ways, a coalition-building effort, not only between the authors brought together in the volume but also with the students and various other readers who choose to engage with the ideas offered in the pages that follow.

THE INSPIRATION AND THE INTENT

"I've been doing intersectionality my whole life. I just didn't call it that."

—Janel Jack, 2019

The genesis for this collection can be found not only within recent currents of turbulence and transformation that show how gender is central to politics at multiple scales, locally, nationally, and globally, but also comes directly from the students in our classes over the last decade or so. In developing this edited collection, we are informed by our experiences in the classroom as we witness the transformation(s) that happen when students first encounter a framework that provides meaning and/or makes sense of their lived experiences. The statement above from one of our students speaks to the significance of intersectionality in giving a name to the realities many of us encounter and seek to challenge. This edited collection comes from our desire to offer scholarship grounded in an intersectional approach that is informed by our experiences as feminist scholars and teachers in political science.

The classroom, for students and professors alike, is a central place in which to consider these currents, and to both learn and "unlearn" in ways that help us to understand the complex meanings, processes, and outcomes they bring and how we might create change. In political science, the structure of our discipline is a barrier to deeply intersectional inquiry and analysis. This is clearly evidenced by the way in which we compartmentalize different aspects of the field, particularly those related to gender, race, sexuality, disability, and Indigeneity—areas of research that are often referred to collectively as "gender and diversity" work within political science.

As Nath, Tungohan, and Gaucher contend, this compartmentalization reinforces a disciplinary structure that understands issues of gender and diversity as "that which is 'other'" and, as such, marginal within the study of politics (2018, 620). As a result, political science has remained a discipline in which the study of gender, race, disability, and Indigeneity are all siloed as "special" or "niche" areas of focus in the study of politics. Thus, while scholars working within feminist, critical race, and anti-oppression frameworks are increasingly drawing on intersectionality to challenge the notion that we can understand any kind of political phenomenon without directly engaging with all aspects of injustice, the structure of political science is itself a major impediment to intersectional scholarship and, according to Tolley, works to maintain the "male-centric" orientation of the discipline (2017, 143). As Tolley further explains, "political science mirrors the world that it analyzes: the gender gaps identified in broader political structures exist in our profession, approaches and scholarly research" (144). While Tolley's focus is particularly on the position of gender in the discipline, the same challenges are present for those working on issues of race, Indigeneity, sexuality, and disability, and therefore none of these areas of inquiry have been "mainstreamed" (i.e., centrally located and incorporated throughout) in political science. Identifying and challenging these silos is part of bringing intersectionality to political science. As Hancock argues, it is "the politics of knowledge production that is at the heart of intersectionality's critique" (2016, n.p.). With this objective in mind, the motivation for this book is four-fold:

First, within the last few years there have been a number of remarkable shifts in politics on the international, national, provincial, municipal, and even street levels that are fundamentally connected to issues of gender. While Canada will remain a key point of reference, the intent of this collection is to illustrate gendered political dynamics at multiple scales: macro, meso, and micro, encompassing global and local trends. Moreover, beyond examining contemporary challenges, this volume explores avenues for change now and into the future.

Second, this volume aims to provide a more complex treatment of both gender and politics, in that gender is examined in light of other collective identities and their intersections, and politics encompasses the institutional and non-institutional political as mutually constitutive, with close attention paid to movement and countermovement politics and their interconnections.

Third, while courses, conferences, and debates in political science have shifted from "women and politics" to "gender and politics," the publications currently available in the discipline largely continue to discuss women and politics but fail to engage with both gender and feminist politics more broadly. For instance, with respect to gender, there is very little scholarship in the field on the timely and complex topics of masculinities and politics and transgender politics (see MacDonald 2017). As a result, political scientists interested in discussing and/or teaching these subjects are forced to turn to publications in other disciplines, such as sociology or cultural and queer studies.

Fourth, this collection showcases the scholarship of a wide and exciting range of scholars who are at different stages of their careers (i.e., in their early, mid, and later years) and from various backgrounds and standpoints. It also features the work of academics affiliated with larger and smaller universities from across Canada, as well as several scholars who are internationally based. Overall, the intent is to foreground research and writing by new and emerging scholars along with more established academics working in innovative, forward-looking areas.

While our contributors are diverse, using multiple forms of analysis and methodologies, they all work to support our anti-oppression, intersectional project and share a commitment to a "praxis perspective" described by Hill Collins and Bilge as involving not "merely apply[ing] scholarly knowledge" to a social or political problem, but instead using "knowledge learned within everyday life to reflect on those experiences as well as on scholarly knowledge" (2016, 42).

THE STRUCTURE AND CONTENTS

Given the foregoing, this volume is divided into two, albeit highly interrelated, sections: part 1, "Transforming Institutions and Ideas: Turbulent Times and Ongoing Struggles," and part 2, "Non-Institutional and Intersectional Politics: Feminisms, Allies, Affect, and Anger." In part 1 we consider the more conventional dimensions of the discipline, although in less conventional ways. Here, the chapters serve to showcase significant subfields in the discipline of political science (e.g., Canadian politics, comparative politics, law and public policy, international political economy, international relations, and political thought/political theory). However, these chapters also illustrate that such subdisciplinary boundaries are often blurred and overlapping. In addition, while the chapters in part 1 deal with key institutions (e.g., legislatures, executives, the judiciary, the media, and the military), the authors provide novel interpretations as they explore these areas with a more ideas-based and actor-based approach.

Indeed, some chapters in part 1 could easily be situated in part 2, and vice versa. For example, because chapter 8, in part 1, considers the social movement implications of "hashtag feminism," it fits very well with the emphases found in part 2. However, it appears in part 1 for several reasons. For a start, in the discipline of political science the media have often been studied as political institutional phenomena, and/or as phenomena with political institutional repercussions. Second, because the chapter also discusses the broader implications of political ideas and discourses, it dovetails well with themes found in other chapters in part 1. Third, by positioning chapter 8 in part 1 we are also making the point that social movements are very much part and parcel of formal politics. Similarly, chapter 10, on the Quebec women's movement, launches part 2, but it could logically appear in part 1, as Quebec politics is crucial to the study of political science in Canada. Moreover, chapter 10 explores how changing forms of the Quebec state are very much connected to the transformations of Quebec feminisms. However, we have chosen this chapter's placement carefully, as it serves as a critical linking chapter between the two parts of the volume and obviously shows their interrelations. Now, for even greater clarity, let us examine the contents of the chapters more systematically.

The first three chapters serve as a backdrop to, and shed light on, several dimensions of Canadian politics in the Justin Trudeau Liberal era. In chapter

1, Alexandra Dobrowolsky critically examines manifestations of contemporary liberalisms, neoliberalisms, and feminisms in Canada and distinguishes them from those in the United States. By tracing the roots of the 2015–19 Liberal government's approach to equality and diversity, she contextualizes its "feminist" discourses and contributions, as well as its supposedly kinder and gentler policies around (im)migration and refugees, ultimately showing how these priorities benefit the few as opposed to the many. In chapter 2, Stephanie Paterson and Francesca Scala home in on the promise and pitfalls of the Trudeau government's gender-based analysis pledges. Through post-structural policy analysis, they reveal that the Trudeau Liberal government's efforts ultimately illustrate *governance feminism* more than feminist government. This is followed by a systematic stocktaking of the Trudeau government's agenda in chapter 3. Here, Jeanette Ashe develops and employs a novel methodology based on 32 indicators to calibrate the extent of gender sensitivity actually at play. Trudeau's poor scorecard ultimately illustrates "Facebook feminism" more than real change.

In chapter 4, we move from parliament and policy to law, the courts, public discourse, and the public arena in Canada. Elaine Craig provides a scathing account of the courts' response to three high-profile sexual assault cases. Women's mistreatment at the hands of judges and lawyers serves to illustrate not only the social and legal phenomena that continue to deter sexually assaulted women from coming forward but also the ongoing role played by discriminatory gender-based stereotypes.

Chapter 5, by Gina Starblanket, provides an important theoretical intervention, drawn from problematic, real-life practices. By examining the power dynamics of settler-colonial violence and how they intersect with other forms of oppression, including heteronormative power relations, Starblanket reveals that gendered identity categories have been "imposed, resisted, and repurposed within Indigenous communities and particularly in movements towards Indigenous decolonization and resurgence." In so doing, Starblanket insightfully distinguishes Indigenous feminist discourse from contemporary discourses around Indigenous masculinity and femininity.

The subfields of Canadian politics and international relations are represented in chapter 6, as Maya Eichler offers a close and careful study of military and defence policy in Canada. After providing an account of its ultramasculinist associations, Eichler assesses recent efforts at reform through an analysis of the military's use of gendered language and gender strategies that include gender balancing, gender mainstreaming, and transforming gendered culture.

Isabel Altamirano-Jiménez exposes the shortfall between Canada's words and its deeds vis-à-vis Indigenous peoples through an account of its mining practices abroad. In chapter 7, she uses the anti-mining struggles of the Zapotec community of Capulalpam, Oaxaca, Mexico as a case study and draws on Indigenous feminist body land sensibilities to highlight Canada's hypocritical practices both locally and globally. In doing so, she brings together insights from the field of international political economy and cutting-edge feminist, Indigenous theorization.

Chapter 8 examines the omnipresent contemporary politics of social media. Various media (e.g., newspapers, radio, and television) have had long-standing effects on both the institutional and non-institutional political not only through "watchdog" roles but also by mobilizing ideas and discourses as well as political actors, including those in civil society, political parties, and the state. And of course the media have also been very much implicated in perpetuating exclusionary portrayals that are gendered, racialized, classed, heterosexist, and the list continues (see for example Tolley 2016; Wagner et al. 2017). However, Tamara A. Small's chapter focuses on the more recent institutional, ideational, and mobilizational manifestations of social media. More specifically, Small weighs the benefits and costs of "hashtag feminism," revealing the transformative impact(s) of online feminist action as well as the challenges (both old and new) that accompany this method of activism in these turbulent times.

In the final chapter in part 1, Toby Rollo provides a contemporary take on long-standing debates in political thought with his review of feminist theory and its treatment of both women and children. In so doing, he focuses on a frequently overlooked aspect of feminist thought: the relationship between childhood and the reproduction of patriarchy. Rollo's co-emancipatory analysis suggests that feminism(s) that fail to engage with children, both as subjects of oppression and agents of resistance, will always be problematic and incomplete.

Part 2 focuses on the non-institutional political, but in ways that show how it very much impacts the institutional political. Chapter 10 opens part 2 and highlights these interrelations, along with the existence and interplay of multiple feminisms, and how both can result in challenges as well as opportunities. The authors, Pascale Dufour and Geneviève Pagé, examine the distinguishing features of the Quebec feminist movement and the pivotal transformations it has recently experienced. These include significantly changed relations with the Quebec state, given funding restrictions and cuts, but also the ideological and theoretical changes that have taken place within the movement as some feminist groups grapple with intersectionality and others forge new linkages, including with Indigenous communities in and beyond Quebec.

In chapter 11, Debra Thompson traces the growth of BLM and its intersectional politics. By vividly portraying its gendered political strategies, she illustrates both the pivotal role of Black, queer women in this movement and the transformative potential of social movements more broadly. Conversely, Alexa DeGagne shows how movement successes and what were once transformative practices can be overtaken by much less progressive forces. In chapter 12 she depicts how the turbulent, radical LGBTQ Pride parades of the past have transformed into the present-day corporate-sponsored, "family friendly," and pro-police celebrations that epitomize Pride's "pinkwashing."

In chapter 13, Sarah Marie Wiebe details Indigenous mobilization and Indigenous women's contributions to environmental struggles that seek to circumvent extractive politics based on colonial governmentality. She draws lessons from her comparative case study of actions taken in Burnaby Mountain on Coast Salish territory in BC and around Mauna a Wākea, the highest mountain in Hawai'i, calling for an environmental justice approach informed by Indigenous feminist thought, ecofeminism, and queer theories.

Chapter 14 considers transfeminist politics transnationally. Chamindra Kumari Weerawardhana calls on scholars of politics and international relations, particularly feminist scholars, to expand their epistemologies by centring the praxis of transfeminist-of-colour activism(s). Transfeminist-of-colour activism, Weerawardhana illustrates, is an advocacy philosophy that offers rich transformative possibilities for intersectional solidarity-building and collaboration that both celebrate differences and go beyond difference.

In chapter 15, Stacy Clifford Simplican builds on feminist scholarship to explain why political science needs to take disability seriously and how disability activists can respond to turbulent times and other movement politics. Disability, she argues, highlights important omissions in our conceptions of citizenship and what counts as "political" behaviour, as well as in intersectional analyses limited to gender, race, class, nationality, and sexuality. She calls for a multi-faceted approach that helps us to better understand the meaning, and major significance, of disability to contemporary politics.

Michael Orsini unpacks the discourses and politics around the governance of body weight in chapter 16. This chapter considers contentious cultural and policy narratives around obesity and fatness, how they are inextricably linked to the affects and emotions they engender and produce, and how these affects and emotions are in turn structured by complex relations around race, gender, class, and disability.

Last but not least, in chapter 17 John Grant and Fiona MacDonald examine the politics of masculinism and masculinity by considering the interplay between the alt-right countermovement, populisms, toxic masculinity, and violence. They outline why political science, particularly feminist political science, will benefit from engaging deeply with these topics and offer insight into how the current political terrain might be challenged through a transformative approach to masculinity/ies.

In sum, the chapters in this volume not only document but try to make sense of these turbulent times, and in so doing seek to identify transformational opportunities now and into the future. Let us now turn to this critical, challenging, and necessary endeavour.

NOTES

1 See the image at https://www.ctvnews.ca/canada/demonstrations-block-traffic-in
   -support-of-indigenous-pipeline-protesters-in-b-c-1.4244872.
2 As editors of this volume on gender and politics, we are compelled to situate
   ourselves and our "authorial position" (de Leeuw and Hunt 2018, 3). We are
   clearly privileged women, not only because we are tenured professors, but
   also because we are white, able-bodied, heterosexual, and cis female Canadian
   citizens. At the same time, as feminist academics and activists we are
   committed to shedding light on multiple power relations, those that sustain
   oppressive practices and those that work to subvert them. Although we are
   ambivalent about ever more present—but often seemingly perfunctory—land
   acknowledgements, as settlers and allies we acknowledge these territories
   in order to recognize historic, and present-day, settler colonialism with its
   multiple and ongoing ramifications. Alexandra Dobrowolsky is the daughter
   of Ukrainian settler-immigrants. She was born in Sudbury, Ontario, which
   is located in the Robinson-Huron Treaty territory, on the lands of the
   Atikameksheng Anishnawbek and the Wahnapitae First Nations and with
   a strong Métis presence. She works at Saint Mary's University, and lives
   in Halifax, Nova Scotia, located in Mi'kma'ki, the ancestral and unceded

territory of the Mi'kmaq People. Fiona MacDonald was born in Aberdeen, Scotland, and settled in Canada as an infant with her Scottish immigrant father and settler Canadian mother. She grew up in Brandon, Manitoba, which is situated in Treaty 1 and 2 territory. She now works at the University of the Fraser Valley in Abbotsford, BC. This territory is the unceded land of the Stó:lō (people of the river).

REFERENCES

Bachrach, Peter, and Morton S. Baratz. 1962. "The Two Faces of Power." *American Political Science Review* 56 (4): 947–52.

Beck, Laura. 2017. "The 49 'Nastiest' Signs from the Worldwide Women's March." *Cosmopolitan*, January 22. https://www.cosmopolitan.com/politics/a8616050/womens-march-washington-best-signs/.

Bone, Kristen Marie. 2017. "Trapped behind the Glass: Crip Theory and Disability Identity." *Disability and Society* 32 (9): 1297–314.

Brown, Wendy. 2015. *Undoing the Demos: Neoliberalism's Stealth Revolution.* 2015. New York: Zone Books.

Budgeon, Shelley. 2011. *Third Wave Feminism and the Politics of Gender in Later Modernity.* Houndmills, UK: Palgrave Macmillan.

Chenowith, Erica, and Jeremy Pressman. 2017. "This Is What We Learned by Counting the Women's Marches." *Washington Post*, February 7. https://www.washingtonpost.com/news/monkey-cage/wp/2017/02/07/this-is-what-we-learned-by-counting-the-womens-marches/?utm_term=.0840454acdfa.

Cotter, Adam. 2016. "Sexual Misconduct in the Canadian Armed Forces, 2016." Statistics Canada, Catalogue No. 85-603-X. https://www150.statcan.gc.ca/n1/pub/85-603-x/85-603-x2016001-eng.htm.

Crenshaw, Kimberlé. 1991. "Mapping the Margins: Intersectionality, Identity Politics, and Violence against Women of Color." *Stanford Law Review* 43 (6): 1241–99.

Dauvergne, Catherine. 2016. *The New Politics of Immigration and the End of Settler Societies.* Cambridge: Cambridge University Press.

de Leeuw, Sarah, and Sarah Hunt. 2018. "Unsettling Decolonizing Geographies." *Geography Compass* 12 (7): e12376. https://doi.org/10.1111/gec3.12376.

Enloe, Cynthia. 2017. *The Big Push: Exposing and Challenging the Persistence of Patriarchy.* Oakland: University of California Press.

Foucault, Michel. 1988. *Politics, Philosophy, Culture: Interviews and Other Writings 1977–1984*, edited by Lawrence D. Kritzman, trans. Alan Sheridan and others. New York: Routledge.

Gibson, Victoria. 2019. "Human-Rights Case Reveals Ontario Considered Removing Sex-Ed Classes Completely." *Globe and Mail*, February 1. https://www.theglobeandmail.com/canada/article-hrto-case-reveals-ontario-government-considered-removing-sex-ed/.

Hancock, Ange-Marie. 2016. *Intersectionality: An Intellectual History*. Oxford: Oxford University Press.

Herman, Edward S., and Noam Chomsky. 2002. *Manufacturing Consent: The Political Economy of the Mass Media*. New York: Pantheon Books.

Hill Collins, Patricia, and Sirma Bilge. 2016. *Intersectionality*. Cambridge: Policy Press.

Ladner, Kiera L. 2003. "Governing within an Ecological Context: Creating an AlterNative Understanding of Blackfoot Governance." *Studies in Political Economy* 70 (1): 125–52.

MacDonald, Fiona. 2017. "Knocking Down Walls in Political Science: In Defence of an Expansionist Feminist Agenda." *Canadian Journal of Political Science* 50 (2): 411–26.

MacMillan, Jennifer. 2017. "Nova Scotia Village Hosts One of the Smallest Women's Marches, but It's Still Mighty." *CBC News*, January 23. https://www.cbc.ca/news /canada/nova-scotia/women-s-march- on-washington-sandy-cove-digby-neck -donald-trump-1.2899568.

May, Vivian M. 2015. *Pursuing Intersectionality: Unsettling Dominant Imaginaries*. New York: Routledge.

Monture-Angus, Patricia. 1995. *Thunder in My Soul: A Mohawk Woman Speaks*. Halifax: Fernwood.

Murphy, Jessica. 2015. "Canada Launches Inquiry into Murdered and Missing Indigenous Women." *The Guardian*, December 8. https://www.theguardian.com /world/2015/dec/08/ canada-40m-inquiry-violence-indigenous-women-justin -trudeau.

Nath, Nisha, Ethel Tungohan, and Megan Gaucher. 2018. "The Future of Canadian Political Science: Boundary Transgressions, Gender and Anti-Oppression Frameworks." *Canadian Journal of Political Science* 51 (3): 619–42.

Ridgeway, Cecilia L. 2018. "Framed before We Know It: How Gender Shapes Social Relations." In *Gendered Lives, Sexual Beings: A Feminist Anthology*, edited by Joya Misra, Mahal Dyer Stewart, and Marni Alyson Brown, 10–16. Thousand Oaks, CA: Sage.

Sparks, Riley. 2014. "Elizabeth May, Judy Rebick Revisit Ghomeshi Comments." *Toronto Star*, October 28. https://www.thestar.com/news/canada/2014/10/28 /elizabeth_may_judy_rebick_revisit_ghomeshi_comments.html.

Starblanket, Gina. 2017. "Being Indigenous Feminists: Resurgences against Contemporary Patriarchy." In *Making Space for Indigenous Feminism,* edited by Joyce Green, 21–41. Halifax: Fernwood.

Stewart, Savannah. 2017. "Concordia's Simone de Beauvoir Institute Launches Feminist University Initiative." *The Link*, October 22. https://thelinknewspaper.ca /article/concordias-simone-de-beauvoir-institute-launches-feminist-university -initia.

Tolley, Erin. 2016. *Framed: Media and the Coverage of Race in Canadian Politics*. Vancouver: UBC Press.

———. 2017. "Into the Mainstream or Still at the Margins? 50 Years of Gender Research in the Canadian Political Science Association." *Canadian Journal of Political Science* 50 (1): 143–61. https://doi.org/10.1017/S0008423916001177.

Wagner, Angelia, Linda Trimble, Shannon Sampert, and Bailey Gerrits. 2017. "Gender, Competitiveness, and Candidate Visibility in Newspaper Coverage of Canadian Party Leadership Contests." *The International Journal of Press/Politics* 22 (4): 471–89.

West, Candace, and Don H. Zimmerman. 2018. "Doing Gender." In *Gendered Lives, Sexual Beings: A Feminist Anthology*, edited by Joya Misra, Mahal Dyer Stewart, and Marni Alyson Brown, 3–9. Thousand Oaks, CA: Sage.

PART ONE

Transforming Institutions and Ideas: Turbulent Times and Ongoing Struggles

1

A Diverse, Feminist "Open Door" Canada? Trudeau-Styled Equality, Liberalisms, and Feminisms

Alexandra Dobrowolsky[1]

Key terms: diversity, equality, human capital, neoliberal feminism, neoliberalism, rollback and rollout neoliberalism, social investment, social liberalism

INTRODUCTION

In the 2015 election campaign, and throughout their 2015–19 term in office, the Justin Trudeau-led Liberals were intent on portraying Canada in a very different light from that of Stephen Harper's three previous Conservative governments (two minority governments in 2006 and 2008 and one majority in 2011), harkening back to an earlier Liberal/liberal era (Hadfield 2017) when Pierre Elliot Trudeau was prime minister (1968–79 and 1980–84). Trudeau senior was known for his views on a "Just Society,"[2] as well as his role in establishing Canada's Charter of Rights and Freedoms, including its commitment to **equality** and constitutional entrenchment of multiculturalism. Now his son championed similar ideals and went further by identifying as a feminist. Since "it was 2015," Justin quipped, a gender-balanced cabinet was long overdue; and he proceeded to proclaim various "feminist" firsts, including two "feminist" budgets and a "feminist" foreign policy agenda (see Eichler in this volume) leading to a "feminist" G7 summit (the June 2018 international meeting of seven world leaders hosted by Canada in Charlevoix, Quebec). An inquiry into missing and murdered Indigenous women and girls (MMIWG) was launched, along with initiatives to support 2LGBTQ communities and a national dialogue on racism. The Liberal government also promised to apply "GBA+" (gender-based analysis plus; see the chapters by Ashe and Paterson and Scala in this volume) to its policy development and upgraded the office of Status of Women of Canada (SWC) to a Department for Women and Gender Equality (WAGE).

Conversely, the Harper government had sought to disempower equality seekers; eradicated markers of equality, both symbolic and institutional (Dobrowolsky 2015); let GBA atrophy; and refused to establish a MMIWG inquiry. It also undercut Canada's multicultural reputation (Abu-Laban 2015) and was accused of sparking an exclusionary "culture war" (Radwanski 2015). Justin Trudeau, on the other hand, proclaimed: "Canada's back" (Canadian Press 2015), welcoming newcomers of all kinds (immigrants, refugees, and asylum seekers) with open arms and "open door" allusions. Some of Trudeau's rhetoric was realized in short order, by, for example, fulfilling the Liberal campaign pledge to admit 25,000 Syrian refugees and by appointing a cabinet that reflected Trudeau's ubiquitous refrain of "diversity is our strength." By 2017, the Liberal government had repealed exclusionary elements of the Conservative government's citizenship act, and by 2018 it had allocated $23 million over two years for multiculturalism and an anti-racist plan (Levitz 2018).

Yet Trudeau's words and deeds contained multiple versions of liberalism and feminism. More specifically, emergent **neoliberal feminism** combined with long-standing market and **human capital** (i.e., skills, knowledge, education, and experience considered to be valuable and marketable) priorities translated into policies that benefited the few rather than the many, when gender, race, and class are taken into consideration. This chapter thus illustrates that the Liberal government's hallmark feminist and immigration initiatives fall short when viewed through the lens of intersectionality, calling into question the depth and breadth of its achievements around equality and **diversity**. The first section reviews different manifestations of liberalism and feminism in Canada, with the United States used as a point of contrast and comparison. The second section shows how a mix of **social investment** and **rollout neoliberal** and neoliberal feminist ideas and practices have influenced Justin Trudeau's agenda. The lack of intersectional analysis in immigration policies' market and human capital logic, at both federal and provincial levels, is explored in section three. Section four considers what all this tells us about the future of transformational gendered politics, equality, and diversity in Canada.

Transformational politics occur when key political actors put progressive ideas into motion with tangible effects. However, ideas, meanings, and discourses can also replicate structural forces as actors seize political opportunities and make political choices, but do so in the context of broader socioeconomic constraints. Thus, as we shall see, such ongoing struggles between agency and structure can also result in retrogressive outcomes.

VARIETIES OF LIBERALISM AND FEMINISM IN CANADA, WITH THE UNITED STATES AS A COUNTERPOINT

Leading historical analysts of political culture have contrasted Canada and the United States (typically disregarding Indigenous contributions; see Henderson 2007). Focusing on the ideas of British colonists in the United States (Hartz 1964), or the key "formative event" of the American Revolution (Lipset 1986), they explain how liberalism, with its prioritization of individualism, antipathy to state interference in people's private lives, and laissez-faire approach to the marketplace, became dominant in the United States. This is then counterposed to Canada's "Tory touch," which gave rise to a combination of liberal, conservative, and socialist ideologies more conducive to an active state (Horowitz 1966; Lipset 1986; Wiseman 1988). Unlike the United States, then, Canada reflected **social liberalism** (Mahon 2009, 50–51), "a synthesis of individualist and collectivist values" that "took greater notice of the social circumstances" that "conditioned individual choices" (O'Connor, Orloff, and Shaver 1999, 49–50).

Canada is also routinely depicted as a "mosaic" as opposed to the American "melting pot." More accurately, Canada had its own assimilationist model (with its racialization of non-British immigrants as well as its genocidal response to Indigenous people), but this was somewhat attenuated in the 1970s by shifts in immigration policy. Moreover, ethnic minority group activism provided the catalyst for a more tolerant discourse of multiculturalism (Kymlicka 2014, 23), and although Pierre Trudeau was very much a liberal individualist, he cultivated multiculturalism in policy and constitutionally as a unifying symbol that would prop up Canadian nationalism and counter Quebec nationalist forces (La Selva 2014, 10).

While P.E. Trudeau-era Charter guarantees made Canada renowned for its "creative mechanisms for accommodating difference" (Kymlicka 2014, 21), particular pivotal movements were the genesis of its multicultural and egalitarian ideals. Collective action resulted in Canada's constitutional entrenchment of group rights, including those for Aboriginal peoples,[3] racial minorities, and persons with disability, as well as the subsequent recognition of discrimination on the basis of sexual orientation (Smith 2005).

Modern "Western feminism grew up as a sister doctrine to liberalism" (Abbey 2011, 1). However, unlike mainstream American feminism's reformist classical liberalism, the dominant strands of feminism in Canada also had a social liberal caste, with significant socialist feminist and, in Quebec, nationalist dimensions (see Dufour and Pagé in this volume). This made Canadian feminisms not only more statist but also more "progressive in many important ways" (Vickers, Rankin, and Appelle 1993, 24). A vivid illustration of the different contexts in question is the fact that American feminist efforts to obtain an equal rights amendment in the US Constitution failed in the 1970s, while pan-Canadian feminist mobilization in the 1980s (albeit with notable dissent in Quebec) resulted in two Charter equality sections (15 and 28), as well as a provision for "affirmative action" (Dobrowolsky 2000).

Despite these contrasts, Canada and the United States have been affected by larger socio-economic forces, producing commonalities that have impacted both the nature and forms of their liberalisms and their equality seekers. For instance, the Great Depression of the 1930s resulted in state interventionism in both countries, while 40 years later a wide-scale economic downturn produced a "crisis of Keynesianism" and prepared the ground for a rise in neoliberal theories and practices (Bradford 1998).

Neoliberalism downsized social programs, deregulated (i.e., provided a freer rein for markets and private companies), and devolved responsibilities onto families and communities. It also became a "peculiar form of reason" configuring "all aspects of existence in economic terms," from "vocabularies, principles of justice, political cultures, habits of citizenship, practices of rule, and above all democratic imaginaries" (Brown 2015, 17). In this way, "distinctly political meanings" such as equality, or an array of policies, including those around social welfare and immigration, gave way to "economic valences" and "market metrics," leading democracies to be conceived as requiring "technically skilled human capital, not educated participants in public life" (177).

Neoliberalism has no "pure" form, but is rather a "complex and often contradictory phenomenon" that encompasses "a diverse range of practices"

(Kantola and Squires 2012, 385). For example, **rollback neoliberalism** involves reconfiguring the state and dismantling its social programs, while offloading responsibilities onto the market, the community, and/or the family. As a result, it encompasses the "destruction or discreditation of Keynesian-welfarist and social-collectivist institutions" (Peck and Tickell 2002, 37) typified by British Prime Minister Margaret Thatcher and American President Ronald Reagan. Rollback neoliberalism has been distinguished from rollout neoliberalism, which is characterized by "the purposeful construction of neoliberalized state forms, modes of governance, and regulatory relations" (Peck and Tickell 2002, 37). In other words, rollback neoliberalism shrinks "the social," whereas rollout neoliberalism spreads economic rationales into broader realms of social existence, perpetuating discourses like "social economy" or "social cohesion" and ones that prevent "social exclusion" rather than promote equality.

Neoliberalism is also not a monolithic, immutable force (Clarke 2008). In 1980s and early 1990s America, the approach was punitive towards some women (i.e., racialized, single mothers, who were especially besieged), while Canada's first neoliberal proponents, Progressive Conservative Prime Ministers Brian Mulroney and Kim Campbell, adopted a "lite" form of neoliberalism (Bashevkin 1998). Here, fully fledged rollback neoliberalism was not effectively implemented until the mid-1990s under Jean Chrétien's Liberals, with, for example, the scaling back and shutting down of supports for women in and outside the state, the delegitimization of so-called "special interests" (i.e., equality seekers), and ever more explicit neoliberal rationales in the field of immigration (Abu-Laban 1998, 2009).

Neoliberalism's spread was neither uniform nor uninterrupted. These ideas took longer to impact the Canadian Supreme Court's decisions around equality (Dobrowolsky 2009a) and other areas of governance, such as Indigenous relations (MacDonald 2011). Moreover, by the late 1990s, upon eliminating Canada's deficit, the Liberals raised spending again. Yet this was not portrayed as welfare state "social spending" but rather social investment (Jenson and Saint-Martin 2003). This "third way" approach, a path between neoliberalism and welfare liberalism, had been sought by US President Bill Clinton (and British Prime Minister Tony Blair), but Prime Minister Jean Chrétien christened it the "Canadian way."

Social investment involved economic rhetoric and calculations. Expenditures occurred in areas that would bring financial returns, such as "investing" in "life-long learning" that would boost marketable education and skills (i.e., human capital). Under Chrétien, supports for early childhood education and addressing child poverty became foci, while his successor, Prime Minister Paul Martin, launched an ambitious national childcare strategy. The presumption was that such investments in children would ultimately produce a better educated and productive citizenry, which, in turn, would fuel economic growth. "Work-life balance" objectives were also popularized. However, employability leading to future economic success was the main driver behind social investment. Although this was not social spending of Keynesian welfare state proportions, some argued that it constituted a break from rollback neoliberalism, while others continued to see it as epitomizing rollout neoliberalism (see Dobrowolsky 2009b).

By 2016, however, there was little debate around the newly elected Harper government's agenda: dismantling institutions and disempowering identities and ideas that championed equality and diversity. This was apparent from the start of Harper's first term, with the cancellation of the Court Challenges Program, a fund supporting equality seekers' litigation strategies (Dobrowolsky 2017, 2018), and extended through to the end of his third term, with the Zero Tolerance for Barbaric Cultural Practices Act. Here, use of the colonial term "barbaric" and the suggestive link to "cultural practices" generated and racialized a sharp divide between those perceived as desirable and undesirable immigrants (Gaucher 2016, 534). In short, because ideals of equality and diversity were still attributed to past Liberal governments, these commitments were to be rescinded and even reversed in the Harper era (Marland 2016).

Throughout these decades, narratives around the "death of feminism" in Canada and the United States abounded (Budgeon 2011, 11). Those who announced this death saw it as the result of self-inflicted wounds and failed to acknowledge the neoliberal repercussions that resulted in the discrediting and dismantling of feminist ideas and practices. Feminism's demise was also wildly exaggerated.

On the global scale, feminism had experienced widespread growth with the creation of "ministries for women, women's bureaux, and gender equality commissions," the establishment of a "feminist arm" of the United Nations, the ratification of the Convention to Eliminate All Forms of Discrimination against Women, some countries' inclusion of gender equity in foreign policy, and the proliferation of feminist non-governmental and transnational organizations (Budgeon 2011, 12–13). By the second decade of the 2000s, feminism was again in the public eye. From Emma Watson's (the actor who portrayed Hermione Granger in the Harry Potter movies) 2014 feminist speech at the United Nations headquarters in New York, which went viral, to a "flurry of self-declared feminist manifestos," there were indications that feminism in the United States and elsewhere had "resurfaced as an important and even influential discourse" (Rottenburg 2017, 330) and later spurred action, with movements like #MeToo "shining a spotlight on gender inequality and demanding accountability" (Gender Equality Advisory Council 2018, 3).

However, mirroring changes borne out of rollout neoliberalism, some of this also reflected a "kind of re-worked equal rights feminism which is compatible with liberal democracy" (McRobbie 2009, 152). Dubbed as neoliberal feminism, because it encompasses gender equality initiatives that become "part of governance structures organized through the normalization and institutionalization of a neoliberal economy paradigm," it is thus a "modernized," "matured" feminism (Budgeon 2011, 13). But this "more respectable 'professional top-down technocratic advocacy on behalf of women's issues on the national and global state,'" critics caution, "ultimately [contributes] to a de-democratization of policy-making" (14).

Unlike the "state feminism" of the 1970s and 1980s, which erected gender equality machineries within the state, neoliberal feminism embraces the logic of the market and turns to its "channels and mechanisms," and thus "gender equality machineries in nation states [become] ever more embedded in neoliberal market reform" (Kantola and Squires 2012, 390, 383). "Feminist" policy priorities are increasingly individualized with a focus on human capital. Brown explains this objective as working "to self-invest in ways that enhance ... [a] figurative credit rating and attract investors" (2015, 33).

To illustrate, consider the goal of "work-family balance." This encourages women to have children and "invest in and cultivate a career" as well as to develop their sense of self, which produces "an individuated feminist subject whose identity is informed by a cost-benefit calculus" (Rottenburg 2017, 331). As Rottenburg argues, this exemplifies a "new form of neoliberal governmentality for middle-class women" as it "activates a more attentive, luminous, and exclusive address to upwardly mobile women" (2017, 331).

In sum, social liberal/social feminist advances of the 1970s collided with neoliberal streamlining and economizing in both rollback and rollout forms. While spending cuts were attenuated somewhat with the social investment ethos of the late 1990s that continued into the 2000s, gender was still largely "written out" (Jenson 2009) of the equation, along with race, Indigeneity, and other realities of Canadian inequality. Then, the anti-egalitarianism of the Harper era in Canada, and the growth of neoliberal feminism outside it, set the stage for equality and diversity's star (discursive) turn under the Liberals.

FEMINIST PRONOUNCEMENTS AND
PROBLEMATIC POLICIES

Justin Trudeau's Liberals alluded to P.E. Trudeau's social liberal era, but given the demise of Keynesian welfare liberalism they instead drew on the social investment-styled policies of Chrétien and Martin. Intent on repudiating the messaging of the Harper government, and since "it was 2015," the Justin Trudeau Liberals also embraced both feminism and diversity. Nonetheless, this increasingly took a more neoliberal hue, reflecting ongoing struggles between structure and agency in a distinctly Canadian context.

In many respects, Trudeau's administration brought welcome support for feminist efforts in and outside the state. For instance, while Harper gutted and attempted to silence the SWC (e.g., burying a study that outlined growing inequality between men and women; see Beeby 2015), the Liberals increased this agency's funding, personnel, and research capacity, recalling earlier, better times for the country's status of women machinery (Harris 2018b). The SWC's standing was further boosted by its 2018 reconfiguration as the Department for Women and Gender Equality (Curry 2018). GBA+ commitments were renewed and there were pledges around the use of intersectional analysis (for details, see Paterson and Scala in this volume).

Beyond achieving gender parity and greater diversity in cabinet, there were also other feminist "firsts," legislatively and otherwise (enumerated in this volume by Ashe, as well as Paterson and Scala). Here the Liberals' 2018 "feminist" budget is particularly noteworthy, as it contained an array of women-focused and women-friendly initiatives, including an allocation of $86 million to a gender-based-violence strategy that would support programs around teen dating, bolster the work of health professionals, and offer resources for sexual assault centres in close proximity to Canadian forces bases (Status of Women Canada 2018).

Trudeau's stance on reproductive freedom is also notable, as he refused to approve Liberal Party candidates who were not pro-choice and his government initially blocked anti-choice groups from obtaining funding from a federal government summer jobs program (groups had to declare that they were supportive of abortion rights to be eligible). However, in response to some public outcry and substantial protests by faith-based groups, the 2019 version of the program simply required applicants to declare that they did not do work that infringed on Canadians' legal rights (Press 2018). Still, later that year, the Trudeau Liberals did pledge to increase their $1.1 billion in international aid devoted to women's health to $1.4 billion (starting in 2023), which would encompass funds dedicated to sexual and reproductive health (Wright 2019).

Reforms were made on multiple fronts; for instance, in 2019, non-binary citizens were allowed to identify with an X, as neither female nor male, on significant government documents (e.g., passports, citizenship certificates, and permanent residency cards). Here the Trudeau government announced that "the change comes as part of its commitment to respect Canadians' 'gender identity, diversity and inclusivity'" (quoted in Burza 2019, n.p.). Foreign Affairs Minister Chrystia Freeland summed up the Liberal government's position overall as follows: "It is [Canada's] role to set a standard for how states should treat women, gays and lesbians, transgendered people, racial, ethnic, cultural, linguistic and religious minorities and Indigenous people" (2017, n.p.).

Trudeau's government clearly wore its feminism proudly, and yet the question arises, Which kind of feminism and why? The first clue comes from the Liberals' 2015 core campaign theme—investing in, and thereby improving the lives of, middle-class families, reflected in their platform title: *Real Change: A New Plan for A Strong Middle Class* (Liberal Party 2015). The feminism Trudeau would go on to promote in office—one that set goals around prosperity and leadership and was activated in policies weighted towards economic returns—would therefore only improve the status of a particular stratum of already privileged women. Despite rhetorical commitments to equality and diversity, we see real gaps in intersectionality in the promotion of a feminism that is more in keeping with neoliberal feminist priorities and practices.

A focus on prosperity is based on a classical liberal assumption that the economic realm is a place of opportunity. This is not the reality for most women. Canadian women are still paid less than men, even though they have "surpassed men in educational attainment, diversified their fields of study at post-secondary institutions, and increased their representation in higher-status occupations" (Pelletier, Patterson, and Moyser 2019, 1). Women are still more likely to be working part-time (Pelletier, Patterson, and Moyser 2019, 7), and more women than men work in precarious jobs. The situation is compounded for women who are poor, racialized, Indigenous, lacking citizenship status, disabled, younger or older, sexual minorities, and so on.

With respect to leadership, the Trudeau Liberals were celebrated for their first-ever gender-balanced cabinet and other forms of representational positioning; and yet Canada was still well behind other countries' advances when it came to women's numerical representation (see Ashe in this volume).

Moreover, this emphasis fits with the neoliberal feminism outlined by McRobbie in that conventional forms of representation and political leadership are
also more accessible for privileged women (McRobbie 2009). The main thrust
of the gender statements in successive Trudeau Liberal budgets was achieving equality of opportunity, especially through encouraging greater workforce
participation among women. The middle class continued to be the prime consideration in the two so-called feminist budgets, with Budget 2017 formally
titled "Building a Strong Middle Class" (Government of Canada 2017), and
Budget 2018 entitled "Equality plus Growth: A Strong Middle Class" (Government of Canada 2018).

While these "feminist budgets" also referenced and attempted to address
poverty and violence, the approach was steeped in the discourse of social
investment. For example, in Budget 2017, evidence of alleviating poverty
came through the Canada Child Benefit Program, "helping to lift thousands
of Canadian children out of poverty," and the highlighting of "investments in
early learning and child care, to support access to child care and allow greater
participation in work, education or training, particularly by mothers" (Government of Canada 2017).

Akin to the late 1990s and early 2000s, when childcare and the discourse
of "work-life balance" had become more prominent, the objective was to
entice women into the paid labour force. Less of a response to long-standing
feminist advocacy around accessible and affordable childcare, this was
more about employability than equality. In fact, Trudeau's first "feminist"
budget of 2017 allocated $7.5 billion over 11 years for targeted childcare
(Anderssen 2017), which fell well short of Prime Minister Paul Martin's
universal childcare strategy of a decade earlier (Radwanski 2017). Neither
"the funds nor the approach" came "close to what the 1968 Task Force on
Child Care or the Royal Commission on the Status of Women" suggested
was necessary for women to be "accorded true equality" (Friendly, Prentice,
and Ballantyne 2018).

Similarly, the Trudeau government's extension of Canada's parental leave
period, from 12 to 18 months, incentivizes women into the paid workforce
and offers an apt illustration of the exclusive nature of such "feminist" policy
measures. The extension accommodates dual-earner families and their work-
life balance but does not provide commensurate income replacement. Parents have the option of more time—18 months—but the amount of money
available will remain the same as for the 12-month period. As Kathleen
Lahey explained: "Spreading out the benefits that are already not sustainable

for single parents or low income working parents is not going to solve the problem" (CBC Radio 2017). Such policies benefit some women—upper-middle-class women who are employed with higher wages and can afford to stay home. For others, the 18-month "option" is a non-starter. Contrary to intersectionality, this policy is more in keeping with the realities of white, upper-middle-class, two-parent families.

Trudeau's resurrection of work-life balance is also telling. This can only be a preoccupation for some women, for example, those who have a well-paid job, support for care work (caring for children, caring for elderly parents, caring for families abroad, and so on), good health, and/or safe work and home environments. This social investment preoccupation is also "an unapologetically middle-class feminism, shorn of all obligations to less privileged women" and those not viewed as "'strivers'" (McRobbie 2013, 120). Such policy priorities pitched as "feminist" in effect create hierarchies among women, who are split along lines of privilege.

Another obvious case of neoliberal feminism came with Trudeau's efforts to cozy up to US president Trump, through his daughter Ivanka, with a $20 million pledge in support of women's entrepreneurialism through the creation of a Canada-United States women's business group (Stone and Slater 2017). Gender equality here is championed strategically and particularly when it enhances "productivity" (Kantola and Squires 2012, 390). Neoliberal rationality celebrates individual entrepreneurialism, and here it combines with liberal feminist discourse as "the conversion of subjects into self-investing human capital dovetails with the notion of professional success as emancipation" (Rottenburg 2017, 344).

It was not at all surprising, then, that Budget 2018 contained a new woman and entrepreneurship strategy (Government of Canada 2018), "set targets for federal procurement from women-led business," allocated "$10-million over five years for women-owned and women-led business to support export opportunities," and provided an additional $250 million through Export Development Canada to "ensure women-led business quick access to available federal resources through partnerships with women business associations" and business development organizations like the Canadian Trade Commissioner Service "to assist Canadian women to build thriving businesses" (Canadian Federation of University Women 2018, 9). Note also how the SWC revamp entailed a name change to the Department of Women and Gender Equality, resulting in the new acronym: WAGE! Such market prioritization is equally explicit when considering immigration.

IMMIGRATION: NEOLIBERALISM WRIT LARGE
WITH LITTLE INTERSECTIONALITY

Canada's immigration policies have always given precedence to labour market needs, but with the consolidation of rollback neoliberalism those with money, skills, qualifications, and official language capacity became the "ideal" migrants (Barber 2008), as they would presumably not constitute a "drain" on resources. Immigrants with capital and human capital were commodified as enhancing economic competitiveness and courted for their economic "payback" (Simmons 2010). Governments shied away from the perceived expense of humanitarian responses such as providing safe haven for asylum seekers and refugees or reuniting family members, and instead the focus on individual capital and marketable skills made economic immigrant selection the top priority. As a consequence, immigration policies came to favour economic immigrant selection over family reunification and refugee resettlement, and as immigration became viewed for its potential profits, it came under greater control of the private sector (Bhuyan et al. 2017).

More explicit class preferences resulted in more implicit gender and race biases (Arat Koç 1999). Income levels and educational opportunities around the world are not equal. When it comes to human capital, more girls than boys are denied an education, and of "the world's 774 million illiterate adults, 2/3 are women" (Gender Equality Advisory Council 2018, 8). This under-education of girls and women around the world makes migration more challenging, in general. More specifically, however, it makes it harder to acquire the necessary language proficiency in English or French required to immigrate to Canada under its Economic Immigration class, wherein every applicant must demonstrate the ability to communicate in one or both of Canada's two official languages. Immigration policies based on market priorities thus favour men who have the requisite money, literacy levels, and credentials. Because the latter are more valued when they are easily translatable, this gives immigrants from certain countries, usually those of the Global North, an edge.

Notions of "skill" are also highly gendered and racialized. Care for children or the elderly, for instance, is not considered to be "skilled" work, and is still disproportionately done by girls and women—nearly three times as much as men (Gender Equality Advisory Council 2018, 12)—and can take a toll on their education levels, attainment of marketable skills, and employment experience. Moreover, care "deficits" result in processes whereby racialized women from the Global South are sought after to provide child and elder care for privileged families in the Global North.

Historically, these realities meant that more women entered Canada through the "family class" immigration category, rendering them "dependent," whereas more men entered through "economic" streams, problematically suggesting that the latter were more "independent" (Creese, Dyck, and McLaren 2008). Rollback neoliberalism translated into reductions of family class immigrants and refugees, and rollout neoliberalism saw expansion in the number and types "economic" pathways, from entrepreneurial and investment streams to the growth of provincial nominee programs (where provinces have more of a role to play in immigrant selection in order to meet their economic needs, and the private sector becomes increasingly involved in immigration). Granted, the numbers of women who possess the requisite capital have grown over time, but misperceptions around who is "dependent" and a welfare "drain" abound, and "most economic applicants are men, and most women who enter Canada via economic streams come as spouses" (Public Policy Forum 2018, 28).

Huge growth in the numbers of temporary foreign workers—for instance, the use of temporary foreign workers in the Atlantic region alone tripled between 2005 and 2012 (Public Policy Forum 2018, 6)—and increased securitization, particularly after the September 11 terrorist attacks in the United States, are but two indicators of the marketized and securitized approach to immigration with its class-based, gendered, and racialized (Amery 2013) preoccupations that became the norm under both the Chrétien/Martin Liberals and Harper Conservatives. However, the former worked to appear more "balanced" in its rhetoric, as the Liberals' 2001 immigration rehaul was called the Immigration and Refugee Protection Act (IRPA). The Conservative agenda was less ambiguous, and included various immigration "crack-downs" with legislation with titles like the Preventing Human Smugglers from Abusing Canada's Immigration System Act.

Gender, race, and class preferences became increasingly apparent with the Harper Conservatives' push for immigrants with better income, education, and skills. Pathways were cleared for high-skilled immigrants with job offers, whereas immigrants' grandparents and family members faced obstacles and blockages to entry into Canada. Both immigration and citizenship became subject to particular kinds of limits (on the resettlement of refugees) and restrictions (citizenship of dual nationals was revoked, and veiled Muslim women were refused citizenship).

This hard-nosed approach was then epitomized by Harper's seeming indifference to a tragic photo of a failed migration effort—a three-year-old Syrian boy, Alan Kurdi, lying face-down on a Mediterranean beach after he, his five-year-old brother, and mother all drowned when their raft capsized (Crane 2018)—which was countered by the Liberals' campaign of a more "compassionate Canada" (Hadfield 2017). The latter reverted to earlier Canadian ideals of supporting immigration of all kinds (i.e., family and economic) and big-heartedness towards refugees and asylum seekers (Dobrowolsky 2017), as with its election promise to admit 25,000 Syrian refugees. Later, Prime Minister Trudeau was photographed handing out winter jackets to newly arrived Syrian refugee children and his "open door" response was summed up in a January 2017 tweet: "To those fleeing persecution, terror & war, Canadians will welcome you, regardless of your faith. Diversity is our strength #/WelcomeToCanada" (Gordon 2017; for more on the significant impact of social media, see Small in this volume). In short, the promise was to buck prevailing trends and pursue immigration measures attendant to asylum seekers, refugees, resettlement, and family frames (Wallace 2018); but over time, the Liberals' more expansive immigration policies and practices stalled, and in some instances were reversed.

In 2016, a total of 25,674 Syrian refugees entered Canada, and 21,751 of these individuals were government assisted. This rapid response to the Liberals' election promise, however, was heavy on the welcoming and light on responding to the actual settlement needs and longer-term services required by the refugees (IRCC 2016). Higher levels of refugee intake were also not constant: the March 2016 immigration plan targeted 44,800 refugees, and this dropped to 43,000 in the 2017 plan. While increases were projected for the future (e.g., a target of 48,700 for 2020), refugee targets were significantly lower than federal targets for high-skilled workers, which were slated to increase from 58,400 in 2016 to a target of 88,000 in 2020 (IRCC 2017).

Granted, the Trudeau government attempted to strengthen family reunification, increasing the number of entry applications for parents and grandparents by abandoning the first-come-first-serve model and instead instituting a lottery system in 2017. When such meaningful matters were left to chance, not merit, this did little to alleviate the distress felt by families. Castigated as a "rushed and deeply flawed program without public consultation," the lottery was nonetheless reinstated in early 2018 (Harris 2018a), but by August, it was abandoned. On the last day of 2018, the government announced it would revert, temporarily, to the old model.

Criticisms of the Liberals' handling of immigration matters intensified after a spike in numbers of cross-border asylum seekers through Quebec, Ontario, and Manitoba. The Conservatives demanded tighter security and suggested that social programs across Canada were "under severe strain due to tens of thousands of unplanned immigrants illegally crossing into Canada" (Crane 2018, 13). Progressive forces pleaded with the government to scrap the Safe Third Country Agreement (Evelyn 2018)—which requires that refugee claimants who arrive in Canada or the US request protection in the first country in which they arrive—for perpetuating not only irregular, but unsafe border crossings. The provinces in question mostly wanted more support from Ottawa to deal with this situation. All this resulted in the Liberals backtracking on their #WelcomeToCanada tweet, and by spring 2019, with the fall election looming, they deployed discourses and practices reminiscent of the Harper government's approach.

Steps were taken to prevent so-called "asylum shopping" with provisions pitched as producing a more "fair" and "efficient" asylum system (Harris 2019). The proposed changes went beyond the Safe Third Country Agreement with the United States, disqualifying refugee claims if they had already been made in any of a greater number of countries deemed to be "safe" (i.e., the four "five eyes" countries that share their intelligence with Canada: the United Kingdom, Australia, New Zealand, and the United States). They also rendered ineligible those whose claims had already been rejected in Canada, or those who had been granted refugee protection elsewhere, depriving some refugee claimants access to full refugee hearings. Moreover, the Liberal government tried to hide these draconian changes to the IRPA by burying them in its April 2019, 400-page, omnibus budget bill, a tactic repeatedly used by the Harper government and widely disparaged.

Civil society and legal organizations, including Amnesty International, the Canadian Council for Refugees, the Canadian Civil Liberties Association, and Canadian Association of Refugee Lawyers, viewed these Trudeau government proposals as "harsh" and "unnecessary" and asserted that "these changes would have a devastating impact on people seeking asylum in Canada" (Canadian Press 2019). Notably, the 2019 budget also allocated $1.05 billion "to improve border enforcement and accelerate asylum processing over the next three years, a sizable jump from C$173.2 million in the previous year's annual budget" (Mackrael 2019). Such funding priorities were more than a little reminiscent of the security preoccupations of previous governments.

Overall, economic considerations remained paramount and key priorities were linked more to prosperity and profitability than equality. Consider here the Trudeau Liberals' prime immigration target: international students. This focus has been decried for its commodification of education, as it relies on international students as a source of revenue through high tuition and fees and then as a source of human capital (Johnstone and Lee 2014). International students thus become a strategic social investment in the future, albeit with little consideration of the difficulties they face at present, from lack of employment opportunities to experiences of racism. This emphasis also calls into question equality commitments as, given the context described above, there tend to be gender imbalances with more male than female international students (Statistics Canada 2015). In addition, global inequalities are perpetuated as wealthy, Global North host countries compete for the "best and brightest" from Global South source countries, thereby contributing to "brain drain" dynamics (Johnstone and Lee 2014).

When the overarching concern is human capital, there is insufficient consideration of equality or precarity. Temporary foreign workers epitomize a situation where there is too little of the former and too much of the latter. A classic example is live-in caregivers, many of whom are racialized women (Tungohen 2013). In a study by Vahabi and Wong, a focus group described live-in caregiving as the "resurrection of slavery in the twenty-first century" (2017, 6). The Harper government made changes to Canada's Live-In Caregiver Program, renaming it the Caregiver Program, with two streams—one for childcare and the other for high medical needs—but it continued to tie workers' immigration status to their employers, perpetuating an "immense power discrepancy ... making it difficult for workers to be forthcoming about abuse" (Bannerjee et al. 2017, 28). Trudeau's Department of Immigration, Refugees, and Canadian Citizenship promised to review the caregiver programs, but then reduced the target number of caregivers (see IRCC 2017) and failed to alleviate the uncertainty around the status of pilot programs geared towards providing caregivers with pathways to permanent residency. New Democrat immigration critic Jenny Kwan noted that the "Liberals' plan shows they intend to continue treating caregivers as 'second-tier economic immigrants'" (quoted in Nuttall 2016). Gender, race, and class issues proliferate, as "95 per cent of the care givers that come to Canada are women from developing countries" (Drolet, quoted in Hennig 2018), perpetuating dynamics whereby privileged women draw on the support of less privileged racialized women in precarious situations. Again, this calls into question commitments to equality and multicultural-ism (Dauvergne 2016).

The federal government's Atlantic Immigration Pilot Program (AIPP) provides another eye-opening example of an economic rationale with insuf-ficient consideration of precarity, but also illustrates growing private sector involvement in immigration. Immigration was identified as a way to redress the east coast's economic, demographic, and labour challenges. Despite highly problematic developments in several Atlantic Canadian provincial nominee program streams, especially when the private sector was left to its own devices (for example, see Baldacchino, 2015; Dobrowolsky 2013), the Trudeau gov-ernment launched the AIPP in 2017. Labour needs were addressed in ways that were welcome to business, through an employer-driven process: jobs could go to foreign workers if employers applied to the program with a reset-tlement plan that would be vetted by settlement organizations and, ultimately, the federal government.

The AIPP's priority streams tend to be gendered (Dobrowolsky 2017), contributing to a pattern where men are wanted for paid work while women are wanted for unpaid work as family members to anchor newcomers to com-munities facing labour shortages and de-population. More broadly, women who enter Canada as spouses of economic principal applicants earn $20,000 less than male principal applicants, but the gap is even wider in Atlantic Can-ada; the 33 per cent gendered wage gap for immigrants in Atlantic Canada is twice the rate of that in Montreal, Toronto, and Vancouver (Public Policy Forum 2018, 27–28). This again renders women as "dependent" and, in turn, can contribute to their isolation and precarity—that is, they can be confined to work in the home or be challenged to find well-paid work outside it. More-over, when employers are entrusted with the responsibility for settlement this calls into question how much they will want to invest in supports for spouses. The business of businesses is attaining profit margins, not address-ing marginalization.

To make matters worse, by September 2019 a CBC News investigation uncovered an illegal job-offer scheme linked to the AIPP. Substantial capi-tal was used to unlawfully circumvent the process and fast track permanent residency: "The problem is that so-called 'ghost' agencies are taking advan-tage of weaknesses in the program. They convince immigrants to turn over sometimes tens of thousands of dollars, paying off select companies to hire the person for no pay or to simply forge their payroll" (MacIvor 2019). This resulted in yet another Atlantic Canadian immigration scandal with gender, race, and class repercussions.

As a final example, the 2018 budget reflected a modicum of intersectional analysis in the form of another pilot program, allocating $31.8 million over three years "for many visible minority newcomer women" in recognition of their "additional barriers including both gender-and-race-based discrimination, [and] precarious or low income employment" (Government of Canada 2018, 62). But here again, we return to the mark of neoliberal feminism, as the ultimate objective is all too familiar: increasing "labour market opportunities."

CONCLUDING COMMENTS

The foregoing suggests that transformational gender politics can occur at the level of ideas, and political actors can put these ideas into effect. However, these actors also operate under structural constraints. In the end, although the Justin Trudeau Liberal government's expressed intentions were fundamentally different from those of Stephen Harper (and President Trump), the former's actions were constrained by liberal and neoliberal influences. Despite seemingly inclusive and expansive discourses, the liberalisms and feminisms at work in the policies examined above benefit the few, not the many, when gender, race, and class are taken into consideration.

The Trudeau Liberals invoked the social liberal equality of old, but actually acted in ways that reflected contemporary social investment, rollout neoliberalism, and neoliberal feminism. Boosting conventional forms of leadership meant gains for the select few, while other pivotal moves dubbed "feminist" were often more about attaining economic and political leverage. Social policies lacked intersectional analyses, as many served a particular type of family: white, upper-middle-class, nuclear, with one stay-at-home-parent or at least a parent whose job is not crucial to the household income. Immigration policies still facilitated economic migration, human capital, and private-sector mandates, despite frames that were more sympathetic to families, refugees, and asylum seekers.

In the end, Trudeau's neoliberal feminism may provide a foothold for some, but crowds out alternatives for many others. A more transformative future would require critically examining the lens of equality of opportunity, middle-class and human capital preoccupations, and highly exclusivist notions of prosperity and leadership. It would mean truly encompassing intersectionality and embracing inclusive policies such as an approach to childcare that is universally accessible, affordable, and flexible. Action plans would be worked out in detail with the affected communities, from tackling gender-based violence in ways that are acutely aware of intersectional oppressions to addressing the precarious circumstances of live-in caregivers and other temporary foreign workers. Research and action with input from a wide range of feminist groups that have been supported with flexible funding would also go a long way in countering the detrimental targeting and perpetuation of a discriminating and ultimately discriminatory neoliberal and neoliberal feminist visions.

As I write this conclusion in the wake of the turbulent 2019 federal election, the Trudeau Liberals have secured a second term and formed a tenuous minority government. And yet, over the past year, ethical breaches around the SNC-Lavalin scandal—which led to the resignations of two powerful, high-profile cabinet ministers, Jody Wilson-Raybould and Jane Philpott (both women, and the former an Indigenous woman, who were subsequently also ousted from the Liberal party)—and photos that emerged early on in the election campaign of a younger Justin Trudeau in black- and brown-face, have become actions and images that have profoundly challenged his government's political, and his own personal, feminist credentials and commitments to equality and anti-racism. And then of course, after the election win came the appointment of Mona Fortier as Trudeau's inaugural Minister of Middle Class Prosperity, offering a final, neoliberal feminist case in point! These highly problematic developments of the past year, in conjunction with the concerns outlined in this chapter, seriously and fundamentally call into question whether Justin Trudeau's Liberal government will ultimately be remembered for championing diversity and feminism of any variety.

DISCUSSION QUESTIONS

1. What are the key differences between classical liberalism, social liberalism, neoliberalism, and social investment?
2. What other ideological influences, beyond the various forms of liberalism discussed in this chapter, have had an impact on gender politics in Canada?
3. Which policies epitomize transformational gender politics? How and why?
4. What would intersectional immigration policies look like?

NOTES

1 I am grateful for helpful suggestions from Fiona MacDonald and the useful feedback from students in the 2018–19 Saint Mary's Political Science Honours Program.
2 This was not without critique, especially in relation to Indigenous people; see, for example, Harold Cardinal's *The Unjust Society* (1999).
3 Although notably lacking was recognition of the inherent right to self-government.

REFERENCES

Abbey, Ruth. 2011. *The Return of Feminist Liberalism*. Montreal: McGill-Queen's University Press.
Abu-Laban, Yasmeen. 1998. "Welcome/STAY OUT: The Contradiction of Canadian Integration and Immigration Policies at the Millennium." *Canadian Ethnic Studies* 30 (3): 190–211.
———. 2009. "The Welfare State under Siege? Neo-Liberalism, Immigration and Multiculturalism." In *Women and Public Policy in Canada: Neo-liberalism and After?*, edited by Alexandra Dobrowolsky, 146–65. Toronto: Oxford University Press.
———. 2015. "The Politics of History under Harper." *Labour/Le Travail* 73 (Spring): 215–17.
Amery, Zaineb. 2013. "The Securitization and Racialization of Arabs in Canada's Immigration and Citizenship Policies." In *Targeted Transnationals: The State, the Media and Arab Canadians*, edited by Jenna Hennebry and Bessma Momani, 32–53. Vancouver: UBC Press.
Anderssen, Erin. 2017. "Liberal Budget's Child-Care Funding Commendable but Won't Help Families Any Time Soon." *Globe and Mail*, April 12. https://www.theglobeandmail.com/life/parenting/liberal-budgets-child-care-funding-commendable-but-wont-help-families-any-time-soon/article34689318/.
Arat-Koç, Sedef. 1999. "Neo-liberalism, State Restructuring and Immigration: Changes in Canadian Policies in the 1990's." *Journal of Canadian Studies* 34 (2): 31–56.
Baldacchino, Godfrey. 2015. "A 'Stopover Place' at Best? Recent Trends in Immigrant Attraction and Retention on Prince Edward Island." In *The Warmth of the Welcome: Is Atlantic Canada a Home Away from Home for Immigrants?*, edited by Evangelia Tastsoglou, Alexandra Dobrowolsky, and Barbara Cottrell, 206–30. Sydney, NS: Cape Breton University Press.
Bannerjee, Rupa, Philip Kelly, Ethel Tungohan, GABRIELA-Ontario, Migrante-Canada, and Community Alliance for Social Justice. 2017. *Assessing the Changes to Canada's Live-In Caregiver Program: Improving Security or Deepening Precariousness*. Pathways to Prosperity Project Study Centre, December.
Barber, Pauline Gardiner. 2008. "The Ideal Immigrant? Gendered Class Subjects in Philippine Canada Migration." *Third World Quarterly* 29 (7): 1265–85.

Bashevkin, Sylvia. 1998. *Women on the Defensive: Living through Conservative Times.* Toronto: University of Toronto Press.

Beeby, Dean. 2015. "Secret Status of Women Report Paints Grim Picture for Canada." *CBC News*, September 7. https://www.cbc.ca/news/politics/status-of -womeninternal-report-1.3214751.

Bhuyan, Rupalee, Daphne Jeyapal, Jane Ku, Izumi Sakamoto, and Elena Chou. 2017. "Branding 'Canadian Experience' in Immigration Policy: Nation Building in a Neoliberal Era." *Journal of International Migration and Integration* 18 (1): 47–62.

Bradford, Neil. 1998. *Commissioning Ideas: Canadian National Policy Innovation in Comparative Perspective.* Toronto: Oxford University Press.

Brown, Wendy. 2015. *Undoing the Demos: Neoliberalism's Stealth Revolution.* New York: Zone Books.

Budgeon, Shelley. 2011. *Third Wave Feminism and the Politics of Gender in Late Modernity.* Houndmills, UK: Palgrave Macmillan.

Burza, Alexandra. 2019. "New Gender 'X' Option on Canadian ID a Mixed Blessing, Say Advocates." *CBC News*, June 4. https://www.cbc.ca/news/canada/kitchener -waterloo/xgender-indicator-1.5162376.

Canadian Federation of University Women. 2018. *CFUW's Overview of the Federal Budget 2018.* 26 March. Ottawa: CFUW.

Canadian Press. 2015. "'We're Back,' Justin Trudeau Says in Message to Canada's Allies Abroad." *National Post,* October 20. https://nationalpost.com/news/politics /were-back-justin-trudeau-says-in-message-to-canadas-allies-abroad.

———. 2019. "Civil Rights Groups Call on Trudeau to Withdraw Changes to Asylum Laws." *Global News*, April 11. https://globalnews.ca/news/5157559/canada-asylum -shopping/.

Cardinal, Harold. 1999. *The Unjust Society.* Vancouver: Douglas & McIntyre.

CBC Radio. 2017. "The Current: 18-Month Parental Leave a Disservice to Women, Says Critic." *CBC Radio*, March 27. http://www.cbc.ca/radio/thecurrent/the -current-for-march-27-the-current-1.4040102/liberal-s-18-month-parental -leave-a-disservice-to-women-says-critic-1.4040118.

Clarke, John. 2008. "Living with/in and without Neo-liberalism." *Focaal* 51: 135–47.

Crane, David. 2018. "Will a New Immigration Crisis Influence the Outcome of the Next Federal Election?" *The Hill Times*, July 2, 13.

Creese, Gillian, Isabel Dyck, and Arlene McLaren. 2008. "The 'Flexible' Immigrant? Human Capital Discourse, the Family Household and Labour Market Strategies." *Journal of International Migration and Immigration* 9 (3): 269–88.

Curry, Bill. 2018. "Ottawa Launches National Pay Equity Legislation and Department for Women and Gender Equity." *Globe and Mail*, October 29. https://www .theglobeandmail.com/politics/article-budget-bill-includes-pay-equity-law -creates-new-department-for-women/.

Dauvergne, Catherine. 2016. *The New Politics of Immigration and the End of Settler Societies.* Cambridge: Cambridge University Press.

Dobrowolsky, Alexandra. 2000. *The Politics of Pragmatism: Women, Representation and Constitutionalism in Canada*. Toronto: Oxford University Press.

———. 2009a. "Charter Champions? Equality Backsliding the Charter and the Courts." In *Women and Public Policy in Canada: Neo-liberalism and After?*, edited by Alexandra Dobrowolsky, 205–25. Toronto: Oxford University Press.

———, ed. 2009b. *Women and Public Policy in Canada: Neo-liberalism and After?*, Toronto: Oxford University Press.

———. 2013. "Nuancing Neoliberalism: Lessons Learned from a Failed Immigration Experiment." *Journal of International Migration and Integration* 14: 197–218.

———. 2015. "That Was Then and This Is Now: The Sad but True Story of a Shrinking Equality Opportunity Structure." In *The Patriation Negotiations*, edited by Lois Harder and Steve Patten, 290–311. Vancouver: UBC Press.

———. 2017. "Bad versus Big: State Imaginaries of Immigration and Citizenship." *Studies in Political Economy* 98 (2): 197–222.

———. 2018. "'Weapons of Mass Distraction'? Migration, Multiculturalism and Citizenship in Two Contrasting Election Campaigns." In *Citizenship as a Regime: Canadian and International Perspectives*, edited by Mireille Paquet, Nora Nagels, and Aude-Claire Fourot, 186–207. Montreal: McGill-Queen's University Press.

Evelyn, Charelle. 2018. "Time to Rethink Canada–U.S. Safe Third Country Deal in Face of U.S. Immigration Sweeps: Amnesty International Researcher." *The Hill Times*, May 30, 6.

Freeland, Chrystia. 2017. "Address by Minister Freeland on Canada's Foreign Policy Priorities." June 6. https://www.canada.ca/en/global-affairs/news/2017/06/address_by_ministerfreelandoncanadasforeignpolicypriorities.html.

Friendly, Martha, Susan Prentice, and Morna Ballantyne. 2018. "Without the Publicly Funded Child Care Now Commonplace in Many Countries, Canada Lacks This Essential Pillar of Support for Women's Equality." *Policy Options*, March 8. http://policyoptions.irpp.org/magazines/march-2018/no-equality-without-universal-child-care/.

Gaucher, Megan. 2016. "Monogamous Canadian Citizenship, Constructing Foreignness and the Limits of Harm Discourse." *Canadian Journal of Political Science* 49 (3): 519–38.

Gender Equality Advisory Council. 2018. "Recommendations from the Gender Equality Advisory Council for Canada's G7 Presidency." https://g7.gc.ca/en/g7-presidency/gender-equality-advisory-council/.

Gordon, Graeme. 2017. "Trudeau Should Probably Stop Telling Desperate Refugees That Everyone Is Welcome in Canada." *CBC News*, April 3. https://www.cbc.ca/news/opinion/trudeau-message-to-refugees-1.4051008.

Government of Canada. 2017. *Budget 2017: Building a Strong Middle Class*. Ottawa: Department of Finance. https://www.budget.gc.ca/2017/home-accueil-en.html.

———. 2018. *Budget 2018: Equality plus Growth: A Strong Middle Class*. Ottawa: Department of Finance. https://www.budget.gc.ca/2018/home-accueil-en.html.

Hadfield, Amelia. 2017. "Maple Life Zeitgeist? Assessing Canadian Prime Minister Justin Trudeau's Policy Changes." *The Round Table* 106 (1): 23–35.

Harris, Kathleen. 2018a. "Liberals Relaunch Family Reunification Lottery Despite Angry Backlash around 'Immigration Fiasco.'" *CBC News*, January 8. https://www .cbc.ca/news/politics/immigration-parents-grandparents-sponsorship-1.4442456.

———. 2018b. "'Small but Mighty': Status of Women Grows from Federal Agency to Full Department." *CBC News*, March 1. https://www.cbc.ca/news/politics/status -women-monsef-budget-1.4556093.

———. 2019. "Liberals Move to Stem Surge in Asylum Seekers—But New Measures Will Stop Just Fraction of Claimants." *CBC News*, April 10. https://www.cbc.ca /news/politics/refugee-asylum-seekers-border-changes-1.5092192.

Hartz, Louis, ed. 1964. *The Founding of New Societies: Studies in the History of the United States, Latin America, South Africa, Canada and Australia*. New York: Harcourt, Brace and World.

Henderson, Ailsa. 2007. *Nunavut: Rethinking Political Culture*. Vancouver: UBC Press.

Hennig, Clare. 2018. "End of Permanent Residency Program for Foreign Caregivers Concerns Workers Group." *CBC News*, February 24. https://www.cbc.ca/news /canada/british-columbia/end-of-permanent-residency-program-foreign -caregivers-1.4549776.

Horowitz, Gad. 1996. "Conservatism, Liberalism, and Socialism in Canada: An Interpretation." *Canadian Journal of Economics and Political Science* 32 (2): 143–71.

Immigration, Refugees, and Citizenship Canada. 2016. *Rapid Evaluation of the Syrian Refugee Initiative*. No E1-2016. Ottawa: Immigration, Refugees and Citizenship Canada.

———. 2017. "Notice: Supplementary Information 2018–2020 Immigration Level Plans." https://www.canada.ca/en/immigration-refugees-citizenship/news /notices/supplementary-immigration-levels-2018.html.

Jenson, Jane. 2009. "Writing Gender Out: The Continuing Effects of the Social Investment Perspective." In *Women and Public Policy in Canada: Neo-liberalism and After?*, edited by Alexandra Dobrowolsky, 25–47. Toronto: Oxford University Press.

Jenson, Jane, and Denis Saint-Martin. 2003. "New Routes to Social Cohesion? Citizenship and the Social Investment State." *Canadian Journal of Sociology* 28 (1): 77–99.

Johnstone, Marjorie, and Eunjung Lee. 2014. "Branded: International Education and 21st Century Canadian Immigration, Education Policy, and the Welfare State." *International Social Work* 57 (3): 209–21.

Kantola, Johanna, and Judith Squires. 2012. "From State Feminism to Market Feminism?" *International Political Science Review* 33 (4): 382–400.

Kymlicka, Will. 2014. "Citizenship, Communities, and Identity in Canada." In *Canadian Politics*, 6th ed., edited by James Bickerton and Alain-G. Gagnon, 21–44. Toronto: University of Toronto Press.

La Selva, Samuel V. 2014. "Understanding Canada's Origins: Federalism, Multiculturalism, and the Will to Live Together." In *Canadian Politics*, 6th ed., edited by James Bickerton and Alain-G. Gagnon, 3–20. Toronto: University of Toronto Press.

Levitz, Stephanie. 2018. "Liberals' Budget Includes $23M for Multiculturalism and Anti-Racism Strategy." *CTV News*, February 28. https://www.ctvnews.ca/politics/liberals-budget-includes-23m-for-multiculturalism-anti-racism-strategy-1.3823101.

Liberal Party of Canada. 2015. *Real Change: A New Plan for a Strong Middle Class.* Ottawa: Liberal Party of Canada.

Lipset, Seymour Martin. 1986. "Historical Traditions and National Characteristics: A Comparative Analysis of Canada and the United States." *Canadian Journal of Sociology* 11(2): 115–55.

MacDonald, Fiona. 2011. "Indigenous Peoples and Neoliberal 'Privatization' in Canada: Opportunities, Cautions and Constraints." *Canadian Journal of Political Science* 44(2): 257–73.

MacIvor, Angela. 2019. "Inside the Illegal Immigration Scheme Targeting Atlantic Canada." *CBC News*, September 16. https://cbc.ca/news/canada/nova-scotia/immigration-fraud-jobs-Atlantic-canada-aipp-1.5281668.

Mackrael, Kim. 2019. "In Shift, Trudeau Begins to Tighten Canada's Welcoming Stance on Refugees." *Wall Street Journal*, March 29. https://www.wsj.com/articles/in-shift-trudeau-begins-to-tighten-canadas-welcoming-stance-on-refugees-11553878130.

Mahon, Rianne. 2009. "Childcare and Varieties of Liberalism in Canada." In *Women and Public Policy in Canada: Neo-liberalism and After?*, edited by Alexandra Dobrowolsky, 48–64. Toronto: Oxford University Press.

Marland, Alex. 2016. *Brand Command: Canadian Politics and Democracy in the Age of Message Control.* Vancouver: UBC Press.

McRobbie, Angela. 2009. *The Aftermath of Feminism: Gender, Culture and Social Change.* London: Sage.

———. 2013. "Feminism, the Family and the New 'Mediated' Maternalism." *New Formations* 80–81: 199–237.

Nuttal, Jeremy J. 2016. "Liberal Immigration Changes Bad News for Caregivers, Says Advocate." *The Tyee*, November 3. https://thetyee.ca/News/2016/11/03/Liberal-Immigration-Changes-Caregivers/.

O'Connor, Julia, Ann Shola Orloff, and Sheila Shaver. 1999. *States, Markets, Families: Gender, Liberalism and Social Policy in Australia, Canada, Great Britain and the United States.* Cambridge: Cambridge University Press.

Peck, Jamie, and Adam Tickell. 2002. "Neoliberalising Space." In *Spaces of Neoliberalism: Urban Restructuring in North America and Western Europe*, edited by Neil Brenner and Nick Theodore, 33–57. Oxford: Oxford University Press.

Pelletier, Rachelle, Martha Patterson, and Melissa Moyser. 2019. "The Gender Wage Gap in Canada: 1998 to 2018." Labour Statistics: Research Papers. Ottawa: Statistics Canada. https://www150.statscan.gc.ca/n1/pub/75-004-m/75-004-m2019004-eng.htm.

Press, Jordan. 2018. "Liberals Drop Contentious Anti-abortion Test for Summer Jobs Funding." *The Canadian Press*, December 6. https://www.cbc.ca/news/politics /liberals-summer-jobs-program-changes-1.4934674.

Public Policy Forum. 2018. *The People Imperative: Come From Away and Stay, Strategies to Grow Population and Prosperity in Atlantic Canada*. Ottawa: Public Policy Forum.

Radwanski, Adam. 2015. "Tories' Culture War Appears to Have Defined Campaign." *Globe and Mail*, October 7, A7.

———. 2017. "For Trudeau's Liberals, Universal Daycare a Distant Dream." *Globe and Mail*, June 16. https://www.theglobeandmail.com/news/politics/for-trudeaus -liberals-universal-daycare-is-a-distant-dream/article35349241/.

Rottenburg, Catherine. 2017. "Neoliberal Feminism and the Future of Human Capital." *Signs* 42 (2): 329–48.

Simmons, Allan. B. 2010. *Immigration and Canada: Global and Transnational Perspectives*. Toronto: Canadian Scholars' Press.

Smith, Miriam. 2005. "Social Movements and Judicial Empowerment: Courts, Public Policy, and Lesbian and Gay Organizing in Canada." *Politics and Society* 33 (2): 327–53.

Statistics Canada. 2015. "Canadian Postsecondary Enrolments and Graduates, 2013/2014." *The Daily*, November 30. https://www150.statcan.gc.ca/n1/daily -quotidien/151130/dq151130d-eng.htm.

Status of Women Canada. 2018. "Strategy to Prevent and Address Gender-Based Violence." July 3. https://cfc-swc.gc.ca/violence/strategy-strategie/index-en.html.

Stone, Laura, and Joanna Slater. 2017. "How Trudeau Recruited a Key Businesswoman, Ivanka Trump." *Globe and Mail*, February 13. https://www .theglobeandmail.com/news/politics/trump-trudeau-to-discuss-women-in -workforce-during-washington-visit/article33996194/.

Tungohan, Ethel. 2013. "Reconceptualizing Motherhood, Reconceptualizing Resistance: Migrant Domestic Workers, Transnational Hyper-Maternalism and Activism." *International Feminist Journal of Politics* 15 (1): 39–57.

Vahabi, Mandana, and Josephine Pui-Hing Wong. 2017. "Caught between a Rock and a Hard Place: Mental Health of Migrant Live-In Caregivers in Canada." *BMC Public Health* 17 (1): 498.

Vickers, Jill, Pauline Rankin, and Christine Appelle. 1993. *Politics as If Women Mattered: A Political Analysis of the National Action Committee on the Status of Women*. Toronto: University of Toronto Press.

Wallace, Rebecca. 2018. "Contextualizing the Crisis: The Framing of Syrian Refugees in Canadian Print Media." *Canadian Journal of Political Science* 51 (2): 207–31.

Wiseman, Nelson. 1988. "A Note on the 'Hartz-Horowitz at Twenty': The Case of French Canada." *Canadian Journal of Political Science* 21 (4): 795–806.

Wright, Teresa. 2019. "Trudeau Pledges More Funding for Reproductive Health Services Worldwide." *The Canadian Press*, June 4. https://www.cbc.ca/news /politics/trudeau-pledges-abortion-funding-1.5161891.

FURTHER READING

Agnew, Vigay. 2009. *Racialized Migrant Women in Canada: Essays in Health, Violence and Equity.* Toronto: University of Toronto Press.

Dauvergne, Catherine. 2016. *The New Politics of Immigration and the End of Settler Societies.* Cambridge: Cambridge University Press.

Dobrowolsky, Alexandra, Sedef Arat-Koç, and Christina Gabriel. n.d. *(Im)migrant Women in Canada: Challenges and Changes.* Policy4Women: Public Space, Public Engagement Briefing Note. Ottawa: Canadian Research Institute for the Advancement of Women. https://www.criawicref.ca/images/userfiles/files /P4W_BN_ImmigrantWomen.pdf.

Gaucher, Megan. 2018. *A Family Matter: Citizenship, Conjugal Relationships and Canadian Immigration Policy.* Vancouver: UBC Press.

Oxfam Canada. 2018. *2018 Feminist Scorecards.* https://www.oxfam.ca/Turning -Feminist-Promises-Into-Progress.

———. 2019. *2019 Feminist Scorecards.* https://www.oxfam.ca/feminist-policy -scorecard-2019/

2

Feminist Government or Governance Feminism? Exploring Feminist Policy Analysis in the Trudeau Era

Stephanie Paterson and Francesca Scala

Key terms: feminist government, gender-based analysis plus, gender results framework, governance feminism, post-structural policy analysis

The 2015 election of the Trudeau Liberals witnessed the re-emergence of a concept long thought to be silenced in Canadian political circles: feminism. After decades of backlash, delegitimizing, and near institutional erasure, Prime Minister Justin Trudeau, a self-proclaimed feminist, brought gender politics back to the centre, seeking not only to establish gender parity in cabinet but also to integrate gender and diversity considerations throughout the whole of government. This **feminist government** (FG), a term taken up in government and media circles, includes a number of initiatives aimed at enhancing diversity and inclusion in government, advocacy, and society. The FG has also made gender and diversity priorities in policy areas previously shielded from feminist intervention, including budgeting, trade, diplomacy, and security. Thus, it is clear that "feminism" has become a key organizing principle for the Trudeau government.

What remains unclear, however, is what exactly is "feminist" about the FG. Indeed, feminism is a contested concept that includes several different ways of knowing, each containing various ideas about what (in)equality means, how it is experienced, what causes it, and how it might be remedied. In this chapter, we undertake **post-structural policy analysis** (PSPA) to tease out what feminism means within the context of the FG, investigating how and to what effect feminist knowledge is taken up and deployed by the government. We are therefore interested not so much in what feminist knowledge *is*, but rather what it *does*. We focus on two pillars upon which the FG is premised: **gender-based analysis plus** (GBA+) and the **gender results framework** (GRF). We argue that the FG is a form of **governance feminism**, defined by Halley et al. as "the installation of feminists and feminist ideas in actual legal-institutional power" (2006, 340). As such, the FG simultaneously expands and narrows feminist knowledge. On the one hand, feminist knowledge is expanded across the "whole of government" and enters areas from which it had previously been excluded. On the other hand, feminist knowledge is narrowed as policy discourse fixes it to a neoliberal understanding of equality that emphasizes equal opportunities, self-reliance, and individual responsibility, thereby limiting how social justice might be conceptualized and achieved.

We begin with a brief discussion of PSPA, followed by an overview of the FG and the role of feminist knowledge and expertise therein. We then turn to an analysis of GBA+ and the GRF to consider how feminist knowledge is taken up in the production of gender inequality and proposed solutions, revealing the simultaneous expanding and narrowing of feminist expertise. We conclude with some reflections on the potential of the feminist agenda to open space for transformative politics.

UNCOVERING "FEMINISM" IN THE FEMINIST GOVERNMENT: POST-STRUCTURAL POLICY ANALYSIS AND GOVERNANCE FEMINISM

In policy studies, policies are typically conceptualized as responses to perceived problems. But problems do not exist objectively "out there"; rather, they must be brought into being to be understood and acted upon. This process of representing reality is the focus of PSPA. This mode of analysis focuses on *representations*, which serve as symbols that fix the meanings of complex phenomena, rendering them amenable to understanding and intervention (Gottweis 2003, 260; see also Bacchi 1999, 2009; Bacchi and Goodwin 2016; Hall 1997; Howarth and Griggs 2012). Given the problem-focus of contemporary policy studies and practice, PSPA centres on problem representations, or what Bacchi (1999, 2009) calls "problematizations." For analysts, it is necessary to interrogate the "work" of representations by illuminating the meanings they produce, as well as what—or who—is silenced or made invisible. It is also essential to unpack the taken-for-grantedness of particular representations by exposing their underlying assumptions and conceptual bases, and by tracing their origins (Bacchi and Goodwin 2016, 17). Finally, we must situate representations within broader social and political relations, examining how they operate in and through social life, reproducing or troubling power relations (Howarth and Griggs 2012).

Key to this approach is understanding how knowledge and expertise are implicated and deployed in governing practices, producing "the kinds of 'subject' we are encouraged to become" (Bacchi and Goodwin 2016, 5). Analytically, then, we want to understand how feminist knowledge—working in tandem with governmental administrative practices—constitutes the problem it seeks to solve. This question has been long debated within the feminist public administration literature. Emerging from earlier debates on the merits of bureaucratic engagement (e.g., Ferguson 1984; Eisenstein 1999), recent literature on state feminism focuses on the conditions under which states respond to feminist claims (e.g., McBride, Mazur, and Lovenduski 2012) and the effects of doing so (e.g., Stratigaki 2004; Verloo and Lombardo 2007; Prügl 2011; Paterson and Scala 2017). In this context, Halley et al. introduced the concept of governance feminism to describe the integration of feminist knowledge and governing, explaining that governance feminism

> piggybacks on existing forms [of] power, intervening in them and participating in them in many, simultaneous, often conflicting, and, in many examples anyway, highly mobile ways. It has found the novelty and civil-society open-texturedness of "the new governance" and "global governance" to be quite hospitable; it seeks not a monopoly of these forms but rather a plentiful presence within them. (2006, 340–41; see also Halley et al. 2018, 2019)

Governance feminism is neither new nor unique to Canada. To be sure, the post-war era saw the emergence of the "Women's State," a multi-nodal approach to gender inequality that included state institutions, arms-length bodies, and funding for movement groups (Rankin and Vickers 2001). Much of this policy architecture resulted from the Royal Commission on the Status of Women, established in 1967, and reflected the demands of white, middle-class, heterosexual, and largely anglophone women (Bunjun 2018; Bromley

2018). Governance feminism in this context reflected a white liberal orientation, as reproductive rights, childcare, and labour market concerns dominated the policy agenda, leaving class-based, racialized, and colonial structures intact. By the 1990s, however, policy capacity had been drastically cut, in what Brodie refers to as the three Ds: "the *delegitimization* of feminism, the *dismantling* of gender-based policy units, and the *disappearance* of the gender subject of public policy" (2007, 167). As women's groups were increasingly maligned as "special interest groups," funding declined and avenues for participation were closed off (Brodie 2007; Knight and Rodgers 2012). Moreover, political discourse and policy increasingly focused on the child, rendering women largely invisible (Dobrowolsky and Jenson 2004).[1] Replacing the multi-nodal approach was an integrated focus on policy analysis in the form of gender mainstreaming, which requires a gender lens to be applied to policy processes and analyses. These forces both heightened and obscured the role of the bureaucracy as a site of gender politics, while at the same time delegitimizing and depoliticizing feminism (Walby 2011).

Central to these processes—and to governance feminism more broadly—is the reassertion of technical expertise in the arena of gender politics and the emergence of a new form of policy worker: the "gender expert" (Bacchi et al. 2005; Paterson 2010). Prügl observes, "At the core of governance feminism is the development of a particular kind of knowledge—feminist legal expertise" (2011, 72), wherein "the authority of these agencies does not derive from the law. Instead, it derives from their application of expertise" (76). In unpacking this expertise, Halley asks a number of questions, including, "Exactly what *forms of feminism* 'make sense' to power elites as they gradually let women in" and "what are the distributive consequences of the partial inclusion of *some* feminist projects? Who benefits and who loses?" (2018, ix; emphasis added). These questions prompt reflection on whose feminism—and relatedly, whose feminist knowledge—is reflected in the state and to what effect, reminding us of the elite elements of feminist knowledge that privilege certain political projects over others. Importantly, once embedded in "the logic of government" (Prügl 2011, 77), this expertise is deployed in ways that make social relations and inequality intelligible and governable. In this way, as a rationality of government, feminist knowledge is a disciplinary force that shapes how we think and speak about gender and broader social relations, and produces significant lived effects across diverse groups.

It is within this context that Trudeau's vision for a FG can be understood. While still nascent and somewhat amorphous, the FG slowly took shape in the back half of his first mandate and is thus far shaped by three pillars: substantive policy measures, institutional commitments, and procedural mechanisms.[2] Substantive policy measures to date include the Feminist International Assistance Policy (FIAP); a more flexible parental leave system that includes a new parental sharing benefit, a use-it-or-lose-it, non-transferrable leave option for the other parent; and increased funding for advocacy groups both domestically, by doubling the money allocated to the Women's Program and abroad through the FIAP.

Several institutional commitments also shape the FG. These include cabinet parity, a commitment to gender budgeting, the National Inquiry into Missing and Murdered Indigenous Women, the LGBTQ2 Secretariat within the Privy Council Office, the Joint/Management Task Force on Diversity and Inclusion in the Public Service, the Multilateral Early Learning and Child Care Framework, the creation of a Centre for Gender, Diversity and Inclusion Statistics within Statistics Canada, a national strategy devoted to preventing and addressing gender-based violence, and the Beyond 150 Feminist Government workshop for public servants. Additionally, in 2018, Status of Women Canada (SWC) was promoted to a full department, the Department of Women and Gender Equality (WAGE), and received a boost of over $100 million in federal funding over five years.

All of these initiatives are supported by two interrelated procedural mechanisms that are central to the FG vision, GBA+ and the GRF. GBA is based on the understanding that policy impacts men and women differently, requiring analysts to apply a gender lens to all policies and programs, ideally at all stages of policy development, implementation, and evaluation (Rankin and Vickers 2001). Although the former Canadian International Development Agency, now Global Affairs Canada, has been doing "social analysis" since the 1970s, GBA spread across the Canadian federal government, and most provinces, in the mid-1990s.[3] In 2011, GBA was renamed GBA+ to signal a shift to a gender-intersectional approach, which acknowledges differences between diverse groups.[4]

Since its adoption, GBA+ has been subject to uneven commitments from elected officials. Although capacity for GBA+ was drastically compromised under the Harper Conservatives, political support for GBA+ increased with the election of the Trudeau government. For example, the 2017 budget was the first federal budget to include a gender statement that was informed by GBA+. Moreover, the 2018 budget was the first gender-sensitive budget in Canada, where every initiative had been subjected to GBA+. Significantly, the budget provided more financial resources to SWC in support of their GBA+ activities. These initiatives were supported by the legislation making SWC a full department within the federal landscape, as well as legislation making gender budgeting mandatory.

Among the long-standing concerns with GBA+ are its limited application and unknown impact.[5] Reports from the Office of the Auditor General (2009, 2015) observed several implementation problems, notably that GBA+ work was of poor quality or simply not done. Similarly, a 2016 report from the Standing Committee on the Status of Women observed that only 29 of the approximately 110 departments and agencies had committed to GBA+ (2016, 4). These reports also noted that there were no mechanisms in place to monitor the outcomes of GBA+. In response, Status of Women Canada, the Privy Council Office, and the Treasury Board Secretariat drafted joint action plans in 2009 and 2016, outlining next steps in addressing these issues.

Towards this end, the Ministry of Finance included the GRF as part of its 2018 budget. The GRF is a "whole of government" framework that provides substantive guidelines for 2018 and future budgeting processes by identifying priority areas, establishing gender equality goals, and providing a list of indicators against which to measure success. It also requires reporting on progress to date and clearly identifying budget actions. The GRF thus speaks to concerns about the transformative potential of GBA+ in the absence of substantive guidelines (e.g., Meier and Celis 2011), explicating the objectives guiding GBA+ and its application to the budget, the goals it seeks to achieve, and the ways in which those goals ought to be measured. In the remainder of this chapter, we apply PSPA to investigate the ways in which GBA+ and the GRF represent the problem of gender inequality.

WHAT'S FEMINIST ABOUT FEMINIST GOVERNMENT? FEMINIST KNOWLEDGE IN GBA+ AND THE GRF

As noted above, GBA+ requires analysts to apply a gender-intersectional lens to all policies and programs, ideally at all stages of policy development, implementation, and evaluation. Reflecting the comprehensive rationality model of policy analysis, in which an optimal solution is chosen from alternatives and subsequently implemented and evaluated, GBA+ proceeds in a linear manner and includes five steps: identify the issue, challenge assumptions, gather the facts (research and consult), develop options and make recommendations, and monitor and evaluate. Moreover, analysts are encouraged to communicate and document results throughout the entire process (SWC 2018a). The GRF offers more guidance to analysts applying GBA+ to budgeting by establishing a clear list of objectives and corresponding indicators. According to the Government of Canada, the GRF is "a whole-of-government tool to track how Canada is currently performing, to help define what is needed to achieve greater equality and to determine how progress will be measured going forward. The framework reflects this government's priorities for gender equality, highlighting the key issues that matter most" (GOC 2018, 219). The GRF is premised on six pillars, each associated with a broad objective and several indicators (GOC 2018, Chapter 5):

1. Education and skills development
    - Equal opportunities and diversified paths in education and skills development;
2. Economic participation and prosperity
    - Equal and full participation in the economy;
3. Leadership and democratic participation
    - Gender equality in leadership roles and at all levels of decision-making;
4. Gender-based violence and access to justice
    - Eliminating gender-based violence and harassment, and promoting security of the person and access to justice;
5. Poverty reduction, health, and well-being
    - Reduced poverty and improved health outcomes;
6. Gender equality around the world
    - Promoting gender equality to build a more peaceful, inclusive, rules-based and prosperous world.

There are 29 indicators associated with the GRF (GOC 2018, 221).

The questions we ask here are: What is represented as the problem, what is silenced or rendered invisible, and to what effect? For both GBA+ and the GRF, the "problem" of gender inequality is represented as a lack of information that can be resolved reactively by detecting potential differential "impacts" (see also Bacchi and Eveline 2010; Paterson 2010). For example, WAGE (formerly SWC) describes GBA+ as "a method for collecting and reviewing data in an unbiased manner, one that leaves aside many of the assumptions that can mask the GBA+ impacts of a given initiative" (SWC

2017). Indeed, the 2016–20 Action Plan, drafted by Status of Women Canada, the Privy Council Office, and the Treasury Board Secretariat, explains, "GBA helps to ensure that the development of policies, programs and legislation includes the consideration of differential impacts on diverse groups of women and men" (SWC 2016, 1). Similarly, the 2018 budget document notes: "Through the deliberate and more consistent use of Gender-based Analysis Plus (GBA+), the Government is able to make evidence-based policy decisions that benefit all Canadians" (GOC 2018, 218). It is further explained: "The Gender Results Framework is aligned with the Government of Canada's policy of GBA+, ensuring that gender is considered in relation to other intersecting identity factors. Wherever possible, and with a view to collecting better data, intersecting identity factors will be considered in the above indicators" (221). In these passages, gender equality can be achieved by way of "better" information; with "better" information, "better" solutions and outcomes will follow. These initiatives are to be supported through the creation of the Centre for Gender, Diversity and Inclusion Statistics, housed within Statistics Canada, which was established to strengthen the capacity of GBA+ (220).

It is this representation of the problem of gender inequality that enables the simultaneous expansion and contraction of feminist knowledge. In representing the problem of gender inequality as a lack of information, GBA+ and the GRF depoliticize social relations, removing them from any consideration of power relations and context (Bacchi and Eveline 2010). For example, in addressing the myths associated with GBA+, WAGE notes: "GBA+ is not advocacy. It is an analytical tool designed to help us ask questions, challenge assumptions and identify potential impacts, taking into account the diversity of Canadians." Similarly, it is explained that "gender equality benefits everyone in a society, and GBA+ can improve the situations of women, men and gender-diverse people. For example, in the same way that women were left out of heart disease research because it was seen as a 'man's disease,' men have historically been overlooked in osteoporosis research. While osteoporosis is often considered a disease of post-menopausal women, men actually account for nearly a third of osteoporosis-related hip fractures" (SWC 2018c, n.p.). In highlighting the potential benefits for men, policy discourse removes the potential of GBA+ to critically interrogate and challenge men and masculinity. In this discursive context, GBA+ is focused on the individual rather than power and relational change; thus, men are not asked to change and masculinity is accepted as given.

Similarly, GBA+ and the GRF are discursively aligned with broader government discourses of efficiency, effectiveness, and economic progress. The GBA+ main page on the WAGE website claims: "Did you know that GBA+ is recognized as a key competency in support of the development of effective programs and policies for Canadians? ... It provides federal officials with the means to continually improve their work and attain better results for Canadians by being more responsive to specific needs and circumstances" (SWC 2018b). The 2018 budget document similarly notes: "Gender budgeting is a conscious effort to understand how decisions affect different people differently, with a view to allocating government resources more equitably and efficiently" (GOC 2018, 218). This discursive alignment not only renders GBA+ and the GRF compatible with traditional bureaucratic discourses, but it also closes off space for forms of knowledge that run counter to—and indeed challenge—Eurocentric, masculinist ways of knowing. Indeed, in emphasizing the technical nature of gender inequality—which can be solved with better information and gender expertise—the situated and experiential knowledge of marginalized groups is rendered invisible (Rankin and Wilcox 2004). Yet it is precisely these forms of knowledge that provide insight into how policy is lived and experienced in the everyday.

Such discursive positioning serves to destabilize the potential threat of feminist knowledge, fixing feminism to a liberal variant and silencing the diverse voices that constitute feminist knowledge. In so doing, it enables its extension to areas such as budgeting, trade, and security. The 2018 budget reports: "The Government will introduce new GBA+ legislation to enshrine gender budgeting in the federal government's budgetary and financial management processes, *extending the reach of GBA+ to examine tax expenditures, federal transfers and the existing spending base, including the Estimates*" (GOC 2018, 220; emphasis added). The budget further notes:

> Canada is committed to eradicating poverty, and building a more peaceful, inclusive and prosperous world. The Government will invest in women's empowerment and gender equality as the best ways to achieve these objectives, grounded in the Agenda 2030 for Sustainable Development. *Numerous studies tell us this is the right course.* It has been estimated that achieving gender equality around the world could increase global GDP by $12 trillion over ten years. And there are strong correlations between gender inequalities and extreme poverty. *For these reasons*

> *and more Canada is pursuing a feminist approach across all its interna-*
> *tional policies and programming, including diplomacy, trade, security, and*
> *development.* (241; emphasis added)

Since GBA+ is simply "good policy analysis" that relies on "better information" in order to improve policy effectiveness, it can and should be extended
across all areas of government (Scala and Paterson 2017b; Paterson and Scala
2017).

If representing the "problem" of gender inequality as one of information
enables the expansion of feminist knowledge throughout the government,
it also narrows it by fixing it to a particular regime of truth wherein equality
is represented as "inclusion." Feminist literature has illuminated the contested meanings of gender equality, including "inclusion," "reversal," and
"transformation" (Verloo 2007; Verloo and Lombardo 2007). These visions
not only demonstrate different ways of thinking about gender equality, but
also contribute to different kinds of solutions. Inclusion here refers to an
understanding of inequality that is rooted in lack; that is, lack of skills or
lack of knowledge about opportunities. Thus, solutions are premised on
"integration" into extant practices and institutions without problematizing
the ways in which those practices and institutions shape individual experiences and contribute to unequal social relations. Reversal extends this
understanding in important ways by acknowledging that women's "unique"
contributions have typically been neglected or undervalued. Here, solutions are premised on recognizing the value of these contributions, such as
women's unpaid care work. Finally, transformation refers to understandings that locate inequality in social relations and power that arise from
socio-political practices and institutions. In other words, solutions aim to
trouble and transform those practices and institutions in more socially just
ways (Fraser 1997).

In narrowing feminist knowledge to "inclusion," the various FG initiatives
obscure the ways in which contemporary socio-political practices and institutions produce the social injustice they seek to solve. For example, GBA+ aims
to detect "differential impact" of policies already designed; thus, analysis is
reactive, aimed at ensuring policy proposals do not disparately burden some
groups over others, rather than proactive, which would inform decisions
before they are made (Bacchi and Eveline 2010; Burt and Hardman 2001). To
clarify, as noted above, the application of GBA+ in the 2017 and 2018 budgets
led to a number of changes to the parental leave program, currently delivered

through the Employment Insurance (EI) system. Reactive GBA+ fails to question whether or not the EI system, which ties eligibility and benefit rates to employment and earnings, is the best way to deliver benefits to parents. Indeed, parental leave programs that are tied to position in the labour market tend to reproduce economic inequality in terms of gender, race, class, and ability (e.g., Pulkingham and Van der Gaag 2004). In short, reactive analysis fails to consider intersectional power relations premised on colonialism, gender, race, class, and so on that shape access to and experiences with states and markets, leaving institutional and ideological contexts unscrutinized (Burt and Hardman 2001).

We can also see this effect in the GRF, whose goals and indicators reflect how feminist knowledge is narrowed. The six pillars address various sites of inequality, including the economy, politics and leadership, and society. However, in discussing inequality within each of these sites, what is problematized are not the practices and institutions that give rise to inequality, but rather the individual choices, or lack thereof, among marginalized groups. As such, "solutions" are limited to individualized and often privatized interventions that aim to "bring people into" existing institutions, such as the market or democratic governance. Such an approach not only renders invisible the role of underlying institutions, such as white heteropatriarchy, in shaping market and political systems, but also obviates transformative change.

This is clear in the objectives associated with each pillar of the GRF. Objectives such as: "equal and full participation in the economy"; "gender equality in leadership roles and at all levels of decision-making"; and "eliminating gender-based violence and harassment, and promoting security of the person and access to justice" (GOC 2018, 221) reveal a taken-for-grantedness regarding the institutional context in which inequality arises. Within this framework, it is not the institutions that require change, but rather marginalized peoples. For example, gender-based violence is represented as problematic not because of violent perpetrators, but because of a lack of data, under-reporting, and non-responsive representatives of the justice system. Thus solutions are premised on providing victims with better information and improving the gender balance of professionals within the legal system so as to empower victims to "tell their stories secure in the knowledge that they will be heard, believed and respected" (334). Here, the GRF makes survivors responsible for reporting their experiences rather than addressing violence itself. The narrowing of feminist knowledge to inclusion is especially apparent with respect to economic inequality regarding education, jobs, and poverty. For example, the GRF highlights the role of education and skills development and employment factors in contributing to inequality. Under the pillar "Education and Skills Development," the primary objective is to establish "equal opportunities and diversified paths in education and skills development" (221). The associated indicators include: "more diversified educational paths and career choices; reduced gender gaps in reading and numeracy skills among youth, including Indigenous youth; and equal lifelong learning opportunities for adults" (221). The language used in these passages masks the ways in which it is lack among women, Indigenous youth, and other marginalized people that is constituted as the problem. For example, when the GRF document explains that "gender segregation in education has led to less gender diversity across occupations and has limited career opportunities for women" (223), it heightens focus on women while neglecting the ways in which patriarchal gender systems privileging masculinity have also limited men's opportunities, particularly in the caring professions. Similarly, it is noted that

> higher levels of education among women have translated into higher wages. However, important gaps remain in both workforce participation and earnings. This partly reflects the different *fields of study* that women and men have pursued, and these choices are often skewed by established norms and institutional barriers formed around gender roles and identities. (222; emphasis in original)

Indeed, one of the key budget actions responding to these indicators is "helping women and underrepresented groups make informed career decisions by *improving the quality of career information and program results*" (224; emphasis in original).

We see similar language concerning "equal and full participation in the economy" (GOC 2018, 224). In justifying this area of intervention, the GRF explains: "Advancing women's economic participation will drive economic growth, while boosting the income of Canadian families. Economic independence means greater financial security of individuals and their families, helping people exercise control over their lives" (225). While this section of the document acknowledges the unequal distribution of care work—as well as wage gaps among Indigenous and immigrant women—emphasis remains on privatized, individual solutions rather than systemic and structural transformation. For example, the lack of affordable childcare is acknowledged as a barrier to women's participation in the labour market, but no mention is made of establishing public childcare programs. Instead, the document boasts of the Multilateral Early Learning and Child Care Framework, which simply tinkers with existing provincial-level programs that favour private systems.

A number of underlying assumptions support these claims, which reinforce the understanding of equality as inclusion. For example, it is assumed gender roles have led to limited female inclusion in male (read: high-paying) jobs such as science, technology, engineering, and math (STEM) fields. Further, it is assumed that the education, skills, and jobs acquired traditionally by white men are aspirational. Notably, no efforts are made to address the historical undervaluing of female-dominated jobs or to encourage more men to enter them; rather, emphasis is on getting women into male-dominated jobs. It is assumed that the market is a neutral arbiter of value and that the role of the state in these matters is to ensure that markets run efficiently and that people have access to good jobs. Together these assumptions leave unscrutinized the white patriarchal capitalist discourse that pervades and shapes policy discourse. In turn, they limit the solutions pursued in addressing inequality and constitute the state as kind, generous, and benevolent, which is reinforced by comments such as: "This chapter presents the details of this results framework and outlines how the Government's plan is helping ensure that everyone has a real and fair chance at success" (GOC 2018, 219). In doing so, the role of economic and political systems in producing and sustaining unequal social relations remains invisible and claims for transformative change are silenced.

CONCLUSION

The election of the Trudeau Liberals in 2015 marked the re-emergence of feminism in Canadian formal political circles. However, we have shown that the FG offers a narrow perspective with which to engage social justice. Premised on feminist knowledge, the FG has included substantive, institutional, and procedural changes that seek to address inequality along intersectional dimensions. Using PSPA, we have demonstrated that feminist knowledge has simultaneously expanded and narrowed within the context of FG. In representing the "problem" of inequality as one of information, policy discourse has enabled the expansion of feminist knowledge into areas such as budgeting, trade, and foreign policy, areas that had previously been shielded from feminist interventions. However, at the same time, feminist knowledge that itself reflects white and class privilege has been narrowed to an understanding of equality as inclusion. In so doing, feminist knowledge is bureaucratized and sanitized, thereby rendering its political means and objectives subject to technocratic scrutiny. As such, the state limits what can be said and by whom, closing off space for transformative politics.

There is, however, reason to be cautiously optimistic about what FG might mean for social politics. The literature on state and market feminism reveals the often ambiguous effects that arise when neoliberal bureaucracies take up feminist knowledge (e.g., McBride, Mazur, and Lovenduski, 2012; Prügl 2017, 2011). Indeed, our previous work has demonstrated the ways gender experts challenge (but also sometimes reinforce) the narrowing of feminist knowledge to that of inclusion, potentially opening space for transformation (e.g., Scala and Paterson 2017ab, 2018; Paterson and Scala 2017). In her analysis of the emergence of feminist ideas within the World Bank, Prügl argues: "In the encounter between feminism and neoliberalism the latter may have the upper hand, but the wholesale defeat of feminist agendas should not be a foregone conclusion. A feminist politics inside hegemonic institutions should not underestimate the subversive potential of powerful ideas" (2017, 48). From this, we are reminded that institutions and practices, while "sticky," are by no means fixed. The space opened by the FG, with its emphasis on diversity, inclusion, and consultation, might yet present opportunities to rethink the ways social relations are constituted in Canada.

DISCUSSION QUESTIONS

1. Is the feminist government a fundamentally different approach to governing than we've historically seen in Canada? Why/why not?

2. Governance feminism occurs when the language of feminism reflects the logic of government. How does this language also reflect white heteropatriarchal capitalism? Are these separate and distinct discourses? Why/why not? Can feminist discourses displace them?

3. Should feminism have an institutional presence in the state? Why/why not?

4. Is feminist activism possible inside the government? Why/why not?

NOTES

1 It should be noted, however, that the impact of these changes was not felt uniformly among groups of women. Indeed, some groups of women, notably Muslim women, are, in fact, "hypervisible" (see Arat-Koç 2012 for a discussion).

2 For a detailed overview and critique of these initiatives, see Oxfam Canada (2017, 2018).

3 See Paterson, Marier, and Chu (2016) for a discussion and overview of provincial-level GBA.

4 For example, racialized women typically fare worse in the labour market than white women; therefore, initiatives aimed at improving employment opportunities and outcomes that fail to address the different experiences and outcomes faced by diverse groups of women risk reproducing inequality along a number of social axes, including gender, race, ability, and class.

5 A number of concerns have emerged regarding the transformative potential of GBA+, including its weak lead agency, emphasis on bureaucratic expertise versus community voices, and persistent privileging of gender as an axis of oppression (Grace 1997; Rankin and Wilcox 2004; Paterson 2010; Hankivsky 2005, 2006, 2012).

REFERENCES

Arat-Koç, Sedef. 2012. "Invisibilized, Individualized, and Culturalized: Paradoxical Invisibility and Hyper-Visibility of Gender in Policy Making and Policy Discourse in Neoliberal Canada." *Canadian Woman Studies/Les cahiers de la femme* 29 (3): 6–17.

Bacchi, Carol. 1999. *Women, Policy, and Politics: The Construction of Policy Problems.* London: Sage.

——. 2009. *Analysing Policy: What's the Problem Represented to Be?* Frenchs Forest, Australia: Pearson.

Bacchi, Carol, and Joan Eveline. 2010. *Mainstreaming Politics: Gendering Practices and Feminist Theory.* Adelaide: University of Adelaide Press.

Bacchi, Carol, Joan Eveline, Jennifer Binns, Catherine Mackenzie, and Susan Harwood. 2005. "Gender Analysis and Social Change: Testing the Water." *Policy and Society* 24 (4): 45–68.

Bacchi, Carol, and Susan Goodwin. 2016. *Poststructural Policy Analysis.* New York: Palgrave Macmillan.

Brodie, Janine. 2007. "Canada's Three Ds: The Rise and Decline of the Gender-Based Policy Capacity." In *Remapping Gender in the New Global Order,* edited by Marjorie Griffin Cohen and Janine Brodie, 166–84. New York: Routledge.

Bromley, Victoria L. 2018. "What's Feminism Done (for Me) Lately?" In *Gender and Women's Studies: Critical Terrain,* 2nd ed., edited by Margaret Hobbs and Carla Rice, 20–34. Toronto: Women's Press.

Bunjun, Benita. 2018. "The Making of a Colonial Archive: The Royal Commission on the Status of Women." *Education as Change* 22 (2): 1–24.

Burt, Sandra, and Sonya Hardman. 2001. "The Case of Disappearing Targets: The Liberals and Gender Equality." In *How Ottawa Spends, 2001–2002: Power in Transition*, edited by Les Pal, 201–22. Montreal: McGill-Queen's University Press.

Dobrowolsky, Alexandra, and Jane Jenson. 2004. "Shifting Representations of Citizenship: Canadian Politics of 'Women' and 'Children.'" *Social Politics* 11 (2): 154–80.

Eisenstein, Hester. 1996. *Inside Agitators: Australian Femocrats and the State.* Philadelphia: Temple University Press.

Ferguson, Kathy. 1984. *The Feminist Case against Bureaucracy.* Philadelphia: Temple University Press.

Fraser, Nancy. 1997. *Justice Interruptus: Critical Reflections on the "Postsocialist" Condition.* New York: Routledge.

Gottweis, Herbert. 2003. "Theoretical Strategies of Poststructuralist Policy Analysis: Towards an Analytics of Government." In *Deliberative Policy Analysis: Understanding Governance in the Network Society*, edited by Maarten Hajer and Hendrik Wagenaar, 247–66. Cambridge: Cambridge University Press.

Government of Canada. 2018. *Budget 2018: Equality plus Growth: A Strong Middle Class.* Ottawa: Department of Finance. https://www.budget.gc.ca/2018/docs/plan/budget-2018-en.pdf.

Grace, Joan. 1997. "Sending Mixed Messages: Gender-Based Analysis and the 'Status of Women.'" *Canadian Public Administration/Administration publique du Canada* 40 (4): 582–98.

Hall, Stuart, ed. 1997. *Representation: Cultural Representations and Signifying Practices*, vol. 2. London: Sage.

Halley, Janet, Prabha Kotiswaran, Rachel Rebouché, and Hila Shamir. 2018. *Governance Feminism: An Introduction.* Minneapolis: University of Minnesota Press.

———. 2019. *Governance Feminism: Notes from the Field.* Minneapolis: University of Minnesota Press.

Halley, Janet, Prabha Kotiswaran, Hila Shamir, and Chantal Thomas. 2006. "From the International to the Local in Feminist Legal Responses to Rape, Prostitution/Sex Work, and Sex Trafficking: Four Studies in Contemporary Governance Feminism." *Harvard Journal of Law and Gender* 29 (2): 335–423.

Hankivsky, Olena. 2005. "Gender vs. Diversity Mainstreaming: A Preliminary Examination of the Role and Transformative Potential of Feminist Theory." *Canadian Journal of Political Science/Revue canadienne de science politique* 38 (4): 977–1001.

———. 2006. "Gender Mainstreaming in the Canadian Context: One Step Forward and Two Steps Back." In *Critical Policy Studies*, edited by Michael Orsini and Miriam Smith, 111–35. Vancouver: UBC Press.

———. 2012. "The Lexicon of Mainstreaming Equality: Gender Based Analysis (GBA), Gender and Diversity Analysis (GDA) and Intersectionality Based

Analysis (IBA)." *Canadian Political Science Review/Revue canadienne de science politique* 6 (2/3): 171–83.

Howarth, David, and Steven Griggs. 2012. "Poststructural Policy Analysis: Discourse, Hegemony, and Critical Explanation." In *The Argumentative Turn Revisited: Public Policy as Communicative Practice*, edited by Frank Fischer and Herbert Gottweis, 305–42. Durham, NC: Duke University Press.

Knight, Melanie, and Kathleen Rodgers. 2012. "The Government Is Operationalizing Neo-liberalism: Women's Organizations, Status of Women Canada, and the Struggle for Progressive Social Change in Canada." *Nordic Journal of Feminist and Gender Research* 20 (4): 266–82.

McBride, Dorothy, Amy Mazur, and Joni Lovenduski. 2012. *The Politics of State Feminism: Innovation in Comparative Research*. Philadelphia: Temple University Press.

Meier, Petra, and Karen Celis. 2011. "Sowing the Seeds of Its Own Failure: Implementing the Concept of Gender Mainstreaming." *Social Politics* 18 (4): 469–89.

Office of the Auditor General. 2009. *Spring Report of the Auditor General. Chapter 1: Gender-Based Analysis*. Ottawa: Office of the Auditor General. http://www1.oag-bvg.gc.ca/internet/English/parl_oag_200905_01_e_32514.html

———. 2015. *Implementing Gender-Based Analysis*. Ottawa: Author. http://www1.oag-bvg.gc.ca/internet/English/parl_oag_201602_01_e_41058.html.

Oxfam Canada. 2017. *2017 Feminist Scorecard*. https://www.oxfam.ca/wp-content/uploads/2017/03/2017_feminist_scorecard_.pdf.

———. 2018. *2018 Feminist Scorecard*. https://www.oxfam.ca/wp-content/uploads/2018/03/feminist_scorecard_2018_turning_feminist_promises_into_progress_infographic.pdf.

Paterson, Stephanie. 2010. "What's the Problem with Gender-Based Analysis? Gender Mainstreaming Policy and Practice in Canada." *Canadian Public Administration* 53 (3): 395–416.

Paterson, Stephanie, Patrik Marier, and Felix Chu. 2016. "Technocracy or Transformation? Mapping Women's Policy Agencies and Orienting Gender (In)Equality in the Canadian Provinces." *Canadian Public Administration* 59 (3): 405–24.

Paterson, Stephanie, and Francesca Scala. 2017. "Gender Mainstreaming and the Discursive Politics of Public Service Values." *Administrative Theory & Praxis* 39 (1): 1–18.

Prügl, Elisabeth. 2011. "Diversity Management and Gender Mainstreaming as Technologies of Government." *Politics & Gender* 7 (1): 71–89.

———. 2017. "Neoliberalism with a Feminist Face: Crafting a New Hegemony at the World Bank." *Feminist Economics* 23 (1): 30–53.

Pulkingham, Jane, and Tanya Van der Gaag. 2004. "Maternity/Parental Leave Provisions in Canada: We've Come a Long Way, but There's Further to Go." *Canadian Woman Studies* 23 (3/4): 116–25.

Rankin, Pauline, and Jill Vickers. 2001. "Women's Movements and State Feminism: Integrating Diversity into Public Policy." Ottawa: Status of Women Canada.

Rankin, Pauline, and Krista Wilcox. 2004. "De-Gendering Engagements? Gender Mainstreaming, Women's Movements and the Canadian Federal State." *Atlantis* 29 (1): 52–60.

Scala, Francesca, and Stephanie Paterson. 2017a. "Gendering Public Policy or Rationalizing Gender? Strategic Interventions and GBA+ Practice in Canada." *Canadian Journal of Political Science* 50 (2): 427–42.

———. 2017b. "Bureaucratic Role Perceptions and Gender Mainstreaming in Canada." *Gender, Work & Organization* 24 (6): 579–93.

Standing Committee on the Status of Women. 2016. *Implementing Gender-Based Analysis Plus in the Government of Canada.* Ottawa: SCSW. http://www.ourcommons.ca /Content/Committee/421/FEWO/Reports/RP8355396/feworp04/feworp04-e.pdf.

Status of Women Canada. 2017. "Research Checklist." Last modified July 18, 2017. http://www.swc-cfc.gc.ca/gba-acs/list-aide en.html.

———. 2018a. "Apply GBA+ to Your Work." Last modified December 4, 2018. http:// www.swc-cfc.gc.ca/gba-acs/apply-appliquez-en.html.

———. 2018b. "GBA+: The Government's Approach." Last modified December 4, 2018. http://www.swc-cfc.gc.ca/gba-acs/approach-approche-en.html.

———. 2018c. "What Is GBA+? Mythbusters." Last modified December 4, 2018. https://swc-cfc.gc.ca/gba-acs/index-en.html#myth.

Status of Women Canada, Privy Council Office, and Treasury Board of Canada Secretariat. 2016. *Action Plan (2016–2020).* Ottawa: SWC. http://www.swc-cfc .gc.ca/gba-acs/plan-action-2016-en.PDF.

Stratigaki, Maria. 2004. "The Cooptation of Gender Concepts in EU Policies: The Case of 'Reconciliation of Work and Family.'" *Social Politics* 11 (1): 30–56.

Verloo, Mieke, ed. 2007. *Multiple Meanings of Gender Equality: A Critical Frame Analysis of Gender Policies in Europe.* New York: CEU Press.

Verloo, Mieke, and Emanuela Lombardo. 2007. "Contested Gender Equality and Policy Variety in Europe: Introducing a Critical Frame Analysis Approach." In *Multiple Meanings of Gender Equality: A Critical Frame Analysis on Gender Policies in Europe,* edited by Mieke Verloo, 201–44. Budapest: Central European University.

Walby, Sylvia. 2011. *The Future of Feminism.* Cambridge: Polity Press.

FURTHER READING

Caglar, Gülay. 2013. "Gender Mainstreaming." *Politics & Gender* 9 (3): 336–44.

Chappell, Louise. 2003. *Gendering Government: Feminist Engagement with the State in Australia and Canada.* Vancouver: UBC Press.

Eveline, Joan, and Carol Bacchi. 2005. "What Are We Mainstreaming When We Mainstream Gender?" *International Feminist Journal of Politics* 7 (4): 496–512.

Findlay, Tammy. 2015. *Femocratic Administration: Gender, Governance, and Democracy in Ontario.* Toronto: University of Toronto Press.

Hankivsky, Olena. 2008. "Gender Mainstreaming in Canada and Australia: A Comparative Analysis." *Policy and Society* 27 (1): 69–81.

Squires, Judith. 2005. "Is Mainstreaming Transformative? Theorizing Mainstreaming in the Context of Diversity and Deliberation." *Social Politics: International Studies in Gender, State & Society* 12 (3): 366–88.

———. 2007. *The New Politics of Gender Equality*. London: Macmillan International Higher Education.

3

Gender Sensitivity under Trudeau: Facebook Feminism or Real Change?

Jeanette Ashe

Key terms: descriptive representation, gender-based analysis plus, gender-sensitive parliament, sex quotas

INTRODUCTION

Canada's 42nd Parliament is often celebrated for its intersectional diversity, with a record number of Members of Parliament (MPs) who are women and/or who identify as Black, Indigenous, or people of colour (BIPOC) elected in the 2015 General Election.[1] Indeed, Liberal Prime Minister Justin Trudeau became an international sensation by appointing Canada's first federal sex-balanced cabinet, inspiring the viral "#becauseits2015" Twitter hashtag (see Small in this volume). A Google search of "Trudeau and feminism" delivers just over one million web hits. However, this narrative of "firsts" contrasts with other indicators that demonstrate that many aspects of Parliament and parliamentary life may still be as insensitive to gender as they have ever been, prompting questions as to just how much "real change" has been achieved.

This chapter explores "turbulent times and transformational possibilities" by developing and employing a new methodology based on 32 key indicators by which to longitudinally explore gender sensitivity in legislatures. This new approach is then used to compare the highly praised Trudeau regime to that of his maligned predecessor, Conservative Prime Minister Stephen Harper, who notoriously avoided discussing women's and gender issues and sought to dismantle equity structures (see Dobrowolsky in this volume). Surprisingly, the comparison shows that despite the heavy equality rhetoric, Trudeau only modestly outperforms Harper in terms of substantive change. Thus, Canada's Parliament is still very much a male-dominated institution, with Trudeau's changes merely layered atop the very same structures that had excluded women and other marginalized groups under the Harper regime. This new method proves a useful way to compare gender sensitivity across time and regimes. In this particular case, it also indicates Trudeau's approach of equality rhetoric over substance might best be described as "Facebook feminism"—as opposed to his campaign slogan of "real change"—which superficially masks and leaves unchallenged deeper, masculinized power structures while at the same time dangerously dampening the urgency for greater gender transformation.

ASSESSING GENDER SENSITIVITY

Concern about gender sensitivity in political institutions is widespread and long-standing, and as parliaments become more diverse, they face increasing pressure to also become more gender sensitive. The Inter-Parliamentary Union (IPU) defines a **gender-sensitive parliament** as responding "to the needs and interests of both men and women in its structures, operations, methods, and in its work" (2011, 6). Founded on the principle of gender equality, it "promotes and achieves equality in numbers of women and men across all of its bodies and internal structures," removes "the barriers to women's full participation," and offers "a positive example or model to society at large" (6). Canada's Parliament is not traditionally viewed as particularly gender sensitive, with the House of Commons and Senate still predominantly reflecting the work and interests of white professional men (see Lovenduski 2005, 2017). Illustrating this is Joan Grace's portrayal of Canada's Parliament as an "inequality regime" in which male privilege runs through its values, policies, and practices (2016, 841).

A key focus of gender-sensitive reform concerns women's **descriptive representation**, defined as legislatures proportionately reflecting the populations they represent in terms of sex, gender, race, ethnicity, Indigeneity, and other social characteristics and shared experiences (Mansbridge 1999). From a normative perspective, Anne Phillips famously argues: "There is no argument from justice that can defend the current state of affairs: and in this more negative defence there is an argument from justice for parity" (1998, 232). The "politics of presence" matters not only for reasons of justice but for matters of legitimacy and policy, with women's descriptive representation linked to substantive representation (Mansbridge 1999; Phillips 1998).[2] For example, Manon Tremblay (2009) shows that women legislators in Canada tend to advance and support legislation for women to a greater degree than men (see also Arscott and Trimble 2013). This trend is seen in other countries, including Sweden, where Lena Wängnerud (2015) finds more gender-sensitive legislation passes when more women legislators are present. Some, however, suggest the descriptive–substantive relationship is complex, as there are no guarantees that women always act for women (see Pitkin 1967). While a clear causal relationship between women's descriptive representation and substantive representation has been somewhat difficult to empirically establish, it is now widely accepted that the two are closely related (Lovenduski 2005). Thus, legislative sex parity is often seen as the overall goal, as the presence of women legislators has at least the potential to transform an otherwise masculine institution into a more gender-sensitive institution.

Phillips encourages exploring systemic descriptive underrepresentation through empirical assessments of parliaments on grounds that "if there were no obstacles operating to keep certain people out of political life, then we would expect positions of political influence to be randomly distributed between both sexes and across all ethnic groups" (1998, 229). Women's disproportional underrepresentation in Canada and in other legislatures presents an irrefutable case for policy action. Influenced by Phillips's argument, today there are few scholars who do not concern themselves with the descriptive representation of women and, increasingly, with other underrepresented groups such as BIPOC and LGBTQ2+ people (see Bird 2016; Tolley 2016; Tremblay 2019).

In terms of empirically assessing the gender sensitivity of parliaments, the IPU's widely cited *Gender-Sensitive Parliaments: A Global Review of Good Practice* (2011) and *Evaluating the Gender Sensitivity of Parliaments: A Self-Assessment Toolkit* (2016) provide a good starting point. These documents offer definitions, assessment advice, and potential questions, but little in the way of detailed methodology and are not intended to facilitate ranking or comparison. In *The Good Parliament*, Sarah Childs (2016) uses the IPU's framework to develop a detailed methodological approach to assessing the diversity sensitivity of the United Kingdom's Parliament during Prime Minster David Cameron's Conservative government. Childs uses a red-amber-green (poor-improved-good) analysis, based on traffic light colours, to document insensitivities and signal if the UK's Parliament is doing badly, well, or if it has "shown some improvement but ... considerably more needs to be done" (2016, 8). Childs's assessment indicates the institution fails to meet the majority of the IPU's gender-sensitive standards.

This chapter builds on the IPU's framework and Childs's work to develop a methodology by which to compare gender-sensitive progress across regimes, using 32 indicators classified into three categories: (1) representation, which contains 12 measures, such as the number of women MPs and committee chairs; (2) infrastructure, which includes 11 measures, such as parental leave and night sittings; and (3) policies and legislation, which consists of nine measures, such as sexual harassment and **gender-based analysis plus** (GBA+).[3] When used for longitudinal comparison, as they are for this study, each indicator is simply scored as "1" when conditions have substantially improved, "–1" when conditions have substantively declined, and "0" for no change.

ASSESSING GENDER SENSITIVITY UNDER HARPER AND TRUDEAU

This chapter tests this new method by assessing gender sensitivity under Conservative Prime Minister Stephen Harper and Liberal Prime Minister Justin Trudeau. As has been described, the Harper regime is often portrayed as hostile to equity, whereas the Trudeau regime is praised for its bold and progressive actions in this area. These two regimes would seem ready for comparison as they exist within the same institutional and cultural context, with Trudeau's Parliament expected to be much more gender sensitive than Harper's. The rest of this section compares the two regimes using 32 indictors grouped into three categories.

Representation

Table 5 provides results for the first suite of indicators associated with descriptive representation across 12 parliamentary bodies. The "Harper" column provides information between 2011 and 2015, with the "Trudeau" column

Table 1 Representation on Parliamentary Bodies: Harper vs Trudeau

Indicator	Harper	Trudeau	Change
Women MPs	25%	27%	1
Women in Cabinet	26%	50%	1
Women Senators	37%	47%	1
Women House Speakers[a]	0	0	0
Women Senate Speakers[b]	0	0	0
Women House Committee Chairs[c]	9%	17%	1
Women Senate Committee Chairs	20%	50%	1
House Committees 50% or More Women Members	0.5%	13%	1
Senate Committee 50% or More Women Members	20%	35%	1
Department of the Status of Women	0	1	1
House Standing Committee on the Status of Women	1	1	0
Senate Standing Committee on Status of Women	0	0	0
Total	–	–	**8/12**

Note: Percentages are rounded.

a Does not include House deputy speakers.
b Does not include Senate deputy speakers.
c The evaluations include only standing committees.

covering the period between 2015 and 2019.[4] The last column scores positive change as "1," no change as "0," and negative change as "-1." Improvements have been made along eight measures: MPs, cabinet, senators, House committee chairs, Senate committee chairs, Senate committees with more than 50 per cent women, House committees with more than 50 per cent women, and increased powers for the Department of the Status of Women, for an overall score of +8/12. Each indicator is explained in detail below.

Based on traditional measures of gender sensitivity, Trudeau's Parliament is clearly more representative in terms of sex, with, for example, historically high numbers of women elected to the House of Commons and appointed to the Cabinet and the Senate.[5] However, aside from a few notable exceptions, such as the striking 25-percentage-point increase in cabinet positions, increases in some other common measures of women's descriptive representation are marginal at best, with, for example, a mere two-percentage-point increase in the number of women MPs elected to Canada's House of Commons.[6] Much more encouraging is the 12.5-percentage-point increase in House committees, with more than 50 per cent women, and the 10-percentage-point increase in the number of women appointed to the Senate.[7] Of some concern, according to the IPU's ranking of women in national parliaments, Canada still lags far behind many other established democracies, and its position dropped by a whopping 22 spots between 2011 and 2019, from 30th to 61st (IPU 2019).

The representation measures also include women's participation in positions of leadership—for example, as speakers and chairs in the House of Commons and Senate standing committees. The IPU stresses that women holding such positions of power and authority can "influence policy direction, present a positive role model to other women, change parliamentary procedures," or "simply ensure a more representative balance" (2011, 17).[8] Yet women remain underrepresented in the upper echelons of parliamentary hierarchies. This trend is seen with House and Senate speaker positions; under Harper all Senate and House speakers were men. This has not changed under Trudeau. This pattern is not altogether surprising, given that only two women have ever held the position in the Senate (in 1974 and 1979) and only one woman has been the speaker of the House (in 1984).[9] To date, there are no measures in place to bring about gender equality, such as a **sex quota** to guarantee the election of women speakers for the next Parliament.[10]

In terms of committee chairs, the IPU suggests women chairs and women's presence on committees are important in so far as their different perspectives matter for the work done, such as reviewing issues and legislation, as well as hearing from women experts on committees (2011, 19). During Harper's regime, women chaired 2 of 24 (9 per cent) of House of Commons standing committees and 3 of 15 (20 per cent) of Senate standing committees. As of January 2019, under Trudeau women chaired 4 of 24 (17 per cent) of House of Commons standing committees (Canadian Heritage, Status of Women, Indigenous and Northern Affairs, and Transport, Infrastructure and Communities), an increase of two since Harper. In terms of Senate chairs, there is now sex parity, with women chairing 8 of the 16 (50 per cent) standing committees, an increase of five women since Harper.[11] Despite the increase in women chairs, women are still disproportionately chairing standing committees dealing with "soft" policy issues such as women's issues and social welfare issues rather than "hard" policy issues such as defence and the economy. As with cabinet positions, this is a long-standing issue in Canada as well as in other parliaments (IPU 2011). The underrepresentation of women chairs of House of Commons standing committees is not simply a supply-side problem; there are more than enough women to fill half of the chair positions.[12] There are currently no mechanisms to address women's underrepresentation as House committee chairs, such as, for example, a sex quota requiring that women chair 50 per cent of committees (see Childs 2017, 2).

Turning next to standing committees with more than 50 per cent women, in the 2011–15 period under Harper, only one House committee—Status of Women—and three Senate committees—Aboriginal Peoples, Official Languages, and Social Affairs, Science, and Technology—had more than 50 per cent women members. Under Trudeau, the number of House committees with more than 50 per cent women members increased by two to three—Status of Women, Foreign Affairs, and Languages—and in the Senate the number increased by three to six—Legal and Constitutional Affairs, National Finance, Official Languages, Human Rights, Rules, Procedures and Rights, and Social Affairs, Science and Technology.[13] Problematically, under Trudeau, 88 per cent (21) of House committees have less than 50 per cent women, but this is still slightly better than under Harper when this figure was 95 per cent.[14] Disconcertingly, two House committees (Fisheries and Transportation) currently have no women members. The numbers are better for the Senate, where under both Harper and Trudeau 75 per cent of committees (12) had less than 50 per cent women members, and currently only one committee (Ethics) has only one woman member (who happens to be the chair). As is the case with women chairs, women members tend to sit on House committees dealing with "soft" as opposed to "hard" issues, but on this front women are doing better in Senate committees. There are no measures in place to formally address the underrepresentation of women on committees, particularly those dealing with harder policy issues. In this respect, it is worthwhile to consider Childs's recommendation to "prohibit single sex/gender select committees and encourage political parties to be mindful of wider representativeness in the election of members to committees" (2017, 3).

In terms of committees dedicated to gender equality, the IPU's report *Gender-Sensitive Parliaments* highlights the influential role they play in "mainstreaming a gender perspective throughout parliamentary work" in so far as they serve as an "incubator for policy ideas related to gender equality" or as a "focal point for women's interest groups in lobbying parliament," and states that "these committees help keep gender equality issues on the agenda for all parliamentarians" (2011, 38). In October 2018, the Status of Women Canada (SWC) agency, as per the Budget Implementation Act 2018, became a full ministry with a full minister, Maryam Monsef, and was renamed the Department of Women and Gender Equality (WAGE). Minister Monsef noted that the Department of WAGE will continue the work that the SWC has been doing since 1976 to promote "equality for women and their full participation in the economic, social and democratic life of Canada," but will now have "greater capacity to do this work that is essential to growing Canada's economy" (SWC 2018a, n.p.). The increase in the powers of the SWC under Trudeau in terms of its transformation into a full department warrants a +1 along this measure.

Unlike the SWC, the powers and mandate of the House of Commons Standing Committee of the Status of Women (FEWO) remain unchanged, as does its relationship to the newly formed Department of WAGE. FEWO's lack of powers is open to considerable criticism; while many of its recommendations are considered by the government, few are implemented, particularly those having to do with legislating gender-based analysis plus (see Grace 2016; Paterson and Scala in this volume). Given the lack of positive change, this measure is given a score of 0. Looking next to the Senate, as of 2019 it still lacks a committee focusing on women and gender equality; thus this measure is given a score of 0.[15] Overall, under Trudeau there have been improvements along 8 of the 12 measures in the "representation" dimension, indicating that there is still some way to go before this dimension is fully gender sensitive.

Infrastructure

The 11 gender-sensitive measures in table 2, on infrastructure, explore the ways Parliament "facilitates the work of members" and "if this privileges some members over others" (Childs 2016, 7; IPU, 2011). Measures along this dimension include "buildings, rules, and practices that underpin the array of members' activities" (Childs 2016, 7). Parliaments were designed by men for men and have had and continue to have a gendered effect on MPs' ability to do their job. Times have changed in so far as not only are there women MPs, but their numbers are growing and, as expected, so too is the number of women MPs giving birth while holding office. Still, the parliamentary infrastructure is not keeping up with these changes. In some ways, Parliament still reflects the outdated family model where MPs have stay-at-home partners who care for their children and other dependents. As shown in table 2, there has been improvement along only one of the 11 measures, parental leave for MPs.

In terms of parental leave, the IPU (2011) sees such a policy as important to making parliaments more family friendly (see also Bittner and Thomas 2017). Budget 2018 included the first ever parental leave program for parliamentarians, prompted, according to House Leader Bardish Chagger, by an

Table 2 Infrastructure

Indicator	Harper	Trudeau	Change
Parental Leave	0	1	1
Childcare Policy	0	0	0
On-Site Childcare during All Sitting Hours	0	0	0
Designated Women-Only Space	0	0	0
Non-members (Infants) Permitted on the House Floor	0	0	0
Night Sittings	0	0	0
Parallel Chamber	0	0	0
Proxy Voting	0	0	0
Videoconferencing	0	0	0
Electronic Voting	0	0	0
Women and Transgender/Gender-Neutral Washrooms	0	0	0
Totals	**0**	**1**	**1/11**

increasing number of women MPs of "childbearing years and MPs with young families" (2018, n.p.).[16] In June 2019, the House of Commons unanimously agreed to new rules to allow MPs to take 12 months of fully paid parental leave from their job when they give birth or adopt, and to miss four weeks of work without penalty prior to their delivery date (Wright 2019). Prior to this change, MPs were not provided parental leave because they did not pay into employment insurance. Rather, they were eligible to take 21 days of medical leave, after which time their pay was deducted $120 per day absent. Further, they had to make arrangements for their absence with their party leadership or whip. Thus, under Harper and for most of Trudeau's tenure, women MPs returned to work shortly after giving birth. For example, MP Christine Moore returned to work only a few days after giving birth to her first child and MP Nikki Ashton returned to work just two weeks after giving birth to twins. In March 2018, Minister of Democratic Institutions Karina Gould became the first sitting minister to give birth while in office and welcomed the long over-due change, saying "it sends a signal that it's acceptable and legitimate" to be both a MP and a new parent (Wright 2019, n.p.).

In terms of childcare policy, the IPU notes childcare policies to be amongst the most important family-friendly changes to parliaments, yet Canada's Par-liament lacks a formal childcare policy for the provision of childcare and its expenses (IPU 2011). While parliamentarians and staff have access to onsite childcare for children aged 18 months to five years of age, there are only 30 spaces, the hours of operation do not reflect the parliamentary sitting times, and there is no drop-in option. There is, however, reason for tempered optimism. The Procedures and House Affairs Standing Committee (PROC) was informed that the House administration had "studied various options regarding offering later hours and a drop-in service for the day care on the parliamentary precinct" but that "these options were found to be problematic and costly due to the uncertainty of usage" (PROC 2016, n.p.). Therefore, one of the recommendations in the PROC's interim report, *Moving toward a Modern, Efficient, Inclusive and Family-Friendly Parliament*, tabled in June 2016, is for the House Administration to proceed with providing flexible childcare services during hours needed by members; however, this would still be at the member's own personal hourly cost.[17] Although there have been no formal changes to the provision of onsite childcare since Harper, PROC indicated it would later "review and evaluate the suitability of whatever services are established" (2016, n.p.).

Unlike the United Kingdom and Finland, Canada's Parliament does not have a women-only space where women members and staff can seek some respite during late-night sittings in a place still disproportionally filled with men (Childs 2017).[18] However, there is a designated family room near the Centre Block for parents caring for young children. There may be some disruption to the family-friendly room and even to onsite childcare as several parliamentary buildings are undergoing rehabilitation work, including the Centre Block, which is expected to take at least 10 years.[19]

Turning next to non-members permitted on the House floor: in Canada, as is the case in most parliaments, only members or officers are allowed on the floor of the House, a tradition that reflects the systemic underrepresentation of women, particularly women with infants and young children (Barnes and Munn-Rivard 2013, 2). This tradition is increasingly challenged by MPs with infants and young families. Breastfeeding in parliaments is now on the rise; for example, in 2016, Australia changed its Standing Orders to permit breastfeeding in the Chamber. In many parliaments, such as Denmark, Finland, and New Zealand, breastfeeding is still not formally permitted, but neither is it ruled out (Childs 2017, 8). Canada also falls into this "grey" category.

While the tradition of formally prohibiting non-members (including infants) on the floor of Canada's House of Commons continues, the speaker permits MPs to bring their infants into the Chamber when it is sitting so long as there is no disruption and the work of the House proceeds without interruption (Barnes and Munn-Rivard 2013, 3). Between 2011 and 2015 three

MPs gave birth, prompting urgency during Harper's government to address this. For example, when former NDP MP Sania Hassainia brought her baby onto the House's floor the speaker initially rejected her but soon allowed her to return, which paved the way for a new precedent of allowing newborns in parents' arms on the floor (Csanady 2015). Allowing infants on the floor while while their parents sit in the House of Commons or on committees will allow members to more fully participate in parliamentary activities and will likely help with the future recruitment and retention of women MPs. The PROC's report on *Moving toward a Modern, Efficient, Inclusive and Family-Friendly Parliament* (2016), however, does not recommend a formal rule change in the Standing Orders to permit infant feeding in the chambers.

Looking to sitting times, late and unpredictable sittings are likely hardest on MPs with caring responsibilities and potentially affect the diversity of Parliament; thus, positive changes to the parliamentary calendar are thought to be among the most family-friendly and gender-sensitive reforms (Barnes and Munn-Rivard 2013, 2; Childs 2016). The fixed parliamentary calendar in Canada was adopted in 1982 and allows the three major adjournments—Easter, summer, and winter holidays—to align with the school calendar. Unlike many other parliaments, Canada's has not discontinued "night sittings." On this matter, the PROC recommends "that House Leaders continue, whenever possible, the informal practice of holding deferred recorded decisions immediately following Question Period" as opposed to evenings and recommends "the Committee commits to undertaking more complete study of this matter during its reviews of the Standing Orders" (2016, n.p.). Reading between the lines, night sittings are not going to be discontinued any time soon.

Parallel chambers, sometime referred to as alternate debating chambers, do not exist in Canada's Parliament but do in other Westminster systems, such as the United Kingdom and Australia. By relieving pressure on the House of Commons a parallel chamber allows for greater flexibility in sitting hours and thus has the potential to increase the gender sensitivity of parliaments (PROC 2016; Childs 2016, 2017).[20] The PROC does not find the addition of a parallel chamber to be overly complicated or expensive, yet it offers no recommendation going forward other than to study it in the future.

Absentee voting, which includes proxy voting, videoconferencing, and electronic voting, is another way to better facilitate the work of MPs who need to be absent from the Chamber "for a restricted set of reasons" (for example, being heavily pregnant or being on parental leave) and still have their votes counted (PROC 2016, n.p.). As of early 2019, all members still must be present in the House and in their assigned seats in order to have their votes recorded. Proxy voting allows MPs to appoint a "proxy" from among other MPs to vote and otherwise act for them. New Zealand's MPs have been using proxy voting since 1996 and Australia's MPs who are breastfeeding have been casting proxy votes since 2008 (PROC 2016). In January 2019, members of the British Parliament voted on a pilot project to allow proxy voting for MPs on parental leave. Yet, like most other parliaments, Canada's still does not allow for proxy voting, and in its report, PROC (2016) made no recommendations allowing for it.[21]

Videoconferencing permits MPs to call in and participate on committee meetings if they are unable to travel to Parliament. Although some provinces formally allow videoconferencing to conduct official parliamentary business, Canada's Parliament does not.[22] There have, however, been instances where members have called in to participate in committee reports, but their virtual presence does not count towards quorum and they cannot vote.[23] As with videoconferencing, electronic voting, sometimes referred to as remote voting, would further facilitate the participation of MPs in the later stages of pregnancy and on maternity, paternity, parental, or caring leave. Although frequently used in the United States, videoconferencing has not arrived at Canada's Parliament (Childs 2017, 21).

Lastly, a parliament's gender-sensitive infrastructure includes women's access to a suitable number of women's washrooms close to both Houses. Over time, more women's washrooms have been added to Canada's Centre Block and at the close of 2018 there were 11 women's washrooms equipped with change tables, with two additional changing tables installed in the women's and men's washrooms located close to the House Foyer (Barnes and Munn-Rivard 2013, 4). While there were some accessible washrooms, there were no transgender or gender-neutral facilities. Given that the rehabilitation of the parliamentary buildings is still in process, current information about family-friendly or gender-sensitive infrastructure for the rehabilitated buildings is not available. In terms of recommendations, PROC (2016) made none on this front; however, the IPU (2011) recommends that parliaments provide enough washroom facilities to accommodate changing demographics.

As seen in table 2 and discussed above, there has been one improvement along the 11 gender-sensitive infrastructure measures from Harper to Trudeau. Notably, some gender-sensitive measures occurred under Harper, including informally allowing non-members on the floor, adding more family-friendly washrooms, and creating a family space. Still, there are several gender-sensitive infrastructure changes in the works and numerous follow-up studies, which could improve Trudeau's future gender-sensitive score. For example, the government's 2018 response to the PROC's *Interim Report on Moving toward a Modern, Efficient, Inclusive and Family-Friendly Parliament* (2016) includes an expression of support for the idea of amending the Standing Orders to formalize the practice of "children being cared for by a Member present in the chamber during sitting" (Hajdu, n.d., n.p.) Further, the government says it will look into "collaborating to schedule votes after Question Period as opposed to in the evening", and "work to publish the 2018 calendar much earlier than in the past to enable MPs to plan their schedules and coordinate with the school calendar" (n.p.). As well, the government is open to considering recommendations to improve the availability and accessibility of childcare services and family/play spaces on Parliament Hill.

Policies and Legislation

Table 3 captures the way in which parliamentary policies and legislation can change the culture of Parliament, for example by implementing codes of conduct, sexual harassment policies, heckling policies, gender-based analysis of legislation, gender-sensitive budgeting, and equity legislation. There have been improvements across three of these nine measures: an increase in committees reviewing legislation using gender-based analysis plus (GBA+), a GBA+ budget, and specific legislation promoting the principle of gender equality. In terms of the other measures, there will likely be future improvements given that the Trudeau government is in the process of addressing some of the concerns in these areas.

None of Parliament's three codes of conduct, the Conflict of Interest Code for Members in the House of Commons, the Conflict of Interest Act, and the Ethics and Conflict of Interest Code for Senators, mention gender equality. Rather, the codes are in place to promote the ethical conduct of parliamentarians and to avoid conflicts of interest for them and their families (Munn-Rivard 2013, 3). Strengthening this is the October 25th, 2018 passing of Bill C-65, An Act to Amend the Canada Labour Code (harassment and violence), the Parliamentary Employment and Staff Relations Act and the Budget Implementation Act, 2017, No. 1, which brings further protections against violence and harassment to all federally regulated workplaces.

The IPU (2011) notes that harassment policies should be an integral part of a parliament's equity strategy and praises Canada on this front as, unlike other

Table 3 Policies and Legislation

Indicator	Harper	Trudeau	Change
Codes of Conduct Mention Gender Equality	0	0	0
Sexual Harassment Policy, MP-to-MP	1	1	0
Heckling Policy	0	0	0
Federal Departments with Legislative Requirement to Report on GBA+	0	0	0
Committees Reviewing Legislation Using GBA+	0	1	1
Systematic Committee Process to Apply GBA+ to Legislation	0	0	0
GBA+ Budget	0	1	1
Specific Legislation Promoting the Principles of Gender Equality	0	1	1
Sex Quotas	0	0	0
Totals	**1**	**4**	**3/9**

parliaments, Canada's has sexual harassment policies. Two policies explicitly deal with sexual harassment. The December 2014 House of Commons Policy on Preventing and Addressing Harassment applies to MPs as employers, staff employed by MPs, House officers, and research officers, but not MP-to-MP relations. However, the June 2015 Code of Conduct for Members of the House of Commons: Sexual Harassment, now a part of the Standing Orders, applies to allegations of sexual harassment between MPs. Under Harper, the MP-to-MP code was added to the appendix of the Standing Orders as a response to the suspension of two Liberal MPs, Massimo Pacetti and Scott Andrews, in November 2014 following complaints by two women NDP MPs. Pacetti sexually assaulted one of the MPs and Andrews sexually harassed the other MP. Although Trudeau removed both MPs from the Liberal caucus the incidents revealed that Parliament had no mechanisms, let alone policies, in place to deal with sexual harassment between MPs (Thompson 2015).

The new MP-to-MP code of conduct, however, is not without problems. In their study "Canada's Member-to-Member Code of Conduct on Sexual Harassment in the House of Commons: Progress or Regress?" Cheryl Collier and Tracey Raney reveal how the code is a "new institutional rule 'nested' inside old intransigent institutions" and thus "not only fails to challenge existing patriarchal norms, but also reinforces and permits them under the guise of change" (2018, 796). The code has serious textual limitations and narrowly defines harassment, pushes the "myth of false reporting," and leads to "victim blaming" (803; see also 803–10). For example, the new code only includes incidents of sexual harassment, defined as "unwanted conduct of a sexual nature that detrimentally affects the work environment," and thus excludes a wider range of gender-based harassment (House of Commons 2015, 3). Gender-based harassment is not explicitly sexual and includes unwanted comments and heckling at women because of their sex (Collier and Raney 2018, 803–04). Further, the code fails to recognize the impact intersecting identities such as race and sexual orientation have upon experiences of harassment (804).

#MeToo's arrival on Parliament Hill further highlights the limitations of the new MP-to-MP code to deal with gender-based harassment. The incidents of misconduct in 2018, let alone instances since the new code's implementation, are too numerous to cite but some standouts include MP Christine Moore accusing MP Erin Weir of inappropriate behaviour and MP Gerry Ritz calling Minister Catherine McKenna "Climate Barbie" (Campbell and McIntyre 2018). The extent of unparliamentary behaviour is further captured in a 2018 survey where close to 58 per cent of women MPs who responded indicated they experienced sexual misconduct while in office by way of unwanted remarks, gestures, and texts, with three MPs reporting sexual assault and four reporting sexual harassment (Smith 2018).

By excluding gender-based harassment the new code does not cover heckling, a practice where MPs "taunt, ridicule and demean (mostly female) parliamentarians" (Collier and Raney 2018, 808). In the PROC's *Interim Report on Moving toward a Modern, Efficient, Inclusive and Family-Friendly Parliament* (2016) heckling is flagged as an ongoing problem and a practice that is not conducive to a respectful workplace, yet the PROC portrays such behaviour as just another part of lively debate and parliamentary culture that is meant to be satirical rather than hurtful. This is not altogether surprising, given that the PROC's report does not challenge the traditional and masculine culture of Parliament; rather, it protects it under the guise of balancing modernization with tradition: "the Committee has attempted to strike an appropriate balance between moving forward as a modern workplace" while "ensuring the long-standing conventions and cultures, which are the foundation of a legislature, are not unduly disturbed" (n.p.).

Thus, so deeply engrained is heckling that Green Party leader and MP Elizabeth May observes, "This is the only workplace in Canada where abuse is routine. It's perfectly acceptable to have people yelling at you, making nasty comments to you, while you're on the floor of the House of Commons doing your work" (Campbell and McIntyre 2018). Indeed, Samara Canada's 2016 report *Cheering or Jeering* finds 69 per cent of MPs feel heckling is a problem and women MPs frequently report hearing heckles directed at their gender and appearance. Most of the 20 per cent of MPs who feel heckling affects their ability to do their job are women (Samara 2016). Still, the PROC's report (2016) does not make any recommendations regarding such "decorum in the House." The MP-to-MP code's omission of heckling, the PROC's failure to address it, and the speaker's inconsistency in calling it out reinforce the idea that such behaviour is "not unparliamentary" (Collier and Raney 2018, 808).

Overall, the code's amendment to include MP-to-MP harassment, while at first glance a positive development, does not address the underlying culture that allows sexual and gender-based harassment to occur in the first place. Given a lack of improvement under Trudeau, the "sexual harassment" measure is given a score of 0.

Next, gender-based analysis (examined by Paterson and Scala in this volume) highlights the different ways legislation impacts women and other marginalized people and how it could be changed to achieve greater gender equality (SWC 2016). As early as 1995, the Government of Canada committed to using gender mainstreaming and to using GBA as a mechanism to "advance gender equality in Canada, as part of the ratification of the United Nations' *Beijing Platform for Action*" (n.p.). **Gender-based analysis plus** takes GBA further and is defined as "an analytical tool used to assess how diverse groups of women, men and gender-diverse people may experience policies, programs and initiatives," with the added "plus" to signify that "analysis goes beyond biological (sex) and socio-cultural (gender) differences" and to recognize that "we all have multiple identity factors that intersect to make us who we are; GBA+ also considers many other identity factors, like race, ethnicity, religion, age, and mental or physical disability" (SWC 2018b).

As of early 2019, only one federal department, Immigration, Refugees and Citizenship Canada, has a legislative requirement to conduct GBA+ and report to Parliament.[24] There is room for some optimism, however, given that the former SWC (now WAGE), the Privy Council Office, and the Treasury Board Secretariat's *Action Plan on Gender-Based Analysis 2016–2020* encourages more federal departments and agencies to conduct GBA+. Moreover, the government has "recently renewed its commitment to GBA+ and is working to strengthen its implementation across all federal departments" (SWC 2016). In terms of committees, there is still no systematic process by which GBA+ is applied. Today, only the House of Commons Standing Committee on the

Status of Women has a formal "mandate" to consider women's equality (Standing Committee on the Status of Women 2019).

Turning to gender-sensitive budgeting, in a 2011 IPU report GBA budgeting is described as "an approach that aims to mainstream gender in economic policy-making and seeks to transform the entire budgetary process" (IPU 2011, 6). Canada is relatively late to the table when it comes to undertaking fulsome gender-sensitive budgeting; for example, Australia's first gender-sensitive budget was in 1984. In its 2016 Fall Economic Statement, the Government of Canada made a commitment to the GBA+ of future budgets, and in 2017 the budget put in a gender statement as a part of the annual budget plan (Government of Canada 2017). While there has been praise for the government's first attempt to undertake gender-based budgeting, there has also been criticism, with some questioning how gender-sensitive it really is. Budget 2017 appears to do what the IPU warned against: it has a separate chapter on women rather than having GBA+ woven through the entire budget (see Anderssen 2017). Budget 2018 goes further than 2017, for example by including parental leave (its shortfalls are examined by Dobrowolsky in this volume). However, there are still many "misses," such as the lack of a national childcare program and lack of new money for affordable and accessible housing (Andrew-Amofah 2018). Both budgets also deliver more tax benefits to rich and middle-class women and men than to those with multiple and intersecting oppressions, such as BIPOC and lower-income women (Howlett 2018). Future budgets could be strengthened by taking a more feminist intersectional analysis to explore innovative ways to increase women's participation in the workplace, such as funding new programs for women with disabilities and for women experiencing domestic violence who also have insecure immigration status (Andrew-Amofah 2018).

Gender equality legislation is another mechanism to facilitate gender equality and gender-sensitive parliaments and is used by governments to "encourage ongoing societal evolution, to redress past discriminations, and to eliminate existing discriminations in domestic law, policies and practices" (Munn-Rivard 2013, 1; IPU 2011, 2). In its report *Gender-Sensitive Parliaments*, the IPU states, "Parliament has a fundamental role to play in ensuring that legislation does not discriminate against men or women and that it promotes gender equality" (2011, 29). Mechanisms for this include gender equality laws and regular parliamentary processes such as debates on legislation (29). Currently, the Charter of Rights and Freedoms in the Constitution Act, 1982 guarantees equality rights (section 15) and extends this guarantee to both sexes (section 28). As well, the Canadian Human Rights Act (CHRA), 1985 protects equality rights and prohibits discrimination on several grounds, including sex (section 2; see Munn-Rivard 2013, 2). Additional legislation like the CHRA can further enhance equalities found in the Charter.

During the Harper period, 16 bills promoting women's and gender equality came before Parliament; however, none passed (see LEGISinfo data for 2011–15).[25] It is worth noting that there was considerable equality backsliding under Harper—not only was there a lack of equality legislation but there were explicit efforts at equality "erasure" (see Dobrowolsky 2009). Trudeau's record is better. From October 2015 to January 2019, seven bills promoting women's and gender equality have come before Parliament and thus far three, all of which are government bills, have passed: C-16, An Act to Amend the Human Rights Act & Criminal Code (sponsored by the Minister of Justice) received Royal Assent on June 19, 2017;[26] C-309, An Act to Establish Gender Equality Week (sponsored by Liberal MP Sven Spengemaan) received Royal Assent on June 21, 2018; and C-210, An Act to Amend the National Anthem (sponsored by Liberal MP Mauril Bélanger) received Royal Assent on February 7, 2018 (see LEGISinfo data for 2015–18).[27] Notably, in 2016, C-237, An Act to Amend the Canadian Elections Act (Gender Equity) (sponsored by NDP MP Kennedy Stewart), designed to increase the representation of women, disabled, and LGBTQ2+ people and BIPOC in the House of Commons, was rejected by the Trudeau government and Conservative opposition after the first reading on February 25, 2016.

Lastly, it is well established that sex quotas for women, used in over 100 countries, offer a fast-track solution to their underrepresentation by creating a temporary demand for women among party selectors (see Gender Quotas Database 2019). For example, some countries entrench reserved seats or legal candidate quotas in their constitutions, while others simply pass new laws. No form of formal quotas is used in Canada's Parliament to increase women's or other marginalized groups' representation, with the latest legislative effort to do so, Bill C-237, An Act to Amend the Canada Elections Act (Gender Equity), rejected. Thus, this measure is given a score of 0.

In summation, the measures in the gender-sensitive legislation category should soon be reassessed given the government's commitment to revisit the recommendations outlined in FEWO's report on GBA+, the newly formed Department of WAGE, the government's promise to undertake more robust gender-sensitive budgets in the future, and the number of gender equity bills before Parliament. Additionally, in 2018 the Liberal Government's motion to review (again) the MP-to-MP code carried unanimously in the wake of the #MeToo movement's arrival on Parliament Hill (see Gilmore 2018). For the time being, however, improvement along only three of the nine measures indicates there is still some way to go before the traffic light turns green along this dimension.

DISCUSSION

As summarized in table 4, the Trudeau government has gained in 12 of the 32 sensitive measures, with most changes occurring in the descriptive representation category. Women's descriptive representation likely but not always leads to substantive improvements for women and can vary between regimes due to the lack of sex quotas. The number and percentage of women in cabinet, women MPs, women senators, and women House and Senate chairs of standing committees have all increased under Trudeau. However, aside from cabinet, and to a lesser extent, the Senate, increases in women's representation in the House and in leadership positions are comparatively small. There has been only one improvement in the infrastructure category and three improvements in the policy category.

In short, Canada's Parliament is now more gender-sensitive than when Stephen Harper was prime minister, but not by as much as might be expected considering Trudeau's #becauseits2015 equality rhetoric. It is a common criticism of Trudeau that he oversells his accomplishments (Wherry 2019). He did manage some significant improvements over a short period, but at the same time, as Liberal MP Anita Vandenbeld, chair of the All Women's Caucus, candidly remarks, Trudeau's sex-balanced cabinet "just glosses over structural barriers that still remain" (Vandenbeld 2017, 103). Indeed, if Trudeau's idea of feminism is reflected in his policy choices, it would be a feminism based on rhetoric and symbolism rather than one committed to real change (see Lovenduski 2005).

Trudeau has had several chances to act instead of appearing to act, with three particularly notable missed opportunities. The first concerns the government's inaction on FEWO's recommendation to implement GBA+ legislation as included in its report *Implementing Gender-Based Analysis Plus in the Government of Canada* (June 2016; see Paterson and Scala in this volume). The second is the government's rejection of C-237, the Candidate Gender Equity Act, designed to increase women's and other groups' representation in the

Table 4 Summary Table

Category	Change Scores
Representation	8/12
Infrastructure	1/11
Policies & Legislation	3/9
Overall	**12/32**

House of Commons. Third is the Trudeau government's decision to renege on its 2015 election promise of electoral reform, and to reject the All-Party Special Committee on Electoral Reform's recommendation to replace Canada's single-member plurality (SMP) electoral system with one that is associated with electing more women, proportional representation.

Grace's in-depth analysis of FEWO provides insight into the government's response to its recommendations: FEWO does not have the "institutional clout and parliamentary capacity to mainstream gender so as to instigate a shift in the dominant male-centric culture within the House" (2016, 841). Grace notes that there are several reasons for this: FEWO's "place within the House ... is best thought of as bounded innovation given the significant challenges the Committee confronts in realizing many of its recommendations." Moreover, the lack of a Senate Committee on the Status of Women prevents "continuity through the legislative system." Further, FEWO's work is undermined by ideological differences and party discipline as seen in the Harper and Trudeau governments' rejection of non-government bills (private member's bills) on women's and gender equality introduced by opposition parties (831). Thus, writes Grace, FEWO's "existence has not shifted the inequality regime within Parliament" (841).

Grace's (2016) points help make sense of the government's rejection of Bill C-237, An Act to Amend the Canada Elections Act (Gender Equity), which would have reduced the reimbursement each registered party received for its election expenses if a party had more than a 10 per cent difference in the number of women and men candidates for the general election. The formula was also designed to incentivize parties to select candidates from other equity-seeking groups, including LGBTQ2+, BIPOC, and disabled people. Although 23 Liberal backbenchers voted with the NDP to support the bill, and it had the support of dozens of non-parliamentary organizations and national and international academics, Trudeau and his cabinet joined with the Conservative MPs to kill the bill 209 to 68. Passing and implementing gender-sensitive legislation is difficult within such a highly partisan, adversarial, and masculine institution for parties, let alone for individual feminist women and men MPs (see Lovenduski 2005). Although C-237 was a private member's bill, the government's outright rejection is out of sync with Trudeau's feminist agenda. This sentiment is captured by Shannon Proudfoot's (2016) article "The Liberals Killed a Bill Promoting Gender Parity in Politics: They Were Wrong."

While the mismatch between change rhetoric and actual reform can be laid at the feet of Prime Minister Trudeau, there are other factors at play. For example, political parties play a substantive role in determining who gets nominated as candidates to stand in elections and, once elected, which MPs are promoted to various positions—for example, House leaders, party whips, committee chairs, and committee members. Thus, it is critical to consider the effects of parties' selection processes on selection outcomes. In 2015, women made up 33 per cent (535) of candidates from the five main parties in Canada (Liberal, Conservative, NDP, BQ, and Greens), only a two-percentage-point increase from the 2011 election.[28] Parties' selection processes in Canada are largely decentralized, with local party members choosing the candidates who run under their party label in each of the 338 seats.[29] As is the case with parties in other countries, parties in Canada follow a ladder of political recruitment that has at least two selection rungs: (1) aspirant candidates apply for nomination in a particular seat by filling out a standard party application form; and if they survive this initial vetting stage they (2) attend a nomination meeting for that particular seat, and local party members either select them or reject them to run as their party candidate.[30] The selection process is designed to filter the many aspirants who apply to the few who secure a candidacy. The concern is not with the winnowing itself; as there are only so many seats, this needs to occur. Rather the concern is with the nature of filtering—whether women and other underrepresented social groups are systemically passed over for the "standard candidate"—usually a white, professional man.

There is considerable interparty variation in parties' selection processes and outcomes, with Scott Pruysers and William Cross (2016) providing a fulsome discussion of these. Parties can apply different equity rules at different selection stages, but to do so they need the support of their leaders and members, which is no small feat. To date, all major national Canadian parties use equality rhetoric (spreading the message of women's representation) and equality promotion (encouraging women to run for office), but none use sex quotas, such as all-women shortlist seats, successfully used by the British Labour Party since the 1990s to artificially increase local party members' demand for women candidates (see Ashe 2017). This is not for lack of trying. Even the NDP, which historically selects the most women candidates and candidates from other equity-seeking groups, failed to pass a member- and constituency-driven equity mandate at its 2016 and 2018 conventions.[31]

Gendered norms influence parties' selection practices and outcomes and are exacerbated by the SMP electoral system, in which parties are encouraged to select the standard candidate, as discussed. It is widely accepted that proportional representative electoral systems are more favourable to women's candidacy and election; thus the Trudeau government's rejection of proportional representation along with its rejection of Bill C-237 keeps intact crucial barriers to women's candidacy and election.

When parties face concerns about their lopsided candidate pools they often take the position that they would like to select more women candidates, but their hands are tied because not enough women come forward (Kenny and Verge 2016). The often-used supply-side argument places blame for women's underrepresentation on women rather than on sexist institutions, including parties' selection processes (Lovenduski 2005). Recent studies on politics and gender prop up the demand-side argument. There are more than enough women seeking candidacies to fill the 169 seats needed for sex parity; however, when women come forward party members still disproportionately choose men (see Ashe 2017).[32] Given this, policy solutions towards a more gender-sensitive Parliament should also be directed at artificially increasing party members' demand for women candidates, for example, through sex quotas for women, while ensuring diversity in parties' candidate pools (supply).

Returning to the theme of transformation, witnesses for FEWO's 2018 study "Barriers Facing Women in Politics" (Standing Committee on the Status of Women 2018) reinforce the recommendations made thus far to increase women's participation in politics and raise new ones. Indeed, several witnesses highlight the role parties and a lack of demand among party selectors for women candidates play in women's underrepresentation and propose the need for the government to use sex quotas to increase their representation. It is unlikely that Canada will change its constitution to require parties use sex quotas to achieve sex parity in the House; thus changing its electoral system would seem a more reasonable way forward (Standing Committee on the Status of Women, 2018). In some countries—for example, Belgium—parties that fail to run sex-balanced candidate lists are disqualified from participating in elections. However, such reforms are unlikely given the government's 2017 rejection of the Special Committee on Electoral Reform's recommendation for electoral reform. Among the milder proposals to increase women's participation is to financially incentivize parties to run more women candidates, as is done in Ireland and France. But, as noted, even this mildest of measures was rejected by Trudeau's government in the form of Bill C-237, the Canada Elections Act (Gender Equity), which witnesses recommend Parliament revisit (Standing Committee on the Status of Women, 2018). Additionally, Elections Canada should be empowered to require political parties to provide additional data on candidate selection contests—on all those who come forward and win or lose their bids. This data can be used to assess party efforts to recruit and select women candidates and to make further recommendations with which to increase their representation. More specifically, Canada's Elections Act should be amended to make mandatory the provision of intersectional data on all aspiring candidates who participate in selection contests, including information on sex, gender identification, race, Indigeneity, physical ability, age, sexual orientation, and class. Such reforms are not unreasonable given the government's recent Bill C-76, the Elections Modernization Act (Standing Committee on the Status of Women Canada, 2018).

Augmenting the recommendations made thus far are those gleaned from comparative analyses of gender sensitivity in other parliaments (see Childs 2017). In terms of improving descriptive representation, data on who participates on parliamentary committees as members and as witnesses should be systemically collected, and if sex imbalance is shown, mechanisms such as quotas should be put in place to bring balance to both. As for infrastructure, although unlikely, MP job-sharing—where two people share the job of one MP—could be considered to achieve greater diversity in so far as it could "help get more parents with children, careers, and more disabled people in Parliament" and encourage them to stay longer (Fawcett Society 2017). Job-sharing has been the topic of considerable exploration in several countries, such as the United Kingdom; however, Canada has yet to undertake such a study. Lastly, in terms of policies and legislation, there is no clear way in which parliaments track how MPs feel about the culture of their workplace and if they feel included or excluded from it. While Canada's Parliament has codes and policies in place to deal with harassment, they are not without problems (see Collier and Raney 2018). There could be more and ongoing opportunities for members to provide feedback on parliamentary culture, which could be used to reform existing codes and implement new codes—for example, around gender-based harassment—where needed (Childs 2017, 13–14; see also Collier and Raney 2018).

Circling back to the overall assessment of Harper v. Trudeau: while Parliament is indeed more gender-sensitive under Trudeau, this is largely due to his personal decision to appoint a sex-balanced cabinet, which both ignores the lack of substantive gender-sensitive changes elsewhere and does not bind future governments. Turning to the theme of "turbulent times and transformational possibilities": while the overall findings are somewhat unexpected, in that at first blush Trudeau is often seen as leading a feminist revolution where Harper is often portrayed in a much less flattering light, they are also understandable, as institutional change is bound to be slow for many reasons, including path dependence.[33] However, there is still reason to hope more could be forthcoming due to pressures from within the parties and from feminist MPs, FEWO, the Department of WAGE, and various feminist organizations, such as Equal Voice.[34]

The results presented in this chapter make a case for undertaking ongoing assessments of Canada's Parliament at regular intervals and to extend these to provincial legislatures and municipalities. Comparing the two regimes reveals that Trudeau's government is more gender-sensitive than Harper's, but not by as much as anticipated. Improvements along only 12 of the 32 measures indicate that the gendered culture of Parliament—its rules and practices—is still largely intact, as highlighted by those critical of Trudeau's treatment of former Liberal ministers Jody Wilson-Raybould and Jane Philpott over the SNC-Lavalin scandal (Harris 2019). The danger in claiming feminism and feminist victories is that it masks the reality that there has been little substantive change. The method used in this chapter to make this assessment could be further improved by including a broader range of data and a wider range of diversity-sensitive indicators to assess intersectionality, and by comparing regimes on a year-by-year basis. All are worth the effort, as they will add to future debates and research as to why some political regimes and not others make a change towards gender sensitivity.

DISCUSSION QUESTIONS

1. In thinking about "turbulent times," what is the value in exploring the gender sensitivity of Canada's Parliament?
2. What can a gender-sensitive assessment reveal about Parliament as a place of work?

3. In thinking about "transformational possibilities," what is needed to make Canada's Parliament more gender sensitive?
4. What are some other measures to include in a gender-sensitive assessment of Parliament?

NOTES

1 In addition to resulting in a record 88 (26 per cent) women elected, a record 57 (17 per cent) BIPOC were elected: 47 (14 per cent) Black and people of colour and 10 (3 per cent) Indigenous Peoples (see Tolley 2015). Notably, the election did not result in a record number of members elected from other politically marginalized groups, such as openly LGBTQ+ people, whose representation is still stuck at 2006 levels. To date, no transperson has been elected to the House or appointed to the Senate (see Lenti 2015).

2 Mansbridge proposes that descriptive representation "enhances the substantive representation of interests" by "improving the quality of deliberation" and by allowing for "adequate communication in contexts of mistrust" and "innovative thinking in contexts of uncrystallized, not fully articulated, interests" (1999, 628).

3 The categories and measures are not fixed; ultimately, they are up to the researcher, but it is recommended that they be guided by those included by the IPU (2011, 2016) and Childs (2016, 2017).

4 The Harper period runs from the beginning to the end of the 41st Parliament (June 2, 2011 to August 2, 2015) and the Trudeau period runs from the beginning of the 42nd Parliament (October 19, 2015) to June 20, 2019, the last sitting day before the general election to elect MPs to the 43rd Parliament (October 21, 2019).

5 Trudeau's cabinet is also more diverse than Harper's in terms of race and ethnicity, with a record two Indigenous people appointed, including one Indigenous woman, and a record five Black and people of colour appointed, including two women. Notably, under Trudeau women hold key portfolios such as Justice (although in January 2019, Jody Wilson-Raybould was demoted from Justice to Veteran Affairs, and in April 2019 Wilson-Raybould and Minister Jane Philpott were expelled from the Liberal caucus over the SNC-Lavalin affair), International Trade, and Indigenous and Northern Affairs. Still, men hold most of the portfolios dealing with "harder" policy issues such as Finance and National Defence, and women are still clustered into portfolios dealing with "softer" policy issues such as Women and Heritage. For the importance of cabinets as sites of representation see Franceschet, Annesley, and Beckwith (2017).

6 The one-percentage-point increase in women MPs since the 2015 general election results from by-elections.

7 The Senate is included in this analysis because the composition of this body, from the speaker to its members, is influenced by the prime minister and in

its legislative role the Senate can both symbolically and substantively alter the gender sensitivity of Parliament. This is captured by the Honourable Senator Renée Dupuis's contribution to the Senate's "Conference on Women's Equality and Parity" (Dupuis 2019). As well, Dupuis acknowledges Trudeau's efforts to increase the number of women senators but challenges the government to go further by amending the Parliament of Canada Act to include "equal representation of men and women in the Senate of Canada." This legislative measure would improve upon Trudeau's "zippering approach" to filling vacancies, which alternates between women and men. Sex parity in the Senate could soon be achieved if such legislation is adopted. The representation of Black people and people of colour in the Senate is close to their representation in the House of Commons; however, the representation of Indigenous Peoples in the Senate is twice as high as in the lower house.

8   On this last point, there are currently no women leaders among the major parties.

9   Women have a better chance at becoming deputy speakers. Under Harper and currently under Trudeau one of the four House deputy speakers has been a woman.

10   The United Kingdom has a sex quota in place to guarantee the election of women deputy speakers (Childs 2016, 8).

11   As with Harper, under Trudeau women are better represented as vice chairs on House committees (14 of the 46, or 30 per cent) and underrepresented as vice chairs on Senate committees (8 of 21, or 38 per cent).

12   This holds even when taking into account that chairs are drawn from the governing party and that chairs cannot be cabinet ministers or parliamentary secretaries. For example, only eight more women are needed for sex parity amongst chairs, and even after removing 17 women ministers and 11 women parliamentary secretaries from the pool of 52 Liberal women MPs, there is a surplus of 24 Liberal women MPs.

13   This excludes the chairs and vice chairs.

14   Under Harper, nine House committees had between 24.9 and 49.9 per cent women, and 14 committees had between 0 and 24.9 per cent women. This has only slightly improved under Trudeau: seven House committees have between 25 and 49.9 per cent women (given there are two more committees with 50 to 74.9 per cent women than under Harper), but 14 committees still have between 0 and 24.9 per cent women.

15   Notably, the All-Party Parliamentary Women's Caucus and the All-Party Parliamentary LGBTQ Caucus were active under Harper and are still active under Trudeau.

16   The first sitting MP to have a baby was Sheila Copps, in 1986.

17   The PROC's report examines "initiatives to make the House of Commons more family friendly for its membership, along with members' staff and those whose work supports Parliament," and contains seven recommendations around the themes of predictability, modernization, and work-life balance (PROC 2016).

18 It does, however, have a parliamentary spousal lounge—open to all spouses and family members.

19 The ongoing rehabilitation of Canada's parliamentary buildings may be followed by going to the "Rehabilitation of the Parliamentary Buildings" website: https://www.tpsgc-pwgsc.gc.ca/citeparlementaire-parliamentaryprecinct/rehabilitation/index-eng.html.

20 Other key features of the parallel chambers in the United Kingdom and Australia include: "They do not possess decision making power; they have a low quorum; and they are more informal in their physical setting, allowing for greater interplay in debate" (Childs 2016).

21 However, vote pairing with another MP in the House of Commons is permitted (Barnes and Munn-Rivard 2013)

22 Nor does Canada's Parliament allow for teleconferencing.

23 Members in BC's and Alberta's legislatures may participate via videoconferencing.

24 So far, only 29 of 110 federal departments have signed on to the House of Commons Standing Committee on the Status of Women's 2009 *Departmental Action Plan on GBA.*

25 Available at https://www.parl.ca/LEGISINFO/Home.aspx. The terms "women" and "gender" were separately entered into LEGISinfo for Harper's two parliamentary sessions, 41(1) and 41(2).

26 Notably, Bill C-16, introduced in Trudeau's 42nd Parliament by NDP MP Randall Garrison, is a variation of Bill C-279, introduced during Harper's 41st Parliament. One of the differences is that C-16 leaves out gender identity in its title.

27 Available at https://www.parl.ca/LEGISINFO/Home.aspx. The method is the same as above for the 41st parliament up until the end of January 2019.

28 In 2015, women made up 31 per cent of Liberal Party of Canada candidates and 20 per cent of Conservative candidates.

29 Typically, only the three major parties—Liberal, Conservative, and NDP—run full slates of candidates in all 338 federal constituencies, with the Bloc Québécois (BQ) only running candidates in Quebec. Forty-three per cent of the NDP's candidates, 28 per cent of BQ candidates, and 39 per cent of Green Party of Canada candidates in 2015 were women.

30 In cases where only one aspirant seeks the candidacy and there is no contest, the aspirant is acclaimed as the party's candidate for that seat.

31 Equity-seeking groups include BIPOC, disabled people, youth, and low-income people.

32 As of 2018, 92 of the 338 MPs are women; therefore, only 77 more women MPs are needed to achieve sex parity.

33 Once institutions are formed, they tend to follow a set path, which in practice can place considerable limitations on them; thus, long-established institutions can act as constraints on what can be done and when something can be done (see Mackay, Kenny, and Chappell 2010).

34 "Founded in 2001, Equal Voice is a national, bilingual, multi-partisan organization dedicated to electing more women to all levels of political office in Canada" (Equal Voice, n.d.).

REFERENCES

Anderssen, Erin. 2017. "Liberals Fall Short with First Gender-Based Federal Budget." *Globe and Mail*, March 22. https://www.theglobeandmail.com/news/politics /federal-budget-2017-women-gender/article34390564/.

Andrew-Amofah, Brittany. 2018. "Budget 2018: Responsiveness to Gender Issues? Not Without Tax Reform." Broadbent Institute Blog, March 2. https://www .broadbentinstitute.ca/bandrewamofah/budget_2018_responsive_to_gender _issues_not_without_tax_reform.

Arscott, Jane, and Linda Trimble. 2013. *Stalled*. Vancouver: UBC Press.

Ashe, Jeanette. 2017. "Women's Legislative Underrepresentation: Enough Come Forward, (Still) Too Few Chosen." *Canadian Journal of Political Science* 50 (2): 597–613.

Barnes, Andre, and Laura Munn-Rivard. 2013. "Gender-Sensitive Parliaments: 1. Advancements in the Workplace." Ottawa: Library of Parliament, April 5. http:// publications.gc.ca/collections/collection_2012/bdp-lop/bp/2012-40-eng.pdf.

Bird, Karen. 2016. "Understanding the Local Diversity Gap: Supply and Demand of Visible Minority Candidates in Ontario Municipal Politics." In *The Political Immigrant: A Comparative Portrait*, edited by Antoine Bilodeau, 180–200. Toronto: University of Toronto Press.

Bittner, Amanda, and Melanee Thomas. 2017. *Mother and Others: The Role of Parenthood in Politics*. Vancouver: UBC Press.

Campbell, Meagan, and Catherine McIntyre. 2018. "Sexual Harassment Has Long Festered on Parliament Hill. Now MPs from All Parties Are Saying 'Enough.'" *Maclean's*, March 7. https://www.macleans.ca/politics/ottawa/sexual-harassment -on-parliament-hill/.

Chagger, Bardish. 2018. *Government Response to the 48th Report of the Standing Committee on Procedures and House Affairs Entitled "Support for Members of Parliament with Young Children."* Ottawa: Leader of the Government in the House of Commons. https://www.ourcommons.ca/content/Committee/421/PROC /GovResponse/RP9755854/421_PROC_Rpt48_GR/421_PROC_Rpt48_GR-e.pdf.

Childs, Sarah. 2016. "The Good Parliament." Bristol: University of Bristol. http:// www.bristol.ac.uk/media-library/sites/news/2016/july/20%20Jul%20Prof %20Sarah%20Childs%20The%20Good%20Parliament%20report.pdf.

———. 2017. "Diversity Sensitive Parliaments: Parliamentary Practice in Comparison, a Briefing." Bristol: University of Bristol.

Collier, Cheryl, and Tracey Raney. 2018. "Canada's Member-to-Member Code of Conduct on Sexual Harassment in the House of Commons: Progress or Regress?" *Canadian Journal of Political Science* 51 (4): 795–815.

Csanady, Ashley. 2015. "Breastfeeding MP Causes a Stir." *National Post*, September 19. https://nationalpost.com/news/politics/breastfeeding-mps-cause-a-stir-in -parliaments-around-the-world-but-with-more-women-running-than-ever-in -canada-it-should-be-the-new-norm.

Dobrowolsky, Alexandra. 2009. "Charter Champions: Equality Backsliding, the Charter and the Courts." In *Women and Public Policy in Canada: Neo-liberalism and After?*, edited by Alexandra Dobrowolsky, 166–86. Toronto: Oxford University Press.

Dupuis, Renée. 2019. "Conference on Women's Equality and Parity." Ottawa: Senate of Canada, April 26. https://sencanada.ca/en/senators/dupuis-renee/external -speeches/2019-04-26-conference-on-womens-equality-and-parity.

Equal Voice. n.d.. "About Equal Voice: Dedicated to Electing More Women to All Levels of Political Office in Canada." https://www.equalvoice.ca/about. Accessed November 4, 2019.

Fawcett Society. 2017. "Job Sharing for MPs Supported by Women Candidates for Most Parties." September 5. https://www.fawcettsociety.org.uk/news/job-sharing -for-mps-supported-by-women-candidates-for-most-parties.

Franceschet, Susan, Claire Annesley, and Karen Beckwith. 2017. "What Do Women Symbolize? Symbolic Representation and Cabinet Appointments." *Politics, Groups, and Identities* 5 (3): 488–93.

Gender Quotas Database. 2019. "Quotas." December 12. https://www.idea.int/data -tools/data/gender-quotas/quotas.

Gilmore, Rachel. 2018. "Motion to Review MP's Sexual Harassment Code of Conduct Carries Unanimously." *iPolitics*, February 1. https://ipolitics.ca/2018/02/01 /motion-review-mps-sexual-harassment-code-conduct-carries-unanimously/.

Government of Canada. 2017. *Budget 2017: Building a Strong Middle Class.* Ottawa: Department of Finance. https://www.budget.gc.ca/2017/home -accueil-en.html.

———. 2018. *Budget 2018: Equality plus Growth: A Strong Middle Class.* Ottawa: Department of Finance. https://www.budget.gc.ca/2018/home-accueil-en.html.

Grace, Joan. 2016. "Presence and Purpose in the Canadian House of Commons: The Standing Committee on the Status of Women." *Parliamentary Affairs* 69: 830–44.

Hajdu, Patty. n.d. "Government Response, Report of the Standing Committee on the Status of Women entitled Implementing Gender-Based Analysis Plus in the Government of Canada." Ottawa: House of Commons. http://www.ourcommons .ca/DocumentViewer/en/42-1/FEWO/report-4/response-8512-421-76.

Harris, Kathleen. 2019. "Trudeau Defends His Feminist Credentials as 2 Expelled Women MPs Insist They Acted on Principle." *CBC News*, April 3. https://www.cbc .ca/news/politics/trudeau-feminist-wilson-raybould-philpott-1.5082634.

House of Commons. 2015. "Appendix II Code of Conduct for Members of the House of Commons: Sexual Harassment between Members." In *Standing Orders of the House of Commons.* http://www.ourcommons.ca/About/StandingOrders /Appa2-e.html.

Howlett, Dennis. 2018. "Budget 2018 Leaves Tax Loopholes That Benefit Rich Men at Women's Expense." *Huffington Post*, March 28. https://www.huffingtonpost.ca /dennis-howlett/budget-2018-gender-equality-women-tax-loopholes_a _23372725/.

Inter-Parliamentary Union. 2011. *Gender-Sensitive Parliaments: A Global Review of Good Practice.* Geneva: Inter-Parliamentary Union. http://archive.ipu.org/pdf /publications/gsp11-e.pdf.

———. 2016. *Evaluating the Gender Sensitivity of Parliaments: A Self Assessment Toolkit*. Geneva: Inter-Parliamentary Union. http://archive.ipu.org/pdf /publications/gender-toolkit-e.pdf.

———. 2019. *Women in National Parliaments*. Geneva: Author. http://archive.ipu.org /wmn-e/classif.htm.

Kenny, Meryl, and Tania Verge. 2016. "Opening Up the Black Box: Gender and Candidate Selection in a New Era." *Government and Opposition* 51(3): 351–69.

Lenti, Erica. 2015. "Why Canada Needs to Elect More LGBTQ Politicians." *Torontoist*, November 4. https://torontoist.com/2015/11/why-canada-needs-to-elect-more -lgbtq-politicians/.

Lovenduski, Joni. 2005. *Feminizing Politics*. Cambridge: Polity Press.

———. 2017. "The Good Parliament and Other Reports." *The Political Quarterly* 88: 306–10.

Mackay, Fiona, Meryl Kenny, and Louise Chappell. 2010. "New Institutionalism through a Gendered Lens: Toward a Feminist Institutionalist?" *International Political Science Review* 31 (5): 573–88.

Mansbridge, Jane. 1999. "Should Blacks Represent Blacks and Women Represent Women? A Contingent 'Yes.'" *Journal of Politics* 61 (3): 628–57.

Munn-Rivard, Laura. 2013. "Gender-Sensitive Parliament: 2. The Work of Legislators." Ottawa: Library of Parliament, April 5. http://publications.gc.ca/collections/collection _2012/bdp-lop/bp/2012-45-eng.pdf.

Phillips, Anne. 1998. *The Politics of Presence*. New York: Clarendon Press.

Pitkin, Hanna, 1967. *The Concept of Representation*. Berkeley: University of California Press.

Procedure and House Affairs Standing Committee (PROC). 2016. *Interim Report on Moving Toward a Modern, Efficient, Inclusive and Family-Friendly Parliament*, 11th Report. House of Commons of Canada, 1st Session, 42nd Parliament, June. http://www.ourcommons.ca/Document Viewer/en/42-1/PROC/report-11.

Proudfoot, Shannon. 2016. "The Liberals Killed a Bill Promoting Gender Parity in Politics: They Were Wrong." *Maclean's*, October 24. https://www.macleans.ca /politics/ottawa/the-liberals-killed-a-bill-promoting-gender-parity-in-politics -they-were-wrong/.

Pruysers, Scott, and William Cross. 2016. "Candidate Selection in Canada: Local Autonomy, Centralization, and Competing Democratic Norms." *American Behavioural Scientist* 60 (7): 781–98.

Samara. 2016. *Cheering or Jeering? Members of Parliament Open Up about Civility in the House of Commons*. Toronto: Samara Canada. https://www.samaracanada .com/research/cheering-or-jeering.

Smith, Joanna. 2018. "MPs Share Stories of Sexual Misconduct on and off the Hill." *The Canadian Press*, January 2. https://www.nationalnewswatch.com/2018/01/02 /mps-share-stories-of-sexual-misconduct-on-and-off-parliament-hill-in-survey/.

Standing Committee on the Status of Women. 2016. *Implementing Gender-Based Analysis Plus in the Government of Canada*, 4th Report. House of Commons of Canada, 1st Session, 42nd Parliament, June. http://www.ourcommons.ca/Content /Committee/421/FEWO/Report s/RP8355396/feworp04/feworp04-e.pdf.

———. 2018. "Barriers Facing Women in Politics." House of Commons of Canada, 1st Session, November 28. https://www.ourcommons.ca/Committees/en/FEWO/StudyActivity?studyActivityId=10006162.

———. 2019. "Committees: FEWO, Standing Committee on the Status of Women." Last modified September 11, 2019. http://www.ourcommons.ca/Committees/en/FEWO.

Status of Women Canada. 2016. *Action Plan on Gender-Based Analysis 2016–2020.* Ottawa: Government of Canada. https://cfc-swc.gc.ca/gba-acs/plan-action-2016-en.html?wbdisable=true.

———. 2018a. *Statement by Minister Monsef on the Introduction on Legislation to Create the Department of Women and Gender Equality (WAGE).* October 29. https://www.canada.ca/en/status-women/news/2018/10/statement-by-minister-monsef-on-the-introduction-on-legislation-to-create-the-department-of-women-and-gender-equality-wage.html.

———. 2018b. "What Is GBA+?" Last modified December 4, 2018. https://cfc-swc.gc.ca/gb a-acs/index-en.html.

Thompson, Elizabeth. 2015. "MPs' New Sexual Harassment Policy Still Keeps Bad Behaviour in the Dark." *iPolitics*, June 8. https://ipolitics.ca/2015/06/08/mps-new-sexual-harassment-policy-still-keeps-bad-behaviour-in-the-dark/.

Tolley, Erin. 2015. "Visible Minority and Indigenous Members of Parliament." Samara, November 26. https://www.samaracanada.com/samarablog/blog-post/samara-main-blog/2015/ 11/26/visible-minority-and-indigenous-members-of-parliament.

———. 2016. *Media and the Coverage of Race in Canadian Politics.* Toronto: UBC Press.

Tremblay, Manon. 2009. "Do Female MPs Substantively Represent Women? A Study of Legislative Behaviour in Canada's 35th Parliament." *Canadian Journal of Political Science* 31: 435–65.

Vandenbeld, Anita. 2017. "Breaking the Parliamentary Glass Ceiling." In *Turning Parliament Inside Out*, edited by Michael Chong, Scott Simms, and Kennedy Stewart, 98–101. Madeira Park, BC: Douglas and McIntyre.

Wherry, Aaron. 2019. "Why Justin Trudeau's Main Foe in 2019 is the Justin Trudeau of 2019." *CBC News*, September 7. https://www.cbc.ca/news/politics/justin-trudeau-2019-election-andrew-scheer-1.5252988.

Wängnerud, Lena. 2015. *The Principles of Gender-Sensitive Parliaments.* New York: Routledge.

Wright, Teresa. 2019. "House of Commons Unanimously Adopts New Parental Leave Policy for MPs." *CBC News*, June 14. https://www.cbc.ca/news/politics/parental-leave-commons-1.5175413.

FURTHER READING

Childs, Sarah. 2016. "The Good Parliament." Bristol: University of Bristol. http://www.bristol.ac. uk/media-library/sites/news/2016/july/2016/20%20Jul%20Prof%20Sarah%20Childs%20T he%20Good%20Parliament%20report.pdf.

Inter-Parliamentary Union. 2011. *Gender-Sensitive Parliaments: A Global Review of Good Practice*. Geneva: Inter-Parliamentary Union.

———. 2016. *Evaluating the Gender Sensitivity of Parliaments: A Self Assessment Toolkit*. Geneva: Inter-Parliamentary Union.

Lovenduski, Joni. 2005. *Feminizing Politics*. Cambridge: Polity Press.

Wängnerud, Lena. 2015. *The Principles of Gender-Sensitive Parliaments*. New York: Routledge.

4

Feminism, Public Dialogue, and Sexual Assault Law

Elaine Craig

Key terms: consent, Ewanchuk, Jian Ghomeshi, legal reforms, #MeToo, public dialogue, rape myth, sexualized violence

The criminal law remains the Canadian state's primary response to the social problem of sexual harm. Problematically, it is difficult to imagine a context in which the detrimental impact of gender-based stereotypes is more readily apparent than in the criminal law's response to **sexualized violence**. Discriminatory social assumptions about sexuality, gender, and rape continue to inform this area of law despite radical changes aimed at eradicating the power of these stereotypes. At the same time, the recent volume and potential impact of **public dialogue** that challenges and disrupts these problematic ways of thinking suggests we are in a unique, and promising era—a turbulent era in which political and legal activism pursued through public dialogue (and social trends such as the **#MeToo** movement) may be disrupting the grip that discriminatory thinking about sexuality, gender, and rape has had on sexual assault law in Canada. The aim of this chapter is to examine, through a case study of three recent high-profile sexual assault cases, whether today's genre of public dialogue has the potential to generate transformative change to both the ways in which law responds to harmful sexual behaviour and its impact on those who turn to the law in response to experiences of sexual violence. The chapter considers the relationship between the social response to these cases (the Ghomeshi case, the discipline of former judge Robin Camp, and the "clearly a drunk can consent" case) and the changes to law and policy that followed these three cases. While challenges to the discriminatory aspects of sexual assault law in Canada have long been a feminist pursuit, there is a newly disruptive character to the ways in which survivors, activists, and the public more generally are engaging with the problem of sexual violence.

The criminal law's response to sexualized violence has been a principal site of feminist political and legal activism in Canada since the mid-twentieth century. This activism motivated decades of **legal reforms**, beginning in the 1970s.[1] Indeed, between the late 1970s and the mid-1990s feminist-driven changes to both the Criminal Code of Canada and the interpretation of sexual assault law by Canadian courts transformed this country's "on the books" legal response to the problem of sexually harmful behaviour. As will be explained, as a consequence of these reforms the law itself in Canada (as opposed to what judges and lawyers do with the law) is quite progressive.

Among others, these changes included laws rejecting empirically unsound and discriminatory stereotypes about sex, gender, and sexualized violence. For example, lawyers are no longer legally permitted to use evidence of a sexual assault complainant's other sexual activity, with the accused or anyone else, to humiliate her or to trigger the **rape myth** that women who are sexually active are less trustworthy or more likely to have consented to the sex at issue in the allegation.[2] Judges are legally prevented from concluding that a child's failure to disclose sexual abuse promptly, or a woman's failure to scream for help during or immediately following a rape, automatically makes their allegation of sexual assault less believable.[3]

In addition, legal recognition of sexual harm was radically broadened to include violations of one's sexual integrity, thus extending the legal concept of non-consensual sexual touching well beyond the heteronormative and narrow construct of sexual violence as penetrative vaginal intercourse.[4] The changes made during this era also included a "yes means yes" affirmative definition of **consent** to sexual touching. This means the criminal law now requires individuals to take reasonable steps to ensure that prospective sexual partners are consenting, and it prevents an accused from arguing that he mistakenly believed the complainant was consenting simply because she did not resist or say no.[5]

As a consequence of activism by community-based anti-violence organizations, front-line workers, feminist politicians and lawmakers, and feminist legal activists, by the end of the twentieth century Canadian sexual assault laws were among the most progressive in the world. Nearly 20 years later, in 2020, it would still be difficult to find a jurisdiction anywhere in which the substantive law of sexual assault, the law "on the books," is more protective of sexual assault complainants than Canada's legal regime.

Yet the actual impact of these groundbreaking reforms has been negligible. For example, despite these changes, reporting rates for sexual assault (non-consensual sexual touching) have not improved. While rates of reporting increased somewhat in the 1980s, this improvement levelled off in the 1990s, and rates have decreased since then (Daly and Bouhours 2010, 565–81). Reporting rates for sexual assault are startlingly lower than for other violent offences (Johnson 2012, 613; Tang 1998, 258). Less than 10 per cent of sexual assault survivors in Canada report their experiences of sexual harm to the police (Kong et al. 2003; Johnson 2006). Conviction rates for sexual assault have been similarly unaffected by these legal reforms. Indeed, some research indicates that rates of conviction for sexual offences actually diminished during the 30-year period over which most of these changes were adopted.[6] Likewise, rates of attrition—the proportion of sexual assaults that are reported to the police but are not pursued due to police and prosecutorial practices—have increased (Johnson 2012, 613). Moreover, there is no evidence that these changes to the law have reduced rates of sexualized violence in Canada.[7] Perhaps most disappointingly, given that the aim of many of these reforms was to protect complainants from the discriminatory and traumatizing treatment they endured as witnesses in sexual assault trials, women continue to report their experiences of the sexual assault trial process as brutal and inhumane.[8]

To summarize, in terms of legal reform, sexual assault law is one of the most successful sites of feminist legal and political activism in Canadian history,[9] yet the measurable impact of these dramatic changes on addressing the social problem of sexual harm, or improving women's experiences with the criminal justice process, has been extremely modest if not inconsequential. This paradox is sometimes referred to as the justice gap in sexual assault law (Temkin and Krahé 2008). The justice gap was one of the factors motivating an effort on the part of many feminist legal scholars in the 1980s and 1990s to critically assess law's capacity to alleviate gender-based oppression and achieve gender equality. The individualized, reactive nature of the criminal law, they argued, will never respond to the underlying systemic norms and attitudes about sex and gender that both perpetuate sexually harmful behaviour and infect every aspect of the legal process used to address allegations of sexual assault (Smart 1989, 48–50).

PUBLIC DIALOGUE AND THE JUSTICE GAP

While academics, sexual assault service providers, and anti-violence activists have been grappling with the justice gap for decades, since 2014 the sexual assault trial process in Canada has also been subject to an unparalleled degree of public and media scrutiny. Indeed, the justice gap in sexual assault law has received unprecedented public attention in Canada in recent years, as exemplified by public responses to, and dialogue surrounding, three cases in particular: the sexual assault prosecution of former Canadian Broadcasting Corporation (CBC) radio host **Jian Ghomeshi**; the disciplinary hearings and ultimate resignation of former justice Robin Camp following his conduct in a 2012 sexual assault trial; and the 2017 acquittal of Halifax taxi driver Bassam Al-Rawi.

The surge in public discourse surrounding each of these three cases focused on the social and legal phenomena that deter women from coming forward, the continued mistreatment of sexual assault complainants at the hands of judges and lawyers, and the ongoing role that gender-based discriminatory stereotypes continue to play in sexual assault trials. While this public dialogue echoed critiques that feminist scholars, law reformers, and activists have highlighted for years, its mediums, format, and volume differed in ways that are noteworthy. For example, it has been conducted through social media (see also Small in this volume) and first person accounts rather than solely through traditional media, and the sustained public focus on this issue over the course of nearly four years is unprecedented. It would be premature to draw conclusions regarding the long-term or permanent impact arising from this public dialogue. That said, these three cases have already inspired legal and government policy developments that may, in the future, help to mitigate the gap between Canada's progressive legal regime and the experiences of those who turn to the criminal justice system following experiences of sexual violence.

The Prosecution of CBC Radio Host Jian Ghomeshi

In the fall of 2014, the CBC fired a high-profile and popular radio show host, Jian Ghomeshi. In the days following his dismissal numerous women disclosed allegations of sexual assault against Ghomeshi. In total, more than

20 women came forward to the media alleging that Ghomeshi had assaulted them—slapped, choked, bit, or punched them—in a sexual context. Ghomeshi was charged with sexual assault, and choking to overcome resistance, in relation to six women.[10]

The allegations against Ghomeshi seemed to amplify an already growing public dialogue focused on inadequacies in the legal system's response to sexualized violence. Traditional media coverage of the case was extensive, both at the time the allegations were made in the fall of 2014 and throughout the duration of his trial in early 2016. The volume of public commentary from lawyers, legal academics, front-line sexual assault service providers, and most importantly survivors of sexualized violence themselves was remarkable (Houpt 2016; Stead 2016).

In 2014, when the allegations against Ghomeshi were reported in the media, much of the public dialogue focused on the fact that none of these women had reported their experiences to the police at the time the alleged incidents occurred.[11] The discussion emphasized the barriers to reporting identified by survivors, chief among them the perceived failings of the criminal justice system and its actors (police, lawyers, and judges) as well as the power imbalance between this successful and well-known radio show host and the women (many of whom also worked in the entertainment industry) who accused him (Tucker 2014b; Phillips 2017). A social media campaign in which survivors recounted previously undisclosed experiences of sexualized violence and explained why they did not report these assaults was initiated a few days after the first set of allegations were reported. It went viral within a few hours. Indeed, within 24 hours almost 8 million people around the world had engaged with #BeenRapedNeverReported on Twitter (Gallant 2014).

A second surge in media coverage and public dialogue occurred in 2016 during, and immediately following, Ghomeshi's trial. In addition to further discourse concerning the barriers to reporting, much of the public dialogue in 2016 focused on two competing interests: the treatment of the three complainants who testified against Ghomeshi, and Ghomeshi's right not to testify and to be presumed innocent. A fraught debate over the presumption of innocence, an accused's right to question his accusers, and the need to protect vulnerable witnesses from traumatic cross-examinations emerged. Defence lawyers spoke publicly about the need to preserve the constitutionally protected rights of the accused (Davies 2016; Rusonick 2016). At the same time, Ghomeshi's lawyer was heavily criticized in the public arena for introducing evidence of the complainants' post-incident conduct with Ghomeshi—second dates, romantic gestures, intimate correspondence, and post-incident sexual activity—to demonstrate inconsistencies or fabrications in their statements to the police and the media and in court.[12]

Ghomeshi was acquitted of all charges. From a legal perspective, this may have been the correct verdict. This is not to suggest that Ghomeshi did not perpetrate these attacks, but rather to agree with the trial judge that the evidence introduced during the trial failed to establish proof of these attacks "beyond a reasonable doubt," which is the legally required degree of certainty in a criminal proceeding. There were a great number of frailties, including inconsistencies and incongruities, in the evidence offered by each of the complainants in R. v. Ghomeshi.[13]

That the decision to acquit Ghomeshi was likely correct has little bearing on the many inadequacies with the process highlighted in the public dialogue surrounding this case. Journalists, protestors, activists, and social media participants raised numerous questions that underlined the failure of Canada's legal system to appropriately and justly respond to incidents of sexual violence. Both traditional and social media were flooded with questions such as: Were the complainants properly prepared in advance by the prosecutors responsible for this case? Did these three women have their own lawyers to assist them throughout this process? Why were they ambushed at trial with decade-old letters and emails they had sent to Ghomeshi containing intimate and sexualized content? Did the pervasive societal distrust of women who allege sexual violation on the part of powerful men lead these women to believe that if they told the police or court about their post-incident amicable interactions with Ghomeshi they were sure to be disbelieved about the assault? In other words, a good deal of the public dialogue focused on the systemic factors that may have caused the complainants in this case to offer testimony that was inaccurate, inconsistent, or incomplete.

Couldn't She Just Keep Her Knees Together? The Response to Robin Camp

Like the Ghomeshi case, the comments of former justice Robin Camp in a 2014 sexual assault trial in Alberta created a near media frenzy (Canadian Judicial Council 2016). Justice Camp's statements in R. v. Wagar were reported around the world and ignited a fierce public policy debate in Canada about the need and desirability of mandatory sexual assault training for judges.

Justice Camp's statements in *Wagar* came to light after his decision to acquit the accused was overturned by the Alberta Court of Appeal.[14] In its decision, the court of appeal suggested that Camp may have relied upon stereotypical thinking in his decision not to convict the accused. The complainant in *Wagar*, a 19-year-old Indigenous woman, alleged that Alex Wagar forced her to engage in sexual intercourse and oral sex after locking her in a bathroom with him during a house party. The accused outweighed her by more than 100 pounds.

During the trial, Justice Camp made a number of statements and asked a number of questions that suggested a deeply flawed understanding of the law of consent heavily informed by stereotypes such as the assumption that women who actually do not want to be raped will fight back or escape. For example, he asked the complainant questions such as: "Why didn't you just sink your bottom down into the basin so he couldn't penetrate you?" and "When your ankles were held together by your jeans, your skinny jeans, why couldn't you just keep your knees together?"[15]

Emblematic of the victim-blaming orientation of many of his questions and statements, Justice Camp referred to the complainant as "the accused" several times during the trial and made assertions such as "the accused hasn't explained why she allowed the sex to happen if she didn't want it."[16] In explaining his reasons for acquitting Wagar, Justice Camp commented that the complainant's "version is open to question. She certainly had the ability, perhaps learnt from her experience on the streets, to tell [him] to fuck off."[17] Statements such as these are entirely inconsistent with the affirmative definition of consent in Canada adopted in the 1990s—a definition that, as noted, rejects the stereotypical notion that a woman who fails to resist can be presumed to have implicitly consented.

Justice Camp's statements and conduct in *Wagar* became the subject of a public inquiry following complaints filed against him with the Canadian Judicial Council (CJC) and a request for an inquiry from the Attorney General of Alberta. The CJC is the body responsible for reviewing complaints against federally appointed judges. Its membership consists of senior judges from each of the provinces and territories. The inquiry committee struck by the CJC to investigate Justice Camp's conduct concluded that he had engaged in misconduct in this trial and unanimously recommended his removal from office. The majority of the CJC agreed with the inquiry committee's recommendation, determining that Justice Camp's statements in *Wagar* demonstrated "obvious disdain" for the law of sexual assault and that "the way in which he conducted himself [was] antithetical to the contemporary values of our judicial system with respect to the manner in which complainants in sexual assault cases should be treated" (Canadian Judicial Council 2017). Although Camp had apologized repeatedly for his statements and undergone both counselling and training in sexual assault law, the CJC determined that, taken as a whole, the impact of his statements on the public's confidence in the judiciary required that he be removed from office. The test for whether a judge should be removed from office is premised on an assessment of whether the judge's misconduct would seriously undermine a reasonable person's confidence in the ability of the judge to properly execute his or her judicial duties in the future (Canadian Judicial Council 1990). Justice Camp resigned on March 9, 2017, shortly after the CJC recommended to the federal minister of justice that he be removed.[18]

A recommendation by the CJC that a judge be removed from office is extremely rare, having occurred only three other times in the council's history (Devlin and Wildeman, n.d.). There is a marked contrast between the CJC's response to Justice Camp's conduct and its resolution of earlier complaints filed against two other judges for very similar conduct.

Consider first the multiple complaints against Justice John McClung of the Alberta Court of Appeal made following his conduct in R. v. Ewanchuk (Canadian Judicial Council 1999). **Ewanchuk** involved a 44-year-old habitual sex offender who lured the complainant, a teenaged woman, into his trailer on the auspices of a job interview. Once inside Ewanchuk began making sexual advances. Each time the complainant said no, Ewanchuk would pause briefly and then escalate his behaviour. The complainant testified that she was fearful that any resistance on her part would result in a violent sexual assault, and as a consequence she lay still and straight while he pushed her back, laid on top of her, ground his genital region into hers, and then removed his penis and rubbed it on her vagina, over top of her underwear.[19]

Ewanchuk was acquitted at trial on the basis that the complainant had not communicated her fear to him and thus he was entitled to rely on the notion of "implied consent." The Crown (as state prosecutors in Canada are called) appealed. In upholding Ewanchuk's acquittal, Justice McClung characterized his actions as "clumsy passes" and "far less criminal than hormonal."[20] He noted that the complainant had had a child out of wedlock and was living with her boyfriend. He stated that "it must be pointed out that the complainant did not present herself to Ewanchuk or enter his trailer in a bonnet and crinolines."[21] (She was wearing shorts and a t-shirt.) Justice McClung suggested that the complainant, who was significantly outsized by Ewanchuk and trapped in his vehicle, could have resolved the situation with a "slap in the face" or a "well placed knee."[22]

Clearly, the intended implication of Justice McClung's statements was that the complainant was sexually experienced and thus capable of fending off her attacker. Her failure to do so, combined with her supposedly immodest attire, suggested that either she was consenting or that she had only herself to blame for the unwanted sexual contact. Lest there be any doubt as to the stereotypical underpinnings of his reasoning in *Ewanchuk*, in an interview with the *National Post* following release of his decision McClung defended his characterization of the complainant, stating that she was "not lost on her way home from the nunnery" (Ohler 1999).

Justice McClung's decision in *Ewanchuk* was appealed to the Supreme Court of Canada, where the acquittal was overturned and a new trial was ordered. The Supreme Court of Canada's decision in *Ewanchuk* reflects the first time a majority of the Court explicitly rejected the stereotype that a complainant's failure to resist implies consent. *Ewanchuk* is famous in Canadian legal circles not only because the Supreme Court's decision in this case is now the leading precedent on the "yes means yes" definition of consent, but also because of Justice McClung's statements about both the complainant and the decision of the Supreme Court to overturn his decision.[23]

As in the case of Justice Camp's conduct in *Wagar*, the CJC received multiple complaints regarding Justice McClung's conduct in *Ewanchuk*.[24] While the stereotypical statements and reasoning of these two judges were very similar, the CJC's response to their conduct differed significantly. Recall that in Justice Camp's case the CJC recommended removal from office following a public inquiry and recommendation of removal from the inquiry committee. In Justice McClung's case, the CJC did not even order an inquiry. While the CJC concluded that it was "simply unacceptable conduct for a judge" to imply that the complainant was "not a nice girl" or that all that is needed to stop a sexual assault is a "well placed knee," and that such conduct can only cause distress to the victim and reflect negatively on the judiciary, the CJC panel reviewing his conduct concluded that even a formal investigation was unnecessary. Astonishingly, the CJC decided that, while inappropriate, his comments did not suggest gender bias and would not shake the public's confidence in his ability to adjudicate future sexual assault allegations in a fair and impartial manner (Canadian Judicial Council 1999).

What explains such a different response from the CJC in these two cases? One might suggest that the difference can be rationalized by the changes to the law of consent that occurred in 1999 after the Supreme Court of Canada overturned Justice McClung's decision in *Ewanchuk*—again, unanimously rejecting for the first time the notion of implied consent based on a woman's failure to resist. In other words, one might assume that because the gender-based stereotypes underpinning McClung's statements and reasoning in *Ewanchuk* had not yet been unanimously rejected by Canada's highest court, his conduct was not as problematic. Conversely, by 2018, when Justice Camp articulated such thinking, the legal definition of consent and its rejection of the stereotype that real victims fight back, or that a woman's attire or lifestyle may imply consent, was well settled and many years old. This explanation seems compelling ... until you consider the CJC's response to the comments of Justice Robert Dewar in a 2011 sexual assault proceeding.

In a sentencing decision in *R. v. Rhodes*, Justice Dewar made several comments that arguably echoed the same type of discriminatory, gender-based assumptions articulated by Justices McClung and Camp.[25] Sentencing decisions, which are issued following a conclusion that the accused is guilty, provide reasons for a trial judge's decision on the penalty to be imposed upon the accused. Rhodes was convicted of sexual assault. Like the complainant in *Wagar*, Rhodes's victim was a young, Indigenous woman. Rates of sexualized violence against Indigenous women are dramatically higher than rates for non-Indigenous women. Moreover, the complex intersection of gender-based stereotypes and racist thinking that obscures the humanity of Indigenous women further distorts sexual assault trials involving Indigenous complainants (Razack 1998).

The accused penetrated the complainant's vagina with his fingers and his penis, anally penetrated her with his penis, and assaulted her genitals with his mouth. Justice Dewar imposed a two-year conditional sentence to be served in the community.[26] In doing so, and despite his finding of forced vaginal, oral, and anal sex, he emphasized that there was no violence knowingly imposed by the accused, and that the complainant did not run away. Echoing the tone and portrayal of the accused's conduct articulated in Justice McClung's statements in *Ewanchuk*, he characterized Rhodes's conduct as that of a "clumsy Don Juan" and stated that "this is a case of misread signals and inconsiderate behavior."[27] Like the victim-blaming orientation reflected in Justice Camp's questions and comments in *Wagar*, he pointed to the fact that the complainant was wearing a tube top without a bra, makeup, and high heels, and he suggested that "sex was in the air" that evening.[28] He said that the complainant was dressed in a way that showed she "wanted to party" (Canadian Judicial Council 2011). Multiple complaints were filed with the CJC following public revelation of Justice Dewar's statements by a journalist who reported on the sentencing decision in *Rhodes* (Kusch 2011).

The CJC's response to Justice Dewar's 2011 statements was more akin to the council's conclusions regarding Justice McClung's conduct than to the outcome a few years later in the Camp case. Highlighting Justice Dewar's acknowledgment of, and apology for, his use of "inappropriate" and "stereotypical language" in the *Rhodes* case and his articulated commitment to pursuing "professional development" in the area of "gender equality," the CJC concluded that other than "formally expressing concern" regarding Justice Dewar's conduct, no other action was necessary. The CJC did not order a formal investigation or public inquiry into Justice Dewar's conduct (which reveals the council's conclusion that his comments did not pose a threat to the public's confidence in his ability to fairly adjudicate sexual assault trials).

To be sure, there were different factors informing each of these three cases of judicial misconduct.[29] However, there were also important similarities regarding the stereotypical assertions about sexual assault, sexual assault complainants, and women in general made by these judges. Moreover, the CJC was clear, even in 1999 and certainly in 2011, that the statements made by Justices McClung and Dewar were informed by outdated, legally rejected, and harmful gender-based stereotypes. What may have changed between 1999/2011 and 2017 is the CJC's recognition of the profoundly damaging effect that this type of judicial misconduct has on public perceptions of the administration of justice and the competency of the judiciary to adjudicate sexual assault trials justly. One possible explanation for this change is the remarkably heightened degree of public dialogue surrounding, and scrutiny of, the legal system's response to sexualized violence that occurred in response to Justice Camp's conduct in *Wagar*.

The Halifax Taxi Driver Case: "Clearly a Drunk Can Consent"

The third of these exceptionally high-profile Canadian sexual assault cases occurred in early 2017. Like the Ghomeshi case and the disciplinary proceeding against former justice Camp, the Halifax taxi driver case, as it came to be known, was the subject of unprecedented national and international media coverage. It sparked public protests and a wave of public dialogue that was highly critical of the legal system.

The case involved the sexual assault prosecution of Bassam Al-Rawi, a former taxi driver in Halifax, Nova Scotia. The police spotted Al-Rawi's parked taxi in an inexplicable location, on a poorly lit street, late at night. The complainant, a 28-year-old woman, was found unconscious in the back seat of Al-Rawi's vehicle, naked from the breasts down, with her legs propped up in a straddle position with one foot on each of the bucket seats in front of her. The police observed Al-Rawi turned towards the back of the vehicle, in between the complainant's legs, with his pants undone and partially low-ered. In addition to her unconsciousness, other signs of the complainant's severe intoxication included her high blood alcohol level, the fact that she had lost control of her bladder and urinated in her clothing, and her com-plete lack of memory of what occurred once she entered Al-Rawi's vehicle. Upon becoming aware of the police officer's presence, Al-Rawi attempted to hide the complainant's urine-soaked underwear and pants, which he was holding in his hands when the police arrived. Prior to the moment when he picked her up in his taxi, 11 minutes before the police found them, the complainant had never met Al-Rawi. The complainant's DNA was found around Al-Rawi's mouth.[30]

Despite all of this evidence, the trial judge concluded that the Crown had not proven that Al-Rawi engaged in non-consensual sexual contact with the complainant. To be convicted of sexual assault, the Crown must prove, beyond a reasonable doubt, that the individual accused of sexual assault knowingly touched the complainant in a sexual manner without her consent. Remov-ing someone's pants and underwear and placing their body in the position in which the complainant was found in this case, if done without the person's consent, constitutes sexual assault. While Judge Lenehan found that Al-Rawi had removed the complainant's clothing, he decided there was no evidence to prove that she had not consented to this activity.[31] As the Nova Scotia Court of Appeal concluded, this was simply wrong.[32] Judge Lenehan ignored sub-stantial evidence indicating that she had not consented to being stripped by Al-Rawi, such as the fact that he was unknown to her, his attempt to hide her clothes, and her lack of memory of the incident.

Judge Lenehan also decided that there was not enough evidence to con-clude that the complainant was too intoxicated to have consented. At a cer-tain level of intoxication individuals become legally incapable of consenting to sexual activity. One of the main issues Judge Lenehan was required to decide in this case was whether the complainant was too drunk to consent to having her clothes removed and her body positioned as it was when the police found her. While it is clear that an unconscious individual cannot consent to the removal of their pants and underwear, it is also clear that up to a certain point of intoxication one is capable of consenting to this activity; thus, Judge Lenehan's legally accurate but carelessly worded, incendiary, and widely reported comment: "Clearly a drunk can consent."[33] While it is true that up to a certain level of intoxication one can consent to sex, the point at which one loses capacity is certainly prior to loss of consciousness. Judge Lenehan's decision about the complainant's capacity to consent was wrong because he equated "too drunk to consent" with unconsciousness rather than some lesser degree of intoxication.

As noted, Judge Lenehan's acquittal of Bassam Al-Rawi generated public outrage. How could this set of uncontested facts, involving police eyewitnesses, result in an acquittal? Sexual assault law expert Elizabeth Sheehy commented that a failure to convict on an evidentiary record of this nature sends the message that "it is open season on incapacitated women" (Kassam 2017). There were public protests, a petition calling for Judge Lenehan's removal from office with 37,000 signatures, and calls for an inquiry into his conduct of the case (Ray 2017). Over 120 complaints of judicial misconduct against Judge Lenehan were filed with the Nova Scotia Judicial Council (Hoskins, Baxter, and Fierlbeck 2018). As was the case with *Ghomeshi* and Camp's conduct in *Wagar*, public dialogue regarding the acquittal included fierce criticism of the legal system's response to sexual assault and demands for change.

A review committee charged with investigating the complaints against Judge Lenehan concluded that there was no evidence of judicial misconduct (Hoskins, Baxter, and Fierlbeck 2018). There is an important distinction between judicial misconduct and judicial error. Judicial errors involve legal mistakes. Judicial misconduct includes explicitly discriminatory statements like those of Justices McClung, Dewar, and Camp. While the committee's conclusion that there was no evidence of judicial misconduct is likely correct, there is no question that Judge Lenehan's decision was filled with legal errors.[34] As is discussed in the paragraphs that follow, his erroneous reasoning in *Al-Rawi*, combined with Justice Camp's decision in *Wagar*, were pointed to by lawmakers advocating in favour of mandatory sexual assault training for Canadian judges.

LOOKING FORWARD: CAN PUBLIC DIALOGUE MITIGATE THE JUSTICE GAP?

The increased public dialogue focused on sexualized violence and the heightened public scrutiny of the legal system's response to sexual assault in Canada since approximately 2014 are undeniable. Less clear is whether this phenomenon will result in improvements to the lived realities, the on-the-ground experiences, of those who participate in the criminal justice process as sexual assault complainants.

Promisingly, there have been social policy and legislative initiatives that are directly attributable to the systemic problems revealed by these three cases. In the aftermath of *Ghomeshi*, the Ontario government adopted an action plan to respond to sexualized violence that included enhanced training, data collection, and mentorship for Crown attorneys aimed at achieving more effective and victim-oriented sexual assault prosecutions. The province also adopted Canada's first pilot project offering sexual assault survivors two hours of state-funded independent legal advice in Toronto, Ottawa, and Thunder Bay (Ontario Government 2015). Since then several other provinces have, with the assistance of funding from the federal government, adopted similar initiatives (Newfoundland and Labrador Justice and Public Safety 2017). In 2018, Ontario announced that it would expand its program to offer independent legal advice to sexual assault survivors in other parts of the province (Ontario Government 2018).

For its part, following *Ghomeshi* the federal government tabled legislation with the specific aim of improving the treatment of sexual assault complainants. Bill C-51 (which has been dubbed "the Ghomeshi rules" by some; Spratt 2017) received Royal Assent in December 2018. It aims to strengthen the laws limiting the kinds of evidence of a complainant's other sexual activity that can be used, clarify the definition of capacity to consent to sexual contact, and require defence lawyers to obtain the court's permission before introducing a complainant's private text messages or email correspondence to demonstrate inconsistencies or fabrications in her testimony.[35]

Bill C-51 also includes an attempt to clarify the definition of consent.[36] This proposed amendment reflects a response to concerns, raised after Judge Lenehan's decision in *Al-Rawi*, that courts have not applied the proper legal test to determine consent in cases involving a complainant who is intoxicated or otherwise incapacitated. The proposed amendment attempts to clarify the circumstances in which a complainant is incapacitated such that they are unable to validly consent to sexual touching.

The impact of law reforms depends on what judges do with them, which is of course an important part of the explanation for the gap between the feminist-inspired reforms of the 1980s and 1990s and the actual impact of these legal changes on the ground. How do judges interpret and apply changes to the law of sexual assault? This raises the prospect of another government initiative that can be directly attributable to the failings of Justice Camp and Judge Lenehan. In the wake of these two cases a private member's bill that would make sexual assault training an eligibility requirement for judicial appointment by the federal government received unanimous approval from the House of Commons. While this Judicial Accountability through Sexual Assault Law Training Act (JUST Act), introduced in 2017 by interim Conservative leader Rona Ambrose, ultimately died in the Senate, it was reintroduced in 2020 by the Liberal government as Bill C-5 an Act to amend the Judges Act and the Criminal Code.[37]

These legislative and policy initiatives can be directly connected to the dramatically increased level of public dialogue regarding sexual assault and in particular public concern regarding, and debate and discussion of, these three exceptionally high-profile cases. Whether the kinds of legal reforms contemplated in Bill C-51 and the JUST Act, or the policy efforts manifested in programs to provide complainants with legal advice and to better train legal professionals, will mitigate the justice gap in sexual assault law remains an open question. The answer likely lies in whether this public dialogue and focus either reflects a change or will inspire a change in social attitudes about sex, gender, and sexualized violence more broadly. As feminists have long pointed out, revising the law of sexual assault remains much easier than changing the sexist and misogynistic attitudes and norms that produced and have reinforced such a discriminatory legal system in the first place. While law reform alone failed to transform the gendered failings of the criminal law's response to sexual harm, perhaps the capacity of these progressive changes to reduce the trauma of trials for complainants and to encourage survivors to report their experiences of sexual violation is still to be achieved. Perhaps the political and legal activism currently being pursued through new forms, and a heightened degree, of public dialogue will be transformative.

DISCUSSION QUESTIONS

1. Can this dramatic increase in public dialogue critiquing the legal system's response to allegations of sexual assault be dismissed as simply a function of social media and its role in changing the form and volume of public dialogue? Or is it more a reflection of social disruption—"turbulent times"?

2. Assuming the rise of social media does serve as an explanatory factor for the public response to cases such as *Ghomeshi*, *Wagar* (Camp) and *Al-Rawi*, does this response nevertheless suggest that a new or different type of legal and political anti-violence activism has emerged? If so, is it capable of changing social attitudes or leading to broad social transformation?

3. Does the standard for removing a judge from office—judicial misconduct that would seriously undermine a reasonable person's confidence in the ability of the judge to properly execute his or her judicial duties—require reconsideration in a post-Ghomeshi, post-#MeToo movement era?

4. Will the legal and policy developments adopted in response to these cases merely widen the justice gap between Canada's progressive legal system and the experiences of sexual assault survivors, or do they offer hope for concrete, transformative improvements to the legal system's treatment of complainants?

NOTES

1 For a comprehensive discussion of the early legislative reforms, see Boyle (1984). For consideration of the reforms achieved in the 1990s and the first decade of the twenty-first century, see Sheehy (2012). For further discussion of Canadian feminist activism in this area of law during the 1980s and 1990s, see Roberts and Mohr (1994).

2 Criminal Code, Revised Statutes of Canada, 1985, c. C-45, s. 276.

3 Ibid., s. 275.

4 An Act to Amend the Criminal Code in Relation to Sexual Offences and Other Offences Against the Person, Statutes of Canada, 1980-81-82-83, c. 125, s. 19.; *R. v. Chase* [1987] 2 S.C.R. 293.

5 *R. v. Ewanchuk* [1999] 1 S.C.R. 330, 169 DLR (4th) 193; Criminal Code, Revised Statutes of Canada, 1985, c. C-45, s. 273.

6 See Daly and Bouhours (2010), who find a significant decrease in Canada in the overall rate of conviction for sexual offences when comparing 1970–89 with 1990–2005.

7 While rates of violent and non-violent crime declined for all other offences between 2004 and 2014, the rate of self-reported sexual assault remained the same (see Codray and Cotter 2014).

8 See generally Sheehy (2012); Regehr et al. (2008)—citing studies by numerous researchers demonstrating negative impacts; Ross (2006)—summarizing research in several countries, including Canada, that reveals the re-traumatization

experienced by sexual assault victims through participation in the criminal justice process.

9 I documented this claim in Craig (2012).

10 See Tucker (2014a). Ghomeshi was prosecuted on, and acquitted of, charges regarding three of these women. Charges with respect to two other women were dropped. Charges involving a sixth women, a former co-worker, were withdrawn after Ghomeshi apologized in court for his sexually inappropriate behaviour towards her and signed a one-year peace bond. A peace bond is a court order involving certain conditions that the accused agrees to comply with—such as not contacting the alleged victim.

11 See e.g. Tucker (2014b); Postmedia News (2014). For a study of the 2014 public dialogue surrounding this case see Phillips (2017).

12 While this criticism is understandable given how traumatic the experience of testifying reportedly was for these complainants, defence lawyers are required to defend their clients vigorously. One of the main methods through which they do this in the context of sexual assault trials is by demonstrating inconsistencies in a witness's statements or, where available, offering evidence that the complainant has been untruthful, misleading, or incomplete in recounting details concerning the allegation or surrounding circumstances (see Decoutere 2016).

13 *R. v. Ghomeshi* [2016] 2016 O.N.C.J. 155, 27 C.R. (7th) 17.

14 *R. v. Wagar* [2015] 2015 A.B.C.A 327.

15 Ibid., trial transcript at 119:10–11, 119:14–15.

16 Ibid., at 437:9.

17 Ibid., at 450:29.

18 See Crawford (2017). Under Canadian constitutional law federally appointed judges can only be removed from office following a joint address of the House of Commons and the Senate (Constitution Act, 1867, 30 and 31 Vict., c. 3.).

19 These factual details from the case are drawn from the work of Backhouse (2017). Backhouse's examination of the case included a review of the trial transcript.

20 *R. v. Ewanchuk* [1998] 6 W.W.R 8 at para. 5 and 21, 57 Alta. L.R. (3d) 235.

21 Ibid., para. 4.

22 Ibid., para. 21.

23 For a rich discussion of the larger controversy concerning Justice McClung's public attack on Supreme Court of Canada Justice Claire L'Heureux-Dubé in response to her concurring decision in *Ewanchuk* (which, in overturning McClung, explicitly identified the stereotypical nature of his reasoning) see Backhouse (2017).

24 The complaints against McClung also included allegations regarding his inappropriate public attack on Justice L'Heureux-Dubé (see Backhouse 2017), and homophobic statements he made in a decision to uphold the Alberta government's exclusion of sexual minorities under its human rights legislation. With respect to the latter, his decision in *Vriend v. Alberta*, [1998] 1 S.C.R. 493 was also overturned by the Supreme Court of Canada.

25 *R. v. Rhodes* [2011] M.J. N.o. 67 (MBQB) (sentencing transcript), 18 February 2011.

26 *R. v. Rhodes* [2011] M.J. N.o. 67 at para. 516 (unreported).

27 Ibid., paras. 509, 512.

28 Ibid., para. 519.

29 One key difference, some would argue, is that Justice Camp's comments were more directly dismissive of Canada's legal regime. However, in content and tone, Justice McClung's decision and public statements reflect a quite similar disregard for the reforms to this area of law.

30 *R. v. Al-Rawi* [2017] Halifax 2866665 (NSPC) (audio trial transcript), 9–10 February 2017.

31 *R. v. Al-Rawi* [2017] Halifax 2866665 (NSPC) (oral decision), 1 March 2017.

32 *R. v. Al-Rawi* [2017] 2018 N.S.C.A. 10.

33 See note 29.

34 As I have argued elsewhere, Judge Lenehan's reasoning may well have been informed by stereotypical thinking (Craig 2017). It did not, however, involve explicitly discriminatory statements about sexual assault law or complainants. See *R. v. Al-Rawi* [2017] Halifax 2866665 (NSPC) (audio trial transcript), February 9–10, 2017.

35 Bill C-51, An Act to Amend the Criminal Code and the Department of Justice Act and to Make Consequential Amendments to Another Act, 1st sess., 42nd Parliament, 2017.

36 Ibid., ss. 19–20.

37 Bill C-337, Judicial Accountability through Sexual Assault Law Training Act, 1st sess., 42nd Parliament, 2017. https://openparliament.ca/bills/42-1/C-337/.

REFERENCES

Backhouse, Constance. 2017. *Claire L'Heureux-Dubé: A Life.* Vancouver: UBC Press.

Boyle, Christine. 1984. *Sexual Assault.* Toronto: Carswell Company.

Canadian Judicial Council. 1990. *Report to the Canadian Judicial Council of the Inquiry Committee Established Pursuant to Subsection 63(1) of the Judges Act at the Request of the Attorney General of Nova Scotia.* Ottawa: Canadian Judicial Council.

———. 1999. "News Release: Panel Expressed Disapproval of McClung Conduct." May 21. Ottawa: Canadian Judicial Council.

———. 2011. "News Release: Canadian Judicial Council Completes Its Review of Complaints Made against Justice Robert Dewar." November 9. https://www.cjc -ccm.gc.ca/english/news_en.asp?selMenu=news_2011_1109_en.asp.

———. 2016. *Report and Recommendation of the Inquiry to the Canadian Judicial Council.* November 29. https://www.cjc-ccm.gc.ca/cmslib/general/Camp_Docs /2016-11-29 CJC Camp Inquiry Committee Report.pdf.

———. 2017. *In the Matter of S. 63 of the Judges Act, RS c, J-1: Canadian Judicial Inquiry into the Conduct of Honourable Robin Camp: Report to the Minister of Justice.* Ottawa: Canadian Judicial Council.

Codray, Shannon, and Adam Cotter. 2014. *Self-Reported Sexual Assault in Canada.* Ottawa: Statistics Canada. https://www.statcan.gc.ca/pub/85-002-x/2017001 /article/14842-eng.htm.

Craig, Elaine. 2012. *Troubling Sex: Towards a Legal Theory of Sexual Integrity.* Vancouver: UBC Press.

———. 2017. "Judging Sexual Assault Trials: Systemic Failure in the Case of R v Bassam Al-Rawi." *Canadian Bar Review* 95 (1): 179–211.

Crawford, Alison. 2017. "Justice Robin Camp Resigns after Judicial Council Recommends Removal." *CBC News*, March 9. https://www.cbc.ca/news/politics /justice-robin-camp-judicial-council-1.4017233.

Daly, Kathleen, and Brigitte Bouhours. 2010. "Rape and Attrition in the Legal Process: A Comparative Analysis of Five Countries." In *Crime and Justice: A Review of Research*, vol. 39, edited by Michael Tonry, 565–650. Chicago: University of Chicago Press.

Davies, Breese. 2016. "Convicting Jian Ghomeshi Will Be Hard—for Good Reason." *Toronto Star*, 2 February. https://www.thestar.com/opinion/commentary/2016/02/02 /convicting-jian-ghomeshi-will-be-hard-for-good-reason.html.

Decoutere, Lucy. 2016. "Lucy Decoutere on the Trauma of the Jian Ghomeshi Trial: 'After Everything I Went Through, Jian Is Free.'" As told to Ruth Spencer. *The Guardian*, March 25. https://www.theguardian.com/world/2016/mar/25/jian -ghomeshi-trial-lucy-de-coutere-interview.

Devlin, Richard, and Sheila Wildeman. n.d. *Judicial Self-Regulation: Between the Ideal and Reality.* Unpublished manuscript in the author's possession.

Gallant, Jaques. 2014. "Twitter Conversation about Unreported Rape Goes Viral." *Toronto Star*, October 31. https://www.thestar.com/news/crime/2014/10/31 /twitter_conversation_about_unreported_rape_goes_global.html.

Hoskins, Frank P., R. Daren Baxter, and Katherine Fierlbeck. 2018. *Decision of the Review Committee.* Halifax: Nova Scotia Judicial Council. http://www .documentclo ud.org/documents/4431083-Review-Committee-Final-Decision .html#document.

Houpt, Simon. 2016, "Jury's Still Out on Media's Role in Ghomeshi Case." *Globe and Mail*, March 25. https://www.theglobeandmail.com/news/national/jury-still-out -on-medias-role-in-ghomeshi-case/article29397973/.

Johnson, Holly. 2006. *Measuring Violence against Women: Statistical Trends 2006.* Catalogue No. 85-570-XIE. Ottawa: Statistics Canada.

———. 2012. "Limits of a Criminal Justice Response: Trends in Police and Court Processing of Sexual Assault." In *Sexual Assault in Canada: Law, Legal Practice, and Women's Activism*, edited by Elizabeth Sheehy, 613–34. Ottawa: University of Ottawa Press.

Kassam, Ashifa. 2017. "Canada Sex Assault Acquittal Signals 'Open Season on Incapacitated Women.'" *The Guardian*, March 7. https://www.theguardian.com /world/2017/mar/07/canada-acquittal-signals-open-season-on-incapacitated-women.

Kong, Rebecca, Holly Johnson, Sara Beattie, and Andrea Cardillo. 2003. *Sexual Offences in Canada.* Catalogue No. 85-002-XIE. Ottawa: Statistics Canada.

Kusch, Larry. 2011. "Judicial Body Reviewing Complaints against Judge." *Winnipeg Free Press*, February 25. https://www.winnipegfreepress.com/breakingnews /Protesters-chant-yes-means-yes-and-no-means-no-116936533.html.

Newfoundland and Labrador Justice and Public Safety. 2017. "Minister Parsons Announces Support for Victims of Sexual Assault." April 25. https://www.releases .gov.nl.ca/releases/2017/just/0425n01.aspx.

Ohler, Shawn. 1999. "Judge Reiterates Belief That Teen Wasn't Assaulted." *National Post*, February 27. https://www.fact.on.ca/newpaper/np990227.htm.

Ontario Government. 2015. *It's Never Okay: An Action Plan to Stop Sexual Violence and Harassment*. https://dr6j45jk9xcmk.cloudfront.net/documents/4593/actionplan -itsneverokay.pdf.

———. 2018. "It's Never Okay: Ontario's Gender-Based Violence Strategy." https:// news.ontario.ca/owd/en/2018/03/its-never-okay-ontarios-gender-based-violence -strategy.html.

Phillips, Dana. 2017. "Let's Talk about Sexual Assault: Survivor Stories and the Law in the Jian Ghomeshi Media Discourse." *Osgoode Hall Law Journal* 54 (4): 1133.

Postmedia News. 2014. "'Been Raped Never Reported': Why 90% of Sex Assault Victims Stay Silent Rather Than Face Trial by Ordeal." *National Post*, November 28. https://nationalpost.com/news/canada/been-raped-never-reported-why-90 -of-sex-assault-victims-stay-silent-rather-than-face-trial-by-ordeal.

Ray, Carolyn. 2017. "Upset, Angry and Confused: Protesters Call for Inquiry into Cabbie's Acquittal." *CBC News*, March 7. https://www.cbc.ca/news/canada/nova -scotia/judge-gregory-lenehan-bassam-al-rawi-cab-driver-sex-assault-protest -inquiry-1.4014155.

Razack, Sherene. 1998. "Race, Space, and Prostitution: The Making of the Bourgeois Subject." *Canadian Journal of Woman and the Law* 10 (3): 338.

Regehr, Cheryl, Ramona Alaggia, Liz Lambert, and Michael Saini. 2008. "Victims of Sexual Violence in the Canadian Criminal Courts." *Victims and Offenders* 3 (1): 99–113.

Roberts, Julian, and Renate Mohr. 1994. *Confronting Sexual Assault: A Decade of Legal and Social Change*. Toronto: University of Toronto Press.

Ross, Mary. 2006. "Restoring Rape Survivors: Justice, Advocacy, and a Call to Action." *Annals of the New York Academy of Sciences* 1087 (206): 218–22.

Rusonick, Reid. 2016. "In Defence of Rigorous Sexual Assault Defences." *Toronto Star*, February 21. https://www.thestar.com/opinion/commentary/2016/02/21/in -defence-of-rigorous-sexual-assault-defences.html.

Sheehy, Elizabeth, ed. 2012. *Sexual Assault in Canada: Law, Legal Practice and Women's Activism*. Ottawa: University of Ottawa Press.

Smart, Carol. 1989. *Feminism and the Power of Law*. New York: Routledge.

Spratt, Michael. 2017. "The Ghomeshi Rules: Bill C-51 Creates Unprecedented Case of Reverse Disclosure." *Canadian Lawyers*, June 19. https://www .canadianlawyermag.com/news/opinion/the-ghomeshi-rules-bill-c-51-creates -unprecedented-case-of-reverse-disclosure/270519.

Stead, Sylvia. 2016. "Public Editor: Ghomeshi Coverage Was Warranted, Necessary." *Globe and Mail*, February 12. https://www.theglobeandmail.com/community/inside-the-globe/public-editor-ghomeshi-coverage-was-warranted-necessary/article28744459/.

Tang, Kwong-leung. 1998. "Rape Law Reform in Canada: The Success and Limits of Legislation." *International Journal of Offender Therapy and Comparative Criminology* 42 (3): 258.

Temkin, Jennifer, and Barbara Krahé. 2008. *Sexual Assault and the Justice Gap: A Question of Attitude*. Oxford: Hart Publishing.

Tucker, Erika. 2014a. "Timeline: Jian Ghomeshi Charged in Sex Assault Scandal." *Global News*, December 3. https://globalnews.ca/news/1647091/timeline-sex-assault-allegations-arise-after-cbc-fires-jian-ghomeshi/.

———. 2014b. "Why Don't Victims or Bystanders Report Sexual Assault?" *Global News*, October 30. https://globalnews.ca/news/1645523/why-dont-victims-or-bystanders-report-sexual-assault/.

FURTHER READING

Powell, Anastasia, Nicola Henry, and Asher Flynn, eds. 2015. *Rape Justice: Beyond the Criminal Law*. London: Palgrave Macmillan.

Sheehey, Elizabeth, ed. 2012. *Sexual Assault in Canada: Law, Legal Practice and Women's Activism*. Ottawa: University of Ottawa Press.

Temkin, Jennifer, and Barbara Krahé. 2008. *Sexual Assault and the Justice Gap: A Question of Attitude*. Oxford: Hart Publishing.

5

Transforming the Gender Divide? Deconstructing Femininity and Masculinity in Indigenous Politics

Gina Starblanket

Key terms: cultural traditions, gender binary, Indigenous feminism, Indigenous femininity, Indigenous masculinity, Indigenous politics, Indigenous womanhood

Over the past few decades, Indigenous studies and **Indigenous politics** scholars have increasingly been attentive to the role of gender in projects of decolonization and Indigenous resurgence. Far from occupying a homogenous place in our methods and theories, it figures variously in diagnoses of colonial and patriarchal violence and also in prescribed remedies. Some have sought to problematize **binary** notions of gender as Western constructs, while others have argued for the revitalization of Indigenous **cultural traditions** through the reclamation of traditional notions of **Indigenous femininity** and **masculinity**. Though such analyses have made important headway in deconstructing the ways in which gender is produced within contexts of colonialism, there is an ongoing need for analyses of the relationship between gender and culture as it emerges within the construction of Indigenous political identities. This chapter traces the ways in which gendered identity categories have been imposed, resisted, and transformed within Indigenous communities and particularly in movements towards Indigenous decolonization and resurgence. In doing so, I draw a distinction between the discourse of **Indigenous feminism** and the discourse on Indigenous femininities and masculinities. What I am most interested in is to what degree the construction of Indigenous political identity stands to grow, or risks being contained, by gender-specific conceptions of Indigeneity such as the re-assertion of "strong" or "healthy" femininities and masculinities. Following the theme of transformation that anchors this collection, this chapter offers insight into the complex relationship between gender and identity within contemporary Indigenous political mobilizations, investigating whether and to what degree the power relations arising from colonial heteronormativity stand to be transformed by discourses of Indigenous feminism, Indigenous masculinities, and Indigenous femininities.

BACKGROUND: GENDER AND COLONIALISM

The highly gendered nature of colonialism is well recognized in Indigenous studies, in terms of the way in which gender both is produced by and also serves to reinforce systems of settler colonialism. Scholars have argued that the imposition of Western gender norms within Indigenous communities has aimed to distort Indigenous notions of identity to render them more consistent with, and easier to regulate within, colonizing social orders. Further, colonial violence against Indigenous women is now understood to have distinctly political aims. As Audra Simpson (2016b) explains in her analysis of the gendered, biopolitical nature of settler colonialism, Indigenous women's and girls' bodies have historically been the targets of violence, not just to clear physical bodies from spaces desired for settlement but also because of what said bodies represent: that is, relationships with land, jurisdiction, processes of reproduction, kinship, and, ultimately, difference from Western systems of law and governance. Thus colonial efforts to minimize and distort Indigenous women's traditional positions within their cultural communities were not merely a byproduct of the patriarchal nature of European societies at the time, but in fact should be understood as a deliberate, enduring, and direct attempt to minimize our political agency. If the extension of settler authority over Indigenous Peoples has required the ongoing marginalization of social and political orders that differ from those of western Europe, then a central part of settler colonialism involves a perpetual (even if evolving) assault upon those who most directly symbolize that difference (Simpson 2016b). Indigenous women's bodies have thus been targeted as dual sites of difference: that is, we have been targeted for our status as Indigenous people who differ from colonizers and as women who differ from western European women.

In colonial contexts, difference represents a threat to the entrenchment and continuity of hegemonic settler societies as well as the means through which violence against Indigenous people is justified. It manifests through a series of binary oppositions that serve to impose violent hierarchies and forms of repression to maintain relations of dominance between the colonizer and colonized (Ashcroft, Griffiths, and Tiffin 1998, 19). The Western tendency to see the world in binary oppositions such as civilized/primitive, guardian/dependant, teacher/pupil, man/woman, and human/nature contributes to the rationalization of processes of colonialism by depicting Indigeneity as always "lesser than"; that is, Indigenous life is representative of a state of depravity and savagery that necessitates salvation, and "civilization." Such characterizations have historically functioned to justify a number of repressive government policies enacted upon Indigenous peoples, including but not limited to the reserve system, vagrancy laws, alcohol prohibitions, the residential school system, the pass system, and other restrictions on Indigenous people's everyday lives.

Binary logics such as those outlined above justify and structure not only the imposition of policies geared towards assimilation but also colonial efforts aimed at appropriation and exploitation (see also Altamirano-Jiménez and Wiebe in this volume). These colonial logics are not relegated to the past—as Simpson and other scholars who are attentive to logics of settler colonialism make clear, the legitimacy of settler political authority is dependent upon the continual reproduction of logics of oppression in the present (Simpson 2016a; Stark 2016; Wolfe 2006). However, attempts to impose dualistic ways of thinking within Indigenous communities have never been seamless projects, as Indigenous philosophies of relationality give rise to conceptions of identity, sexuality, kinship, and relations with creation that weave in and out of or entirely defy categorical ways of thinking. Furthermore, the valuation of one category, such as man, over another category, such as woman, is a foreign mode of thought, as Indigenous laws direct us to exercise equal appreciation for the gifts of all beings across their differences. Indeed, while many aspects of these dichotomies have been internalized by Indigenous Peoples over time, colonial attempts to create gendered subjects such as the male patriarch and domesticated, subservient woman have never been straightforward (Hokowhitu 2016). Nevertheless, patriarchy has over time become a characteristic of many Indigenous communities, as the societal valuation of masculinity over femininity and indeed the legislated priority given to Indigenous men through the Indian Act and other mechanisms have resulted in the subordination of Indigenous women from outside and within our cultural communities (Green 1997; Carlson and Steinhauer 2013).

Just as the experiences of Indigenous men have been shaped by gendered *and* colonial power relations, so too have those of Indigenous women. Indigenous women have different experiences of gendered oppression than non-Indigenous women, and experiences of colonial oppression that are distinct from those of Indigenous men. Modes of analysing oppression that are based on either the colonizer/colonized or man/woman binaries are therefore inherently limited, as Indigenous women's experiences of oppression cannot be fully comprehended through simplistic analyses of patriarchy as a phenomenon that manifests uniformly across cultural and temporal distinctions (Mohanty 1988). Nor can they be analysed through homogenous analyses of colonialism as impacting all Indigenous Peoples in a similar manner (Green 2007). Rather, Indigenous women occupy multiple worlds that place greater value on whiteness (couched in the language of progress and civilization), on heteronormativity and misogyny (both Indigenous and non-Indigenous), and on a range of other hierarchies and structures of oppression.

Gendered social and political structures are amplified in conditions of colonialism, as they lead to the creation of complex relations of power both within and outside of Indigenous communities. In attempts to resist the gendered and sexualized nature of racism and colonialism, there has been a move over time to address violent and damaging representations of Indigeneity while reclaiming and redefining them within Indigenous communities. Such representations include dichotomous treatments of Indigenous Peoples, such as the Indigenous woman as the virtuous Indian princess or the sexually licentious squaw, or the Indian man as the noble savage or bloodthirsty warrior. However, in the process of rejecting these caricatures and the highly gendered and racist assumptions they embody, notions of culturally grounded identity have become inescapably caught up with questions of authenticity within Indigenous communities.

Indigenous studies scholarship has sought to reject colonial gender binaries as alien to pre-contact Indigenous communities, while simultaneously repurposing gender categories through the contemporary construction of culturally rooted or authentic Indigenous subjectivities. Here I turn to the various treatments of gender in contemporary Indigenous scholarship in the interest of mapping out the trajectory of the field and contextualizing many present and future challenges. In doing so, I draw a distinction between the bodies of work that I term "Indigenous femininities" and "Indigenous masculinities," and the critical methodological approaches offered by **Indigenous feminism**.

INDIGENOUS FEMININITIES, FEMINISMS, AND MASCULINITIES

I must begin this section by clarifying that in exploring the discourses of Indigenous masculinity and femininity, my intent is not to lend legitimacy to categories of man/woman themselves. As a socio-political construct that implicates both men and women in particular ways, gender is, however, a worthy site of analysis; and this is particularly true with respect to the ways in which it intersects with other formations of power that impact Indigenous Peoples' existences relative to one another and to colonizing orders. I am primarily interested in the relationship between gender and Indigeneity and in tracing the possibilities and limitations of constructing contemporary framings of Indigeneity through notions of tradition that give rise to culturally grounded ideals of femininity and masculinity.

My first area of focus is the body of work on "Indigenous femininity." By engaging with the concept of femininity, I am not referring to the qualities or attributes that are quintessentially associated with women across cultures, but to the ways in which treatments of femininity or womanhood manifest within Indigenous communities, and particularly when they are invoked as a source of politicized identity. This includes the ways in which representations of Indigenous femininity are produced within Indigenous communities as responses to gendered constructions of identity that were imposed through colonialism, or in efforts to refuse or subvert such representations. While the socio-political significance of Indigenous femininity has also been articulated in many contexts by Indigenous feminists seeking to centre women's agency and voices relative to malestream Indigenous leaders and organizations, I see the discourses on Indigenous femininity and feminism as having several distinct features.

The body of writings, teachings, and creative productions about and for Indigenous women has been relatively well established for some time. Many of these works find their origins in the desire to refuse or subvert colonial efforts to define Indigenous women's subjectivity. The ability to be self-determining, including the ability to live in accordance with our own understandings of Indigeneity, is vital not just to Indigenous women's identities but to collective movements towards self-determination and nation-building. If the contemporary violences and crises faced by Indigenous women are a consequence of colonialism's drive to devalue Indigenous women, then the remedy that follows is the deconstruction of patriarchy and the re-empowerment of Indigenous women. The prescription that is often invoked to work towards this project of empowerment is a renewed appreciation and respect for Indigenous women's inherent gifts. Such gifts include Indigenous women's intimate association with creation and water as those who can bring forth life, and who thus occupy important positions in kinship systems and in the governance of our relations with creation. In efforts to turn away from colonial productions of gendered subjectivity, Indigenous reclamations of gender have often involved a turn inwards, towards a form of cultural identity that is instead grounded upon spiritual and biological sources. Indeed, Indigenous women's teachings often relate to our roles and responsibilities within the many relationships we inhabit—with our families, communities, the spirit world, and other beings that form part of creation.

While culturally and geographically specific, there are certain shared attributes in the ways in which Indigenous femininity is generally constructed. These include determinations of women's location within Indigenous communities as centrally maternal or as those who have a primary responsibility for nurturing and maintaining good relationships. Associated teachings include knowledge relating to pregnancy, birthing rituals, and gender and age-specific roles and ceremonies. For instance, there is an enormous value placed on giving birth in Indigenous communities, which as Emma LaRocque (2017) notes implicates women even when motherhood is conceptualized as a moral ethic rather than a biological responsibility. Other codified behaviours, such as the wearing of a skirt as a symbol of connectedness with mother earth (Allen 1992; Anderson 2016), teachings surrounding how/where to walk and to sit, and expectations relating to modest dress are also grounded upon cultural and spiritual beliefs relating to womanhood and femininity.

Often, such roles are directly associated with the preservation and transmission of cultural knowledge. For instance, the figure of the Indigenous woman as the centre and wheel of life, and as keeper or carrier of culture, situates women as essential to the vitality of Indigenous group culture. These metaphors emerge as particularly salient within decolonial discourses that are grounded upon the reclamation of authentic or pre-contact cultural practices.

Indigenous women's teachings are represented as central to the health and well-being of Indigenous communities, positioning our ability to embody and maintain cultural traditions as a powerful way of resisting and subverting colonial efforts to diminish our power and authority. The need for culturally grounded remedies to gendered oppression is evidenced by the potential benefit to Indigenous communities as a whole, which also positions Indigenous femininities in contradistinction to the purportedly individualistic orientation of Indigenous feminist work. Thus notions of balance, complementarity, and relationality are frequently invoked to contextualize Indigenous women's roles, behaviours, and responsibilities within communities.

The construction of the Indigenous feminine identity can be understood as part of a broader move among Indigenous Peoples to counter colonial identity constructions. As LaRocque (2010) writes, Indigenous Peoples' resistance to gross misrepresentation and marginalization can take place through a number of techniques. The first involves efforts to re-humanize ourselves by emphasizing Indigenous names, social and familial roles, relationships, feelings, and so on. This technique is in response to the colonial devaluation of Indigenous identity as something that should be voluntarily relinquished, outlawed, assimilated, legislated away, reduced to the status of a cultural minority, appropriated, or otherwise vacated of meaning. The second is the drive to re-establish the viability of Indigenous cultures by emphasizing an idealized Indigeneity, such as the ways in which Indigenous cultures are represented as egalitarian or matriarchal vis-à-vis Euro-Canadian patriarchal society. The third is to reverse binary ways of thinking such as the civilized/savage dichotomy, charging settlers rather than Indigenous Peoples as being the perpetrators of gratuitous levels of violence. Many scholarly, artistic, and creative productions have taken up this latter project by pointing out the violence and death Indigenous peoples have experienced as a result of colonial policies such as the criminalization of cultural and political activity, rations policies that resulted in disease and starvation, forms of torture and abuse endured through residential schools, and other forms of suffering perpetuated at the hands of colonial authorities.

Efforts to highlight the violence of colonialism by way of contrast can also be seen in scholarship and cultural productions that seek to reverse gender binaries, such as the assertion of culturally grounded Indigenous femininities as more highly respected and revered than Western conceptions of womanhood, which are often oppressive. Increasingly, this reversal is also being deployed through the assertion of "healthy masculinities" relative to the forms of "toxic masculinity" that characterize patriarchal societies and that have been internalized by many Indigenous Peoples in contexts of colonialism. This leads into the next and related body of work that I want to explore: that is, the growing body of work on "Indigenous masculinities."

Over the past decade, a number of publications on Indigenous masculinity have surfaced in the United States and Canada, leading scholars such as Brendan Hokowhitu (2016) to deem this body of work a recent and burgeoning subfield in Indigenous studies. Indeed, a number of publications in Canada have decisively adopted the label of "Indigenous masculinities" to describe theorizations geared towards healing from the violences suffered by Indigenous men, while also putatively engaged in the work of purging "toxic masculinities" from Indigenous Peoples' collective systems. Yet as scholars such as Billy-Ray Belcourt (2016a) have argued, the idea that the study of Indigenous masculinities is new overlooks the ways in which Indigenous studies scholarship has always centered the Indigenous male subject in its treatment of Indigeneity, colonialism, resistance, and now resurgence. Declarations of Indigenous masculinities as an emergent area of study neglect to acknowledge the ever-present backdrop against which the field of Indigenous studies and its canons, methods, and actors have taken shape.

The normative force of Indigenous masculinities is evident when one contemplates the ways in which Indigenous women's concerns, priorities, and voices have continually been relegated to the margins of the discipline (Green 2002, 2017; LaRocque 1996; Monture-Angus 2002). As early as the late 1980s, Indigenous women scholars such as Patricia Monture-Angus described the hostility that Indigenous women have faced in the academy, writing that "the harassment I have experienced is based on a gendered (or sexualized) construction of the 'good Indian'" (2002, 282). In terms of both the construction of knowledge in the academy and Indigenous efforts to organize politically, masculinity has formed the central force against which Indigenous women have had to push back to get the supposed "women's issues" onto the radar (Green 1993). Masculinity has long shaped the social, political, and economic institutions and practices in Indigenous communities in so far as women's voices and experiences have been positioned in contrast to it and have had to come up against it to make space for our particular conditions and aspirations to be understood. Nevertheless, there are certain distinctive features about the academic discourse on Indigenous masculinity that have emerged over the past ten years.

The purpose of the Indigenous masculinities scholarship is twofold: first, it seeks to deconstruct the impacts of colonial violence upon Indigenous men; and second, it seeks to engage in the reclamation of culturally grounded notions of Indigenous masculinity as part of movements towards decolonization and resurgence (Tengan 2008; McKegney 2014; Innes and Anderson 2015). The premise of this scholarship is that the exorcism of violent, heteronormative conceptions of gender that were imposed as part of colonialism can make possible the rise of more virtuous and culturally appropriate conceptions of masculinity. This, in turn, will contextualize why it is that Indigenous men have been implicated in Indigenous women's oppression, while also affecting movement towards healthier social relations. The discourse on Indigenous masculinities invokes "toxic masculinities" as a byproduct of the colonial condition through an attempt to theorize the intersections between the man/woman and colonizer/colonized binaries. Rather than simply looking to patriarchy and colonialism as a referent through which to explore the operation of power and privilege, the discourse situates the identity category of Indigenous masculinity both as a problem and remedy through a treatment of the relationship between gender and culture that parallels the discourse on Indigenous femininities.

The primary difference between the writings on Indigenous femininities and masculinities is that **Indigenous womanhood** tends to be attributed with more innate characteristics owing to an inherent spiritual or biological connection. While "the spiritual" is seen to be decisively political, this remains an indirect route towards Indigenous women's empowerment, as cultural revitalization is said to bring about more just social and political relations over time. Indigenous masculinities, while also employing reconstructed notions of gender as a means of empowerment, seek an explicitly social *and* political reconstruction of male roles and responsibilities. Despite these differing approaches, they similarly treat the relationship between gender and Indigeneity as having the political purchase needed to overcome heteronormative patriarchy both within and beyond Indigenous communities. These treatments of Indigenous masculinity and femininity locate gender as both empowering and disempowering: a gender-based analysis is said to be useful in deconstructing the disempowering features of Western gender binaries as they have been imposed onto Indigenous peoples, but it also represents a way of reclaiming Indigeneity. Culturally informed gender roles and teachings are seen as empowering as they are reflective of our philosophical beliefs but also represent a fundamental difference from that of the West.

Despite arguably representing an empowering project for many Indigenous Peoples, the linking of culture and gender through the articulation of Indigenous feminine/masculine subjectivities also bears certain limits. In resisting social and political constructions of gender that have been deployed in the service of colonialism and turning towards an understanding of gender that is based on an inherent spiritual or biological capacity, the discourse on Indigenous femininity often neglects to engage with the ways in which gender can also be socially and politically constructed in disempowering ways within Indigenous communities. That is, there is a distinct assumption that while Western conceptions of gender are inherently bad, Indigenous understandings of gender are far more virtuous due to their spiritual or cultural foundations. In making this assumption, Indigenous femininities and masculinities fail to acknowledge how the production of Indigenous gendered subjectivities can exclude, marginalize, or contain the ways in which particular bodies are able to live in accordance with their teachings in the present and future.

For instance, Emily Snyder (2018) describes how the attachment of Cree law to static constructions of Indigenous femininity limits the possible ways in which Cree legal traditions can be embodied by Indigenous Peoples in the present. She argues that the consequence of essentialist treatments of womanhood means that the good relations our laws are directed towards realizing are only ever achievable for a select few, rendering other Indigenous Peoples devoid of a future wherein they can live through Indigenous laws without repressing or distorting their identities to align with gendered attitudes and behaviours. Situating Indigenous women's power as linked to our capacity as potential life givers nests the possibilities for Indigenous women's empowerment within heteronormative identity categories. Such constructions restrict the variety of ways in which Indigenous bodies can exist in spiritual or cultural spaces. Furthermore, the creation of the gendered Indigenous subject as a central figure in decolonization/Indigenous resurgence movements limits the possible means through which Indigenous Peoples can work towards the creation of self-determining futures.

INDIGENOUS FEMINIST INTERVENTIONS

Alongside the scholarship on Indigenous femininities and masculinities, there has also been a growing body of Indigenous feminist scholarly, creative, and activist work in recent decades. When I describe Indigenous feminism as a distinct field, I do not intend to deny the long history of resistance to heteropatriarchal and colonial forms of repression that Indigenous women have been engaging in throughout history. Labelling Indigenous women's resistance as a recent phenomenon denies this long and engaged work, minimizing Indigenous women's agency relative to mainstream feminist movements. However, it is also important not to conflate all writings on and by Indigenous women as a coherent body of work. Not only are Indigenous women's works culturally diverse, they are also driven by distinct political commitments and epistemological orientations. Each of these projects serves important purposes, and collapsing them all into the category of "Indigenous women's writings" does them an incredible disservice by homogenizing their nature and intent. Just as the scholarship written by Indigenous men cannot be collapsed into the singular category of Indigenous masculinities, there is an associated need to parse out the particular ideological and political orientations of Indigenous women's writings in order to appreciate the full breadth and depth of our scholarly contributions. This is not to deny the similarities or possibilities for solidarity between Indigenous feminists and scholars who write about Indigenous femininities or masculinities, but to make clear their connections and points of departure.

Relative to the discourse on Indigenous femininities, Indigenous feminists, for the most part, have not articulated a wholehearted rejection of feminine attributes or cultural attachments that exist within Indigenous communities. Rather, they problematize the implications of representations of Indigeneity or femininity that invoke innate, essential qualities, regardless of their spiritual or cultural grounding. Further, they have sought to address the ways in which representations of both femininity and masculinity give rise to gendered norms and expectations that may implicate or marginalize Indigenous peoples. While not monolithic, Indigenous feminists tend to adopt a more layered and multifaceted understanding of identity, one that is not overdetermined by socio-political expectations of what femininity or masculinity should look like, whether they are culturally grounded or not.

One of the most prevalent critiques of feminism relates to its supposedly homogenizing tendencies: that is, that it either privileges the way in which power operates in relations between men and women at the expense of a substantive analysis of colonial power, or offers only reductive engagements with Indigenous Peoples' experiences (Monture-Angus 1995; Moreton-Robinson 2000; Tohe 2000). Such critiques have been deployed towards Indigenous women who have adopted feminist identities, but also towards organizations such as the Native Women's Association of Canada, which was falsely accused of privileging equality over Indigenous Peoples' rights to self-government during constitutional discussions (Green 1993). Despite analyses that depict Indigenous feminists as pawns of the women's movement who naively allow homogenous notions of gender to obscure or overdetermine our identity as Indigenous Peoples, no Indigenous feminist that I am aware of has ever privileged the need to foreground analyses of the power relations between man/woman over colonizer/colonized. On the contrary, the defining feature of Indigenous feminism has been not just a willingness but an absolute need to understand these systems of power as intimately interconnected.

Indigenous feminism looks at how power operates along multiple axes—we do not attend to colonial relations of power and gendered forms of oppression merely as isolated phenomena but as systems of power that intersect and culminate both within and outside of Indigenous communities. Increasingly, we are working to be attentive to other markers that shape the different locations of Indigenous Peoples, such as sexuality, socio-economic status, age, ability, geography, and so on. While there is still much work left on this front, the willingness of Indigenous feminists to understand power as operating in multiple sites and scales offers an important methodological approach to attend to its intersections and variations. Indigenous feminists argue that power needs to be examined for the ways that it is imposed on Indigenous people, but also the ways in which it is internalized and repurposed within Indigenous communities to the disadvantage of many. While all Indigenous Peoples have been impacted by colonial violence, Indigenous feminists also recognize that said violence has impacted us differently and are interested in unpacking that difference.

One of the most foundational distinctions between Indigenous femininities and Indigenous feminism is that the latter works to make space for the political significance of Indigenous women's voices and existences to be taken seriously in *all of their diverse manifestations*, while working to address patriarchy and misogyny in *all forms and contexts*. Thus, Indigenous feminists refuse to understand gendered oppression only as a consequence of colonialism. Rather, we are committed to deconstructing and problematizing the ways in which gender can be socially and politically constructed by Indigenous Peoples as well, and to addressing these dynamics in our own creative, intellectual, and activist works.

Indigenous femininities and masculinities scholars frequently cite the egalitarianism or matrilineality of pre-contact Indigenous communities to suggest that conditions of colonialism, rather than gender, represent the overarching site of power that should be analysed. As heteropatriarchy was propagated in many ways through colonialism, proponents of this position maintain that attending to colonial violence will create space for the return of culturally informed modes of social and political organization to effect more balanced relations. Yet the project of overcoming colonial gender roles in the present cannot simply be oriented to the revitalization of heteronormative articulations of Indigeneity that advance *a priori* depictions of culture and tradition as a catch-all remedy to settler colonialism. As Billy-Ray Belcourt has observed, there are several traps involved in investing in the past as a way of remedying the violence of the present, as past ways of being were context-specific and cannot be merely reproduced in the present by those who have never experienced those same contexts (2016b, 11). Furthermore, the linking of gender fluidity to the past restricts queerness to a spiritual world that is selectively invoked within contemporary contexts while failing to disrupt gender categories altogether, thus preventing the imagination of new modes of existence into the future. Rather than invoking a past that is largely inaccessible and ignoring the ways in which gendered power structures have become constitutive of the present, Belcourt advocates for a politics of a form that we do not yet know, a break with our habitual referents of gender, culture, and tradition.

MOVEMENTS TOWARDS NON-BINARY METHODOLOGIES

Owing largely to the work of Indigenous queer theorists and Indigenous feminists, there is a growing call in Indigenous scholarship to think beyond gender binaries in order to imagine ways of being Indigenous in the present and future that are not contained by ontologies of gender or tradition (Belcourt 2016b; Hunt 2015; LaRocque 2017; Simpson 2017). Such scholars are demonstrating the various ways in which the attachment of Indigeneity to a pre-contact femininity or masculinity delimits the breadth of possible ways of engaging in decolonial resistance, of being Indigenous in the contemporary world, or of working towards future existences that aren't themselves shaped by pre-existing notions of what gendered relations, balance, or complementarity might look like. In other words, these works demonstrate how our attachments to the past and specifically to a gendered past narrow the possibilities for transformation, for rupturing through the binaries that all too often configure Indigenous Peoples' lives. As Sarah Hunt writes, the linking of Indigenous health and wellness to gendered roles and teachings highlights the need for an Indigenous gender analysis that displaces gender norms, one that restores the health and humanity of Indigenous Peoples beyond the gender binary (2015, 116). Instead of devoting ourselves to revitalized notions of masculinity or femininity as the pathway through which we might achieve decolonization, wellness, or empowerment, our efforts may be better focused on becoming more conscious of the limitations that Indigenous people place on ourselves through pre-existing assumptions of what culturally grounded notions of gender—or gender-lessness—should look like.

The imperative to move beyond binary treatments of gender and culture does not involve rejecting cultural teachings and traditions altogether, but disrupting entrenched ways of thinking that preclude our ability to understand them in a more fluid and generative way. The recent work of Leanne Betasamosake Simpson provides an important example of how Indigenous Peoples can work towards non-binary ways of thinking in conceptualizing new political arrangements while also grounding ourselves upon our own worldviews and philosophical foundations.

Simpson's writings are noteworthy as they trouble binary notions of gender while also reflecting a deep commitment to her own cultural teachings and practices. The theory that she draws on is the traditions and knowledge that she carries as an Anishinaabe Kwe, and, importantly, she does not regard it as static dogma. Of significance in Simpson's approach is the way in which she has always acknowledged the gendered and heteronormative impacts of colonialism as damaging but has never let them overwrite her understanding of Indigeneity. Her writings about the violences of colonialism have never been totalizing, foregrounding women's agency and power within conversations about the land, creation, nation-building, and colonial resistance. Further, she embodies an approach that represents the so-called "women's issues" and "broader political issues" not as mutually exclusive but as inextricably bound up in one another.

Simpson's early works employed explicitly gendered references to tradition in conceptualizing decolonization, advocating for the reclamation of women's traditional teachings and practices, such as those relating to motherhood and child-rearing, and positioning these as intimately linked to the process of nation-building (Simpson 2006). While she has continued to foreground the urgent need for Indigenous Peoples to configure our social and political practices upon our own teachings and philosophies, over time she has increasingly emphasized the need to be attentive to the role of gender in the formation of Indigenous subjectivities. Her recent writings demonstrate that one can respect and honour cultural traditions even when engaging critically with how they are represented and invoked, and their associated function and implications.

Simpson's broadening and dynamic approach to storytelling elucidates the transformative possibilities that emerge when one moves beyond binary treatments of gender. For instance, in a number of different contexts she has drawn on the story of the origins of maple syrup to illustrate the significance of understanding land as pedagogy. In her first published telling of the story, the main character is Gwiiwzens, the figure of a boy (Simpson 2013). Then, in a 2014 publication, she relays a similar story while framing the main character as a girl, Kwezens, noting that the story can and should be told using all genders. Finally, in her 2017 publication *As We Have Always Done*, Simpson again tells the story through reference to Binoojinh, a non-binary child. Here she draws on Anishinaabe terminology to allow for greater movement and fluidity of cultural knowledge. Binoojinh thus serves an important theoretical and methodological function, demonstrating that Indigeneity does not have to be conceptualized along gendered lines and that in fact when we allow slippage beyond these various forms of containment, our teachings can take on a far greater spectrum of possible iterations and adaptations into the future. Indeed, the transformative potential of traditional teachings can be either limited by static renditions or unleashed through dynamic and relational tellings. The gender fluidity of the main character disrupts binary ways of thinking about cultural traditions while also revisiting gender binaries through cultural knowledge, which in turn broadens the bases and questions through which we think about both Indigeneity and gender.

Simpson's various treatments of the story's main character elucidate the ways that dynamic engagements with Indigenous intellectual and cultural traditions allow them to be heard by a wider range of people and applied in a wider range of contexts. Utilizing a non-binary main character gives rise to different teachings, messages, and possible takeaways for the reader that are not based on an association with any subject position the reader must identify with. In sum, it creates space for different possible ways of being Indigenous, of understanding one's relationship with the land and learning from it in contemporary and future contexts. She notes that Indigenous methods aimed at "queering resurgence" must be driven by more than just inclusion, as inclusion involves a process of making space for queer forms of Indigeneity within normative categories, or within straight worlds (Simpson 2017, 134). Rather, we need forms of analysis that are attentive to the limits of these conceptual categories and are committed to deconstructing their foundations. Simpson advocates for the imagination of new ways of being Indigenous, never pre-empting what these methods should look like but being cautious of the conditions that can foreclose upon them.

While Simpson's work exemplifies a distinct shift in Indigenous scholarship, it is also one that remains rare and fraught with complexities on the ground level. She is certainly aware of this, as she references her own community-based work and the tensions and challenges of addressing gendered dynamics as they arise within cultural practices and traditions to implicate particular bodies in different ways. In my view, the grounded nature and awareness of the corporeality of these questions is the most interesting dimension of her work. Exploring the ways in which bodies interact with, are empowered by, or are repressed by normative orders, she draws attention to the contours of structures of oppression that are not always experienced universally. Here I am reminded of Sara Ahmed's (2012) discussion of the visibility of institutional walls as most readily apparent to those who are engaged in the on-the-ground work involved in regularly coming up against them.

Ahmed suggests that a critical orientation to institutions emerges in the process of encountering them, which in turn allows for greater consciousness of the factors that sustain their permanence. She uses the example of a "brick wall," which keeps its place even when theoretical commitments to change have been advanced. This metaphor helps elucidate the limits of purely theoretical projects geared towards being reflexive and critical in how one imagines change, or in one's attitude towards institutions. While perhaps universally recognized as a barrier, the permanence of a brick wall is particularly visible to those who regularly engage in the practical labour of challenging it. To those who do not come up against it, such as those who do not feel that its associated norms and habits exclude or contain their existence, the wall is either unapparent or appears to be open, permeable, and malleable. She writes that perhaps "the categories in which we are immersed as styles of life *become explicit when you do not quite inhabit them*" (2012, 178; emphasis in original). In relation to the current conversation, the institutional walls being encountered are identitarian categories of masculinity and femininity, rendered even more immovable by notions of culture and tradition. Yet these binary ways of thinking are not merely forms of conceptual containment, as they alternately implicate, privilege, homogenize, exclude, erase, and lead to violence against Indigenous bodies.

Certainly, the vision of queer Indigeneity offered by Simpson is not arrived at seamlessly, and, as Ahmed notes, the practical labour involved in regularly challenging the walls that configure our lives can be both exhausting and seemingly never-ending. Perhaps the key is not to focus on the practicality or viability of any given endpoint, but to work through a process that continually challenges the conceptual forms of containment that preclude new ways of thinking so as not to pre-empt what the future holds through rigid attachments to gender or tradition. As Belcourt writes in his discussion of queer Indigeneity, our conditions of possibility as Indigenous Peoples are intimately attached to our ability to think about Indigeneity as "categorically messy" and "without referent and without any agreed upon meaning," in a state of being that "refuses to attach to any one history, biology, or geography" (2016b, 29). In his view, the greatest number of possibilities for moving beyond the reification of gender and tradition exist in the spaces-in-between, in the methodologies that may appear nonsensical to some but that provide the requisite points of departure from our entrenched ways of thinking. Thinking of transformation as departure can be challenging, as it requires a willingness to critically interrogate and perhaps rid ourselves of the attachments that continue to hold many of our relations down.

CONCLUSION

This chapter has endeavoured to demonstrate that colonial and gendered power relations are complex systems that must be addressed from many angles, including those that may appear to be distinct or inconsistent political projects. Certainly, the highly gendered and sexualized nature of colonialism highlights the necessity of an analytical frame that is attentive to the relationship between gender and colonialism, in order to understand the foundations and ongoing power dynamics of colonial violence and oppression in a comprehensive way. However, I have also sought to interrogate whether the repurposing of gender roles upon culturally informed foundations is necessarily empowering to all who are implicated by them, and also to reflect on how they might foreclose ways of being that lie outside of normative orders. It is in the deconstruction of these conceptual and material forms of containment, and movement beyond them, that we might come to find the greatest possibilities for engaging in a politic that is truly transformative.

DISCUSSION QUESTIONS

1. What are some of the ways that understandings of womanhood and manhood differ across cultures? What are some of the similarities?
2. Identify some of the entrenched ways of thinking that you can see in the world around you. Can you reflect on the meaning of symbols and language used in institutions you interact with on a daily basis?
3. What gendered expectations and norms have you experienced in your life? Did you find them to be empowering? Disempowering? Both?
4. Have you ever tried to question or interrogate your family's or community's traditions? What did you find most difficult about this process?

REFERENCES

Ahmed, Sara. 2012. *On Being Included: Racism and Diversity in Institutional Life.* Durham, NC: Duke University Press.

Allen, Paula Gunn. 1992. *The Sacred Hoop: Recovering the Feminine in American Indian Traditions.* Boston: Beacon Press.

Anderson, Kim. 2016. *A Recognition of Being: Reconstructing Native Womanhood.* Toronto: Canadian Scholars' Press.

Ashcroft, Bill, Gareth Griffiths, and Helen Tiffin. 1998. *Key Concepts in Post-Colonial Studies.* London: Psychology Press.

Belcourt, Billy-Ray. 2016a. "Can the Other of Native Studies Speak?" *Decolonization: Indigeneity, Education, & Society*, February 1. https://decolonization.wordpress .com/2016/02/01/can-the-other-of-native-studies-speak/.

———. 2016b. "A Poltergeist Manifesto." *Feral Feminisms* 6: 22–32.

Carlson, Nellie, and Kathleen Steinhauer. 2013. *Disinherited Generations: Our Struggle to Reclaim Treaty Rights for First Nations Women and Their Descendants.* Edmonton: University of Alberta Press.

Green, Joyce. 1993. "Constitutionalizing the Patriarchy: Aboriginal Women and Aboriginal Government." *Constitutional Forum* 4 (1–4): 110–20.

———. 1997. "Exploring Identity and Citizenship: Aboriginal Women, Bill C-31, and the Sawridge Case." PhD diss., University of Alberta.

———. 2002. "Transforming at the Margins of the Academy." In *Women in the Canadian Academic Tundra: Challenging the Chill*, edited by Elena Hannah, Linda Paul, and Swani Vethamany-Globus, 85–91. Montreal: McGill-Queen's University Press.

———. 2007. "Taking Account of Aboriginal Feminism." In *Making Space for Indigenous Feminism*, edited by Joyce Green, 20–32. Halifax: Fernwood.

———. 2017. "ReBalancing Strategies: Aboriginal Women and Constitutional Rights in Canada." In *Making Space for Indigenous Feminism*, 2nd ed., edited Joyce Green, 166–91. Halifax: Fernwood.

Hokowhitu, Brendan. 2016. "History and Masculinity." In *Sources and Methods in Indigenous Studies*, edited by Chris Andersen and Jean O'Brien, 195–204. Milton Park, UK: Taylor & Francis.

Hunt, Sarah. 2015. "Embodying Self-Determination: Beyond the Gender Binary." In *Determinants of Indigenous Peoples' Health*, edited by Margo Greenwood, Sarah de Leeuw, Nicole Marie Lindsay, and Charlotte Reading, 104–19. Toronto: Canadian Scholars' Press.

Innes, Robert & Kim Anderson, eds. 2015. *Indigenous Men and Masculinities: Identities, Legacies, Regeneration*. Winnipeg: University of Manitoba Press.

LaRocque, Emma. 1996. "The Colonization of a Native Woman Scholar." In *Women of the First Nations: Power, Wisdom, and Strength*, edited by Christine Miller and Patricia Chuchryk, 11–17. Winnipeg: University of Manitoba Press.

———. 2010. *When the Other Is Me: Native Resistance Discourse, 1850–1990*. Winnipeg: University of Manitoba Press.

———. 2017. "Métis and Feminist: Contemplations on Feminism, Human Rights, Culture and Decolonization." In *Making Space for Indigenous Feminism*, 2nd ed., edited by Joyce Green, 53–71. Halifax: Fernwood.

McKegney, Sam. 2014. *Masculindians: Conversations about Indigenous Manhood*. Winnipeg: University of Manitoba Press.

Mohanty, Chandra Talpade. 1988. "Under Western Eyes: Feminist Scholarship and Colonial Discourses." *Feminist Review* (30): 61–88.

Monture-Angus, Patricia. 1995. *Thunder in My Soul: A Mohawk Woman Speaks*. Halifax: Fernwood Publishing.

———. 2002. "On Being Homeless: One Aboriginal Woman's 'Conquest' of Canadian Universities." In *Crossroads, Directions and a New Critical Race Theory*, edited by Francisco Valdes, Jerome McCristal Culp, and Angela P. Harris, 274–87. Philadelphia: Temple University Press.

Moreton-Robinson, Aileen. 2000. *Talkin' Up to the White Woman: Aboriginal Women and Feminism*. Brisbane: University of Queensland Press.

Simpson, Audra. 2016a. "Consent's Revenge." *Cultural Anthropology* 31 (3): 326–33. https://doi.org/10.14506/ca31.3.02.

———. 2016b. "The State Is a Man: Theresa Spence, Loretta Saunders and the Gender of Settler Sovereignty." *Theory & Event* 19 (4).

Simpson, Leanne. 2006. "Birthing an Indigenous Resurgence: Decolonizing Our Pregnancy and Birthing Ceremonies." In *Until Our Hearts Are on the Ground: Aboriginal Mothering, Oppression, Resistance and Rebirth*, edited by Jeannette Corbiere Lavell and Dawn Memee Lavell-Harvard, 25–33. Bradford, ON: Demeter Press.

———. 2013. *The Gift Is in the Making: Anishinaabeg Stories*. Winnipeg: Portage & Main Press.

———. 2014. "Land as Pedagogy: Nishnaabeg Intelligence and Rebellious Transformation." *Decolonization: Indigeneity, Education & Society*, 3 (3), 1–25.

———. 2017. *As We Have Always Done: Indigenous Freedom through Radical Resistance*. Minneapolis: University of Minnesota Press.

Snyder, Emily. 2018. *Gender, Power, and Representations of Cree Law*. Vancouver: UBC Press.

Stark, Heidi Kiiwetinepinesiik. 2016. "Criminal Empire: The Making of the Savage in a Lawless Land." *Theory & Event* 19 (4).

Tengan, T.P.K. (2008). *Native Men Remade: Gender and Nation in Contemporary Hawai'i*. Durham, NC: Duke University Press.

Tohe, Laura. 2000. "There Is No Word for Feminism in My Language." *Wicazo Sa Review* 15 (2): 103–110.

Wolfe, Patrick. 2006. "Settler Colonialism and the Elimination of the Native." *Journal of Genocide Research* 8 (4): 387–409.

FURTHER READING

Barker, Joanne. 2017. *Critically Sovereign: Indigenous Gender, Sexuality, and Feminist Studies*. Durham, NC: Duke University Press.

Belcourt, Billy-Ray. 2016. "A Poltergeist Manifesto." *Feral Feminisms* 6: 22–32.

Hokowhitu, Brendan. 2016. "History and Masculinity." In *Sources and Methods in Indigenous Studies*, edited by Chris Andersen and Jean M. O'Brien. Milton Park, UK: Taylor & Francis.

Hunt, Sarah. 2015. "Embodying Self-Determination: Beyond the Gender Binary." In *Determinants of Indigenous Peoples' Health*, edited by Margo Greenwood, Sarah De Leeuw, Nicole Marie Lindsay, and Charlotte Reading, 104–19. Toronto: Canadian Scholars' Press.

Green, Joyce, ed. 2017. *Making Space for Indigenous Feminism*, 2nd ed. Winnipeg: Fernwood Publishing.

Simpson, Leanne. 2017. *As We Have Always Done: Indigenous Freedom through Radical Resistance*. Minneapolis: University of Minnesota Press.

Snyder, Emily. 2018. *Gender, Power, and Representations of Cree Law*. Vancouver: UBC Press.

6

How Gender Became a Defence Issue: A Feminist Perspective on Canadian Military and Defence Policy

Maya Eichler

Key terms: essentialism, feminist defence policy, gender balancing, gender mainstreaming, gender neutrality, military, non-essentialism, transformation of gendered military culture, Women, Peace and Security

Military and defence policy is an area of political life that requires much more sustained citizen engagement, and specifically feminist engagement. The **military** is a key institution of the modern state, central to its sovereignty and legitimacy. As such, the military is a powerful institution that demands state resources and shapes political and social life. The military is an important site of feminist investigation for both political and analytical reasons. It claims a large part of societal resources, diverting them away from non-militarized security concerns that disproportionately impact women's lives, such as human security and food security. The military is also a deeply gendered institution, dominated by men and informed by masculinized values. It privileges characteristics stereotypically associated with dominant norms of masculinity, such as strength, aggression, courage, and toughness, over characteristics stereotypically associated with femininity, such as pacifism, empathy, vulnerability, or weakness. The military derives its status, in part, through its association with dominant notions of masculinity, while also shaping broader societal understandings of what it means to "be a man." The waging of war has historically been one of the grounds used to justify women's subordination to men. Countries across history and geography have excluded women from active participation in war, designated women as requiring male protection in war, and characterized women as too weak to fight (Goldstein 2001).

The Department of National Defence (DND) and the Canadian Armed Forces (CAF) make up Canada's largest government department in terms of personnel and budget. They have 119,000 employees[1] and a budget of close to $20 billion (DND and CAF 2018; Government of Canada 2018). The military represents Canada and Canadian interests abroad, while acting as a tool of nation-building domestically. In the early twenty-first century, the Canadian military has been engaged across the globe, with its largest and most significant engagement in Afghanistan from 2001 to 2014. Canada is no exception when it comes to the gendering of its military. Historically, Canada's military leadership resisted women's inclusion in combat. Forced to open all military occupations to women in 1989, the military grudgingly adopted a gender-neutral stance. **Gender neutrality** was a way to downplay the significance of gender without having to confront the deeply masculinized nature of military and defence policy in Canada.

Against this backdrop, the change in rhetoric from the Canadian military and defence leadership that began in 2015 is striking. That year, the chief of the defence staff—the country's top military leader—acknowledged sexual misconduct in the CAF as a systemic problem and vowed to eliminate it. The Canadian military also for the first time ordered an external survey of its members on the issue of sexual harassment and sexual assault. In 2016, the CAF committed to integrating a gender perspective into all military planning and operations, while the Canadian government announced its adoption of a feminist foreign policy. In early 2018, the minister of defence, Harjit Sajjan, stated that Canada was taking a feminist approach to its military. The past few years have been "turbulent times" in regards to gender and Canadian military and defence policy, but do these developments indicate substantive change? How do we best understand the adoption of feminist concerns into the masculinized sphere of military and defence policy in Canada? Has there been a transformation of institutional policy or rather a co-optation of feminist advocacy? And what would a truly **feminist defence policy** look like?

As I argue in this chapter, the adoption of feminist concerns into Canadian military and defence policy is double-edged. It is the result of national and international feminist and civil society efforts to transform the military and defence sphere as well as a way for militaries to re-legitimate themselves and strengthen their operational effectiveness. It is a positive development that the Canadian military and defence establishment has begun to go beyond gender blindness and gender neutrality to consider **gender balancing, gender mainstreaming**, and the **transformation of gendered military culture**. The integration of a gender lens or feminist approach has potential (as discussed by Paterson and Scala in this volume). However, in the context of the military, it requires careful feminist monitoring to avoid a situation where gender primarily serves an instrumental purpose for the institution. A truly feminist defence policy would go beyond mere inclusion of women and a focus on operational effectiveness. It would seek guidance from feminist activists and scholars to challenge dominant notions of defence that rely on masculinized and militarized values.

This chapter consists of four sections. First, I offer a brief overview of feminist insights into militaries and defence policy and of strategies for change. Second, I outline the history of gender integration in the CAF to illustrate the legacy of discrimination against women and efforts to address it. Third, I show how the emergence of a global **Women, Peace and Security** agenda is shaping Canadian defence policy. Finally, I examine Canada's 2017 defence policy through an analysis of its gendered language and strategies, which include gender balancing, gender mainstreaming, transformation of gendered culture, and, to a lesser extent, explicitly feminist goals. In conclusion, I assess the "transformational possibilities" of the adoption of gender concerns into military and defence policies in Canada during these "turbulent times."

While gender may be the military's most defining feature, it is important to note that gender works in conjunction with other structures of discrimination. The CAF has long been not only a male-dominated and masculinist institution but also a heteronormative, racialized, ableist, and white settler institution (Poulin and Gouliquer 2012; George 2016). This chapter focuses on the gendered history and transformational potential of the military, and only in passing addresses these intersecting structures. This is due to the dearth of research that examines intersectional and non-binary gender experiences in the CAF, but also reflects the dominance of a binary gender frame in and beyond military and defence policy.

GENDER, MILITARIES, AND DEFENCE POLICY: THEORETICAL CONSIDERATIONS

Feminist research on militaries and defence issues exists in various disciplines, foremost in international relations, security studies, military sociology, critical military studies, and women and gender studies. I highlight three main insights from this body of research here—a non-essentialist understanding of the gendered nature of war and peace, the gendered construction of defence concepts, and militaries as gendered institutions. Then I discuss different approaches to reforming and potentially transforming gendered militaries and defence policy.

Essentialism assumes that women and men are naturally associated with different characteristics, whereas **non-essentialism** emphasizes the social and discursive construction of stereotypical gender traits. The starting point for feminist research on militaries and defence issues is the insight that there is no inherent link between women, femininity, and peace, or between men, masculinity, and war. There is nothing "natural" or "essential" about women's under-representation in the military and defence sector. Instead, specific military and defence policies and historical, cultural, social, and economic contexts have produced gendered and binary understandings of war and peace and of masculinity and femininity (Enloe 2000; Eichler 2014). Rather than reproducing the dualism of "warrior men" and "pacifist women," feminists emphasize that constructions of gender and defence are mutually constitutive (Cockburn 2010).

Central concepts of defence policy rely on gender for their meaning. As feminist scholars argue, the interests of the male-dominated state and its male citizens shape dominant definitions of security. Feminist scholars are critical of the appeal that militarized security continues to have in domestic and global politics and seek to develop alternatives to current security narratives and policies (Wibben 2011). They suggest reconceptualizing security from the perspective of ordinary women (and men) and going beyond militarized security to focus on the personal, economic, environmental, or physical dimensions of security (Tickner 2001). The concept of protection used in defence policy and discourse is also gendered. It is based on a dichotomy of masculinized protectors vis-à-vis feminized populations in need of protection, justifying the subordination of women and others (Stiehm 1982; Young 2003; Sjoberg 2013). Despite the gendered ideology of protection, defence policies and military operations often have disproportionally negative impacts on women. Military conflict tends to increase incidents of violence against women, including sexual violence.

Militaries are the central institution for the promotion and enforcement of defence policy and have long been structured in gendered ways. Militaries have relied on notions of femininity and masculinity, such as women in need of protection or men as soldiers and protectors (Enloe 2000). While the warrior has endured as "a key symbol of masculinity" (Morgan 1994), women's and men's roles in war are not static. Women's presence in Western militaries has significantly expanded since the 1970s as a result of political and social changes (Carreiras 2006). These changes include the shift from conscription to volunteer forces, militaries' search for new sources of "manpower" (Enloe 2000), feminist advocacy for equal citizenship (Feinman 2000), the changing nature of warfare (Elshtain 2000; Tait 2015), and, more recently, international gender mainstreaming instruments such as United Nations Security Council Resolution 1325 (UNSCR 1325)[2] on Women, Peace and Security (Obradovic 2014). Notwithstanding women's increased military participation, feminist scholarship shows that many Western militaries remain male-dominated organizations that are hostile towards women.

But can militaries change? What is the scope of their transformational potential? Feminists have historically been divided on this question. Liberal feminists have argued for women's inclusion into the defence realm, for their "right to fight" as full citizens of the state. Radical feminists have identified militarism as one of the main sources of, and justifications for, unequal gendered power relations. They have argued that challenging militaries and ending war is a necessary component of the broader feminist struggle for social change (Cockburn 2010). But in the early twenty-first century, feminists need to grapple with a more complex reality, one in which states wage wars in the name of protecting women's rights,[3] militaries are lifting women's combat bans and actively recruiting women, and foreign policies are declared to be feminist. Claire Duncanson and Rachel Woodward (2016) challenge feminists to ask how militaries can be "regendered" or "degendered" in ways that challenge their unequal gender order. They go beyond earlier feminist debates that were polarized between advocating for women's "right to fight" and opposing women's co-optation into militarism.[4] Instead, they argue that we need to consider and pay attention to the possibilities of transforming military institutions. In practice, today's militaries and defence departments are increasingly integrating gender concerns into their policies and operations.

Policy-makers and advocates are adopting a range of approaches aimed at reforming and potentially transforming the military and defence sector. In this context, it is important to distinguish four different strategies, sometimes applied in conjunction. The liberal feminist approach, most often adopted by policy-makers, focuses on gender balancing. Gender balancing aims to increase the number of women in the foreign and defence sector. This "add women and stir" approach tends to treat gender as synonymous with women and does not tackle the underlying gendered power relations that exclude women in the first place. Gender mainstreaming is a second strategy used to reform the gendered sphere of military and defence policy. As per a widely cited definition, "mainstream-ing a gender perspective is the process of assessing the implications for women and men of any planned action, including legislation, policies or programmes, in all areas and at all levels" (UN ECOSOC 1997). Gender mainstreaming aims to change processes within institutions such as the military to avoid gender-discriminatory outcomes. A third strategy is the transformation of gendered military culture, which aims not just at correcting gender imbalance or gender-discriminatory outcomes but at transforming a military culture that privileges men and masculinities and creates imbalances of power and privilege between men and women (as well as others who do not fit the masculinized norm of soldiering; e.g., racialized men, injured men, non-binary or LGBTQ2S+ per-sonnel, etc.). What is at stake in transforming gendered military culture is the very construction and redefinition of the identity of the soldier and of concepts such as security and protection in ways that no longer privilege masculinity over femininity. Finally, an explicitly feminist strategy is the most substantively trans-formational. It seeks not just to reform militaries but to undo the root causes of women's global gender subordination, which include militarism and the wag-ing of war. Such a strategy makes anti-militarism, gender equality, and women's rights the driving goals of policy and programming. All four of these strategies draw on feminist insights but exist along a continuum from moderate reform to radical change. Policy-makers and advocates do not always agree on the meaning and effectiveness of these strategies, as we will see below. In my view, all strate-gies need to work in concert to achieve lasting change and require monitoring and input from feminists within the military and beyond.

GENDER AND THE MILITARY IN CANADA: A NATIONAL AND HISTORICAL PERSPECTIVE

The Canadian military, like other Western militaries, is a gendered institution with deeply masculinized roots and a long history of discriminating against women. Women's full inclusion in the military has been resisted and their presence has primarily reflected personnel needs, especially in feminized occupations such as medical and clerical work. Until 1989, the military maintained a gender quota, a "minimum male requirement" determining the minimum percentage of male service members for each occupation, and completely excluded women from the combat arms (Winslow and Dunn 2002). Furthermore, until 1992, the CAF did not permit lesbian as well as gay and transgender personnel to serve, and engaged in a concerted campaign to "purge" them (Poulin and Gouliquer 2012). Pressure from outside the institution—a combination of legal, civil society, and media pressure—was crucial to ending these discriminatory policies. In the decades since, the Canadian military has adopted a variety of approaches to women and gender: continued resistance towards women's integration; an official gender-neutral approach that accepts women's presence in the military but does not aim to transform its gendered culture; and more recently an instrumentalist approach that defines women's presence as positive for operational effectiveness.

Human rights legislation, as well as the growing feminist advocacy of the 1960s, led to increased awareness of the discrimination that women faced across sectors. The 1970 report by the Royal Commission on the Status of Women included six recommendations (out of 167) specifically on the military. The Canadian Human Rights Act (1978) and Section 15 of the Charter of Rights and Freedoms (1982) strengthened the cause to end the military's discrimination against women (Winslow and Dunn 2002). In the 1980s, the case of women's exclusion from the military's combat arms was brought to the Canadian Human Rights Tribunal.[5] At the time, the CAF leadership resisted women's full integration, arguing that women were not up to the physical demands of combat operations and would undermine unit cohesion (Robinson 1985). However, the Human Rights Tribunal ruled that "there is no risk of failure of performance of combat duties by women sufficient to justify a general exclusionary policy."[6] As a result of the tribunal ruling, all occupations were immediately opened to women, except for submarine service (opened to women in 2001).

In response, the Canadian military chose an approach of gender neutrality that aimed at removing explicitly discriminatory policy and focused on discounting gender differences. As Karen Davis explains, the military "sought to satisfy the minimum requirements of the CHRT [Canadian Human Rights Tribunal] ruling" (2013, 2). This led to the removal of legal barriers that discriminated against women, but the military's gendered culture was largely left intact. The embrace of gender neutrality was not sufficient to change the military's gendered culture, which remained rooted in ideals of (heterosexual and white) warrior masculinity defined in opposition to femininity (see also Grant and MacDonald in this volume). During Canada's war in Afghanistan (2001–14) the military augmented its gender-neutral approach by emphasizing women's instrumental value to operations. For example, the military emphasized the usefulness of female soldiers to conduct security checks on female civilians and liaise with local populations. Media coverage of Canada's war in Afghanistan reflected the tension between the gender-neutral and instrumentalist approaches to women. It painted a picture in which Canadian female soldiers in Afghanistan had both achieved the status of "equal" warriors *and* brought gender-specific "feminine" skills to their jobs (Chapman and Eichler 2014). Such a contradictory construction, in which female soldiers are seen as equal to, and still as different from, male soldiers, did little to challenge masculinity as the norm of soldiering and to acknowledge women as soldiers in their own right.

The military has also adopted an instrumentalist approach in how it deals with the problem of sexual violence in its ranks. While media reports had drawn attention to sexual harassment and sexual assault in the military since the 1990s, it was only in 2014—in response to another series of media reports—that the chief of the defence staff ordered an external review into the matter (in the context of broader turbulent times around these issues, see Craig in this volume). The *External Review into Sexual Misconduct and Sexual Harassment in the CAF*, known as the Deschamps Report, was released in 2015 and documented a sexualized culture that is hostile towards female and lesbian, gay, bisexual, transgender, and queer/questioning (LGBTQ) members (Deschamps 2015). The first external survey on sexual misconduct in the CAF, conducted in 2016 by Statistics Canada, confirmed the findings of the Deschamps Report. It found that four in five military members reported "seeing, hearing or experiencing inappropriate sexual or discriminatory behaviour" in their workplace during the previous 12 months, and that more than one in four women in the Regular Force and close to one in three women in the Reserves had experienced sexual assault during their military service (Cotter 2016). In response to the Deschamps Report, the military embarked on what it called "Operation HONOUR," a mission aimed at eradicating sexual misconduct in the CAF. As the operational order for Operation HONOUR by the chief of the defence staff explains: "Harmful and inappropriate sexual behaviour involving members of the CAF is an operational readiness issue, incongruent with our ethics and values, and wrong" (DND and CAF 2015). While the military leadership has condemned sexual misconduct in general, it has emphasized the instrumental value of addressing sexual misconduct for the institution.

Whereas prior to 1989 the military argued that women in the combat arms were harmful to operational effectiveness, today including more women and ending sexual misconduct are defined as important for operational effectiveness. The recent acknowledgement of sexual misconduct by the CAF indicates some positive change. But the history of how the military has approached gender should make us cautious. Despite the removal of gender discriminatory policy, masculinized constructions of soldiering and a masculinized culture continue to dominate in the CAF and limit women's military integration. In early 2019, women represented 15.7 per cent of the Canadian military, but remained concentrated in non-combat roles such as medical, dental, clerical, and other support occupations and were virtually absent from the combat arms and special forces (DND and CAF 2019; Lane 2017). This presents the CAF with a major dilemma as it seeks to respond to new global developments such as the Women, Peace and Security agenda.

WOMEN, PEACE AND SECURITY: THE GLOBAL CONTEXT AND ITS IMPACT ON CANADA

Gender is a concern to national militaries such as the CAF but has also become established as a global security issue. The passage of UNSCR 1325 on Women, Peace and Security in October 2000 was an international breakthrough for women's organizing as it marked the first time in the UN's history that a UNSC resolution relating to peace and security mentioned women and acknowledged the importance of a gender perspective. UNSCR 1325 calls for the protection of women and girls during armed conflict and their participation in peacekeeping, conflict resolution, and the prevention of conflict. There have since been seven follow-up resolutions that deal with related issues, such as sexual violence. Together UNSCR 1325 and its follow-up resolutions are referred to as the Women, Peace and Security agenda.

However, action has not necessarily followed the rhetoric of UNSCR 1325. To mark the fifteenth anniversary of the adoption of UNSCR 1325, the UN conducted a global study of the resolution. It found that national action plans on the implementation of UNSCR 1325 have been slow to take off and a focus on women's protection and victimization has sidelined discussions on women's participation. As Phumzile Mlambo-Ngcuka, UN under-secretary-general and executive director of UN Women, states in the foreword to the global study on UNSCR 1325: "There remains a crippling gap between the ambition of our commitments and actual political and financial support. We struggle to bridge the declared intent of international policymaking and the reality of domestic action" (UN 2015, 5). Still, UNSCR 1325 has spurred both the North American Treaty Organization (NATO) and the European Union to adopt UNSCR 1325 as the normative framework for their international deployments. The Women, Peace and Security agenda also informed Sweden's adoption of a feminist foreign policy in 2015.

Canada was at the forefront of global efforts to adopt UNSCR 1325 in 2000, playing an important role as one of the non-permanent members of the UNSC at the time. In 2001, Canada initiated the Group of Friends of 1325, a coalition of UN member states, UN agencies, and civil society groups that coordinate actions to promote implementation. This group convenes meetings with stakeholders, for example the 2015 meeting addressing sexual exploitation and abuse by UN peacekeepers. Nonetheless, Canada was slow to develop its own action plan on the implementation of UNSCR 1325. The first Canadian National Action Plan (CNAP) was adopted only in 2010 and civil society groups and feminist researchers were critical of its lack of a dedicated budget. Typical of national action plans in Western countries, the first CNAP also had an outward-looking focus geared towards international operations while understating the importance of gender mainstreaming Canada's domestic institutions (Women's International League for Peace and Freedom 2015). The 2017–22 CNAP addresses these critiques to some extent.

In early 2016, the Women, Peace and Security agenda received a boost when the Canadian chief of the defence staff passed a directive committing to apply a gender perspective (through gender-based analysis+ [GBA+]) to all CAF planning and operations (DND and CAF 2016). The directive reiterates Canada's international commitments to gender mainstream its defence policy through UNSCR 1325 and its follow-up resolutions, as well as NATO directive 40–1. It recognizes that women's and men's experiences differ, that the same process may have differential outcomes for them, and that gender intersects with other identity categories such as culture, sexuality, and age (hence the +). The directive's goal is that all CAF members will develop competency in GBA+ and be able to apply it in their day-to-day work. At the same time, the directive defines GBA+ as a way to improve operational effectiveness, focusing narrowly on the instrumental value of gender and intersectional perspectives to the CAF and DND (DND and CAF 2016). As a result of this directive, the CAF has established three gender advisor positions and has committed to having gender advisors on all operations. The implementation of the Women, Peace and Security agenda also informed Canada's 2017 defence policy, as I discuss next.

CANADA'S NEW DEFENCE POLICY: ASSESSING THE GENDER TURN

Women have been virtually absent in the making of Canadian defence policy. Canada has had only one female prime minister and one female minister of defence (Kim Campbell served in both positions). Defence policy making in Canada has not just excluded women's voices but has been gender-blind, based on the assumption that gender is not a relevant category to consider. For example, the *Canada First Defence Strategy* from 2009 made no mention of gender or women, other than for the perfunctory mention of the "women and men" of the Canadian Forces (DND and CAF 2009). Canada's 2017 defence policy, *Strong, Secure, Engaged* (DND 2017), departs from this legacy of gender blindness. In the consultation period that led up to the policy, gender perspectives were more prominent than they had ever been in Canadian debates on defence—as a result of the adoption of gender perspectives by the 2015–19 Trudeau government (see Ashe, Dobrowolsky, and Paterson and Scala in this volume). But the consideration of gender was not as robust as in other government policy reviews, reflecting the greater resistance of the military and defence sector. While the government's international assistance review asked for input on how to apply a feminist lens throughout all of Canada's international assistance activities, a gender lens was included in the defence policy review as an afterthought, with the last-minute addition of a separate expert roundtable on gender perspectives.

The 2017 defence policy is embedded within the broader framework of a feminist foreign policy and feminist international assistance policy. It focuses on two gender concerns in particular: changing the gender make-up and gendered culture of the CAF and integrating gender perspectives into international military operations. As the 2017 defence policy states: "The Canadian Armed Forces is committed to gender equality and providing a work environment where women are welcomed, supported and respected" (DND 2017, 21). However, gender equality issues are dealt with within the broader framework of "Leveraging Canada's Diversity" (23). This reflects the more recent shift in the military's approach towards both instrumentalizing gender and collapsing gender within broader diversity issues (outlined in the military's "strength through diversity" platform and its diversity strategy). As the defence policy states: "The Canadian Armed Forces is committed to demonstrating leadership in reflecting Canadian ideals of diversity, respect and inclusion, including striving for gender equality and building a workforce that leverages the diversity of Canadian society" (23). The defence policy also commits to increase the percentage of women from 15 per cent in 2016 to 25 per cent by 2026. It is argued that "this [increase] will not only contribute to positive Canadian Armed Forces culture change, but will also increase overall operational effectiveness" (23). As this statement illustrates, the Canadian military and defence leadership is emphasizing the instrumental value of having greater diversity, including gender diversity, both for operational effectiveness and culture change. Culture change was one of the key recommendations of the Deschamps Report and is recognized in the 2017 defence policy as necessary for addressing sexual misconduct in the CAF. Operation HONOUR is also mentioned, as is the need for "Promoting a Culture of Leadership, Respect, and Honour" (27).

The integration of GBA+ into all military planning and operations is another key feature of the defence policy (DND 2017, 24). But again, the instrumental value of doing so is emphasized: "Incorporating gender perspectives into the preparation, conduct, and evaluation of missions enables the Canadian Armed Forces to increase operational effectiveness and enhance understanding of the challenges faced by populations at risk in areas of armed conflict or natural disaster" (85). At the same time, gender equality is mentioned as a core value informing international operations: "Canadian international engagement will be guided by the core Canadian values of inclusion, compassion, accountable governance, and respect for diversity and human rights. The goal of gender equality permeates all of these core values" (61). Gender equality informs Canada's broader values that shape its international operations, but gender equality is not seen as a goal of military and defence policy itself.

As this brief review of Canada's 2017 defence policy suggests, gender has become a key defence policy concern. This new and noteworthy development is the culmination of national pressures to reform the CAF and international commitments through the Women, Peace and Security agenda. The 2017 defence policy mentions a number of different strategies to address gender concerns: from increasing the number of women in the CAF (gender balancing), to applying GBA+ (gender mainstreaming), to addressing sexual misconduct through Operation HONOUR (transforming gendered military culture). Working towards gender equality is mentioned but is least developed as a strategy and not linked to an explicitly feminist strategy for change.

The inclusion of a range of strategies to achieve change is positive. However, there are also serious concerns about whether the 2017 defence policy indicates real transformation. While Canada has officially adopted a feminist foreign policy and a feminist approach to the military, it has not explicitly adopted a feminist defence policy. Despite the integration of gender concerns, defence policy in practice continues to reflect the security and interests of the state and not of women, whether white, racialized, cisgender, transgender, straight, or queer. A feminist defence policy would shift our focus from state to human—in particular, women's—security, and to non-militarized forms of security, such as economic, food, or environmental security (Eichler 2016). As the submission to the 2016 defence policy review by the feminist organization Canadian Voice of Women for Peace argued: "It is vital that the Government of Canada reconceptualise the meanings of defence and security away from militarism and instead to sustainable development and disarmament" (Lorincz 2016, 2). The aim of an explicitly feminist defence policy would be not only to increase the number of women in the defence sector and integrate a gender perspective but to shift how we define security. An explicitly feminist defence policy would conceptualize gender equality beyond mere inclusion and define it as an objective of policy (Eichler 2016). With the 2017 defence policy, the Trudeau government has largely limited gender to employment equity and operational issues, as well as attempts to transform the gendered military culture, but not emphasized gender equality itself as a goal of military and defence policy or redefined how we understand security.

Feminist observers have emphasized that de-militarization must occur if Canada is truly committed to feminism (Tuckey 2017). In fact, the 2017 defence policy indicates more of a re-militarization than a de-militarization of Canadian defence policy. The integration of gender concerns took place within a broader focus on investing in and growing the Canadian military. It includes a commitment to increase defence spending "from $18.9 billion in 2016–17 to $32.7 billion in 2026–27" (DND 2017, 11), with new investments going to procurement and the well-being of service members, as well as an increase in personnel. As Andrea Lane argues in her analysis of the new policy: "Beyond the money, however, the Trudeau government has gone even further to position itself as serious, security-minded, and supportive of its military. For example, there is a new aggressive role for the CAF in the cyber domain, marking for the first time that Canada will be attacking, not merely defending, in this arena. Other acquisitions also allude to a robust, active, and offensive vision for the CAF" (2018, 274). Much of the language of the defence policy is masculinized, relying on gendered tropes of combat-readiness, security, and strength. The prominent integration of gender concerns marks a decided turn away from gender-blind policies of the past. However, this inclusion of feminist-informed language may convey a more benign image of the Canadian military and state than is warranted.

CONCLUSION

This chapter has assessed the "transformational possibilities" of integrating gender concerns into Canadian military and defence policy during these "turbulent times." Military and defence policy has undergone considerable change since the 2000s. This change reflects broader shifts in gendered militarism in the West. Militaries have deeply masculinized legacies, but today they are finding ways to integrate women and gender in attempts to re-legitimate themselves and improve operational effectiveness. Women and gender perspectives are integrated into the global security structure through UNSCR 1325 and its follow-up resolutions, while some countries have adopted explicitly feminist foreign policies. As this chapter has argued, Canada's 2017 defence policy commits to various strategies of integrating gender concerns into military and defence policy, from gender balancing, gender mainstreaming, and transforming gendered culture to valuing gender equality. But it has not gone so far as to redefine the meaning of security in less masculinized and militarized terms or to adopt an explicitly feminist defence policy.

There remain serious contradictions between the goals of military and defence policy, with their focus on operational effectiveness and state interests, and the goals of gender equality at the heart of feminist theory and practice. This speaks to the issue of whether a feminist defence policy is possible or whether it is a contradiction in terms. A feminist defence policy would go beyond gender balancing and gender mainstreaming to challenge the persistent masculinized and state- and military-centric view of defence. It would require redefining the gendered basis of soldiering, protection, and security. Only when we challenge the gendered foundations of defence and make gender equality an explicit goal of military and defence policy are we likely to be able to transform (re-gender or de-gender) militaries themselves. In the meantime, feminists need to pursue a dual strategy of critically engaging ongoing efforts aimed at integrating gender into military and defence policy while offering a deeper critique of the ways in which military and defence policy continue to be informed by dominant notions of masculinity. A truly transformative integration of gender concerns into military and defence policy will depend on the engagement and scrutiny of stakeholders in civil society—most importantly, feminist activists and researchers.

As gender has become established as a key defence issue in Canada, a feminist perspective on military and defence policy becomes even more crucial to assessing the changing relationship between gender and the politics of war and peace. But not only is the relationship between gender and the politics of war and peace evolving during these "turbulent times," so is our society's and our military's understanding of gender. In 2019, the Canadian military updated its policy on transgender personnel and included language on non-binary personnel into its departmental plan for GBA+. In response, feminist research on the Canadian military will also need to continue to better integrate intersectional and non-binary perspectives, so that feminists can inform the "transformational possibilities" that are emerging.

DISCUSSION QUESTIONS

1. Do you believe militaries are inherently masculinized or can they be re-gendered or de-gendered?
2. What transformation do you think should occur within the military to enable gender equality?
3. What needs to change to make the military a welcoming and safe place for cisgender, queer, transgender, and racialized women?
4. Do you think a feminist defence policy is possible?

NOTES

1 This number includes 68,000 Regular Force members, 27,000 Reserve Force members, and 24,000 civilian employees.
2 Resolution 1325 on Women, Peace and Security, 2000; UN doc. no. S/RES/1325.
3 The use of women's rights discourse to justify military intervention was most prominently on display in the US-led war in Afghanistan that started in 2001, but

became a key feature of the broader global war on terror in the early twenty-first century (see Hunt and Rygiel 2006).

4 For examples of these earlier feminist debates, see, for example, Carter (1996); Elshtain (2000).

5 Canadian Human Rights Tribunal decision in *Brown v. Canadian Armed Forces* (T.D. 3/ 89), 20 February 1989.

6 Ibid., p. 31.

REFERENCES

Carreiras, Helena. 2006. *Gender and the Military: Women in the Armed Forces of Western Democracies*. New York: Routledge.

Carter, April. 1996. "Should Women Be Soldiers or Pacifists?" *Peace Review* 8 (3): 331–35.

Chapman, Krystel, and Maya Eichler. 2014. "Engendering Two Solitudes? Media Representations of Women in Combat in Quebec and the Rest of Canada." *International Journal* 69 (4): 594–611.

Cockburn, Cynthia. 2010. "Militarism and War." In *Gender Matters in Global Politics*, edited by Laura Shepherd, 105–15. London: Routledge.

Cotter, Adam. 2016. "Sexual Misconduct in the Canadian Armed Forces, 2016." *Statistics Canada*, November 28. http://www.statcan.gc.ca/pub/85-603-x/85-603 -x2016001-eng.htm.

Davis, Karen. 2013. *Negotiating Gender in the Canadian Forces 1970–1999*. PhD diss., Royal Military College of Canada.

Department of National Defence. 2017. *Strong, Secure, Engaged: Canada's Defence Policy*. Ottawa: Government of Canada. https://www.canada.ca/en/department -national-defence/corporate/reports-publications/canada-defence-policy.html.

Department of National Defence and the Canadian Armed Forces. 2009. *Canada First Defence Strategy*. http://www.forces.gc.ca/en/about/canada-first-defence -strategy.page.

———. 2015. *CDS OP Order – OP HONOUR*. Ottawa: Chief of Defence Staff, August 14. https://www.canada.ca/en/department-national-defence/services/benefits -military/conflict-misconduct/operation-honour/orders-policies-directives/cds -operation-order.html.

———. 2016. *CDS Directive for Integrating UNSCR 1325 and Related Resolutions into CAF Planning and Operations*. Ottawa: Chief of Defence Staff, January 29. https:// www.canada.ca/en/department-national-defence/services/operations/military -operations/conduct/cds-directive-unscr-1325.html.

———. 2018. "Mandate of the Department of National Defence and the Canadian Armed Forces." Last modified September 24, 2018. http://www.forces.gc.ca/en /about-us.page.

———. 2019. "Women in the Canadian Armed Forces: Backgrounder." National Defence and the Canadian Armed Forces, March 7. http://www.forces.gc.ca/en /news/article.page?doc=women-in-the-canadian-armed-forces%2Fizkjqzeu.

Deschamps, Marie. 2015. *External Review into Sexual Misconduct and Sexual Harassment in the Canadian Armed Forces*. Ottawa: Government of Canada, March 27. http://publications.gc.ca/site/eng/9.801509/publication.html.

Duncanson, Claire, and Rachel Woodward. 2016. "Regendering the Military: Theorizing Women's Military Participation." *Security Dialogue* 47 (1): 3–21.

Eichler, Maya. 2014. "Militarized Masculinities in International Relations." *Brown Journal of World Affairs* 21 (2): 81–93.

———. 2016. "A Feminist Defence Policy for Canada?" Invited submission to the Defence Policy Review. http:/fgpaapp.forces.gc.ca/en/defence-policy/review/docs/halifax/eichler-halifax-submission.pdf.

Elshtain, Jean Bethke. 2000. "'Shooting' at the Wrong Target: A Response to Van Creveld." *Millennium: Journal of International Studies* 29 (2): 443–48.

Enloe, Cynthia. 2000. *Maneuvers: The International Politics of Militarizing Women's Lives*. Berkeley: University of California Press.

Feinman, Ilene Rose. 2000. *Citizenship Rites: Feminist Soldiers and Feminist Antimilitarists*. New York: New York University Press.

George, Tammy. 2016. "Be All You Can Be or Longing to Be: Racialized Soldiers, the Canadian Military Experience and the Impossibility of Belonging to the Nation." PhD diss., University of Toronto.

Goldstein, Joshua S. 2001. *War and Gender: How Gender Shapes the War System and Vice Versa*. Cambridge: Cambridge University Press.

Government of Canada. 2018. *Budget 2018: Equality plus Growth: A Strong Middle Class*. Ottawa: Department of Finance. https://www.budget.gc.ca/2018/home-accueil-en.html.

Hunt, Krista, and Kim Rygiel, eds. 2006. *(En)Gendering the War on Terror: War Stories and Camouflaged Politics*. Hampshire, UK: Ashgate.

Lane, Andrea. 2017. "Special Men: The Gendered Militarization of the Canadian Armed Forces." *International Journal* 72 (4): 463–83.

———. 2018. "Manning Up: Justin Trudeau and the Politics of the Canadian Defence Community." In *Justin Trudeau and Canadian Foreign Policy: Canada among Nations 2017*, edited by Norman Hillmer and Philippe Lagassé, 261–84. London: Palgrave MacMillan/Springer International.

Lorincz, Tamara. 2016. "From Preventative Diplomacy to Sustainable Peace: A Gender-Based, Eco-Feminist and Nonviolent Approach to Canadian Defence and Security Policy." The Canadian Voice of Women for Peace's submission to the Defence Policy Review public consultation. http://vowpeace.org/wp-content/uploads/2016/08/From-Diplomacy-to-Sustainable-Peace_VOW-Submission-FINAL.pdf.

Morgan, David H.J. 1994. "Theater of War: Combat, the Military, and Masculinities." In *Theorizing Masculinities*, edited by Harry Brod and Michael Kaufman, 165–82. London: Sage.

Obradovic, Lana. 2014. *Gender Integration in NATO Military Forces: Cross-National Analysis*. Farnham, UK: Ashgate.

Poulin, Carmen, and Lynne Gouliquer. 2012. "Clandestine Existences and Secret
    Research: Eliminating Official Discrimination in the Canadian Military and
    Going Public in Academia." *Journal of Lesbian Studies* 16 (1): 54–64.
Robinson, Shirley M. 1985. "Women in Combat: The Last Bastion." *Canadian
    Woman Studies/Les Cahiers De La Femme* 6 (4): 99–103.
Sjoberg, Laura. 2013. *Gendering Global Conflict: Toward a Feminist Theory of War.*
    New York: Columbia University Press.
Stiehm, Judith. 1982. "The Protected, the Protector, the Defender." *Women's Studies
    International Forum* 3 (3–4): 367–76.
Tait, Victoria. 2015. "Gender and the 21st Century Threat Environment." *The Journal
    of the Royal Canadian Military Institute (RCMI)* 75 (1): 5–9.
Tickner, J. Ann. 2001. *Gendering World Politics: Issues and Approaches in the Post-Cold
    War Era.* New York: Columbia University Press.
Tuckey, Sarah. 2017. "The New Era of Canadian Feminist Foreign Policy." Canadian
    International Council, December 18. https://thecic.org/the-new-era-of-canadian
    -feminist-foreign-policy/.
United Nations (UN). 2015. *Preventing Conflict, Transforming Justice, Securing Peace:
    A Global Study on the Implementation of UNSCR 1325.* New York: UN Women.
United Nations Economic and Social Council (UN ECOSOC). 1997. *UN Economic
    and Social Council Resolution 1997/2: Agreed Conclusions.* Geneva: UN ECOSOC,
    July 18. https://www.refworld.org/docid/4652c9fc2.html.
Wibben, Annick. 2011. *Feminist Security Studies: A Narrative Approach.* London:
    Routledge.
Winslow, Donna, and Jason Dunn. 2002. "Women in the Canadian Forces: Between
    Legal and Social Integration." *Current Sociology* 50 (5): 641–67.
Women's International League for Peace and Freedom. 2015. *Women, Peace and
    Security Webinar: Feminist Foreign Policy.* YouTube video, 1:55:11, November 5.
    https://www.youtube.com/watch?v=fry3LgQEbUc
Young, Iris Marion. 2003. "The Logic of Masculinist Protection: Reflections on the
    Current Security State." *Signs: Journal of Women and Culture in Society* 29 (1):
    1–25.

FURTHER READING

Deschamps, Marie. 2015. *External Review into Sexual Misconduct and Sexual
    Harassment in the Canadian Armed Forces.* Ottawa: Government of Canada,
    March 27. http://publications.gc.ca/site/eng/9.801509/publication.html.
Enloe, Cynthia. 2000. *Maneuvers: The International Politics of Militarizing Women's
    Lives.* Berkeley: University of California Press.

7

Free Mining, Body Land, and the Reproduction of Indigenous Life

Isabel Altamirano-Jiménez

Key terms: body land, communalism, free mining, re-member, resource extraction

In recent years, and in various ways, Canada has expressed commitments to the Truth and Reconciliation Commission's Calls to Action vis-à-vis Indigenous Peoples. However, this chapter illustrates how Canada's actions, at home and internationally, more accurately reflect the tensions between the imperative of pursuing natural **resource extraction** and protecting the rights of Indigenous Peoples. Often narratives of good governance, white civility, and promises of employment generation serve to conceal current processes of dispossession and the violence sustaining the racially structured national and global Canadian mining industry (Butler 2015, 6–7). Unprecedented investments in mining operations negatively impact Indigenous communities through the degradation and pollution of their lands and water sources, limitations on their access to natural resources, and the displacement of people from their lands (Willow 2016; WEA/NYSHN 2016). These impacts are also gendered and generational. In Canada, the report by Women Earth Alliance and the Native Youth and Sexual Health Network (WEA/NYSHN) shows that the connection between land, body, and extraction creates a powerful intersection for North American Indigenous communities, one that threatens their very survival and is often ignored (2016, 2). In Latin America, Indigenous feminists use the term body-territory-land to evoke the connection between their struggles against resource extraction and gendered violence (Cruz Hernandez 2016; Cabnal 2010).

This chapter examines the connection between **free mining** (laws allowing access to a large area of land for the purpose of securing access to mineral deposits and establishing mining above other activities), land, and body. Focusing on the anti-mining struggle of the Zapotec community of Capulalpam, Oaxaca, Mexico, this chapter shows that the reclamation of Indigenous people's fundamental sovereignty over their bodies cannot be separated from the historical and contingent relationships between resource extraction, the state, and colonialism (see also Wiebe in this volume). I use the unified concept of "**body land**"[1] to evoke not only the impacts of resource extraction on the human and non-human worlds but also the transformational, decolonial possibilities that arise from Indigenous women's embodied practices of resistance and refusal. Mexico provides an important case study given Canada's political and economic relations with Mexico (recently renewed through the renegotiation of the North American Free Trade Agreement [NAFTA], linking Canada, Mexico, and the United States). Moreover, this case study illustrates the ways in which settler states, corporations, and political elites coordinate efforts to control resource-rich areas of the world, erasing Indigenous Peoples.

Combining Indigenous feminism with an historical analysis of mining law and critical political economy, this chapter shows how contemporary colonialism and dispossession manifest through free trade agreements, narratives of development, and the legality of imposed property regimes. These colonial power relations manifest between the Global North and South and between states and Indigenous governments. This chapter first maps an Indigenous body land framework that accounts for how the experiences of gendered, sexualized, racialized, colonized, and transborder bodies intersect with the movement of capital and the fixity of extraction. Second, it provides an historical account of how different property regimes have served to reconfigure the body land connection through the production of a "colonial underground" (Scott 2008) that shapes how the surface of the land is experienced. Third, it analyses the outcomes produced by the imposition of free mining in Mexico. While free, prior, and informed consent is an essential standard of Indigenous self-determination in both national and international law, the legal strategies used to gain access to Indigenous land raise questions about who consents and how consent is manufactured. To clarify, Mexico municipalities, including Indigenous municipalities, constitute a third level of government with jurisdiction over their lands. Lastly, by exploring the connection between body and land, this chapter documents the community's embodied experiences of resource extraction not only through the experience of harms but also through the collective actions that render bodies, land, and communities in ways that are more promising for transformational, decolonial politics.

BODY LAND: AN INDIGENOUS FEMINIST RESEARCH FRAMEWORK

Body land encompasses different dimensions of Indigenous feminist politics. For example, according to the United Nations Special Rapporteur on the Rights of Indigenous Peoples, Victoria Tauli-Corpuz, we "cannot delink the fight of Indigenous peoples for their land, territory and resources from the violence that is committed against Indigenous women" (Rowlands 2016, n.p.). Similarly, in Latin America, Indigenous feminists and activists have pointed out that the body cannot be separated from the land. They explicitly use the term "body land" to convey the fact that what happens on the land has negative effects on Indigenous women's bodies (Cruz Hernandez 2016; Cabnal 2010; Paredes 2011). Although Indigenous feminists and Indigenous women's organizations have reported the gendered effects of resource extraction on local social life and relationships (Amnesty International 2016; WEA/ NYSHN 2016; Deoanandan and Dougherty 2016; McDonnell 2014; Sweet 2014; Altamirano-Jiménez 2013), the link between land and body is seldom taken into consideration (Altamirano-Jiménez 2013; WEA/NYSHN 2016), concealing the processes through which Indigenous social and cultural reproduction is threatened. I argue that body land is a unified concept that captures both the expansive detrimental repercussions of colonial resource extraction and the generative capacities of Indigenous women's embodied practices of resistance and refusal. As an Indigenous feminist analytic, body land refers to the ontological relationship—that is, a way of being in the world— between Indigenous people and territory/place.

To elaborate, in Indigenous worldviews, the body cannot be separated from the landscape one shares with highly heterogeneous beings with which we develop an intense and continuous relationship. From this point of view, territory "can be understood as a network of relationships produced by different forms of life" (Cruz et al. 2017, 13, my translation). In Nahuatl, the term "altepetl" or "water mountain" signifies community, a social unit. According to Lopez Austin (1994), this term conveys the interdependence between a community of people, natural forces, and non-human beings inhabiting the territory. Interactions among human beings, earth, and non-human beings evoke thousands of intersections that are driven by people's actions and inactions and correlate to seasonal cycles and community governance (see also Wiebe in this volume). These interactions are central to how Indigenous communities govern themselves and organize responsibilities along gender lines.

Moreover, from a Zapotec perspective, territory is not divided into surface and subsurface or different silos of resources. As Aquino Centeno (2011) observes, water and forest are sacred forms of life on the ground. The subsoil, on the other hand, represents the roots, the seeds that make possible the existence of mountains, water, plants, and so on. Thus, the subsurface is part of the spiritual, symbolic, and material life of Indigenous communities.

Colonialism certainly altered such intimate, sensual, embodied relationships to land. Europeans imagined Indigenous territories as places of plunder and waste. In the digital era, modern settler states and corporations coordinate efforts to map and control resource-rich areas, continuing to render human and non-human life non-existent (Gómez-Barris 2017, 8). Moreover, these long-standing efforts to suppress and colonize Indigenous life have produced footprints in body land. As Indigenous feminists have noted, "The historical violence produced by extraction has left marks in our territory-bodies as well as in our lands when our rivers and lagoons are polluted and as women we still need to provide for our families" (Cruz et al. 2017, 13). Thus, Indigenous Peoples' lives are entangled with colonial state institutions, practices, and actions (see also Wiebe and Starblanket in this volume).

By centring the connection between body and territory, Indigenous feminists insist on the need to historicize Indigenous struggles and the continuity of colonial mining. Such insistence, however, does not mean that land and bodies are the same in an essentialist sort of way. Rather, it means that bodies are territories that need to be defended and protected and that what happens on the land has corporeal effects. When resource extraction and dispossession occur, people are rendered disposable, forced to migrate or endure everyday environmental harm and gendered violence, or criminalized for opposing such economic projects. Thus, seeing both Indigenous lands and bodies as territories of material, cultural, historic, and symbolic life, including those bodies that have been de-territorialized, means that struggles for bodies and lands cannot be separated. These are struggles for the social and cultural reproduction of Indigenous life.

Body land, therefore, highlights the potential of bodies coming together to resist as well as to **re-member**[2] communities. Because memories, histories, dreams, harms, and desires live in bodies, re-membering is about being with one another in community to collectively imagine other futures. As an Indigenous feminist political practice, body territory is not only about the vulnerability of the body but also about the possibility of unbodying the body and "render[ing] again," both collectively and individually, in ways that are positive and liberating (Belcourt 2017, 40). As Quechua activist Julieta Paredes notes, Indigenous women work on their bodies while simultaneously working to build the territories they can inhabit without violence and with the freedom to explore their sexuality, dreams, and desires (2010, 205–06).

ACCOUNTING FOR THE COLONIAL UNDERGROUND

Edward Said argued that "the actual geographical possession of land is what colonialism is about" (1994, 78). Colonialism, however, involved more than land. Before colonialism could even succeed, it had to render Indigenous bodies and territories extractible, devaluing other human/non-human interactions and relationships (Gómez-Barris 2017, 18). Colonialism, imperialism, racism, and uneven gender relations were instrumental in the process of separating body land.

To illustrate, the search and large-scale extraction of silver and gold in what would become Mexico brought immense wealth to Spain at the expense of millions of Indigenous labourers and Black slaves. In the Spanish Iberian legal tradition, precious metals were considered the prerogative of the Catholic queen and based on a system of classification that reflected the racialized division of the colonial society. What is more, this type of land ownership divided into surface and subsurface rights, and while Indigenous Peoples experienced various dimensions of colonization on the land, what happened underground also fundamentally altered Indigenous lives. This "colonial underground" (Scott 2008) was spiritually and physically traumatic, and socially, economically, and environmentally destructive, altering Indigenous Peoples' relationships to land. In many Indigenous communities, underground spaces were revered. For example, caves were, and still are, considered ceremonial places and mountains where gold was found were thought to be sacred. Over time, the practices associated with colonial mining transformed these underground spaces into locales associated with evil and greed.

Although mining was central to the colonial economy in Mexico, it did not develop evenly across regions. In Oaxaca, mining was not a central activity until the late 1700s, when labour was drafted from Indigenous communities. While it is well documented that Indigenous men were coerced to work at the mines, women also participated in the mining complex by selling food and candles and providing services (Velasco Murillo 2013, 12). Although Indigenous people became integrated into the market, colonial protection of Indigenous communal ownership of land, as well as women's work within their communities, sustained their collective social reproduction.

After the Mexican independence movement of 1810, the colonial legal mining legislation was initially maintained with minimal change. However, the prospect of immense wealth drove British mining companies to urge their government to secure a free trade agreement with the newly formed country (Brown 2012, 92). In exchange for Mexico's being admitted into the community of "civilized nations," meaning European countries, England demanded access to mining resources in Mexico. "Speculation of loans and mining stocks soon produced an economic crisis, which was met with further changes in tax and property regimes and tariffs with the purpose of revitalizing the mining industry in the second half of the century" (Hernández Chávez 2006, 125). The *Leyes de Reforma* or Reform Laws facilitated the creation of a land market aimed at preventing the accumulation of "wastelands" in the hands of the Catholic Church and Indigenous communities. The latter were considered an obstacle to the modernization of the country, particularly in those regions where they constituted the majority of the population and controlled huge tracts of land collectively (Arrioja Díaz Viruell 2010, 146).

In 1884 and 1892, the mining law was modified to substitute the Spanish colonial mining code with an English property regime that granted ownership of the subsoil to landowners. In British North America, free mining had been formally enshrined in western Canada in the British Columbia Gold Fields Act of 1859 and in the United States by the American General Mining Law of 1872 (Hoogeveen 2015, 126), which allowed companies and individual prospectors to stake a mineral claim without the consent of Indigenous Peoples. Facilitated by an emergent geological science that emphasized the purity of minerals and the rise of industrial capitalism, the dispossession of Indigenous lands not only accelerated in the nineteenth century in Canada and the United States but the practice was naturalized as news of gold "discovery" spread.

In Mexico, the adoption of free mining produced a number of *fundos mineros* or mining estates in different regions of the country as American mining companies capitalized on the newly opened opportunity. By the 1900s, 81 per cent of the mining property was concentrated in American hands. New machinery and techniques, as well as infrastructure to connect the country, accelerated shipment of ore to Europe from remote places such as Oaxaca. Unlike mining in northern Mexico, mining in Oaxaca occurred on a small scale and Indigenous people participated in this economic activity without abandoning their traditional subsistence activities.

In the early 1900s, several important mining conflicts regarding working conditions exploded in the country, some of which merged with the Mexican revolution movement of 1910, driving private investors away. After the movement ended—and in an attempt to regain control of mining property—Article 27 of the Mexican Constitution of 1917 re-established the Iberian division of surface and subsurface ownership. While the state claimed the subsoil, Indigenous Peoples maintained full ownership of the surface. Moreover, Article 27 established provisions to collectively retain national ownership of land, resources, and water. Ironically, despite this legislation, by the 1970s the state only owned 15 per cent of the mining property in Mexico (Tetreault 2014, 2). In 1982, when oil prices dropped, Mexico found itself unable to repay its debt and was forced to implement policies dictated by the International Monetary Fund and the World Bank (Altamirano-Jiménez 2013).

FREE MINING AND INDIGENOUS RIGHTS: WHO CONSENTS?

In the early 1990s, as NAFTA was being negotiated, Canadian geological expertise, risk capital, and ideas about "good governance" became dominant (Gonzalez Rodriguez 2011, 18) to avoid charges that NAFTA practices of dispossession were racist and violent. In what was now a neoliberal context, law and economic rationalism were used to make arguments in favour of transforming Mexico's so-called backward economy into a modern one. This would be done by giving capital the legitimate right to dispossess people and eradicate their livelihoods. To illustrate, in anticipation of the implementation of NAFTA, the Mexican government was "encouraged" to make several constitutional changes and legislative changes to Article 27 of the Constitution and the Mining Law, which have had serious consequences for Indigenous Peoples (see World Bank 1991). For example, Article 27 of the Mexican Constitution of 1917 was rewritten to undermine Indigenous and peasants' control over their agricultural communal lands and *ejidos*, land plots granted by the state, which were individually held but could not be sold nor bought. Article 27 had effectively shielded about half of Mexican territory from the market by recognizing Indigenous communities' ownership of land, woodlands, and water. This article also established the state's ownership of the subsurface.

The reforms of 1992 made two important changes. First, ejido lands were privatized and could thus be sold, mortgaged, and rented for the purpose of creating a land market. Moreover, while previously land plots were granted mainly to males, women had historically participated in agricultural activities and accessed land and resources based on customary practices (Altamirano-Jiménez 2013, 83). However, as part of the changes to Article 27 women lost the right to inherit land. On the other hand, the communal ownership of agrarian communities in forested areas remained inalienable.

At this time, the Mining Law was also changed to legally establish free mining once again. For instance, the Mexico Mining Restructuring Project's objectives included fostering foreign investment, providing access to communal lands, implementing a mineral rights policy, and eliminating royalty payments. Importantly, Article 6 of the Mining Law was transformed to deem mineral exploration, exploitation, and processing as of public benefit, ensuring that these activities took precedence over any other land use. In addition, regulations regarding environmental assessments were practically ignored, facilitating exploration for and exploitation of minerals.

Mining concession holders can now demand that land occupied by towns become vacated to facilitate their endeavours (Bacon 2013, 44). Not surprisingly, Mexico became the number one destination for Canadian mining investment, which constitutes 74 per cent of foreign investment (Delgado Ramos 2010; Garibay 2010; Garibay and Balzaretti 2009). Representing itself as a civil, liberal, democratic country, the Canadian state actively promoted the interests of Canadian mining companies. Using diplomatic relations, influencing Mexico and other host countries' regulatory regimes, and advancing earth science knowledge centres, the Canadian state has been instrumental in positioning mining companies as key players of the global economy (Butler 2015 10). By 2006, according to Bacon, 61 million hectares of land had been given in concessions and by 2010 this more than doubled to 126 million hectares (2013, 43–44). In the state of Oaxaca, 770,000 hectares have been granted in concessions, most without the knowledge of the communities affected.

In 1990, Mexico ratified the International Labour Organization's Convention 169. Importantly, the convention introduced the base concept of free, prior, and informed consent that had been driven by the global Indigenous movement (Sawyer and Gomez 2012). In 1991 this country modified Article 4 of the Constitution to recognize the "pluricultural" nature of the Mexican state and the right of Indigenous Peoples to self-determination. In 1995, Oaxaca became the first state to change its local constitution to implement the rights of Indigenous Peoples as recognized in the Constitution.

With these changes, national law and NAFTA rules functioned to override the recognized territorial jurisdiction of Indigenous Peoples. On the one hand, the federal government can grant concessions to the underground. On the other, mining activities cannot be performed without having access to the surface, which is owned by Indigenous communities and municipalities. This situation raises important questions over who consents and how states, corporations, and political elites manufacture consent. The priority afforded to mining activities in relation to other land uses creates critical grey areas and power imbalances, which are often manipulated by mining companies. In order for Indigenous communities to defend their territories, they have had to interact with a complex set of national and international rules and legislation that together expose the contradictions between the recognition of Indigenous rights and the power afforded to the extractive industries.

CAPULALPAM: THE STRUGGLE TO DEFEND INDIGENOUS COMMUNAL LAND

It is not possible to understand the Zapotec community of Capulalpam's refusal of a Canadian open pit mine without considering the community's historical experience of the colonial underground and its struggle to maintain control over its territory and social reproduction. As Salvador Aquino Centeno (2011) contends, the subsurface is not disconnected from the collective identity and historical memory of the community. Capulalpam is a Zapotec town and a municipality located in the Juarez Highlands. Like many other Indigenous communities in Oaxaca, Capulalpam is governed by Indigenous laws or the so-called Indigenous normative systems. These are bodies of legal principles, practices, and governance institutions that preceded and survived state sovereignty. Indigenous communities, **communalism**,[3] and rights to land and water find their origin in these systems.

The region is covered with pine and pine-oak forests, which have been communally owned and sustainably managed since the late 1980s. However,

Capulalpam is no stranger to mining, which began in 1870 when gold and silver reservoirs were found. Mining was then represented as the economic activity that was supposed to finally bring "progress" to Oaxaca, especially the highlands. By the early 1900s, the Natividad mine had become the richest operation in Oaxaca, employing Zapotecs and other Indigenous Peoples from different communities. For over a century, generations of men and women worked at the Natividad mine, socializing as unionized miners while fulfilling their community obligations as Zapotecs (McNamara 2007). Conflicts over labour conditions were a constant feature of this activity. Many ex-miners still associate the underground with exploitation, accidents, deaths, and meagre salaries. In fact, the tensions between the mining company and miners over labour conditions lasted until early 1993, when the mining union was finally dismantled just before NAFTA was implemented. By the 1970s, when mining started to decline, many Indigenous people opted to migrate, putting at risk the very social reproduction of many communities in the highlands.

Meanwhile previously, in 1954, the community learned that the federal government had granted a timber concession to a paper mill company (Fábrica de Papel Tuxtepec, FAPATUX) in the region without their consent (Barton Bray and Merino 2004). Despite the legal protection of Indigenous communal lands and forests, once the permit was granted the community could not decide how much timber was extracted from its territory, nor could it negotiate the price (Mraz Bartra 2013, 77). In the early 1980s, when the permit was about to expire, community members initiated an intense process of organizing with the purpose of regaining their forest. They created the Organization for the Defense of Natural Resources in the Juarez Highlands to cooperate with other forested communities and initiated a legal process against the federal government (Altamirano-Jiménez 1998). In 1981, a woman from Capulalpam learned of the government's plans to renew and extend the timber concession. She quickly mobilized other women and together they decided to act. Women destroyed the bridge used by the timber trucks, literally using their bodies to prevent them from getting out of the community. Men soon followed them. Despite women's central role in recovering communal forest, their participation has remained invisible. The fact that communal landholders' representation is family-based—and that women often perform work that does not count as a form of active citizenship within the community—has contributed to obscuring their contribution. However, it is not possible to ignore that women were also central to building a sense of the communal and the values and practices that prefigure the collective actions of the community.

In 1983, the forest concession was finally cancelled. The movement to stop the timber concession was crucial to developing a communal vision of forest management based on reciprocity and a communal governance system that aims at benefiting both the community and the environment. To community members, forests are living entities that exist as a result of the relationships between human and non-human beings sharing the territory. In the community's view, the defence of their forests was an act of self-determination. As part of it, the community designated its own protected areas, which became part of the Early Action Areas (this was a program implemented by the federal government to promote community conservation) and Capulalpam was to receive payment for ecosystem services from the federal government. The community also developed economic projects, including a toy shop and an ecotourism company. In the view of the mayor, "these projects have been central to preventing the migration of our people" (García Martínez 2015, n.p.).

While Capulalpam and other communities in Oaxaca have been internationally praised for their communally managed forests, Indigenous organizations, environmentalists, and academics have rung the alarm that such areas are at risk due to the intensification of mining and the energy sector. In 2000, the community heard rumours that a Canadian mining company, Continuum Resources, had bought the old Natividad mine. The Ministry of Economic Development had granted 50,000 hectares of Indigenous land in the Juarez Highlands, violating the community's Indigenous surface rights. The community demanded that the company explain to the communal assembly why it did not ask for the community's consent. Confident that a former mining community would welcome back such activity, the company argued that mining would create jobs and development in the highlands. The community refused. Continuum Resources's representatives accused the community of opposing progress and continued with its activities. The new expansive mining project extended underground tunnels to forest and aquifer areas, where the company illegally captured water until several water springs disappeared (*La Jornada*, October 7, 2007, n.p.).

Once again, the community mobilized to stop mining. In this process, memories of the past were central to bringing people together in the present. As noted in an ex-miner's testimony:

> We do not forget those who died at the mine, we do not forget those who were intoxicated by poisonous gases in the mine's tunnels, we do not forget the exploitation, we do not forget the sexual exploitation and violence

> that women endured, we do not forget that it was our medicine women
> who took care of those who became ill, not the mine's clinic. We know
> that mining has nothing for us. (quoted in Méndez García 2017, 15)

These memories and felt experiences stand at odds with the mining industry's official registers, which emphasize jobs and economic rationality. In the case of this community, memory has been central to evoking a past and the possibility of defending an Indigenous future. Besides collecting ex-miners' testimonies, old and young community members walked their territory identifying the changes contemporary mining has produced in the landscape. Moreover, the municipal government and the head of the agrarian communal assembly, with the support of the citizens' assembly, initiated a lawsuit against the mining company for operating on communal lands without the communal assembly's consent. As noted by the mayor of the community, "Here, no individual can grant permission to access our territory. Here, consent is a communal issue because the territory is Capulalpam's communal heritage" (Vélez Ascencio 2011, n.p.). In the lawsuit, instead of appealing to the Indigenous collective rights recognized in the Mexican Constitution of 1991, this community positioned itself as a precolonial community whose primordial communal land titles were recognized by the Spanish Crown in 1599, exposing the problem of recognizing rights that protect culture but not land.

While the community emphasized the impact of resource extraction on bodies and territory, neither bodies nor territory can be reduced to sites of pollution. Rather, in this process, the defence of Zapotec land and bodies becomes an everyday struggle for an Indigenous future. Unlike the mining of the past, under current regulations mining concessions often include water concessions, forcing communities to compete with mining companies for water use permits (Méndez García 2017; Mraz Bartra 2016;). Moreover, the newly found sources of gold and silver are located in sensitive areas such as a sacred mountain, aquifers, and the community biological reserve. As the Capulalpam Manifesto stated: "A community without water has no life on which future generations can depend on. We must defend our future" (No a la Mina Org 2007).

Once again, women played an important yet invisible role—one that was behind the scenes or under-acknowledged—when the legal strategy followed by the municipal and agrarian authorities was not enough. Women blockaded the community's road entrance. Women and their families also organized and participated in a blockade in Oaxaca city to refuse mining in their territory.

While men are often concerned with the process of granting concessions, explorations, and negotiations, women are concerned with environmental degradation, the community's well-being, and the possibility of having a Zapotec future (Méndez García 2017; Mraz Bartra 2016). In rejecting mining, Zapotec women link environmental degradation with health, illness, and death. While working above ground, Indigenous women were affected by what happened in the colonial underground. From this perspective, the community's determination to protect the environment cannot be reduced to an environmental act; rather, it is a collective attempt at protecting a communal way of being in the world. According to Zapotec thinker Martínez Luna, communalism can be understood as an ideology of self-recognition that centres Zapotecs' thought and refusal of dispossession (2010, 80).

Importantly, while communalism has brought people together to resist colonialism, it has also received some criticism for being exclusionary and posing serious political challenges for women. For example, how can women demand access to communal lands without compromising the kinship relations that have historically served to protect Indigenous lands from dispossession? How can they defend their body territory while also building the territory where they can freely dream, be safe, and have a voice? When asked to reflect on the challenges confronting women in Capulalpam, one woman stated: "I would say it is building more horizontal gender relations" (quoted in Méndez García 2017, 72).

Capulalpam's anti-mining struggle has extended beyond the community by establishing relationships with other regional, national, and international anti-mining organizations. At the same time, this struggle is also in tension with a neighbouring, yet relatively new, community, Natividad, which supports mining. In 2005, in an attempt to co-opt the Capulalpam anti-mining movement, the Mexican federal government granted Capulalpam the designation of "magic town," a title that highlights the historical, cultural, and aesthetic qualities of small towns. Although the community has capitalized on this denomination, tensions exist regarding who benefits from this program and from showcasing the cultural traditions of this town. At the same time, Capulalpam has used the platform provided for such denominations to continue to express its refusal to mining (Méndez García 2017, 218).

In 2006, the Canadian mining company was finally found to be in serious violation of waste disposal procedures and was ordered to halt activities. However, the concession remained open. In 2011, the community learned that another Canadian mining company was planning an exploration project. Once again, the community refused it. The communal assembly confirmed it would not consent to the project, noting: "The community of Capulalpan, exercising our rights as an Indigenous and peasant municipality, refuses permission to the companies Natividad, Minera Teocuitla, Continuum Resources, Arco Exploration, or companies using any other name to carry out exploration or exploitation of minerals in our lands" (quoted in Bacon 2013, 51). While Indigenous communities have no control over mining concessions, the inalienability of Indigenous communal land rights and the community's collective response have provided the strength to temporarily stop mining once again.

In 2013, at the Encounter of Mesoamerican Peoples held in Capulalpam, representatives from Indigenous communities from Latin America, the United States, and Canada confirmed: "No to Mining, Yes to Life" (Encounter of Mesoamerican Peoples 2013, n.p.). Refusal of mining is not only about rejecting extraction but also about creating something new: an Indigenous project in which Indigenous Peoples can live with freedom and dignity. At this meeting, Indigenous participants emphasized the need for communities to strengthen their governance systems and institutions, including the communal assembly and cargo system. Capulalpam's representatives noted that their community's success in interrupting mining will depend on their communal actions and knowledge. For example, Indigenous organizations often note that mining companies foster and capitalize on community divisions and the lack of Indigenous women's land rights in order to gain access. Thus, a communal, organized response has the potential to counteract Canadian mining companies' actions and render the collective body in liberating ways.

CONCLUSION

In this chapter, I have explored the connection between land and body and documented the struggle of the Zapotec community of Capulalpam against Canadian mining. While some argue that Canada's problematic prominence in resource extraction is recent, I have shown that its actions and inactions are part of an historic, resource-based colonial project that continues to this day. Rather than turning away from the imperial ambitions of its mother country, Canada has embraced and perpetuated them (Deneault and Sacher 2012) through mining practices at home and abroad that epitomize settler colonialism. I also hope to have demonstrated how the embodied experiences of gendered, sexualized, racialized, and colonized bodies intersect with the movement of global capital and the fixity of resource extraction. I focused on the community's embodied experience of mining not only through the harms it has experienced but also through the collective response that defends a Zapotec future while opening the space for Indigenous women to demand more horizontal gender relations.

By looking into questions of surface and subsurface ownership and free, prior, and informed consent, I have shown the legal intricacies and dissonances created by the establishment of free mining and the recognition of Indigenous rights in Mexico. I have also demonstrated how dispossession is never only about land and minerals but about bodies and other human/non-human interactions that are rendered invisible.

DISCUSSION QUESTIONS

1. What is free mining and how has it affected Indigenous Peoples?
2. What does an Indigenous feminist analysis of Indigenous Peoples' relationships to territory have to offer social sciences?
3. How do states, corporations, and political elites cooperate to advance resource extraction?
4. How is gender implicated in processes of natural resource extraction?

NOTES

1 Body land will be explained more fully later in the chapter, but it is used as a means of conveying the ontological relationship between Indigenous bodies and territory/place, and thus captures both the expansive detrimental repercussions of colonial resource extraction and the generative capacities of Indigenous Peoples' embodied practices of resistance and refusal.
2 The term "re-member" refers to the practice of being with one another, building community to collectively imagine other political possibilities.
3 Communalism can be understood as an ideology of self-recognition that centres Zapotecs' thought and refusal of dispossession.

REFERENCES

Altamirano-Jiménez, Isabel. 1998. "De eso que llaman moviemiento indio y su proyecto identitario 1970–1994." Senior honours thesis, National School of Anthropology and History (ENAH).

———. 2013. *Indigenous Encounters with Neo-liberalism: Place, Women and the Environment.* Vancouver: UBC Press.

Amnesty International. 2016. "Out of Sight, Out of Mind: Gender, Indigenous Rights and Energy Development in British Columbia". London: Amnesty International. https://www.amnesty.ca/sites/amnesty/files/Out%20of%20Sight%20Out %20of%20Mind%20ES%20FINAL%20EN%20CDA.pdf.

Aquino Centeno, Salvador. 2010. "La lucha por el control del territorio en Calpulalpan: Diferentes maneras acerca de la compresión del subsuelo, el oro, la plata, la ley y el capital." Paper presented at Jornada Mesoamericanas III, October.

———. 2014. "La experiencia de explotación del oro y la plata en Capulalpam de Méndez, en la Sierra Zapoteca de Oaxaca." In *Movimiento Indígena en América Latina*, vol. 3, edited by Fabiola Escarcéga et al., 268–74. Mexico City: UAM-CIESAS-Centro de Estudios Andino Mesoamericanos. http://www.academia .edu/15906168/Movi miento_ind%C3%ADgena_en_Am%C3%A9rica_Latina _Vol_III.

Arrioja Díaz Viruell, Luis Alberto. "Dos visiones en torno a un problema: las tierras comunales indígenas en Oaxaca y Michoacán, 1824–1857." *Relaciones* 124 (31): 143–85. http://www.scielo.org.mx/pdf/rz/v31n124/v31n124a6.pdf.

Bacon, David. 2013. *The Right to Stay Home: How US Policy Drives Mexican Migration.* Boston: Beacon Press.

Barton Bray, David, and Leticia Merino. 2004. *La experiencia de las comunidades forestales en Mexico.* Mexico City: Instituto Nacional de Ecología.

Belcourt, Billy-Ray. 2017. *This Wound Is a World.* Calgary: Frontenac House Poetry.

Brown, Kendal W. 2012. *A History of Mining in Latin America: From the Colonial Era to the Present.* Albuquerque: University of New Mexico Press.

Butler, Paula. 2015. *Colonial Extraction: Race and Canadian Mining in Contemporary Africa.* Toronto: University of Toronto Press.

Cabnal, Lorena. 2010. *Feminismos diversos: el feminismo comunitario.* Madrid: ACSUR-Las Segovias.

Cruz, Delmy Tania, et al. 2017. *Mapeando el cuerpo-territorio: Guía metodológica para las mujeres que defienden el territorio.* Quito: CLACSO, Instituto de Estudios Ecológico del tercer Mundo.

Cruz Hernandez, Delmy Tania. 2016. "Una Mirada muy otra a los territorios cuerpos femeninos." *Solar* 12 (1): 35–46. http://revistasolar.org/wp-content /uploads/2017/07/3-Una-mirada-muy-otra-a-los-territorios-Cuerpos-femeninos .-Delmy-Tania-Cruz-Hern%C3%A1ndez.pdf.

Delgado Ramos, Giancarlo. 2010. "Presentation." In *La ecología política de la minería en América Latina: Aspectos socioeconómicos, legales y ambientales de la megaminería*, edited by Giancarlo Delgado Ramos, 1–9. Mexico City: UNAM-CIICH.

Deneault, Alain, and William Sacher. 2012. *Imperial Canada Inc.: Legal Haven of Choice for the World's Mining Industries.* Vancouver: Talonbooks.

Deoanandan, Kalawatie, and Michael Dougherty, eds. 2016. *Mining in Latin America: Critical Approaches in the New Extraction.* New York: Routledge.

Encounter of Mesoamerican Peoples. 2013. "Collectivo Oaxaqueño por la Defensa de los Territorios." Colectivo Oaxaqueño en Defensa de los Territorios, January 21. http://endefensadelosterritorios.org/2013/01/21/declaratoria-encuentro-de -pueblos-de-mesoamerica-si-a-la-vida-no-a-la-mineria/.

García Martínez, Anayeli. 2015. "Mujeres de Capulálpam: la defensa del territorio frente a la explotación minera." *La Jornada*, 8 November. https://www.proceso .com.mx/420151/mujeres-de-capulalpam-la-defensa-del-territorio-frente-a-la -explotacion-minera-dejar-en-borrador.

Garibay, Claudio. 2010. "Paisajes de acumulación minera por desposesión campesina en el México actual." In *La ecología política de la minería en América Latina: Aspectos socioeconómicos, legales y ambientales de la megaminería*, edited by Giancarlo Delgado Ramos, pp. 133–82. Mexico City: UNAM-CIICH. http:// biblioteca.clacso.edu.ar/Mexico/ceiich-unam/20170502045538/pdf_1467.pdf.

Garibay, Claudio, and Alejandra Balzaretti. 2009. "Goldcorp y la Reciprocidad Negativa en el Paisaje Minero de Mezcala, Guerrero." *Desacatos* 30: 91–110.

Gómez-Barris, Macarena. 2017. *The Extractive Zone: Social Ecologies and Decolonial Perspectives*. Durham, NC: Duke University Press.

Gonzalez Rodriguez, José de Jesús. 2011. "Minería en México: Referencias generales, regimen fiscal, concesiones y propuestas legislativas." Working paper no. 121. Mexico City: Centro de Estudios de la Opinión Publica.

Hernández Chávez, Alicia. 2006. *Mexico: A Brief History*. Los Angeles: University of California Press.

Hoogeveen, Dawn. 2015. "Sub-Surface Property, Free-Entry Mineral Staking and Settler Colonialism in Canada." *Antipode* 47 (1): 121–38.

López Austin, Alfredo. 1994. *Tamoachan and Tlalocan*. Mexico City: Fondo de Cultura Económica.

Martínez Luna, Jaime. 2010. "The Fourth Principle." In *New World of Indigenous Resistance: Noam Chomsky and Voices from North, South and Central America*, edited by Lois Meyer and Benjamín Maldonado Alvarado, 85–101. San Francisco: City Lights Books.

McDonnell, Emma. 2014. "The Co-constitution of Neo-liberalism, Extractive Industries, and Indigeneity: Anti-mining Protests in Puno, Peru." *Extractive Industries and Society* 2 (1): 112–23. http://dx.doi.org/10.1016/j.exis.2014.10.002.

McNamara, Patrick. 2007. *Sons of the Sierra: Juárez, Díaz and Ixtlán, Oaxaca 1855–1920*. Chapel Hill: University of North Carolina Press.

Méndez García, Elia. 2017. *De relámpagos y recuerdos: Minería y tradición serrana por la lucha por lo común*. Guadalajara: Universidad de Guadalajara-CIESAS Jorge Alonso.

Mraz Bartra, Anna Lee. 2013. "Los haceres de la sociedad en torno al medio ambiente: Capulálpam de Méndez, Sierra Juárez, Oaxaca, México." *Sociedad y Ambiente* 1 (3): 78–88.

No a la Mina Org. "Manifiesto de Capulapan de Méndez." May 2007. https:// noalamina.org/latinoamerica/mexico/item/614-oaxaca-mexico-la-mineria-y -la-defensa-de-los-recursos-naturales-en-la-sierra-norte.

Paredes, Julieta. 2011. *Hilando Fino, desde el feminismo comunitario*. La Paz: Comunidad Mujeres Creando Comunidad.

Rowlands, Lyndal. 2016. "Justice for Berta Caceres Incomplete without Land Rights: UN Rapporteur." Common Dreams, May 14. https://www.commondreams.org /news/2016/05/14/justice-berta-caceres-incomplete-without-land-rights-un -rapporteur.

Said, Edward. 1994. *Culture and Imperialism*. New York: Vintage Books.

Sawyer, Suzana, and Edmund T. Gomez. 2012. *The Politics of Resource Extraction: Indigenous Peoples, Multinational Corporations and the State*. Basingstoke, UK: Palgrave Macmillan.

Scott, Heidi. 2008 "Colonialism, Landscape and the Subterranean." *Geography Compass* 2 (6): 1853–69.

Sweet, Victoria. 2014. "Rising Waters, Rising Threats: The Human Trafficking of Indigenous Women in the Circumpolar World of the United States and Canada." Legal Studies Research Paper Series 12 (1). http://ssrn.com/abstract=2399074.

Tetreault, Darcy. 2016. "Free Market Mining in Mexico." *Critical Sociology* 42 (4–5): 643–59.

Velasco Murillo, Dana. 2013. "Laboring above Ground: Indigenous Women in New Spain's Silver Mining District, Zacatecas, Mexico, 1620–1770." *Hispanic American Historical Review* 93 (1): 3–32.

Vélez Ascensio, Octavio. 2011. "Impugnan concesiones mineras en Oaxaca". *La Jornada*, May 17. http://media.jornada.com.mx/2011/05/17/estados/034n1est.

Women's Earth Alliance and Native Youth and Sexual Health Network. 2016. "Violence on the Land, Violence on Our Bodies. Building an Indigenous Response to Environmental Violence." Berkeley and Toronto: WEA/NYSHN. http://landbodydefense.org/uploads/files/VLVBReportToolkit2016.pdf.

World Bank. 1991. *Staff Appraisal Report: Mexico, Mining Sector Restructuring Project*. May 30. http://documents.worldbank.org/curated/en/539581468299976772 /pdf/multi-page.pdf.

FURTHER READING

Estes, Nick, and Jaskiran Dhillon, eds. 2019. *Standing with Standing Rock: Voices from the #NODAPL Movement*. Minneapolis: University of Minnesota Press.

Wiebe, Sarah Marie. 2017. *Everyday Exposure: Indigenous Mobilization and Environmental Justice in Canada's Chemical Valley*. Vancouver: UBC Press.

Willow, Anna. "Indigenous ExtrActivism in Boreal Canada: Colonial Legacies, Contemporary Struggle and Sovereign Futures." *Humanities* 5 (3): 55. https://doi .org/10.3390/h5030055.

Women's Earth Alliance and Native Youth and Sexual Health Network. 2016. "Violence on the Land, Violence on Our Bodies: Building an Indigenous Response to Environmental Violence." Berkeley and Toronto: WEA/NYSHN. http://landbodydefense.org/uploads/files/VLVBReportToolkit2016.pdf.

The Promises and Perils of Hashtag Feminism

Tamara A. Small

Key terms: digital feminism, digital mediated consciousness raising, digilante, hacktivism, hashtag feminism, slacktivism

The Calgary Stampede is perhaps not the first thing that comes to mind when considering the transformation of feminism. The Calgary Stampede is an iconic Canadian event; billed as "The Greatest Outdoor Show on Earth," it is one of the world's largest rodeos and attracts millions of visitors to the City of Calgary each summer. In 2015, the hashtag #SafeStampede began to surface in response to the belief that "problematic sexualized behaviors and representations common to large festivals" had developed at the Stampede (Felt, Dumitrica, and Teruelle 2018, 73). The #SafeStampede campaign began on Twitter as a way to share personal stories of sexual harassment and raise awareness. More recently, it has grown to include a celebration of positive and respectful behaviour during the Stampede. The #SafeStampede campaign has even been endorsed by the Stampede organizers. #SafeStampede is a Canadian example of an important digital trend referred to as **hashtag feminism**. According to Mendes, Ringrose, and Keller (2018), it is one of the most popular forms of feminist activism today.

Communication technology, from brochures to radio to television, has long played an important role in formal politics. This chapter focuses on the highly political and gendered repercussions of social media. Here not only the institutional aspects but also the ideational (e.g., the impact on public discourse) and practical repercussions (e.g., as a form of mobilization) of social media are explored in terms of both these "turbulent times" and their "transformational possibilities."

The objective of this chapter is to explore the promises and the perils of hashtag feminism. The practical ramifications of digital technologies in contemporary gender politics are both transformational and turbulent. While hashtag feminism has roots in previous waves of feminism, it is wholly new in its method. Without a doubt, digital technologies such as Twitter have transformed and reinvigorated feminist movements by providing a new venue for feminist activities, especially among younger women. At the same time, however, this new venue has created new challenges for feminism and reignited old ones.

FEMINISM MEETS THE INTERNET

Digital technologies have been around for more than two decades. With more than four billion people worldwide using the internet and the average internet user spending around six hours per day using internet-connected devices and services (McDonald 2018), there are few areas of social, economic, cultural, and political life that have remained untouched. Almost from the very beginning, scholars have a focused on the relationship between democracy and digital technologies. The mobilization hypothesis, for instance, suggests that the internet creates greater opportunities for participation and political engagement. This is because digital technologies offer both political actors and the public "democratic potentials" that did not exist in the broadcast era (Bentivegna 2002, 54). The internet is interactive, inexpensive, decentralized, hypertextual, has great informational capabilities, and is multimedia. According to the mobilization hypothesis, digital technologies can lower the cost, both financially and temporally, of acquiring political information and participation, thereby creating opportunities for people from groups who have traditionally participated less in the formal political process (e.g., women, younger people, people of colour, Indigenous people) to increase their participation (Delli and Carpini 2000; Norris 2001). Moreover, digital technologies have created new modes of engagement that did not exist in the offline world, which can be used to allow people to express political views and engage in politics (Jensen, Jorba, and Anduiza 2012).

Politics in all its facets, including governments, political parties, legislators, interest groups, social movements, and individual citizens, has moved online. Feminist politics and activism is no different, as cyber-feminism, **digital feminism**, or online feminism is about "harnessing the power of online media to discuss, uplift, and activate gender equality and social justice" (Martin and Valenti 2013, 6). Indeed, some posit a very special relationship between digital technologies (especially social media) and feminism, in the sense that they have created a "new," or fourth, wave of feminism (see Baumgardner 2011; Munro 2013; Aitken 2017). Although, the notion of "waves" is contested and there appears to be little conceptual clarity of what constitutes the "fourth wave," nonetheless, Baumgardner suggests that different forms of mobilization appeared around 2008, when a critical mass of "tech-savvy and gender-sophisticated" feminists began to use the internet to express themselves (2011, n.p.).

In this period, there was a burst of online feminist activity, including blogs, e-zines, newsletters, YouTube videos, and social media accounts. Digital feminism can be considered transformative in that this activity is thought to be dominated by younger women, who now use the power of social media to grapple with many of the same issues that feminists of previous waves did (Aitken 2017; Looft 2017). While questions arise over whether increased use of digital technologies is sufficient to delineate a new era of feminism (Munro 2013), and regardless of whether a new wave exists or not, this chapter will show how and why an array of feminists are online and in a big way.

Within the realm of activism, digital technologies are seen to have the capacity to complement or expand repertoires of collective action for social movements such as feminism (Van Laer and Van Aelst 2010). Social movements, off- and online, seek to both affect public opinion and persuade institutional actors such as governments and political parties to pursue issues they advocate. In terms of complementing activism, digital technologies are an organizing, mobilizing, and communication tool for activists (Raynauld, Lalancette, and Tourigny-Koné 2016). For activist groups, digital technologies provide a quick, easy, and cost-efficient way to communicate with supporters, share information, raise awareness, and/or solicit financial support (van der Graaf, Otjes, and Rasmussen 2016). Digital technologies not only have supported or complemented real-world collective action, they also have expanded the realm of activism by creating new, virtual realms that are based completely in digital technologies (Van Laer and Van Aelst 2010). Activities such as **hacktivism**[1] (Gunkel 2005), Facebook groups, alternative media, and hashtag activism are examples. There is no offline version of these forms of collective action; they exist on and because of digital technologies.

The capacities to complement and expand collective action are both present in digital feminism. SlutWalk and the 2017 Women's March on Washington are just two examples of the former. The SlutWalk movement began in Toronto after a police officer, in a talk to female students at York University, advised that not dressing like a slut was a way to avoid victimization. Students used social media to organize a protest against slut-shaming in Toronto in 2011; this led to SlutWalk protests in cities around the world, which continue to date. More recently, the Women's March on Washington began as a grassroots campaign on Facebook following the election of US President Donald Trump (Nicolini and Hansen, 2018). In a short time frame, social media were used to organize the march and attract hundreds of thousands of protesters to Washington, DC, while smaller protests took place around the world (Lapowsky 2017). Hashtag feminism is an example of the latter, a virtual collective action repertoire. Hashtag feminism is a subset of hashtag activism. According to Phillip Howard, hashtag activism is "what happens when someone tries to raise public awareness of a political issue using some clever or biting keyword on social media" (quoted in Brewster 2014, n.p.). Prominent examples of hashtag activism include #Kony2012, #BlackLivesMatter, and #ALSIceBucketChallenge.

Hashtag activism is a social media phenomenon. Because of this, it is worth briefly discussing social media, especially Twitter, in more detail. Social media allow users to easily create, share, collaborate, and communicate with other users (Small 2016). Twitter is a type of social media called a micro-blog, where users can post a 280-character message or "tweet."[2] Despite the character limit, tweets can convey a lot of information due to the inclusion of photos, videos, and shortened links to other web content. A hashtag is another way that users can convey particular information within a tweet; it is a keyword or phrase that describes a tweet, connects it to other information, and aides in content searching (Small 2011). Hashtags were not developed by Twitter; rather, they were a community-driven convention that started in 2007. They are now used in other social media such as Facebook and Instagram and are part of everyday speech (Kanski 2017). Twitter is one of the world's most popular websites; it ranks 12th on Alexa's top 500 sites on the web at the time of writing (Alexa 2017). Tweets have the capacity to be seen by a large audience when using popular hashtags, and because Twitter accounts are often not private (as compared to Facebook). Some hashtags gain considerable traction and begin to "trend"—perhaps even being listed in a "trends for you" sidebar in the application.

As this chapter will show, hashtags have the capacity to bring women's issues to the forefront of the political and public agenda. Table 5 lists a small sample of notable feminist hashtags of the past few years. This is by no means a representative list of feminist hashtags; they were merely selected to demonstrate the variety and diversity of feminist hashtags that have come into public consciousness in the Western (mainly American) context. Though a number of Canadian-born hashtags did trend during the Jian Ghomeshi affair (see Craig in this volume), including #BeenRapedNeverReported, #IBelieveLucy, #IBelieveSurvivors, and #WeBelieveSurvivors, it does appear that hashtag feminism is a global trend. For example, #aufschrei is a German hashtag that shares experiences of sexism and sexual assaults. Still in use today, it was the German hashtag of the year in 2013 (Drüeke and Zobl 2016). In response to a satirical video on sexual abuse, rape, and the culture of blaming the victim in India, #victimblaming arose (Guha 2015). In South Korea, the hashtag #iamafeminist trended for three months in 2015 and was important in initiating activism against misogyny both on- and offline in that country (Kim 2017). From these examples (and those in table 5), we can see that feminist hashtags often arise out of real situations and contemporary discussions and they often challenge contemporary sexism, misogyny, and rape culture (Mendes, Keller, and Ringrose 2019). In examining the academic literature and popular discussions of feminist hashtags since 2013, it becomes evident that they have brought a significant number of benefits to the feminist movement. However, the same affordances that make Twitter a great tool for feminists also create a number of issues. I now turn to a discussion on the promises and perils of hashtag feminism.

THE PROMISES OF HASHTAG FEMINISM

This section explores four opportunities that Twitter provides to feminist activism: **digital mediated consciousness raising**; space for intersectional feminism to flourish; support for participants; and public awareness of feminist issues. Twitter creates a "space—even a community" for communication, discussion, debate, support, and awareness of the issues facing modern women and girls (Golbeck, Ash, and Cabrera 2017, para. 11).

Consciousness raising is the first opportunity offered by hashtag feminism (Murphy 2013; Clark 2014; Mendes, Keller, and Ringrose 2019).

Table 5 Notable Feminist Hashtags

Hashtag	Year	Creator	Description	Example Tweet
#SolidarityIsForWhiteWomen	2013	Mikki Kendall	Used to air grievances about the problematic behaviour of mainstream white feminists. It was intended to be "Twitter shorthand for how often feminists of colour are told that the racism they experience 'isn't a feminist issue'" (Kendall 2013).	I want everyone who got offended by #solidarityisforwhitewomen to interrogate why white women are trying to claim & re-frame Black history.
#NotYourAsianSidekick	2013	Suey Park	Created to push the conversation of Asian American feminists into the broader feminist discourse. Also used to focus on stereotypes of Asian-American women in the media.	We're still waiting for u to hire Asian American writers and comedians. We are not a punch line #SaturdayNightlies #NotYourAsianSidekick.
#BringBackOurGirls	2014	Obiageli Ezekwesili	In response to the abduction of 276 Nigerian schoolgirls in 2014. Used to call for action by Nigerian and international governments.	112 of their former schoolmates are still being held captive by #BokoHaram. The fight continues to #BringBackOurGirls!
#YesAllWomen	2014	Unknown	Appeared following the 2014 Isla Vista killings. It is used to share examples or stories of misogyny and violence against women.	An adult man literally just barked at me from his car ... #YesAllWomen.
#WhyIStayed	2014	Beverly Gooden	Used to illuminate why it is so difficult for women to leave abusive relationships. It developed in response to the video of Baltimore Ravens linebacker Ray Rice assaulting his wife (then fiancée) Janay Palmer in an elevator.	#WhyIStayed ... because I didn't think anyone would believe me.
#safetytipsforladies	2014	Hilary Bowman-Smart	A sardonic hashtag about how tired women are of being told to do stupid, ineffective, unrealistic things to avoid being raped.	don't be anywhere. 100% of rapes happen in places & locations #safetytipsforladies.

Hashtag	Year	Creator	Description	Example
#RapeCultureIs When	2014	Zerlina Maxwell	Used to contribute to awareness of the various perceptions of rape culture.	#rapecultureiswhen they are still calling this convicted rapist a "swimmer" in headlines.
#BeenRaped NeverReported	2014	Antonia Zerbisias and Sue Montgomery	A Canadian hashtag developed in response to women coming forward with allegations of violent encounters with Jian Ghomeshi in the press rather than to law enforcement. #IBelieveLucy, #IBelieveSurvivors, and #WeBelieveSurvivors are other hashtags related to the Ghomeshi sexual assault trial.	Ibelievelucy #ibelievewomen And yes, I've been raped (more than once) and never reported it. #BeenRapedNeverReported
#AskHerMore	2015	Representation Project	A campaign of the Representation Project to call out sexist reporting and suggest ways to (re)focus on women's achievements.	Defining a woman by the way she wore her hair is insulting and it's particularly insulting given Barbara Bush's legacy. We expect more of you, @NPR #AskHerMore.
#distractingly sexy	2015		Used by female scientists who tagged photos of themselves with this hashtag in response to a speech given by a British Nobel Laureate about women in the laboratory being a distraction.	Feeling pretty #distractinglysexy sitting in a snow bank waiting for a bird to show up. #fieldworkfun.
#MeToo	2017		Used to demonstrate the prevalence of sexual assault and harassment, especially in the workplace. It follows the public revelations of sexual misconduct allegations against film producer Harvey Weinstein.	I was a good scientist but I needed to do something more than fight this everyday. I moved away from science to education. Good choice for me but sad that I couldn't stay in the field I love most. Signed. #metoo.

Consciousness raising is not a new practice within feminism. Starting in (at least) the second wave, consciousness raising occurred in small groups and face-to-face conversations, creating a space for women to share personal experiences of gender discrimination (Sowards and Renegar 2004). The difference here is that the consciousness raising occurs through hashtags on Twitter. As a form of digital mediated consciousness raising, hashtag feminism provides "a better understanding of feminist politics and acts as a low-barrier entrance for other types of (feminist) activism and political engagement" (Mendes, Keller, and Ringrose 2019, 5). As table 5 shows, each hashtag can bring a different feminist issue to the forefront. For instance, #MeToo and #distractinglysexy focus on workplace issues. The 2017 re-launch of the hashtag #MeToo has its roots in Hollywood. It followed the public revelations of sexual misconduct allegations against film producer Harvey Weinstein. More recently, it has become a global movement by bringing the issues of workplace harassment and sexual violence into the public consciousness. The hashtag #distractinglysexy is a more sardonic hashtag with a serious purpose. It raises issues around the complexity of women working in STEM.[3] It arose after a speech by Nobel Prize winner Tim Hunt, where he talked about the "trouble with girls" in labs at a conference of science journalists in 2015. Of this, he said: "Three things happen when [women] are in the lab, you fall in love with them, they fall in love with you, and when you criticise them they cry" (quoted in Ratcliffe 2015). Accompanying the hashtag, female scientists posted comical photos of themselves in the types of clothing and/or equipment they wear to conduct their daily work, including lab coats, goggles, and full body hazmat-style suits, highlighting that women in labs are there to perform their jobs and are not sex objects. These examples show that some hashtags have the capacity to make visible the "injustices and abuses" that "hide in plain sight" (Thrift 2014, 1091).

The reach of hashtag feminism can be extensive. Because hashtag feminism takes place on popular social media, this conversation moves beyond small group conversations, instead becoming a sustained transnational conversation between women and girls. The #MeToo hashtag was used 12 million times in the first 24 hours, in many languages, including Arabic, Farsi, French, Hindi, and Spanish (CBS/AP 2017; Mahdavi 2018). Feminist hashtags allow people to see issues of gender-based violence, rape culture, and workplace harassment not as personal problems but as structural problems that exist in a wide variety of socio-political contexts (Mendes, Ringrose, and Keller 2018). Moreover, hashtag feminism provides an entry for women and girls, especially younger ones, to participate in broader feminist activity.

Related to this digital mediated consciousness raising, hashtag feminism is seen as a space for intersectionality to flourish by allowing a multiplicity of voices across sexuality, race, and class lines to be heard and demand recognition (Clark 2014). The literature suggests that Twitter allows women of colour to "speak to each other across borders and boundaries" (Loza 2014). Table 5 highlights two such hashtags, #SolidarityIsForWhiteWomen and #NotYour-AsianSidekick. Both are attempts to raise intersectional issues within online feminist discourse. Created by Black feminist Mikki Kendall, #SolidarityIs-ForWhiteWomen focused on challenging the white feminist movement and the exclusion of people of colour from mainstream feminism (Loza 2014). Williams (2015) also highlights the importance of Twitter for Black feminists. She notes that the hashtags that developed about the Black victim in the Steubenville rape case[4] allowed women of colour to unite and inform. This is especially important as she contends that white feminists did not initially take on the Steubenville rape case. The intention behind #NotYourAsianSide-kick, according to hashtag creator Suey Park, was to create a new space for Asian American feminism and for a discussion on the stereotypes and racism directed towards Asian women (BBC Trending 2013; Capachi 2013). In the first 24 hours, the hashtag was used more than 45,000 times worldwide. A more recent intersectional hashtag is #MuslimWomensDay. The 2017 hashtag was established to allow young Muslim women to define their own stories of what it means to be a contemporary Muslim woman and to push back against Islamophobic stereotypes of Muslim women (Pennington 2018). These examples provide evidence of "people of colour resisting authority, opting out of conforming to the status quo, and seeking liberation, all by way of documentation in digital spaces" (Conley 2014, 1111). While women of colour see hashtag feminism—and social media more broadly—as an inclusive and participatory space, as per the mobilization hypothesis, there is also a tension where an intersectional difference can be seen as dividing the movement, an issue I discuss later in this chapter.

While hashtag feminism, as a form of digital mediated consciousness raising, has the capacity to affect the direction of the feminist movement, it also has a personal impact on participants. Many commentators suggest that the sharing of experiences, especially those related to sexual violence, allows participants to get and provide support to others within the digital space (Murphy 2013; Clark 2016). We see evidence of this in the empirical analyses of hashtag feminism. Mendes, Ringrose, and Keller (2018) conducted interviews with hashtag feminism participants and note that the public response garnered by tweeting was considered unexpected but meaningful by participants. Support could be in the form of the tweet being "favourited" or "retweeted," or through a direct message from a stranger. Support was also mentioned by participants who engaged in an anti-sexism in science hashtag study (Golbeck, Ash, and Cabrera 2017); 56.2 per cent of respondents felt they received support from the broader community.

Beyond the benefits of hashtag feminism *within* the community of women and girls, it also has the capacity to raise awareness *outside* of it, within the broader public discourse (see the discussion on public discourse by Craig in this volume). As mentioned, the term "trending" describes when a hashtag becomes extremely popular at a particular time. When this happens, the hashtag is listed on the main page of Twitter. The older media (e.g., broadcast and newspaper), or legacy media, pay attention to what is trending. Journalists use Twitter as a tool for finding and researching story ideas (Hermida 2013). For many, their experience with #MeToo, #WhyIStayed, or #BeenRapedNeverReported will not be from being a participant in the hashtag or even being on Twitter; they will read or watch about the trending hashtag in the news. Clark analysed the news media coverage of #WhyIStayed and argues that it had an "amplification effect" for the movement. Indeed, the coverage of #WhyIStayed was favourable to the movement because the media published "stories that worked from the assumption that domestic violence victims should not be blamed for their own abuse" (2016, 799). The hashtag was covered extensively in major media outlets such as *Time*, *BBC*, and *Al Jazeera*. Moreover, hashtag creator Beverly Gooden was featured in numerous television broadcasts and penned editorials in papers such as the *New York Times* (Gooden 2014). Similarly, Williams (2015) argues that Black feminists used hashtags such as #StandWithJada, #JusticeForJada, #JadaCounterPose, and #SupportJada to spread information about the victim in the Steubenville rape. In doing so, they eventually brought the story to the attention of the media. When legacy media take up a hashtag, the message of the movement permeates the broader public consciousness, creating a conversation beyond feminist circles. While it is important not to assume causation, it appears that this broader conversation can sometimes have real-world impacts (Rivers 2017). Indeed, Tim Hunt resigned his academic position in light of the #distractinglysexy comments. #BringBackOurGirls put pressure on the Nigerian and US governments (Khoja-Moolji 2015), while #AskHerMore shamed journalists into asking different questions to female actors and athletes (The Representation Project, n.d.). To be sure, not all feminist hashtags are taken up by legacy media. Even though the Indian hashtag #victimblaming received some coverage in Western media, it was virtually ignored by the media in India (Guha 2015).

The four opportunities discussed, and the examples provided, should demonstrate the transformational power of digital technologies within gender politics. It would be a mistake to suggest that these issues and topics would not be discussed if not for digital technologies; that said, they transform the reach and the place in public discussion of women's issues.

THE PERILS OF HASHTAG FEMINISM

Despite the aforementioned opportunities for hashtag feminism, turbulence has invariably arisen. Of late, there are a number of criticisms to be found in popular feminist media. For instance, Zoe Strimpel argues that hashtag feminism is lazy. She writes:

> "Me too" is intended to demonstrate just how widespread is the sexual harassment of women and to galvanise as many women as possible to "speak out," to "tell their stories"—curiously dated phrases that echo the consciousness-raising lingo of the feminist movement in the 1970s. Except that unlike the Women's Liberation Movement of the 1970s, this is just hashtag feminism. It is full of grievance but utterly lacking in solutions or even ideas. (2017, n.p.)

Some of the challenges of hashtag feminism are related to the nature of digital technologies, while others are related to broader issues of feminism. The first challenge is **slacktivism**. It should be pointed out that the accusation of slacktivism is associated with many online activist activities, not just hashtag feminism. Slacktivism, a portmanteau of slacker and activism, is a pejorative term suggesting that many online political actions have little real-world impact. Social media makes political action so easy that its main purpose is increasing "the feel-good factor of the participants" rather than real social or political change (Christensen 2011, para. 3). For instance, some see the "liking" or joining of charities, political organizations, or political issues on Facebook as slacktivism. Indeed research suggests that these activities actually make it less likely for people to engage in meaningful offline activities such as donating (Kristofferson, White, and Peloza 2013).

Hashtag feminism suffers from similar accusations, as highlighted by Strimpel (2017) above. Hashtag feminists participate indirectly from a distance rather than engaging in real-world organizations or on the streets. For instance, while posting a tweet about why one stayed or a picture of oneself in an unsexy lab uniform may be cathartic for the participants, they seem insufficiently linked to larger organization and movement regarding gendered violence or women in STEM. To what extent do these tweets even effect political and social changes to these issues? As slacktivism, social media does not allow for a sustainable network of activists to be developed. Rather, a trending hashtag gives the impression of connectivity among individual social media users who are actually unconnected.

The slacktivism accusation is debatable: as we have seen, hashtag feminism is extremely important to those who participate in it. Julia Schuster's (2013) research suggests slacktivism accusations within the movement might be the result of generational differences among feminists—between the so-called third and fourth wavers. Her research suggests there are differences between older and younger feminists in New Zealand both in terms of their technology use (one group is online, the other less so) and the methods used by each group. On this latter point, Linder et al. (2016) note that younger people do not distinguish between off- and online activism. For them activism is activism regardless of where it takes place; therefore, they are engaging in it.

Internet trolls are another challenge of hashtag feminism. The term is internet slang for a person who makes a deliberately offensive, inflammatory, or provocative statement online (Underwood and Welser 2011). Like slacktivism, internet trolling is not necessarily a hashtag feminist problem per se; instead, it relates more to the nature of digital technologies. That said, women and girls face significant challenges on the internet. An Australian study found that more than three-quarters of Australian women under the age of 30 have faced some form of online harassment (Norton by Symantec 2016). They suggest that online harassment of women and girls is becoming an "established norm." Looking at online feminist activities, Mendes, Ringrose, and Keller (2018) came to similar conclusions. Their survey found trolling and online abuse a common experience, with 72 per cent of survey respondents reporting harassment in response to their feminist views and challenges to rape culture online. Similarly, Golbeck, Ash, and Cabrera (2017) found that roughly 70 per cent of their survey respondents listed trolling as the main disadvantage to participation. Some suggest that the trolling of women is a unique type of trolling. Mantilla (2015) calls this behaviour "gendertrolling," while Jane (2016) calls it "gendered e-bile." This type of trolling is character-ized by gender-based insults and vicious language (e.g., ugly, bitch, fat, slut, etc.), and often features threats of violence. Indeed, the threat of rape is fre-quently used in response to women online (Cole 2015), as are death threats. Moreover, Mantilla (2015) suggests this type of online harassment tends to be sustained over a long period of time by a number of coordinated attackers.

Research also shows that online feminists are developing coping strategies for dealing with trolling and harassment. This includes blocking the accounts of online harassers or avoiding engagement with them—as the old adage says, "Don't feed the trolls" (Mendes, Ringrose, and Keller 2018). Another option for dealing with attackers is engaging in **digilante** (a portmanteau of digi-tal and vigilante) tactics such as calling out and/or attempting to "name and shame" attackers (Jane 2016, 285). These types of activities are necessary, as law enforcement bodies, policy-makers, and digital technology companies have yet to produce adequate responses to online harassment and the trolling of women. Indeed, Twitter has recently been called out by Amnesty Interna-tional (2018), suggesting that the social media giant is undermining the rights of women by allowing abuse against women to flourish on its platform. Twit-ter launched a campaign called "Standing with Women Around the World" in 2018 to address these issues. It remains to be seen if Twitter can tangibly address the online harassment that exists within its application. Until then, Twitter remains a space where women are not free from violence.

Earlier, I suggested that intersectionality was an opportunity and a chal-lenge for feminist movements online. As mentioned, hashtags such as #YesAllWhiteWomen, #NotYourAsianSidekick, #whitewomenprivilege, and #SolidarityIsForWhiteWomen were created to call out white feminists. While they are important for women of colour in feminist movements, these hashtags have led to concerns that Twitter is a "toxic" and "divisive" space for feminism. In her popular essay "The Trouble with Twitter Feminism," Megan Murphy writes: "For the most part, I haven't found Twitter to be a positive experi-ence. And I'm not just talking about harassment from misogynists, I'm talk-ing about the internal shit. The mean girls–style popularity contest so many of those on feminist Twitter engage in" (2013, n.p.). Adele Wilde-Blavatsky, in a *Huffington Post* (UK) essay, accused #SolidarityIsForWhiteWomen of being "particularly guilty of such 'white women bashing'" (2013, n.p.). Other feminists decried the airing of dirty laundry within the movement on Twit-ter and the lack of unity among feminists. #StopBlamingWhiteWomen and #WeNeedUnity developed in response. These types of criticism, particularly of Black feminists, have led to further criticisms of the criticizers (see Park and Leonard 2014). According to Risam, "white feminists rather conservatively rewrite intersectional critique into simply making trouble, while, comically, suggesting that people who foreground race in their analysis are the real racists" (2015, n.p.). To be sure, the intersectional divides of race, gender identity, and sexuality existed in the feminist movement from the very earliest waves, but Twitter has solidified these criticisms into a series of hashtags and made them very public.

The final peril of hashtag feminism is that the anti-feminist countermovement has also made its way on to Twitter. "Operation Lollipop" is one notable example. Around 2014, a hashtag began trending on Twitter: #EndFathersDay. It featured tweets suggesting that Father's Day was a holiday that celebrates misogyny. One of the earliest tweets came from Phoebe Kwon, who describes herself as a "Lesbian, Korean American, Feminist": "#EndFathersDay because men shouldn't even be allowed around children." After about six months, it was revealed that a group on 4chan[5] started the hashtag under the name "Operation Lollipop." This group masqueraded as women of colour by creating fake Twitter accounts to post provocative tweets that made feminists look extreme. Indeed, the photo of "Phoebe Kwon" was simply a stock photo of an Asian woman. Until that was known, this hashtags trended as fake Twitter users, and eventually real ones, began using it. It became more noticeable when people began to react to it. Indeed, at its height, #EndFathersDay had been tweeted 60,000 times. Moreover, news organizations like Fox and Friends discussed #EndFathersDay at its height. Overall, "Operation Lollipop" sought to delegitimize online feminists. What is interesting about this case is that "Operation Lollipop" appeared to understand the online feminist movement. By using hashtags, they showed that they understood the growing importance of Twitter to these so-called fourth wavers. Moreover, by masquerading as women of colour, the members of "Operation Lollipop" also demonstrated that they understood the complex and fraught relationship between feminists of colour and white feminists online, discussed earlier. According to Ganzer (2014), 4chan was successful in damaging the online feminist community's reputation.

#WomenAgainstFeminism or WAF is another example of a backlash hashtag. It was created in response to the #YesAllWomen campaign in 2004. #WomenAgainstFeminism is used by those who reject feminism and the feminist label. Beyond the hashtag, WAF also has a website, Facebook page, and YouTube channel. A common trope is the posting of a selfie with a handwritten sign responding to the statement "I don't need feminism because ..." For instance: "I don't need feminism because I believe in equality, not entitlements and supremacy. I don't need feminism because I made my *own* choice to be a stay at home mom and my working husband should NOT be harassed. I don't need feminism because regretting sex doesn't make it rape."

Other WAF tweets include text and images that mock feminism, using caricatures such as the man-hating feminist or the unattractive feminist (Young 2014). According to Christiansen and Høyer (2015), these posts centre on themes such as modern feminism not representing the person's posting the critique, and that feminists continually portray women as victims and deprive women of agency. Moreover, DeKeseredy, Fabricius, and Hall-Sanchez (2015) are concerned that WAF helps to fuel the online men's rights movement. The WAF countermovement is not unsubstantial. At the time of writing, the Facebook page of Women Against Feminism had 45,253 likes. Other countermovement hashtags of this type include #FeminismIsCancer, #FeminismDestroys, and #antifeminist. There are also numerous sexist hashtags found on Twitter such as #LiesToldByFemales, #IHateFemalesWho, #RulesForGirls, #MyGirlfriend-NotAllowedTo, #ThatsWhatSlutsDo, and #ItsNotRapeIf. These hashtags promote sexism by suggesting that men are responsible for regulating women's behaviour and by promoting rape myths (Fox, Cruz, and Lee 2015). Another hashtag, #NotAllMen, was a response to #YesAllWomen. While the hashtag #NotAllMen and the broader "Not All Men" movement acknowledges that rape, sexism, and misogyny are real, they suggest that not all men participate in such behaviours and are intended to address generalizations about how men behave. That said, critics of #NotAllMen suggest it "articulates a defensive rebuttal against feminist critiques of sexism and misogyny" (Thrift 2014, 1091). To be sure, anti-feminist positions are not new; however, the same opportunities presented to feminists through social media are also available to those who seek to oppose and belittle the movement. And like the feminist movement, these counter-hashtags have also captured the attention of the media and, therefore, the broader public (see Young 2014).

CONCLUSION

This chapter has explored hashtag feminism, mainly in the Anglo-American context. There is growing academic attention to this topic. Indeed, the journal *Feminist Media Studies* has dedicated at least three "Commentary and Criticism" sections to the discussion of various hashtags (many of which are cited in this chapter). Drawing on this important work, this chapter shows that hashtag feminism is a new digital collective action repertoire that has developed out of the affordances of Twitter. Hashtag feminism exists only because Twitter exists. Twitter takes disparate users and enables communities of conversation about the ongoing problem of violence against girls and women and issues within the feminist movement (Mendes, Ringrose, and Keller, 2018). While the rhetoric in these hashtags is not particularly new, how it looks is very different. As we have seen, hashtag feminism provides a large group of people the opportunity to engage in activism—raising awareness of issues within and outside of the movement. Dobrowolsky (2014) has suggested that the feminist movement was in need of reinvigoration; long-term activists were worn out and the movement had not captured the imagination of younger women. Hashtag feminism has provided one type of reinvigoration, especially among younger women. Hashtag feminism can also have real-world effects on politics and government.

In the months following the insurgence of #MeToo, several female Members of Parliament spoke out about the toxic sexist culture on the Hill (Campbell and McIntyre 2018). And several countries, including Canada, introduced legislation aimed at strengthening and expanding laws surrounding sexual violence and harassment.[6] At the same time, however, hashtag feminism is not without its problems. Some are new problems that plague all sorts of activist organizations within digital technologies. Other "new" digitally mediated issues are problems of feminism that existed long before the internet. Ironically, it is the same features that have been a boon for feminism on Twitter that have also caused a number of problems for the movement.

Hashtag feminism is just one form of online feminism. Initiatives such as Hollaback! have also been created online. Hollaback! is a grassroots initiative to raise awareness about and combat street harassment. Starting in 2010 in the United States, Hollaback! is now a global movement. Digital technologies have allowed for the establishment of feminist magazines such as *Bustle* and *Jezebel*. There are also feminist blogs, vlogs, and podcasts where feminists create and produce their own content. Feminist gaming is also a subset of this category. Moreover, as mentioned, digital technologies have been crucial in complementing feminist activism offline. Protests can be organized, publicized, and documented in ways that did not exist before. Traditional feminist organizations such as Planned Parenthood can be supported through online donations. That said, because of the trending potential of Twitter, hashtag feminism is an extremely important and popular type of digital feminism.

The tension between transformation and turbulence can be seen in the fact that the term "fourth-wave feminism" remains in debate in the literature and the movement. There can be little doubt that digital technologies have been transformative for the feminist movement. Twitter allows for a mobilizing of participation and networking for feminism worldwide in ways that could not happen in the pre-internet world.

DISCUSSION QUESTIONS

1. In what ways have the internet and social media transformed the feminist movement?
2. Is hashtag feminism a form of slacktivism?
3. What is an internet troll? Is gender-based trolling different than other forms of trolling?
4. Why is intersectionality both good and bad for digital feminism?
5. Do the promises of hashtag feminism outweigh its perils?

NOTES

1 Hacktivism draws on the creative use of digital technologies for the purposes of facilitating online protests, performing civil disobedience in online spaces (Gunkel 2005). Groups like WikiLeaks epitomize hacktivist practices.
2 Tweets were originally restricted to 140 characters and were increased to 280 characters in November 2017.
3 STEM refers to the fields of science, technology, engineering, and mathematics, which have historically low participation among women.
4 The Steubenville rape case occurred in Steubenville, Ohio, in 2012, when a high school girl, incapacitated by alcohol, was publicly and repeatedly sexually assaulted by her peers, several of whom documented the acts on social media. The case raised numerous issues of rape culture as the media coverage portrayed the perpetrators as promising football players and the victim as a drunk (Penny 2013). Two of the men were convicted in juvenile court for the rape of a minor the following year.
5 4chan is an English-language imageboard website that has been instrumental for the formation or popularization of several internet memes and internet pranks. Users generally post anonymously. Indeed, the hacktivist group Anonymous developed out of 4chan.
6 For examples, see Bill C-65, An Act to Amend the Canada Labour Code (Harassment and Violence); the Parliamentary Employment and Staff Relations Act; and the Budget Implementation Act.

REFERENCES

Aitken, Mel. 2017. "Feminism: A Fourth to Be Reckoned With? Reviving Community Education Feminist Pedagogies in a Digital Age." *Concept* 8 (1): 1–18.

Alexa. 2017. "Alexa Top 500 Global Sites." Alexa: An Amazon Company. https://www.alexa.com/topsites. Accessed May 11, 2017.

Amnesty International. 2018. "Online Abuse of Women Thrives as Twitter Fails to Respect Women's Rights." Amnesty International, March 21. https://www.amnesty.org/en/latest/news/2018/03/toxic-twitter-online-abuse-and-violence-against-women/.

Baumgardner, Jennifer. 2011. "Is There a Fourth Wave? Does It Matter?" Feminist.com. https://www.feminist.com/resources/artspeech/genwom/baumgardner2011.html.

BBC Trending. 2013. "#NotYourAsianSidekick Goes Global." *BBC News*, December 16. https://www.bbc.com/news/blogs-trending-25399314.

Bentivegna, Sara. 2002. "Politics and New Media." In *The Handbook of New Media*, edited by Leah A. Lievrouw and Sonia Livingstone, 50–61. London: Sage.

Brewster, Shaquille. 2014. "After Ferguson: Is 'Hashtag Activism' Spurring Policy Changes?" *NBC News*, December 14. https://www.nbcnews.com/politics/first-read/after-ferguson-hashtag-activism-spurring-policy-changes-n267436.

Campbell, Meagan, and Catherine McIntyre. 2018. "The #MeToo Reckoning Comes to Parliament Hill: 'I Am Done. I Am Mad.'" *Macleans.ca*, March 7. https://www.macleans.ca/politics/ottawa/sexual-harassment-on-parliament-hill/.

Capachi, Casey. 2013. "Suey Park: Asian American Women Are #NotYourAsianSidekick." *Washington Post* (blog), December 17. https://www.washingtonpost.com/blogs/she-the-people/wp/2013/12/17/suey-park-asian-american-women-are-notyourasiansidekick/.

CBS/AP. 2017. "More Than 12M 'Me Too' Facebook Posts, Comments, Reactions in 24 Hours." *CBS News*, October 17. https://www.cbsnews.com/news/metoo-more-than-12-million-facebook-posts-comments-reactions-24-hours/.

Christensen, Henrik Serup. 2011. "Political Activities on the Internet: Slacktivism or Political Participation by Other Means?" *First Monday* 16 (2). http://firstmonday.org/article/view/3336/2767.

Christiansen, Alex Phillip Lyng, and Ole Izard Høyer. 2015. "Women against Feminism: Exploring Discursive Measures and Implications of Anti-feminist Discourse." *Globe: A Journal of Language, Culture and Communication* 2: 70–90.

Clark, Rosemary. 2014. "#NotBuyingIt: Hashtag Feminists Expand the Commercial Media Conversation." *Feminist Media Studies* 14 (6): 1108–10.

———. 2016. "'Hope in a Hashtag': The Discursive Activism of #WhyIStayed." *Feminist Media Studies* 16 (5): 788–804.

Cole, Kirsti K. 2015. "'It's Like She's Eager to Be Verbally Abused': Twitter, Trolls, and (En)Gendering Disciplinary Rhetoric." *Feminist Media Studies* 15 (2): 356–58.

Conley, Tara L. 2014. "From #RenishaMcBride to #RememberRenisha: Locating Our Stories and Finding Justice." *Feminist Media Studies* 14 (6): 1111–13.

DeKeseredy, Walter S., Alexis Fabricius, and Amanda Hall-Sanchez. 2015. "Fueling Aggrieved Entitlement: The Contribution of Women against Feminism Postings." *CRIMSOC: The Journal of Social Criminology* 4: 1–25.

Delli Carpini, Michael X. 2000. "Gen.Com: Youth, Civic Engagement, and the New Information Environment." *Political Communication* 17 (4): 341–49.

Dobrowolsky, Alexandra. 2014. "The Women's Movement in Flux: Feminism and Framing, Passion, and Politics." In *Group Politics and Social Movements in Canada*, 2nd ed., edited by Miriam Catherine Smith, 151–78. Toronto: University of Toronto Press.

Drüeke, Ricarda, and Elke Zobl. 2016. "Online Feminist Protest against Sexism: The German-Language Hashtag #aufschrei." *Feminist Media Studies* 16 (1): 35–54.

Felt, Mylynn, Delia Dumitrica, and Rhon Teruelle. 2018. "Social Media Obstacles in Grassroots Civic Mobilizations." In *Proceedings of the 9th International Conference on Social Media and Society*, 71–81. New York: Association for Computing Machinery. https://doi.org/10.1145/3217804.3217899.

Fox, Jesse, Carlos Cruz, and Ji Young Lee. 2015. "Perpetuating Online Sexism Offline: Anonymity, Interactivity, and the Effects of Sexist Hashtags on Social Media." *Computers in Human Behavior* 52 (November): 436–42.

Ganzer, Miranda. 2014. "In Bed with the Trolls." *Feminist Media Studies* 14 (6): 1098–100.

Golbeck, Jennifer, Summer Ash, and Nicole Cabrera. 2017. "Hashtags as Online Communities with Social Support: A Study of Anti-Sexism-in-Science Hashtag Movements." *First Monday* 22 (9). http://www.ojphi.org/ojs/index.php/fm/article/view/7572.

Gooden, Beverly. 2014. "Why We Stayed." *New York Times*, 13 October. https://kristof.blogs.nytimes.com/2014/10/13/why-we-stayed/?_r=2.

Guha, Pallavi. 2015. "Hash Tagging but Not Trending: The Success and Failure of The News Media to Engage with Online Feminist Activism in India." *Feminist Media Studies* 15 (1): 155–57.

Gunkel, David J. 2005. "Editorial: Introduction to Hacking and Hacktivism." *New Media & Society* 7 (5): 595–97.

Hermida, Alfred. 2013. "#JOURNALISM: Reconfiguring Journalism Research about Twitter, One Tweet at a Time." *Digital Journalism* 1 (3): 295–313.

Jane, Emma A. 2016. "Online Misogyny and Feminist Digilantism." *Continuum* 30 (3): 284–97.

Jensen, Michael J., Laia Jorba, and Eva Anduiza. 2012. "Introduction." In *Digital Media and Political Engagement Worldwide*, edited by Eva Aduiza, Michael J. Jensen, and Laia Jorba, 1–15. Cambridge: Cambridge University Press.

Kanski, Alison. 2017. "5 Ways the Hashtag Influenced Our Culture." *PR Week*, August 23. https://www.prweek.com/article/1442689.

Kendall, Mikki. 2013. "#SolidarityIsForWhiteWomen: Women of Color's Issue with Digital Feminism." *The Guardian*, August 14. https://www.theguardian.com/commentisfree/2013/aug/14/solidarityisforwhitewomen-hashtag-feminism.

Khoja-Moolji, Shenila. 2015. "Becoming an 'Intimate Publics': Exploring the Affective Intensities of Hashtag Feminism." *Feminist Media Studies* 15 (2): 347–50.

Kim, Jinsook. 2017. "#iamafeminist as the 'Mother Tag': Feminist Identification and Activism against Misogyny on Twitter in South Korea." *Feminist Media Studies* 17 (5): 804–20.

Kristofferson, Kirk, Katherine White, and John Peloza. 2013. "The Nature of Slacktivism: How the Social Observability of an Initial Act of Token Support Affects Subsequent Prosocial Action." *Journal of Consumer Research* 40 (6): 1149–66.

Lapowsky, Issie. 2017. "The Women's March Defines Protest in the Facebook Age." *WIRED*, January 21. https://www.wired.com/2017/01/womens-march-defines -protest-facebook-age/.

Linder, Chris, Jess S. Myers, Colleen Riggle, and Marvette Lacy. 2016. "From Margins to Mainstream: Social Media as a Tool for Campus Sexual Violence Activism." *Journal of Diversity in Higher Education* 9 (3): 231–44.

Looft, Ruxandra. 2017. "#girlgaze: Photography, Fourth Wave Feminism, and Social Media Advocacy." *Continuum* 31 (6): 892–902.

Loza, Susana. 2014. "Hashtag Feminism, #SolidarityIsForWhiteWomen, and the Other #FemFuture." *Ada New Media* (blog), July 7. https://adanewmedia.org /2014/07/issue5-loza/

Mahdavi, Pardis. 2018. "How #MeToo Became a Global Movement." *Foreign Affairs*, March 6. https://www.foreignaffairs.com/articles/2018-03-06/how-metoo-becam e-global-movement.

Mantilla, Karla. 2015. *Gendertrolling: How Misogyny Went Viral*. Santa Barbara, CA: Praeger.

Martin, Courtney E., and Vanessa Valenti. 2013. *FemFuture: Online Revolution*. New Feminist Solutions series, vol. 8. New York: Barnard Center for Research on Women.

McDonald, Nathan. 2018. "Digital in 2018: World's Internet Users Pass the 4 Billion Mark." *We Are Social USA*, January 30. https://wearesocial.com/us/blog/2018/01 /global-digital-report-2018.

Mendes, Kaitlynn, Jessica Ringrose, and Jessalynn Keller. 2018. "#MeToo and the Promise and Pitfalls of Challenging Rape Culture through Digital Feminist Activism." *European Journal of Women's Studies* 25 (2): 236–46.

———. 2019. *Digital Feminist Activism: Girls and Women Fight Back against Rape Culture*. Oxford: Oxford University Press.

Munro, Ealasaid. 2013. "Feminism: A Fourth Wave?" *Political Insight* 4 (2): 22–25.

Murphy, Meghan. 2013. "The Trouble with Twitter Feminism." *Feminist Current* (blog), December 18. https://www.feministcurrent.com/2013/12/18/the-trouble -with-twitter-feminism/.

Nicolini, Kristine M., and Sara Steffes Hansen. 2018. "Framing the Women's March on Washington: Media Coverage and Organizational Messaging Alignment." *Public Relations Review* 44 (1): 1–10.

Norris, Pippa. 2001. *Digital Divide: Civic Engagement, Information Poverty, and the Internet Worldwide*. New York: Cambridge University Press.

Norton by Symantec. 2016. "Norton Study Shows Online Harassment Nears Epidemic Proportions for Young Australian Women." Symantec, March 8. https://www .symantec.com/en/au/about/newsroom/press-releases/2016/symantec_0309_01.

Park, Suey, and David J. Leonard. 2014. "In Defense of Twitter Feminism." *Model View Culture*, February 3. https://modelviewculture.com/pieces/in-defense-of -twitter-feminism.

Pennington, Rosemary. 2018. "Making Space in Social Media: #MuslimWomensDay in Twitter." *Journal of Communication Inquiry* 42 (3): 199–217.

Penny, Laurie. 2013. "Laurie Penny on Steubenville: This Is Rape Culture's Abu Ghraib Moment." *New Statesman*, March 19. https://www.newstatesman.com /laurie-penny/2013/03/steubenville-rape-cultures-abu-ghraib-moment.

Ratcliffe, Rebecca, and Agencies. 2015. "Nobel Scientist Tim Hunt: Female Scientists Cause Trouble for Men in Labs." *The Guardian*, June 10. https://www.theguardian .com/uk news/2015/jun/10/nobel-scientist-tim-hunt-female-scientists-cause -trouble-for-men-in labs.

Raynauld, Vincent, Mireille Lalancette, and Sofia Tourigny-Koné. 2016. "Political Protest 2.0: Social Media and the 2012 Student Strike in the Province of Quebec, Canada." *French Politics* 14 (1): 1–29.

Risam, Roopika. 2015. "Toxic Femininity 4.0." *First Monday* 20 (4). http://firstmonday .org/ojs/index.php/fm/article/view/5896.

Rivers, Nicola. 2017. *Postfeminism(s) and the Arrival of the Fourth Wave: Turning Tides*. London: Palgrave Macmillan.

Schuster, Julia. 2013. "Invisible Feminists? Social Media and Young Women's Political Participation." *Political Science* 65 (1): 8–24.

Small, Tamara A. 2011. "What the Hashtag? A Content Analysis of Canadian Politics on Twitter." *Information, Communication & Society* 14 (6): 872–95.

———. 2016. "Two Decades of Digital Party Politics in Canada: An Assessment." In *Canadian Parties in Transition*, 4th ed., edited by A. Brian Tanguay and Alain-G. Gagnon, 388–408. Toronto: University of Toronto Press.

Sowards, Stacey K., and Valerie R. Renegar. 2004. "The Rhetorical Functions of Consciousness-Raising in Third Wave Feminism." *Communication Studies* 55 (4): 535–52.

Strimpel, Zoe. 2017. "I've Had Enough of MeToo 'Hashtag Feminism' and Its Intellectual Laziness." *The Telegraph*, October 17. https://www.telegraph.co.uk /women/life/had-enough-metoo-hashtag-feminism-intellectual-laziness/.

The Representation Project. n.d. "#AskHerMore." The Representation Project. Accessed May 11, 2017. http://therepresentationproject.org/the-movement /askhermore/

Thrift, Samantha C. 2014. "#YesAllWomen as Feminist Meme Event." *Feminist Media Studies* 14 (6): 1090–92.

Underwood, Patrick, and Howard T. Welser. 2011. "'The Internet Is Here': Emergent Coordination and Innovation of Protest Forms in Digital Culture." In *iConference '11: Proceedings of the 2011 iConference*, 304–11. New York: Association for Computing Machinery.

van der Graaf, Amber, Simon Otjes, and Anne Rasmussen. 2016. "Weapon of the Weak? The Social Media Landscape of Interest Groups." *European Journal of Communication* 31 (2): 120–35.

Van Laer, Jeroen, and Peter Van Aelst. 2010. "Internet and Social Movement Action Repertoires: Opportunities and Limitations." *Information, Communication & Society* 13 (8): 1146–71.

Wilde-Blavatsky, Adele. 2013. "Stop Bashing White Women in the Name of Beyonce: We Need Unity Not Division." *The Huffington Post* (UK), December 20. https://www.huffingtonpost.co.uk/adele-tomlin/white-feminism_b_4477351.html

Williams, Sherri. 2015. "Digital Defense: Black Feminists Resist Violence with Hashtag Activism." *Feminist Media Studies* 15 (2): 341–44.

Young, Cathy. 2014. "Stop Fem-splaining: What #womenagainstfeminism Get Right." *Time*, July 24. http://time.com/3028827/women-against-feminism-gets-it-right/.

FURTHER READING

Mantilla, Karla. 2015. *Gendertrolling: How Misogyny Went Viral*. Santa Barbara, CA: Praeger.

Mendes, Kaitlynn, Jessalynn Keller, and Jessica Ringrose. 2019. *Digital Feminist Activism: Girls and Women Fight Back against Rape Culture*. Oxford: Oxford University Press.

Thrift, Samantha C. Forthcoming. "Digital Feminism: Subverting the Neoliberal Chill in Canada." In *Digital Politics in Canada: Promises and Perils*, edited by Tamara A. Small and Harold Jansen. Toronto: University of Toronto Press.

Women and Children First! Childhood, Feminisms, and the Co-emancipatory Model

Toby Rollo

Key terms: children, co-emancipation model, colonialism, decolonial, gender theory and gender critique, infantilization, maternal feminism, patriarchy

INTRODUCTION

In this chapter, I examine how the main traditions of feminist thought have interpreted the relationship between **children** and **patriarchy**, with a focus on the potential for the liberation of children alongside women. These questions are critical to the emancipatory aims of critical feminist and **gender theory** because strong elements of patriarchy can be inadvertently preserved when children are missing from analyses. It is as children, for instance, that we are socialized into gender roles and first acquire patterns of heteropatriarchal thinking and behaviour (Maccoby 1988). To overlook childhood, then, is to overlook one of the most significant moments in the reproduction of patriarchy. Likewise, the degrading conceptualization of women as mere child-bearing and child-rearing subjects depends on a prior conceptualization of children as degraded beings who debase those associated with them. These deep links between the conceptualization of both women and children under patriarchy, if ignored, inhibit our ability to fully reconceptualize women and gender categories in productive and liberating ways.

Most traditions of feminism have a complicated history with the figure of the child (Baird 2008; Burman 2012; Burman and Stacey 2010; Galatzer-Levy 2015; Hetherington 1998; Thorne 1987). On the one hand, it is feminist theorists and activists who have been largely responsible for revealing how children are positioned within patriarchy, in part by showing how intimate relationships within the domestic private sphere constitute a domain of power and, therefore, a domain of politics (Rosen and Twamley 2018). Feminists point to evidence from various fields of study that show how children and youth represent a class of people who suffer from discrimination, objectification, exclusion, harassment, and violence precisely *because* they are children (see Bell 1995; Flasher 1978; Pierce and Allen 1975; Thompson 1975; Turner and Matthews 1998; Westman 1991; Young-Bruehl 2012). Yet on the other hand, some mainstream feminist approaches focus on women in ways that subordinate or erase the oppression of children under patriarchy, "rendering children largely absent from the social world and sociological consideration except as objects of socialisation" (Rosen and Twamley 2018, 4).

Within the dominant currents of feminist thought that *do* recognize issues of domination related to childhood, most have concluded that the liberation of women is inextricably linked to the liberation of children, in what I will refer to as the **co-emancipation model** of freedom from patriarchy. Co-emancipation models tend to include the following assumptions: that it is predominantly in childhood that heteropatriarchal gender norms and binaries are coercively inculcated and reproduced; that children, therefore, represent the first and most vulnerable victims of heteropatriarchal violence; and, as a result, that the liberation of women from patriarchy cannot be disassociated from the liberation of children. Co-emancipation models also acknowledge that children are not simply passive objects and victims, but also exercise their own forms of agency and resistance (Esser et al. 2016).

To illustrate, let us first turn to the exemplar of co-emancipatory feminist scholarship and activism, Shulamith Firestone, and her classic text *The Dialectic of Sex*. Firestone famously describes the link as more than just shared oppression:

> Women and children are always mentioned in the same breath ("Women and children to the forts!"). The special tie women have with children is recognized by everyone. I submit, however, that the nature of this bond

is no more than shared oppression. And that moreover this oppression is intertwined and mutually reinforcing in such complex ways that we will be unable to speak of liberation of women without also discussing the liberation of children, and vice versa. (1970, 72)

It has become all the more pressing in our present "turbulent times," given the contemporary rise of right-wing movements and patriarchal politics, that we come to grips with the complex relationship between childhood, feminism, and gender theory. Unfortunately, in the decades that have followed Firestone's conceptualization of liberation, a general understanding of how the child features in the broader scope of feminist thinking has failed to emerge.

My intention in this chapter, therefore, is to map out how the child fits into various models of feminist theory and gender theory more broadly, to identify where and perhaps why the co-emancipatory model emerges or fails to emerge. The chapter begins with prevalent Western feminist approaches and concludes with the interpretations of intersectional feminists, for whom the child's experiences of domination are not restricted to gender but also include race, **colonialism**, age, and ability. I will proceed by first tracing out early liberal feminism's treatment of the child as an obstacle to freedom and how this approach informed subsequent iterations of socialist feminism within which the child was viewed as an object of uncompensated labour. I then turn to radical feminist thought and the deep tensions within it between a co-emancipatory model and a model in which the child was taken to represent women's biological and social enslavement. Perceived shortcomings within liberal, socialist, and radical feminisms gave rise to **maternal feminist critiques** and the argument that almost all dominant Western feminist theorizations had been structured by a form of liberal individualism that isolated women from their relationships with others, especially children. I then discuss how feminist theory expanded rapidly in the late twentieth century, giving rise to gender theories such as queer theory and transfeminism. The contribution of gender theory has been to highlight how a romanticized vision of the child has been weaponized to deny the dignity and equality of LGBTQIA peoples, in part by imposing strict gender conformity on children so as to affirm traditional heteronormative ideas of love and the family. I conclude with a discussion of how Black feminisms and Indigenous feminisms have revealed how heteropatriarchy works together with racism and colonialism. These approaches offer an intersectional **decolonial** critique that is more thoroughly co-emancipatory, affirming how children have been victims of patriarchy as well as agents of anti-patriarchal resistance, and thus paving the way for a genuinely transformational gender politics.

EARLY WESTERN FEMINISMS

Liberal Feminism

By the nineteenth century, in many Western countries feminist thought was actively informing social and political movements that championed women's formal equality and full citizenship, including participation in electoral politics. The suffragettes argued for enfranchisement on the grounds that women possessed the same reasoning capacities as men and should therefore qualify as autonomous persons with access to the full schedule of formal civil and political rights held by individuals. Later, in the mid-twentieth century, liberal feminists involved in second-wave feminism extended that struggle to women's reproductive rights, entry into the labour force, and other informal barriers to equality.

Within most of these classic liberal feminist movements, the child represented the embodiment of the primal or animal nature that was used to justify the natural exclusion of irrational human beings from the privileged domain of politics. Feminists argued that women's biological association with the debased nature of birthing and nurturing had resulted in their relegation to the private sphere and the domestic roles of mother and housewife. From this perspective, women were bound to home and hearth by patriarchal chains justified by the biology of childbearing, which in turn created barriers to entry into the public sphere and prohibited them from attaining economic and sexual independence from men.

Moreover, because of this association with children and childhood, women were depicted as impeded by a child-like incompetence, a view expressed by the nineteenth-century German philosopher Arthur Schopenhauer, who wrote in his essay "On Women" that the limitations placed on women are natural precisely because of the natural link between women and children:

> Women are directly adapted to act as the nurses and educators of our early childhood, for the simple reason that they themselves are childish, foolish, and short-sighted—in a word, are big children all their lives, something intermediate between the child and the man, who is a man in the strict sense of the word. (1970, 81)

In this context, feminist emancipation was principally envisioned as freedom from natural exclusion and imposed domesticity, but not in ways that recognized how the child, too, was degraded and excluded under patriarchy.

Early liberal feminists such as Mary Wollstonecraft confronted patriarchal **infantilization** by asserting that women are capable of the same degree of rational maturity available to men, even if they often failed to cultivate these qualities and remained child-like. In her *Vindication of the Rights of Woman*, for example, Wollstonecraft lamented the "childish passions" that plagued women of her time (1891, 402). Unfortunately, this line of argument affirmed the idea of natural exclusions and the degraded nature of childhood, effectively reinforcing the vision of freedom and agency as belonging exclusively to the historically masculine virtue of mature reason and rationality. In this respect, early liberal feminism tended to reinforce rather than challenge the patriarchal categories of public and private, political and domestic, freedom and servitude, rational and emotional, humanity and mere nature.

In failing to extend a critique of patriarchy to children, early liberal feminism had also preserved one of the basic logics of racist and colonial dehumanization: the infantilization of groups. Tragically, many early feminists actively rejected the possibility of emancipation for Black and Indigenous peoples on the grounds that they, unlike white women, were destined to remain perpetual children (Field 2014). The degraded figure of the child was preserved as the paradigm of natural subordination so that Black and Indigenous peoples could be depicted as child races in need of discipline and tutelage (Kromidas 2014; Nandy 1985, 2007; Rollo 2018a, 2018b; Shweder 1982; Mills and LeFrançois 2018). This logic of patriarchal authority adopted by liberal feminists, as Anne McClintock has noted, allowed imperial expansion to be "figured as a linear, nonrevolutionary progression that naturally contained hierarchy within unity: paternal fathers ruling benignly over immature children" (1995, 45).

Socialist Feminism

During the industrial age, severe economic inequalities and brutal working conditions motivated some feminist thinkers to focus on the role of capitalism in the oppression of women. Socialist feminists observed that within the oppressive capitalist class structure women represented the most exploited group of workers. They drew attention to the unpaid labour performed by women in the domestic sphere, where caring for children was entirely uncompensated, as well as in the exploitation of working women, who were compensated much less than men. For many, the idea of class itself must be seen as historically gendered, with women representing the first and most consistently exploited class in any economic order (Engels 1884; Lerner 1986).

Where liberal feminisms had generally positioned the child as an obstacle to freedom, socialist feminisms tended to view the child as an object of unpaid labour, the responsibility for which fell disproportionately on women. Liberal and social-ist feminists agreed that children should be relegated to schools, and although they disagreed on the ultimate value of education (i.e., whether the function of education was to promote individual freedom or class freedom), they shared a commitment to a doctrine of natural progress according to which individuals and groups must pass through stages towards a more quintessentially rational "human" form of life. Thus, while Marx was deeply troubled by the plight of child labourers under capitalism, it is also true that in Marxist and socialist feminisms children were not viewed as agents or even as an oppressed class. Socialists orga-nized the transfer of children from factories into schools, in part because children were viewed as having nothing to add to the workers' struggle. Whatever oppres-sion the child might experience could be addressed once the adults overthrew their capitalist oppressors—a form of trickle-down emancipation.

In both liberal and socialist feminisms, then, the child has often featured as a patriarchal obstacle to the freedom of women, imposing an unjust and backward life from which women ought to be liberated so that they might flourish, like men, into fully autonomous agents. Unfortunately, in situating the figure of the child as a primitive antecedent to the fully human maturity of men (and now women), feminism retained rather dangerous ideas of natural exclusion that were immediately repurposed to depict non-European peoples as occupying a histori-cal, superstitious, animistic, and child-like stage of cultural development. Indeed, in her famous work *The Second Sex*, Simone de Beauvoir herself demonstrates how modern feminism often engaged in degrading infantilization of groups, in this case, Indigenous Peoples: "The peoples who have remained under the thumb of the goddess mother, those who have retained the matrilineal regime, are also those who are arrested at a primitive stage of civilization" (1989, 76).

Radical Feminism

From the foundations built by the liberal and socialist feminist traditions, a more radical brand of feminism emerged in the mid-twentieth century. Although internally diverse and factional, radical feminisms generally agreed that patriarchy is much more than just one form of discrimination among others. Rather, patriarchy was understood as the basic architecture of modern power, a foundational ordering principle of Western social, economic, and political life. Patriarchy is understood to inform—fundamentally—modern society and its definition of full humanity (as *mankind*), such that any critique or challenge requires a revolutionary remaking of virtually all modern institutions and relationships defined and constructed by patriarchy. The opinions of radical feminists diverged and intersected in interesting ways with respect to what kinds of challenges were required, and the resulting tensions have been especially significant when it came to children. On the one hand, radical feminists often identified reproductive biology and child-rearing as an existential form of oppression that could be overcome through reproductive technologies. On the other hand, radical feminists were also the first to articulate a vision of co-emancipation, arguing that patriarchy oppresses women and children equally.

Many, including prominent radical feminist and co-founder of the (American) Women's Liberation Movement, Shulamith Firestone, seemed to subscribe to both of these positions. Firestone argued for the use of artificial reproductive technologies to free women from the burden of childbearing (1970, 138), but unlike liberal and socialist feminists she also wished to abolish the degraded category of the child altogether. Firestone claimed that feminists must struggle to dissolve the distinction between adulthood and childhood, along with the dubious patriarchal binary oppositions separating private and public, domestic and political, human and nature, freedom and servitude. Drawing from Marxist historical materialism, Firestone argued that the fates of women and children are inextricably intertwined, in part because women are themselves categorized as children. Firestone went so far as to refer to feminists as "ex-child and still oppressed child women" (104). In this sense, the subordination of children was identified as the earliest and most fundamental form of patriarchal oppression, since the conceptualization of women as irresponsible and irrational was itself predicated on a biological and cultural link to the more primordial fallen and slavish nature of children.

Yet Firestone's approach often paralleled the child liberationists of her time, those who tended to argue for extending the rights enjoyed by adults to children (see Holt 1974). In the end, emancipation would involve nothing less than the "full self-determination, including economic independence, of both women and children" (Firestone 1970, 207). Like child liberationists, Firestone tended to gloss over the differences that do exist between younger and older human beings, leading to a libertarian view of the child as an autonomous economic agent as well as some rather controversial views on the sexuality of children and youth (98). Aside from these moments of overreach, however, Firestone and radical feminists like her were responsible for bringing the issue of patriarchal oppression of children into feminist discourse. Where modern liberal feminism decried the growing romanticization of childhood vulnerability and innocence that ensnared women in traditional childbearing and child-rearing roles, Firestone observed that children were equally victimized by such designations. The idealization and objectification of children under the *adult* gaze is not unlike the experiences of women under the venerating *male* gaze: "To be worshipped is not freedom," she observed (74).

The co-emancipation model advanced by radical feminists had alerted mainstream feminism to the oppression of both women and children under patriarchy, but the radical interpretation of childbearing as natural enslavement, along with the erasure of important differences between adults and children, was considered too extreme for most mainstream scholars and activists. Radical feminism precipitated a shift in feminist interrogations of patriarchy, leading to a recognition that the universalizing liberal individualist lens tended to conflate women with men as well as children with adults. At the same time, mainstream feminist thinkers were compelled to reconsider motherhood and the constitutive relationships between women and children.

Maternal Feminism

Maternal feminist ideas have a long history. Maternal feminisms associated with first-wave feminism viewed childbearing and child-rearing as aspects of women's superior virtuous capacities as citizens. More recent iterations contend that while mothering and child-rearing can be used as a tool of patriarchal oppression, they need not be rejected as *inherently* oppressive (Held 1993; Rich 1976; Ruddick 1989). These maternal feminists were responsible for rethinking pregnancy, birth, and child-rearing as a challenge to the patriarchal order, along with important lessons on how to revolutionize thinking about politics and society. Thus, today, many maternal feminists call for a reorientation of political life away from abstract principles of justice towards a relational ethics of care. The relationship between mothers and children—what Sara Ruddick called "maternal thinking"—is understood as universally emancipatory because mothering is not just a feminine virtue but rather "a paradigm for human relations in general (Ruddick 1989); in this view, everyone, including men, has the capacity to become a 'mothering person'" (Crivello and Espinoza-Revollo 2018, 142).

Contemporary maternal feminisms are deeply suspicious of the liberal ideal of the unencumbered individual and its influence on twentieth-century feminism: "Women raised on a diet of liberal feminism in the period after feminism's second wave find that equality is attainable only so long as they are child free" (Thomson and Baraitser 2018, 69). For while there is injustice in intimidating women into having children, there is also injustice in conflating freedom with the absence of children, especially in a way that reinforces the rather patriarchal definition of freedom or liberty as a life unburdened by responsibilities to young people. From this perspective, the idea of the autonomous and independent liberal subject has been disastrous when applied to "thinking about either women or children" (Rosen and Twamley 2018, 9) as well as corrosive to any "recognition of children's and women's social interdependency" (Carulla 2018, 64). The maternal ideal here is to be understood not as traditional motherhood but as a political ethos: "a lifelong intersubjective and relational need to care and to be cared for" (Nolas, Sanders-McDonagh, and Neville 2018, 232). Contemporary maternal feminists offered the first genuine challenge to the masculine virtues of abstract rationality, which they identified as harboured in previous incarnations of women's liberation as well as in the earlier notion that relationships of care are the sole privilege of women. In contrast to the abstract individualism inherent in liberal equality models, "the political ethics of care acknowledges that human relations are between unequal and interdependent persons" (Crivello and Espinoza-Revollo 2018, 142). Freedom and autonomy are therefore relational rather than individual and, in the domains of law and politics, they should be recognized as being generated *with* others and their particular needs (see Nedelsky 2011).

Not all theorists of care are maternal feminists—many feminist disability scholars (see Clifford Simplican in this volume), for instance, have different approaches to care and mothering (see Hall 2002)—but in recognizing the interdependence of human beings, who are bound by relations of care, maternal feminists became some of the first to develop a co-emancipatory model of liberation that extended to all relations inflected by patriarchal domination. In other words, by challenging the notion of the solitary liberal individual, these feminists began to lay bare the modes of oppression at the intersections of race, class, and gender for both women and children. As we shall see further on, maternal feminists were heavily influenced by the work of Black and Indigenous women, who pioneered the intersectional approach.

FEMINIST THEORY: RECENT CONTRIBUTIONS AND CHALLENGES

Contemporary reactions to feminist and gender-critical movements often centre on the alleged risk these ideas pose for the sanctity of childhood and the innocence of vulnerable children. This anxiety over the well-being of the child reveals how those concerned with preserving traditional gender roles and identities recognize that childhood is the primary site in which traditional patriarchal relations are reproduced and, therefore, potentially disrupted. The child is, in this sense, at the centre of heteronormative politics. We find a direct response to these anxieties in the tradition of **gender critique**, which is heavily informed by LGBTQIA analyses of heteropatriarchy and the social construction of gender binaries in childhood.

LGBTQIA Theory

Gender critique has initiated deep interventions into a host of issues previously covered by feminists, such as amendments to maternal feminism that encompass "queer and trans mothering practices" (Thomson and Baraitser 2018, 71). Gender theorists have also exposed how the figure of the child is deployed to normalize heteronormative reproductive relationships to the exclusion of non-gender-conforming sexualities and family structures (Dyer 2016; Edelman 2004; LeFrançois 2013; Lesnik-Oberstein 2010). They have detailed how queer parents must contend with the fact that heteropatriarchal gender binaries are coercively imposed on children by society in ways that preserve dominant categories of sex and gender (Epstein 2005).

Although not often explicit, the focus of gender critique on the heteronormative socialization of children entails a strong co-emancipatory claim. The myriad formations of heteronormative coercion and violence are learned early, in the family, and so it is only when children are no longer a central target and tool of heteropatriarchal culture that the liberation of LGBTQIA peoples can be genuinely established. Current debates around gendered washroom facilities (Cavanagh 2010), and gay-straight alliances in schools (Toomey and Russell 2013; Walls, Kane, and Wisneski 2010) highlight the deep connections between gender-critical movements and childhood experience. These emerging discussions demonstrate how the resistance of children themselves to strict gender conformity embodies a radical disruption of patriarchal society previously overlooked by many feminist thinkers.

Black and Indigenous Feminisms

The work of Black, Indigenous, and women of colour feminisms has uncovered the extent to which patriarchy has played a role in global patterns of domination associated with imperialism, colonialism, and slavery. Feminists of colour were some of the earliest critics of patriarchy and likewise remain at the forefront of scholarship and activism that seek to address issues faced by BIPOC women and children, including refugees and irregular migrants. The association known as Grassroots Women, for instance, was an anti-imperialist, feminist organization in East Vancouver, Canada, initiated in the 1980s by the Philippine Women Centre in order "to question the very basis of the neoliberal state and the capitalist organisation of childcare and reproductive labour, and to resist the exploitation and oppression of working-class women and children" (Edwards 2018, 47). Similar associations have emerged in the decades since to confront the way immigration and domestic labour policies disproportionately affect racialized women and children (Tungohan 2013).

Black feminist traditions interrogate the ways that patriarchy interacts with racism to subjugate Black women and how white liberal and socialist feminisms tend to exclude these particular struggles of Black women from emancipatory frameworks. Like radical feminists, Black feminists observe that patriarchy constitutes a foundational structure of modern society, but they are also attuned to the way sexism intersects with the history of African slavery in the subordination of Black women (cf. Curry 2017). For many Black feminists, maternal feminist scholarship was guilty of centring the experiences of white women, for whom patriarchy is experienced along the dimensions of sex and gender. Black women who choose to have children have also to contend with gendered racism, which manifests in institutions of education and child welfare, where Black women endure disproportionately high levels of scrutiny by government agencies and Black children experience disproportionate levels of surveillance and abuse. It was insights such as these that were largely overlooked by mainstream analyses of race and gender and that led to the development of what came to be called feminist standpoint theory (Hill-Collins 1990), which holds that those in marginalized positions are better positioned to identify and conceptualize power relations than those occupying positions of privilege.[1] bell hooks, for example, was one of the few after Firestone to observe that patriarchal violence begins with the child: "The most common forms of patriarchal violence are those that take place in the home between patriarchal parents and children. The point of such violence is usually to reinforce a dominator model, in which the authority figure is deemed ruler over those without power and given the right to maintain that rule through practices of subjugation, subordination, and submission" (2004, 24). Given the limits of white feminist theory to fully recognize the experiences of racialized childhood, Black feminists developed practices of co-emancipation in which the liberation of Black children was foregrounded.

As with most radical feminists, Black feminisms observe that women's allegedly degrading roles in childbirth and child-rearing leads them to be conceptualized as ignorant and childish by association. But this dynamic is exacerbated by the fact that Black peoples are also dehumanized through the infantilization of non-European peoples as members of a primitive "child-race." The supposed cultural immaturity of people of colour is a colonial premise, one that is preserved in white emancipatory models, including, historically, those of feminists (Rollo 2018a). The view that people of colour exist in a state of civilizational childhood, and that "mature" white European society has a burden to educate and discipline the child-like peoples of the world, presupposes the naturalized patriarchal dominance of rational adult over irrational child. In essence, in so far as the child stands as the perennial archetype of primitive existence and natural subjugation, it also serves to anchor the modern racial and patriarchal order.

Alongside Black feminism, Indigenous feminisms have unveiled how patriarchy and colonialism are mutually reinforcing (Maracle 1996; Stewart-Harawira 2017), and they challenge the ways in which patriarchal colonialism targets Indigenous women and children in the ongoing project of genocide and dispossession (Starblanket 2017). In many Indigenous legal and political traditions, men, women, other genders, and children are recognized as equals with unique gifts and responsibilities within their communities. Like maternal feminism, these feminists tend to view mothering as empowering rather than oppressive (Anderson 2016; Nickel 2017). Indigenous feminisms, broadly speaking, are relational in their approach and, unlike most other forms of feminism, view relationships of mutual responsibility as extending to other species as well as to particular territories, lands, and waters (see Green 2017).

These relationships are often central to the sovereignty of Indigenous nations, knowledges and practices require intergenerational transmission, so it is precisely these connections to territories that settler colonialism sought to disrupt by targeting Indigenous women and children. As Anishinaabe scholar Leanne Betasamosake Simpson relates, early settlers were frustrated by the fact that many Indigenous Peoples exhibited "a style of parenting and education that generated a different kind of governance, a different kind of leadership, and a different kind of nation." Colonial nation builders "recognized that the destruction of Indigenous women and children was the fastest way to remove Indigenous Peoples from the land," and likewise "the fastest way to destroy nations." Because Indigenous children are the inheritors of Indigenous ways of being, which are often deeply opposed to heteropatriarchal relations of domination, it was necessary that settler colonial policies "were designed to target children" (2013, n.p.). Decolonial practices that centre children are important in recovering from the near destruction of Indigenous concepts of childhood and parenting: "Rebuilding Indigenous nations requires us to rebuild our childrearing practices" (Pace-Crosschild 2018, 193). As Starblanket (in this volume) and others explain, many Indigenous feminists are seeking to expunge the elements of heteropatriarchy that have seeped into Indigenous ways of life, in part by taking up practices of rematriation in which women (and gender-non-conforming members of the community) reoccupy their legal and political roles (Kuokkanen 2016). These practices can be facilitated by returning to the traditional land-based education of children and youth (Simpson 2011, 2014).

CONCLUSION

In this brief introduction to the relationships between children, feminism, and gender theory a number of concerns have been raised. There are legitimate concerns, for instance, over how effective mainstream feminisms have been in eliminating heteropatriarchal ideas and assumptions from their theoretical frameworks. Almost half a century has passed since Firestone called for the liberation of both women and children, a call that mainstream feminisms have not fully acknowledged:

> We must include the oppression of children in any programme for feminist revolution or we will be subject to the same failing of which we have so often accused men: of not having gone deep enough in our analysis, of having missed an important substratum of oppression merely because it didn't directly concern us. (1970, 104)

There are a number of factors behind the reticence to embrace a co-emancipatory model. Most significant, perhaps, is that mainstream feminism remains heavily influenced by liberal (and to a lesser extent socialist) ideologies. As a consequence, mainstream feminism has yet to fully engage with childhood studies and embrace the argument, as Firestone did, that childhood is itself a site of patriarchal oppression. Liberalism tends to privilege the criticisms of power advanced by individuals who can represent their interests, such as an interest in being free of oppressive patriarchal domesticity. Liberal approaches are much less likely to take on the more onerous and difficult project of challenging the fundamental existence of an informal, political, private domestic sphere characterized by inequality and coercion. Put another way, children are still viewed as emblematic of the domain of home and housework that liberal feminisms seek to preserve yet *from which* women are to be liberated.

In the same way that many Black feminisms often centre the child in combating racist heteropatriarchy (Patton 2017), so, too, do many Indigenous feminisms identify decolonization as a process that requires the co-emancipation of Indigenous women and children from patriarchal domination. The co-emancipatory struggle championed by early radical feminists and embodied in the practices of Black and Indigenous scholars and activists centres on cultivating relations of care in addition to the use of reason and its cognate facilities (e.g., intelligence, acumen, sophistication). Relations of care are arguably more important because they are the only form of political agency accessible to beings of all ages and capacities and the only value around which political conditions of genuine equality and difference can be established and sustained.

The liberal view of freedom from domesticity and childhood has proven robust. It presents victims of patriarchal exclusion and domination with a seductive choice: Either gain freedom for oneself by endorsing reason as a threshold and sole criterion of inclusion, a criterion established by dominant patriarchal society in order to preserve the profitable categories of natural exclusion based on irrationality. Or, reject the masculine veneration of reason along with its exclusions but in doing so be charged with abandoning the only readily available form of emancipation, emancipation by oneself for oneself. In response, mainstream liberal and socialist feminisms appear to have accepted the Faustian liberatory bargain to varying degrees. By contrast, within dominant Western currents of gender theory, contemporary maternal feminists and LGBTQIA scholarship present a co-emancipatory and more robustly transformational gender politics. Alongside these dominant currents, Black and Indigenous feminisms continue to promote the most substantively intersectional vision of co-emancipation and, therefore, appear to lead the anti-patriarchal struggle in both theory and practice.

DISCUSSION QUESTIONS

1. What are some reasons that, despite forceful arguments for a co-emancipatory project offered by radical, Black, and Indigenous feminisms, the struggles of children under patriarchy remain overlooked in most mainstream feminist theories and practices?
2. What alternative conceptions of the child and childhood might better serve feminists and gender theorists in critiquing and resisting patriarchy?
3. What untapped possibilities for rich and productive dialogue on co-emancipation might emerge between feminist and gender theory and other social justice movements concerned with race and colonialism?
4. How might a recovery of a broad and inclusive co-emancipatory model of feminism be essential to contend with the rise of radical patriarchal politics?

NOTE

1 Standpoint theory is somewhat complicated by the fact that everyone has lived as a child under patriarchy, along with the recognition that both young boys and girls are victims of the patriarchal violence required to reproduce patriarchal relations and institutions from generation to generation. Meditations on Black lesbian mothering articulated by Audre Lorde (1984) bring to light how violence against children inculcates the model of domination, especially among young boys, who are targeted so that they can emerge as adults who sustain heteropatriarchal white supremacy. Likewise, as bell hooks argues, "the first act of violence that patriarchy demands of males is not violence towards women. Instead patriarchy demands of all males that they engage in acts of psychic self-mutilation, that they kill off the emotional parts of themselves. If an individual is not successful in emotionally crippling himself, he can count on patriarchal men to enact rituals of power that will assault his self-esteem" (2004, 66).

REFERENCES

Anderson, Kim. 2016. *A Recognition of Being: Reconstructing Native Womanhood*, 2nd ed. Toronto: Women's Press.

Baird, Barbara. 2008. "Child Politics, Feminist Analyses." *Australian Feminist Studies* 23 (57): 291–305.

Bell, John. 1995. "Understanding Adultism." Somerville, MA: YouthBuild. http://actioncivics.scoe.net/pdf/Understanding_Adultism.pdf.

Burman, Erica. 2012. "Deconstructing Neoliberal Childhood: Towards a Feminist Antipsychological Approach." *Childhood* 19 (4): 423–38.

Burman, Erica, and Jackie Stacey. 2010. "The Child and Childhood in Feminist Theory." *Feminist Theory* 11 (3): 227–40.

Carulla, Susana Borda. 2018. "When the Rights of Children Prevail over the Rights of Their Caretakers: A Case Study in the Community Homes of Bogotá, Colombia." In *Feminism and the Politics of Childhood: Friends or Foes*, edited by Rachel Rosen and Catherine Twamley, 50–65. London: UCL Press.

Cavanagh, Sheila L. 2010. *Queering Bathrooms: Gender, Sexuality, and the Hygienic Imagination*. Toronto: University of Toronto Press.

Crivello, Gina, and Patricia Espinoza-Revollo. 2018. "Care Labour and Temporal Vulnerability in Woman–Child Relations." In *Feminism and the Politics of Childhood: Friends or Foes*, edited by Rachel Rosen and Catherine Twamley, 139–54. London: UCL Press.

Curry, Tommy. 2017. *The Man-Not: Race, Class, Genre, and the Dilemmas of Black Manhood*. Philadelphia: Temple University Press.

De Beauvoir, Simone. *The Second Sex*. Trans. H.M. Parshley. New York: Vintage Books.

Dyer, Hannah. 2016. "Queer Futurity and Childhood Innocence: Beyond the Injury of Development." *Global Studies of Childhood* 7 (3): 290–302.

Edelman, Lee. 2004. *No Future: Queer Theory and the Death Drive*. Durham, NC: Duke University Press.

Edwards, Merryn. 2018. "Working-Class Women and Children in Grassroots Women." In *Feminism and the Politics of Childhood: Friends or Foes*, edited by Rachel Rosen and Catherine Twamley, 40–49. London: UCL Press.

Engels, Fredrich. 1884. *The Origin of the Family, Private Property, and the State*. London: Penguin Books.

Epstein, Rachel. 2005. "Queer Parenting in the New Millennium: Resisting Normal." *Canadian Women's Studies* 24 (2–3): 7–14.

Esser, Florian, Meike S. Baader, Tanya Bets, and Beatrice Hungerland, eds. 2016. *Reconceptualising Agency and Childhood: New Perspectives in Childhood Studies*. New York: Routledge.

Field, Corinne. 2014. *The Struggle for Equal Adulthood: Gender, Race, Age, and the Fight for Citizenship in Antebellum America*. Chapel Hill: University of North Carolina Press.

Firestone, Shulamith. 1970. *The Dialectic of Sex: The Case for Feminist Revolution*. New York: Morrow and Co.

Flasher, Jack. 1978. "Adultism." *Adolescence* 13 (51): 517–23.

Galatzer-Levy, Robert M. 2015. "Women and Children Last: Reflections on the History of Child Psychoanalysis." *The Psychoanalytic Study of the Child* 69 (1): 108–45.

Green, Joyce, ed. 2017. *Making Space for Indigenous Feminism*, 2nd ed. Black Point, NS: Fernwood.

Hall, Kim Q. 2002. "Feminism, Disability, and Embodiment." *National Women's Studies Association Journal* 14 (3): 7–13.

Held, Virginia. 1993. *Feminist Morality: Transforming Culture, Society, and Politics*. Chicago: University of Chicago Press.

Hetherington, Penelope. 1998. "The Sound of One Hand Smacking: History, Feminism and Childhood." *Journal of Australian Studies*, 22 (59): 2–7.

Hill-Collins, Patricia. 1990. *Black Feminist Thought: Knowledge, Consciousness, and the Politics of Empowerment*. New York: Routledge.

Holt, John. 1974. *Escape from Childhood: The Needs and Rights of Children*. Boston: E.P. Dutton.

hooks, bell. 2004. *The Will to Change: Men, Masculinity, and Love*. New York: Atria Books.

Kromidas, Maria. 2014. "The 'Savage' Child and the Nature of Race: Posthuman Interventions from New York City." *Anthropological Theory* 14 (4): 422–41.

Kuokkanen, Rauna. 2016. "Indigenous Women's Rights and International Law." In *The Handbook of Indigenous Peoples' Rights*, edited by Corrine Leonard and Damien Short, 129–45. New York: Routledge.

LeFrançois, Brenda A. 2013. "Queering Child and Adolescent Mental Health Services: The Subversion of Heteronormativity in Practice." *Children and Society*, 27 (1): 1–12.

Lerner, Gerda. 1986. *The Creation of Patriarchy*. Oxford: Oxford University Press.

Lesnik-Oberstein, Karín. 2010. "Childhood, Queer Theory, and Feminism." *Feminist Theory* 11 (3): 309–21.

Lorde, Audre. 1984. *Sister Outsider: Essays and Speeches by Audre Lorde*. Berkeley, CA: Ten Speed Press.

Maccoby, Eleanor E. 1988. "Gender as a Social Category." *Developmental Psychology*, 24: 755.

Maracle, Lee. 1996. *I Am Woman: A Native Perspective on Sociology and Feminism*. Toronto: Raincoast Books.

McClintock, Anne. 1995. *Imperial Leather: Race, Gender, and Sexuality in the Colonial Contest*. New York: Routledge.

Mills, China, and Brenda A. LeFrançois. 2018. "Child as Metaphor: Colonialism, Psy-governance, and Epistemicide." *World Futures* 74 (7–8): 503–24.

Nandy, Ashis. 1985. "Restructuring Childhood, Ideology of Adulthood." *Alternatives*, 10 (3): 359–75.

———. 2007. "Paternal Deceits." *New Internationalist*, 1 October. https://newint.org/features/2007/10/01/roots.

Nedelsky, Jennifer. 2011. *Law's Relations: A Relational Theory of Self, Autonomy, and Law*. New York: Oxford University Press.

Nickel, Sarah A. 2017. "'I Am Not a Women's Libber Although Sometimes I Sound Like One': Indigenous Feminism and Politicized Motherhood." *American Indian Quarterly* 41 (4): 299–335.

Nolas, Sevasti-Melissa, Erin Sanders-McDonagh, and Lucy Neville. 2018. "'Gimme Shelter'? Complicating Responses to Family Violence." In *Feminism and the Politics of Childhood: Friends or Foes*, edited by Rachel Rosen and Catherine Twamley, 225–40. London: UCL Press.

Pace-Crosschild, Tanya. 2018. "Decolonising Childrearing and Challenging the Patriarchal Nuclear Family through Indigenous Knowledges: An Opokaa'sin Project." In *Feminism and the Politics of Childhood: Friends or Foes*, edited by Rachel Rosen and Catherine Twamley, 191–98. London: UCL Press.

Patton, Stacey. 2017. *Spare the Kids: Why Whupping Children Won't Save Black America*. New York: Beacon Press.

Pierce, Chester M., and Gail B. Allen. 1975. "Childism." *Psychiatric Annals* 5: 266–70.

Rich, Adrienne. 1976. *Of Woman Born: Motherhood as Experience and Institution*. New York: W.W. Norton & Co.

Rollo, Toby. 2018a. "The Color of Childhood: The Role of the Child/Human Binary in the Production of Anti-Black Racism." *The Journal of Black Studies* 49 (4): 307–29.

———. 2018b. "Feral Children: Settler Colonialism, Progress, and the Figure of the Child." *Settler Colonial Studies* 8 (1): 60–79.

Rosen, Rachel, and Catherine Twamley. 2018. "The Woman-Child Question: A Dialogue in the Borderlands." In *Feminism and the Politics of Childhood: Friends or Foes*, edited by Rachel Rosen and Catherine Twamley, 1–20. London: UCL Press.

Ruddick, Sara. 1989. *Maternal Thinking: Toward a Politics of Peace*. Boston: Beacon Press.

Schopenhauer, Arthur. 1970. *Essays and Aphorisms*. London: Penguin Books.

Shweder, Richard A. 1982. "On Savages and Other Children." *American Anthropologist* 84 (2): 354–66.

Simpson, Leanne Betasamosake. 2011. *Dancing on Our Turtle's Back*. Peterborough, ON: Arbeiter Ring.

———. 2013. "Honour the Apology." https://www.leannesimpson.ca/writings/2013/7/23/honour-the-apology.

———. 2014. "Land as Pedagogy: Nishnaabeg Intelligence and Rebellious Transformation." *Decolonization: Indigeneity, Education & Society* 3 (3): 1–25.

Starblanket, Gina. 2017. "Being Indigenous Feminists: Resurgences against Contemporary Patriarchy." In *Making Space for Indigenous Feminism*, 2nd ed., edited by Joyce Green, 21–41. Black Point, NS: Fernwood.

Stewart-Harawira, Makere. 2017. "Indigenous Feminism as Resistance to Imperialism." In *Making Space for Indigenous Feminism*, 2nd ed., edited by Joyce Green, 124–39. Black Point, NS: Fernwood .

Thompson, Paul. 1975. "The War with Adults." *Oral History* 3 (2): 29–38.

Thomson, Rachel, and Lisa Baraitser. 2018. "Thinking through Childhood and Maternal Studies: A Feminist Encounter." In *Feminism and the Politics of Childhood: Friends or Foes*, edited by Rachel Rosen and Catherine Twamley, 66–82. London: UCL Press.

Thorne, Barrie. 1987. "Re-visioning Women and Social Change: Where Are the Children?" *Gender and Society* 1 (1): 85–109.

Toomey, Russell B., and Stephen T. Russell. 2013. "Gay–Straight Alliances, Social Justice Involvement, and School Victimization of Lesbian, Gay, Bisexual, and Queer Youth: Implications for School Well-Being and Plans to Vote." *Youth & Society* 45 (4): 500–22.

Tungohan, Ethel. 2013. "Reconceptualizing Motherhood, Reconceptualizing Resistance: Migrant Domestic Workers, Transnational Hyper-Maternalism and Activism." *International Feminist Journal of Politics* 15 (1): 39–57.

Turner, Susan M., and Gareth B. Matthews, eds. 1998. *The Philosopher's Child: Critical Perspectives in the Western Tradition*. Rochester, NY: University of Rochester Press.

Walls, N. Eugene, Sarah B. Kane, and Hope Wisneski. 2010. "Gay–Straight Alliances and School Experiences of Sexual Minority Youth." *Youth & Society* 41 (3): 307–32.

Westman, Jack C. 1991. "Juvenile Ageism: Unrecognized Prejudice and Discrimination against the Young." *Child Psychiatry & Human Development* 21 (4): 237–56.

Wollstonecraft, Mary. 1891. *A Vindication of the Rights of Woman: With Strictures on Political and Moral Subjects*. London: T. Fisher Unwin.

Young-Bruehl, Elisabeth. 2012. *Childism: Confronting Prejudice against Children*. New Haven, CT: Yale University Press.

FURTHER READING

Rosen, Rachel, and Katherine Twamley, eds. 2018. *Feminism and the Politics of Childhood: Friends or Foes*. London: UCL Press.

Spyrou, Spyros, Rachel Rosen, and Daniel Thomas Cook, eds. 2018. *Reimagining Childhod Studies*. London: Bloomsbury Academic.

PART TWO

Non-institutional and Intersectional Politics: Feminisms, Allies, Affect, and Anger

10

Gender and Feminist Mobilizations in Quebec: Changes within and outside the Movement

Pascale Dufour and Geneviève Pagé

Key terms: alliances, intersectional, intersectional turn, mobilization, nationalism, Quebec women's movement, trajectory

While the women's movement in the rest of Canada (as well as Britain and the United States) was "on the defensive" (Bashevkin 1998) and faced a period of decline from the 1980s onward, the **Quebec women's movement** flourished and diversified, not only creating cross-solidarities with progressive movements and organizations, such as unions and other community groups as well as Quebec feminist intellectuals, but also remaining strong enough to significantly influence the Quebec state and its public policies. These differences can be explained, in part, by the historical struggles for Quebec's independence that have had a fundamental influence on the Quebec women's movement, creating both opportunities and constraints. In Quebec, the delineation of the national community has changed over time with respect to the rest of Canada, but also within Quebec itself. The existence of the political project of Quebec sovereignty (sustained by social and political forces) creates ambiguities in terms of who constitutes the dominant majority group (Bilge 2010). In other words, although Québécois/es constitute a distinct minority in Canada, they are the majority in Quebec, raising questions about who exactly constitutes or qualifies as the "we" of the Québécois majority. The answers to this question are multiple and varied. They also oscillate between "civic" nationalist responses based on political formulations of the nation, and "ethnic" **nationalism,** based on ethnic markers and often racialization.

These debates have been important to the development of the feminist movement, starting with its historical connections to the Quebec nationalist movement of the 1960s (Lamoureux 2001; Mills 2004; Pagé 2012, 2015). In the past, the relationship between the nationalist and feminist movements played a dynamic role in fostering the latter, both securing financial support and creating recurrent political opportunities to push for progressive reforms. However, since the late 1990s "turbulent times" within the nationalist movement, along with developments that include: the introduction of managerial modes of operation by the state; the rising voices of women of colour, im/migrant women, Indigenous women, and LGBTQI2S+ advocates; and the transformations of feminism and its organizations, have resulted in discordant dynamics between feminisms and nationalisms. As a result, the past successes of the Quebec women's movement, even when anchored in institutions and institutional practices, have not guaranteed transformative developments for the future. In this chapter, we offer a detailed examination of how and why the Quebec women's movement and its constitutive groups are facing important challenges both from outside and within the movement.

The story we tell in this chapter might appear monolithic and not inclusive enough of alternative and marginalized narratives of the history of different Quebec feminisms. This is due in part to our focus on mainstream feminist organizations and the challenges they face. Of course, these histories are multiple and complex. In each period, voices from Black, Indigenous, and lesbian/queer feminists disputed what feminism should be in Quebec. But unlike in other provinces, these contestations were mostly voiced by individuals instead of organizations (with some notable exceptions, such as the organization Quebec Native Women, discussed later in this chapter) and the literature documenting these voices is rare and very dispersed. This undoubtedly influences the story we are presenting, where nationalism has served both as an engine for the development of feminist demands and a barrier to the expression of diversities. While our account is limited by the scant empirical work available to date, there is a new generation of students in the process of documenting these issues (see for example Labelle 2019).

In the first section of this chapter, we consider the changes that feminist groups face in relation to the Quebec state and its institutions. We also look at ideological and theoretical changes inside the movement, due to the rapidly changing society surrounding it. In the second section of the chapter, we examine why feminists in Quebec are at a crossroads, facing both challenges and opportunities. The future of the movement and its potential for "transformative politics" will greatly depend on the capacity of activists to negotiate more robust **intersectional politics**, deal with different forms of racialization, and position the movement within a rapidly changing social and political context.

THE SHRINKING FOUNDATIONS OF THE QUEBEC WOMEN'S MOVEMENT

Despite its many successes over the last several decades, the destabilized foundations of the Quebec women's movement can be understood by exploring two main developments: the transformation of its relationship with the state, and the position of the movement in a larger political field in and beyond the state, given transformations within the movement itself and its capacity to act as a unified force.

Transformations of the Movement vis-à-vis the State

The Quebec women's movement differed from others elsewhere, such as those in western Europe that laid the foundations for—and/or grew in reaction to—the rise of the welfare state after World War II (Orloff 2009). Social and family policies regulated mainly through state institutions were denounced by many western European feminists as patriarchal and not responsive to women's needs, often because they relied on women's unpaid domestic work. In contrast, in Quebec, because the welfare state emerged slightly later (in the 1960s), the contemporary feminist movement, along with other social groups, developed parallel to it (Favreau 2017) and thus was able to influence it and propose political alternatives that were later incorporated into the state. A classic example is childcare services, which first developed as an autonomous initiative in the 1970s, and then were gradually incorporated and extended into state policy in the 1990s through the *Centres de la petite enfance*, a publicly subsidized and controlled service.

The influence of the Quebec feminist movement was not unidirectional in that it did not consist only of lobbying the state from without; it also called for a transformation of the state from within. The movement was called on to participate in many state initiatives, such as consultation tables on domestic violence or working on ways to improve women's health. Consequently, the movement became highly institutionalized, not only through state funding but also by acting as a meaningful political representative—that is, having formal seats in state structures, and, in some cases, holding formal consultative roles.[1]

Despite the close relations between the movement and the state, the movement was still able to be both a strong and effective opponent of problematic state actions and a leader in calling for progressive reforms. For example, in 1995 the women's movement organized a march across the province, *La Marche du pain et des roses* (the bread and roses march), which later yielded concrete gains on such issues as pay equity and social assistance (Dufour 2008; Graefe 2001). As a result, women's groups' relationships with the state were considered simultaneously cooperative and confrontational (Lamoureux 1994; White et al. 1992; Jetté 2008).

However, by the start of the 2000s, when the Quebec state decided to cut investments in social policies and community group funding, the movement was shaken on several fronts.[2] The Quebec women's movement was challenged in its capacity to be sustained by organizations that act as opponents to the state and serve the population through alternative services (as with women's shelters). This diminished its ability to intervene in the political process—a trend that other types of community organizations were and are facing as well. As a result, the defunding of localized community groups (especially combative ones), and the restructuring of the ways services are delivered and public decisions are made, led to the following question: Are any of these societal groups still capable of continuing their advocacy roles in and against the state (Masson 2012)?

Compounding the matter, since the early 2000s institutionalized community groups have been compelled by the state to adopt a "management" style of governance, which involves dedicating more time to accountability and the standardization of service delivery in order to secure funding. This means that less time can be devoted to their core missions and to advocacy. Furthermore, a policy of "state modernization" was adopted in 2003. This "re-engineering of the state" created agencies in charge of implementing public policies that favoured public-private partnerships (PPPs) for social service delivery. These PPPs introduced service contracts (*ententes de services*) with social groups and redefined them as "partners in the delivery of services" (Depelteau,

Fortier, and Hébert 2013, 17). As "partners," groups were treated as private agents, submitted to criteria of quantitative efficiency, and became preoccupied with short-term planning and more individualized approaches to the delivery of services, instead of collective action. For example, the 2003 health and social services reform privileged the implementation of population-based approaches, clinical projects, limited contracts, and results-based evaluations, which fostered a climate of fear and uncertainty among women's and community organizations that firmly opposed being included in the reform.

Nonetheless, in 2004, the Ministry of Health and Social Services (MHSS) restated its commitment towards women's groups and did not alter its community funding program (Masson 2012). A decade later, however, the Philippe Couillard Liberal government implemented a new program (the Gaétan Barrette health reform overhaul), replacing the previous arrangement with women's and community groups. Since then, discussions and negotiations with both the community sectors and regional agencies and the MHSS have been strained (Rivard 2017, 2018).

During the same period, a new actor was able to gain in prominence in this PPP logic: private foundations, such as the Chagnon foundation. Private foundations had previously been much less prevalent in Quebec than elsewhere in Canada (Ducharme and Lesemann 2012). These new private funders challenged the decision-making structure of social groups (which were accountable mainly to their members and decidedly democratic when it came to determining how to combat social problems), forcing them to adopt top-down decision-making processes and to rely on scientific expertise instead of the expertise developed by service users. In other words, these private foundations directly challenged the community organizations' principles. Not all groups worked with private foundations, but they increasingly became a source of funding for community groups (Depelteau, Fortier, and Hébert 2013), especially as alternative sources withered away.

Despite these changes and challenges, the capacity of the Quebec women's movement has not experienced a straightforward decline. As Masson (2012) has shown, Quebec state-society relationships present a hybrid picture in which competing logics coexist. For instance, the aforementioned managerial approach still rivals the "social liberal" (see Dobrowolsky in this volume) logic inherited from the past. In Quebec, then, women's organizations still have access to core funding instead of depending only on limited, project-funding resources, as has been the case elsewhere in Canada. Thus, the future remains uncertain: it will depend in part on the capacity of the movement to create resistance, building on and joining with other oppositional forces, all of which are necessary to advance a feminist agenda in turbulent times. To explain further, an examination of significant shifts within the movement is necessary.

Transformations within the Movement

Revisiting the history of the Quebec women's movement is beyond the scope of this chapter (for more on this history see Trudel 2009), but it is useful to point out some key differences between the Quebec feminist movement and its Canadian counterparts to understand the current transformations. As argued elsewhere (Pagé 2012, 2015), the Quebec feminist movement in the 1960s and 1970s developed in part by using a national liberation discourse—one grounded in class struggle and in anti-imperialist and anti-colonialist theories from the Global South—which saw francophone women as on the losing end of three systems of oppression: patriarchy, capitalism, and colonialism. Although in retrospect it seems problematic to understand white francophone women as oppressed by colonialism (they were also descendants of colonizers and profited from the colonization of Indigenous communities), most political and economic institutions in Quebec were then controlled by the English-speaking minority. Even as the "Quiet Revolution"[3] started to change this pattern, the critique of the anglophones' stronghold provided by the nationalist movement and the political project the latter proposed resonated strongly with francophone women. Thus, (white) feminists—especially the revolutionary ones— saw themselves as needing to battle multiple interacting systems of oppression,[4] and saw national liberation as one aspect of their struggle. Although the relationship between the feminist movement and the nationalist movement has always been conflictual (Lamoureux 2001; de Sève, Lamoureux, and Maillé 1999), it was nonetheless a major factor in Quebec feminism's **trajectory** and explains why it moved away from its Canadian counterparts, which were more invested in federalism. It also helps us to understand why the Quebec women's movement developed different understandings of "community," the Québécois "we," oppression, and the path to liberation.

In addition to nationalism, the strong influence of a radical materialist feminist tradition,[5] imported from France in the 1980s, continued to distance the Quebec feminist movement from its Canadian counterparts (Pagé 2012; Lamontagne 2017). This tradition served to maintain a strong structural analysis of the commonality of women's oppression even while recognizing different contexts and experiences (Juteau 2010).

Yet, as Quebec society changed—francophones now control most political and some economic institutions in Quebec—the underclass is no longer associated with a language marker but with a racial marker. In other words, leading voices in the Quebec women's movement who linked gender, class, and nationalist struggles were increasingly contested by racialized women and women from a new generation who faced differently configured economic challenges and introduced new dimensions of intersectional politics. For example, Muslim women and their allies have argued that religious discrimination (particularly linked to the wearing of a headscarf) is one of the main barriers to Muslim women's economic participation, more so than class or gender, thus expanding the conceptual ground for women's oppression.

This trajectory helps to explain why certain groups in the movement—Indigenous and racialized women, anglophone and allophone women—have experienced greater marginalization than (white) francophone women, and when the former struggled to gain a voice, resistance occurred and instability emerged within the feminist movement (Campbell-Fiset 2017). While this dynamic is also present in the rest of Canada, leading Quebec feminists (white and francophone) resisted these challenges longer, as Maillé (2017) argues, and they were even more reluctant to integrate contemporary postcolonial and intersectional feminist approaches into their analyses. Again, this occurred because (white) francophone Quebec feminists historically saw themselves as victims of colonization (by the anglophones) and as racialized and oppressed, and thus drew upon earlier forms of intersectional politics having to do with gender, class, and nation (Pagé 2015). As mentioned in the introduction to this chapter, we cannot yet speak of the extensive organizational expression of collective voices of Black feminists and Muslim feminists in Quebec. Several attempts to create specific organizations have failed (for example, after the Women's March of 2017), although a succession of networked individuals have maintained the pressure.

At the same time, however, other particularities of the Quebec women's movement highlight its strengths. As in other Western societies, the movement is ideologically diverse (there are liberal feminists and leftist groups as well as different branches of radical feminism; for an overview, see Rollo in this volume). But this plurality has not prevented common actions through time that have created pathbreaking organizational forms and struggles. For instance, the creation of the influential umbrella organization the *Fédération des femmes du Québec* (FFQ; federation of Quebec women) in 1966 and the establishment of the Quebec Council on the Status of Women in 1973 brought together different strands of feminism and spurred the growth of similar organizations across Canada. In the 1980s and 1990s, feminists working in concert resulted in landmark legislative gains, such as the Pay Equity Act in 1996, and feminist groups in Quebec led the way in mobilizing for front-line intervention in social services, popular education, violence against women, employment services, and childcare, and in the cultural sphere. And so, while feminist umbrella organizations and state-tied bodies withered away in the rest of Canada by the 1990s, this was not the case in Quebec.

Nonetheless, more recently, the challenges outlined above have gradually taken their toll. For example, the FFQ now appears fragile and its ability to play its role as the leading federation of feminisms is increasingly in question. To elaborate, in the 1990s and early 2000s the FFQ emerged as the main (albeit always contested) leader of the movement, federating local and regional groups and gaining credibility on the political scene. This was especially evident in its organization of the 1995 Marche du pain et des roses, mentioned earlier, which led to the FFQ's privileged role as a national interlocutor in negotiations with the Quebec state (Maillé 2000, 99; Masson 2012, 48). The success of the 1995 march then inspired members of the FFQ and other Quebec feminists to create and lead the first global action of the World March of Women in 2000, furthering the legitimacy of the FFQ as a leader in the women's movement in Quebec and on both the local and the international scene (Giraud and Dufour 2010). However, since the early 2000s this leadership has been undermined by successive (federal) funding cuts that have had concrete effects on the FFQ (such as the reduction in permanent staff positions from seven in 2009 to two in 2018), greatly limiting the **mobilization** capacity of the organization and the feminist movement as a whole.

Moreover, this financial uncertainty has contributed to internal crises. In 2011, in an effort to revitalize and reunite the movement, the FFQ launched *Les États généraux de l'action et de l'analyse feministes* (EGF; the Estates General of Feminist Action and Analysis), a series of province-wide consultations with groups and individuals discussing the direction and priorities of the movement for the next 20 years. Although impressive in its magnitude, this two-year mobilization effort did not convert into a strong political force able to effectively negotiate with the government and make concrete gains, in part due to the rapid decline of the FFQ.

Still, these turbulent political times—and the waning strength and influence of the FFQ—should not be interpreted as a decreasing capacity of the women's movement as a whole, as other networks and voices have emerged (for example, the 2017 Women's March, organized all around the world) to challenge the FFQ's position as the only legitimate state interlocutor. Nonetheless, the future is unclear, given several challenges and opportunities to which we will now turn.

QUEBEC FEMINISMS AT A CROSSROADS

What lies ahead for the Quebec women's movement will greatly depend on the capacity of activists to deal with the following challenges and respond to new claims in a changing political context.

Key Challenges

In 2008, an academic conference, *Faut-il réfuter le Nous femmes pour être féministe au XXIe siècle?* (Must we refute "We women" to be feminist in the twenty-first century?), was held in Montreal and dealt directly with the question of who constitutes the "we" of Quebec feminism. This was an attempt to deal with the rifts that had opened within the movement and marked the beginning of what we will call the **intersectional turn**, and both the empowerment and instability that came with it.

In 2006 and 2007, several controversies emerged in the Quebec media around the notion of "reasonable accommodation," which called for necessary and appropriate modifications and adjustments to rules and norms to ensure that people with disabilities or others with specific requirements (for example, religious practices) had the ability to exercise their rights on an equal basis with others. Tensions were high as cleavages within the women's movement were exacerbated by the media, which expressed outrage at certain "accommodations"[6] conceded to minorities and deemed them to be discriminatory for women. For example, in April 2006 the media inaccurately reported that the Hasidic (orthodox Jewish) community had asked a YMCA facility to install frosted-glass windows (which directly faced the back of their synagogue) in its training room in order to hide women exercising from the view of Hasidic children.[7] The province-wide consultation on "reasonable accommodations" that followed in 2008—the Bouchard-Taylor Commission—was intended as a vehicle for resolving the controversies at stake, but instead served as the Quebec version of much broader "culture versus gender" or "multiculturalism versus feminism" debates taking place elsewhere, including the rest of Canada.

In Quebec, the specific question of whether religious accommodations were endangering women's rights deepened divisions among feminists. For some, the Quebec feminist project means transcending religious traditions (historically Catholic, and now more diverse) and promoting both secularism and equality. This translates into questioning religious accommodations and, eventually, it means staunchly opposing the wearing of religious symbols and garb by state employees. Particular attention is paid to the headscarf, as this subset of Quebec feminists see it as a symbol of women's oppression (i.e., an accommodation of culture, here religion, trumped gender equality). However, this position had the effect of stigmatizing Muslim women and racializing many (im)migrants, particularly those of North African origin. Intentionally or not, it contributed to the marginalization of racialized women, while minimizing the inequality and violence experienced by them in non-racialized dominant groups.

For other Quebec feminists, their rights (cultural, religious, or gender equality) should be simultaneously defended and recognized without hierarchies; they argue for the strongest inclusion of differences possible within the movement and its demands. These feminists are more influenced by contemporary, postcolonial, and intersectional feminist perspectives. They are denounced by feminists who are wary of accommodations and the resurgence of religion and accuse them of destroying gains made by feminists over the years, endangering the secular project (or Quebec's specificity), and selling out to Canadian multiculturalism (Saint-Louis 2018).[8]

The États généraux du féminisme (EGF) between 2011 and 2013 were in part designed to address these tensions, and became the battlefield for what Marie-Ève Campbell-Fiset describes as the "intersectional turn." Over this period, the FFQ pushed to adopt an intersectional framework and was faced with resistance from "universalist feminists" (Campbell-Fiset 2017), who advocated minimizing differences among women in order to foreground women's common oppression.

As a case in point, in 2013, a new feminist group, *Pour le droit des femmes du Québec* (PDFQ; for the rights of Québécois women), claimed in the media to be a counterweight to the FFQ. PDFQ not only criticized the FFQ's support of women's right to wear the headscarf, but also accused the FFQ of adopting an individualist and Islamic feminist agenda. This confrontation between PDFQ and the FFQ continued in 2019 as debates around Bill 21, An Act Respecting the Laicity of the State—which prohibits all employees of the state in a position of authority (including teachers) from wearing religious symbols (including headscarves)—crystallized the divide. Although the number of individuals and groups opposing intersectionality is small, they are vocal and virulent (Pagé and Pires 2015), and have powerful ties to the media and government. Many justify their opposition to the public display of religious symbols through an interpretation of the history of Quebec feminism as having opposed religion (given the historic dominance of the Catholic Church in Quebec and its role in the oppression of women) since the 1960s (Jacquet 2017). They not only support a secular Quebec, but link this support to the rise of the nationalist movement and gains from the Quiet Revolution onwards (Lamoureux 2018), as discussed above. In this case, even if some (white) nationalist feminists showed an early proto-intersectional analysis of multiple and simultaneous oppressions, nationalist feminism in Quebec is now more intransigent and less open to newer intersectional demands and needs from women of colour and other marginalized women.

And so, the struggle is ongoing. Another vivid illustration of the conflicts and contestations at play occurred in 2017, when the FFQ made headlines with the election of its first transgender president, Gabrielle Bouchard. At this time, some Quebec feminists publicly challenged the idea that Bouchard could represent women, including Diane Guilbault, who left the FFQ in 2013 to form PDFQ.

This narrow understanding of women's rights places limits on new and/or more expansive conceptions of feminism, as well as redefining the political priorities and strategies that they require. As just one illustration, when the organization Quebec Native Women (QNW) asks for "nation to nation" recognition by the FFQ, QNW is not only questioning an egalitarian project sustained by white feminists, but is also challenging the very conception of a Quebec territorial collectivity or a political unit. Put differently, when Quebec's racialized women ask for more space in struggles and confront the movement's white privileges, they also disrupt the dominant representation of Quebec women as exploited and oppressed by the anglophones (men and women).

As a result, the path to an inclusive movement that is sensitive to differences becomes more difficult in Quebec than in the rest of Canada. To emerge from this conundrum, the movement needs to redefine feminism without feeling that the position of the "Quebec nation" is necessarily under threat. Moreover, the rethinking of the "we" used by privileged white feminists to include a diversity of positions and histories and to take several dimensions of oppression into consideration (Dorlin 2008) is not enough; the movement needs to redefine the Quebec "we" as a territorial collectivity existing as a diverse collective entity. Nevertheless, these turbulent times do offer opportunities for the Quebec women's movement to re-invent itself and the multiple feminisms it expresses.

Some Opportunities

Several contentious episodes in Quebec's political life have provided some opportunities for the Quebec feminist movement to build new **alliances** and adopt new demands. We focus here on two types of alliances that are especially important for future transformative developments.

Anti-racism and a New Anti-colonialism

In 2012 and 2013, grassroots Indigenous groups mobilized across Canada under the banner of Idle No More. The Quebec chapter of Idle No More was launched in January 2013 by Widia Larivière, an Algonquin and a Quebecer, and Mélissa Mollen-Dupuis, who is Innu. Idle No More thus highlighted the concerns of another collective social actor in Quebec: Indigenous communities in general and Indigenous feminists in particular. While the FFQ had worked for some time to improve its relationship with Indigenous women's organizations, the relationship was fraught with difficulties. However, the 2004 signing of the *Déclaration solennelle de solidarité* (solemn declaration of solidarity) between the FFQ and QNW, whereby women from two different nations (noted above) came together to express their solidarity and support of each other's struggles, constituted a significant milestone. This recognition of women belonging to different nations was a clear step forward from the Quebec nationalist tradition and in the direction of a more inclusive movement. This declaration, combined with the awareness raising done as part of the EGF (2011–13), the Idle No More campaigns, and broader actions around Missing and Murdered Indigenous Women and Girls (MMIWG), were all steps in the right direction for the Quebec women's movement. Yet, a number of issues still need to be addressed in terms of how this newfound solidarity is expressed and acted upon.

The struggle over the integration of an intersectional framework during the EFG was also an important moment of awareness raising about the real presence and the concrete consequences of systemic racism. It seems that—at least among members of the FFQ—there is considerable consensus that colonialism and racism towards Indigenous and racialized women have

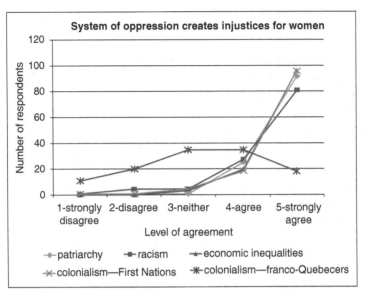

Figure 1 Number of respondents (dis)agreeing with the statement "Patriarchy/racism/economic inequalities/colonialism against First Nations/ colonialism against franco-Quebecers creates injustices for women"

Source: Pagé and Pires 2015, 30

far more detrimental effects on the lives of these women than "colonialism against Franco-Quebecers" (Pagé and Pires 2015, 30), as shown in figure 1 above.

The graph shows that while more than 80 respondents strongly agreed that patriarchy, racism, economic inequalities, and colonialism towards First Nations create injustices for women, only 18 strongly believed that colonialism against franco-Quebecers does the same. This transformation of the feminist paradigm offers opportunities to build a stronger, more inclusive movement that can integrate the priorities of a diverse group of women—including Indigenous and racialized women, but also queer and trans people[9]—and potentially bridge the gap between anglophone and francophone feminists, as well as connect with other activists. Thus, recent transformations and debates can lead to new solidarities in feminism in order to both recognize differences among women and the necessity to consider the articulation of oppression (Szczepanik et al. 2010). Yet, this progress is also slowed by the dearth of organized groups representing the interests of Muslim women, Black women, immigrant women, and other racialized women. This task often falls on the shoulders of individual women involved in the movement.

These recent transformations in the movement are slowly affecting some campaigns. For example, the demands of the 2015 World March of Women embodied both the integration of an intersectional analysis and the recent alliance with Indigenous women. Titled "*Libérons nos corps, notre terre et nos territoires*" (Let's liberate our bodies, our land [earth] and our territories), the manifesto written for this event [10] worked to integrate an understanding of how our bodies, our environment, and our territories are colonized, marginalized, and subjected to violence and external control through the different capitalist, colonial, racist, ableist, and patriarchal imperatives. We also see a strong presence of environmental preoccupations—presented in connection with issues of Indigenous control of the land—and opposition to the precedence of capitalist profit over health and environmental preoccupation (see Altimarano-Jiménez and Wiebe in this volume). This example shows how the feminist movement can produce more inclusive discourses that allow for the different preoccupations of activists to come under the same banner and have transnational influence (see Masson, Paulos, and Beaulieu Bastien 2017).

#MeToo and Mass Renewal?

Parallel to this type of mobilization, in Quebec, as in the rest of Canada, the resurgence of awareness of sexual violence as an issue started a few years before the #MeToo movement, with the 2014 trial of well-known CBC radio host Jian Ghomeshi (see Craig and Small in this volume). This brought issues of sexual violence to the forefront of the media, including social media, and led to the creation of the hashtag #BeenRapedNeverReported, which created space for disclosures and in turn translated into #AgressionNonDénoncée. These two hashtags mobilized more than eight million users in Canada (Savard-Moisan 2017; Pelletier 2015). In Quebec in 2015 the *Regroupement Québécois des Centres d'aide et de lutte contre les agressions à caractère sexuel* (an organization that consolidates sexual assault centres in Quebec) launched the campaign #OnVousCroit (#WeBelieveYou) to celebrate and support all the women who were courageous enough to disclose while sending a clear message to the population about what women need.

As a result, when #MeToo (#MoiAussi) arrived in Quebec in 2017, it landed on fertile ground. These social media grassroots movements have clearly brought issues of sexual violence awareness not only to the forefront of the feminist agenda but also to the broader provincial political agenda, with the minister responsible for higher education and the status of women, Hélène David, pushing for the adoption of Bill 151, An Act to Prevent and

Fight Sexual Violence in Higher Education Institutions, along with major funding promises for prevention and support of victims of sexual violence.

CONCLUSION

As this chapter demonstrates, both external and internal forces have fundamentally challenged the Quebec women's movement and its relationships with the state and institutions. Yet feminist activists are in the process of inventing new ways of being and acting as feminists. As Staggenborg and Taylor claimed:

> We firmly believe that social movements based on fundamental social cleavages do not die out, but scale down and retrench to adapt to changes in the political and social climate. After the period of intense mobilization in the 1960s and early 1970s, many women's movement organizations managed to remain alive and grow, new organizations continued to form, and new tactics were added to the feminist repertoire. The movement continued within institutions, in other social movements, and in cultural venues. (2005, 48)

And so, at the time of writing this chapter, the Quebec feminist movement can be described as alive and well, even as it undergoes profound transformations. As we have shown in this chapter, the challenges facing the Quebec movement are not shaking feminism itself, but rather some of the problematic universalizing formulations it has adopted, along with the positions of some (dominant) groups within it. Nevertheless, as Alexa Conradi, past president of the FFQ, notes: "Feminism might be in fashion today, but the issue of its political power is still in question. The answers are, in part, in the hands of activists" (2017, 53, our translation).

DISCUSSION QUESTIONS

1. How does the historical predominance of white feminists in the Quebec feminist movement continue to shape contemporary debates?
2. What could be an intersectional reformulation of the #MeToo campaign in Quebec?

3. Can feminism still coexist with nationalism?
4. What are the main tensions within the Quebec's women's movement and what are some avenues to move beyond them?

NOTES

1 In 2001, the adoption of *La politique de reconnaissance et de soutien de l'action communautaire* formalized the funding of groups defined as "autonomous," including the vast majority of women's groups, and recognized their expertise in the field (see White et al. 2008).

2 It is commonly agreed that, in Quebec, the neoliberal turn happened later than elsewhere in Canada, in 2003 with the Jean Charest Liberal government. Nonetheless, social funding and rationales behind social policies were being transformed as early as the end of the 1980s, with the second Robert Bourassa Liberal government (1985–94). Yet concrete changes affecting women's and community groups only occurred later, and it is only since 2014, with the Philippe Couillard Liberal government, that women's groups' relations with the state have dramatically deteriorated.

3 The period from 1960 to 1970, known as "the Quiet Revolution," involved important social, cultural, political, and economic transformations. For example, the Quebec state took over control of education and welfare from the Catholic Church. This revolution resulted in gains that included opportunities for access to public, francophone post-secondary schools, and the design of unique welfare policies specific to Quebec's needs, as well as the development of francophone-led industry and business.

4 Although the term "intersectionality" was not used by Quebec feminists, some had conceptions of interacting systems of oppression that were similar (see Pagé 2012 for more details).

5 The radical materialist feminists are influenced by Marxist political theories and consider that structurally, the sexual division of labour (inside and outside the household) and the appropriation of women's bodies are the cornerstone of women's oppression. They thus view both class and gender systems as interacting sources of oppression.

6 Most of the examples of "accommodations" used to support the media outcry turned out to be either false, greatly misrepresented, or private arrangements between clients and businesses (and thus not "reasonable accommodations" as per the legal term; Bouchard and Taylor 2008). For an excellent postcolonial analysis of the ensuing legislation proposed by the government—the Quebec Charter of Values—see Haince, El-Ghadban, and Benhadjoudja 2014.

7 In fact, the reality was that the YMCA was replacing its windows and opted to use frosted-glass windows instead of regular windows with shades based on a survey of its members and in consultation with the Jewish community.

8 In the view of some Quebec sovereigntists, the reasonable accommodation principle is the spearhead of Canadian multiculturalism, promoting community rights and ignoring or diminishing the recognition of Quebec (francophone) specificity as a whole. The theory and practices of multiculturalism have always been contested in Quebec due to the centrality of French language and culture. As a result, Quebec has adopted and promoted "interculturalism" instead of multiculturalism.

9 For more information on these issues, see Tourki 2017.

10 The manifesto can be found in French only at: http://www.ffq.qc.ca/wpcontent /uploads/2014/12/Texte-de-r%C3%A9flexion-MMF-2015.pdf.

REFERENCES

Bashevkin, Sylvia. 1998. *Living through Conservative Times: Women on the Defensive.* Chicago: University of Chicago Press.

Bilge, Sirma. 2010. "'… Alors que nous, Québécois, nos femmes sont égales à nous, et nous les aimons ainsi': la patrouille des frontières au nom de l'égalité de genre dans une 'nation' en quête de souveraineté." *Sociologie et Sociétés* 42 (1): 197–226.

Bouchard, Gérard, and Charles Taylor. 2008. *Building the Future: A Time for Reconciliation.* Commission Report. Québec: Gouvernement du Québec.

Campbell-Fiset, Marie-Ève. 2017. "Analyse d'un backlash intramouvement: les états généraux de l'action et de l'analyse féministes (2011–2014)." Master's thesis, Université du Québec à Montréal.

Conradi, Alexa. 2017. *Les angles morts.* Montreal: Remue-Ménage.

de Sève, Micheline, Diane Lamoureux, and Chantal Maillé. 1999. *Malaises identitaires: échanges féministes autour d'un Québec incertain.* Montreal: Remue-Ménage.

Depelteau, Julie, Francis Fortier, and Guillaume Hébert. 2013. "Les organismes communautaires au Québec: financement et évolution des pratiques." Institut de recherche et d'informations socio-économiques (IRIS), May. https://cdn.iris -recherche.qc.ca/uploads/publication/file/Communautaire-WEB-02.pdf.

Dorlin, Elsa. 2008. *Sexe, genre et sexualités: introduction à la théorie féministe.* Paris: PUF.

Ducharme, Élise, and Frédéric Lesemann. 2012. "Philanthropie et fondations privées: une nouvelle gouvernance sociale?" *Lien social et politique* 65: 203–24.

Dufour, Pascale. 2008. "Des femmes en marche: vers un féminisme transnational?" In *Le Québec en mouvements,* edited by Francis Dupuis-Déri, 57–70. Montreal: Lux.

Favreau, Louis. 2017. *Mouvement communautaire et État social.* Montreal: PUQ.

Giraud, Isabelle, and Pascale Dufour. 2010. *Dix ans de solidarité planétaire: perspectives sociologiques sur la Marche mondiale des femmes.* Montreal: Remue-ménage.

Graefe, Peter. 2001. "Whose Social Economy? Debating New State Practices in Québec." *Critical Social Policy* 21 (25): 34–58.

Haince, Marie-Claude, Yara El-Ghadban, and Leïla Benhadjoudja. 2014. *Le Québec, la Charte, l'autre: et après?* Montreal: Mémoire d'encrier.

Jacquet, Caroline. 2017. "Représentations féministes de 'la religion' et de 'la laïcité' au Québec (1960–2013): reproductions et contestations des frontières identitaires." PhD diss., Université du Québec à Montréal. https://archipel.uqam.ca/9827/.

Jetté, Christian. 2008. *Les organismes communautaires et la transformation de l'État-providence*. Québec: Presses de l'Université du Québec.

Juteau, Danielle. 2010. "'Nous' les femmes: sur l'indissociable homogénéité et hétérogénéité de la catégorie." *L'Homme et la société* 2 (176–77): 65–81.

Labelle, Alexie. 2019. "Why Participate? An Intersectional Analysis of LGBTQ People of Color Activism in Canada." *Politics, Groups, and Identities*, published online.

Lamontagne, Amélie. 2017. "'Je ne veux pas être condamnée au viol à perpétuité, et toi?' Luttes féministes québécoises contre les violences sexuelles (1970–1983)." Master's thesis, Université de Montréal. https://papyrus.bib.umontreal.ca/xmlui/handle/1866/20669.

Lamoureux, Diane. 2001. *L'amère patrie: féminisme et nationalisme dans le Québec contemporain*. Montreal: Remue-ménage.

———. 2018. "Feminism and Nationalism in Quebec." In *Gendering Nationalism*, edited by Jon Mulholland, Nicola Montagna, and Erin Sanders-McDonagh, 187–202. New York: Palgrave.

Lamoureux, Jocelyne. 1994. *Le partenariat à l'épreuve*. Montreal: Éditions Saint-Martin.

Maillé, Chantal. 2000. "Féminisme et mouvement des femmes au Québec: un bilan complexe." *Globe* 3 (2): 87–105.

———. 2007. "Réception de la théorie postcoloniale dans le féminisme québécois." *Recherches féministes* 20 (2): 91–111.

Masson, Dominique. 2012. "Changing State Forms, Competing State Projects: Funding Women's Organizations in Quebec." *Studies in Political Economy* 89 (1): 79–103.

Masson, Dominique, Annabel Paulos, and Elsa Beaulieu Bastien. 2017. "Struggling for Food Sovereignty in the World March of Women." *The Journal of Peasant Studies* 44 (1): 56–77.

Mills, Sean. 2004. "Québécoises deboutte! Le Front de libération des femmes du Québec, le Centre des femmes et le nationalisme." *Mens* 4 (2): 183–210.

Orloff, Ann Shola. 2009. "Gendering the Comparative Analysis of Welfare States: An Unfinished Agenda." *Sociological Theory* 27 (3): 317–43.

Pagé, Geneviève. 2012. "Feminism à la Quebec: Ideological Travelings of American and French Thought (1960–2010)." PhD diss., University of Maryland. https://drum.lib.umd.edu/handle/1903/12740.

———. 2015. "Est-ce qu'on peut être racisées, nous aussi?: Les féministes blanches et le paradoxe du désir de racisation." In *Le sujet du féminisme est-il blanc ? Femmes racisées et recherche féministe*, edited by Naïma Hamrouni and Chantal Maillé, 133–54. Montreal: Remue-ménage.

Pagé, Geneviève, and Rosa Pires. 2015. *L'intersectionnalité en débats: pour un renouvellement des pratiques féministes au Québec*. Montreal: Fédération des femmes du Québec and Service aux collectivités, UQAM.

Pelletier, Francine. 2015. *Second début: cendres et renaissance du féminisme*. Montreal: Atelier 10.

Rivard, Sébastien. 2017. "Nouvelle ronde de travaux sur le partenariat entre les organismes communautaires et les établissements de santé." Montreal: Bulletins du RIOCM, February.

——. 2018. "Nouvelles du PSOC—formulaire 2018–2019, refonte du programme, crédits alloués et cadre de partenariat." Montreal: Bulletins du RIOCM, January.

Saint-Louis, Jean-Charles. 2018. "Parler de la 'diversité' au Québec: une étude généalogique des discussions récentes sur le pluralisme et la citoyenneté." PhD diss., Université du Québec à Montréal. https://archipel.uqam.ca/11748/.

Savard-Moisan, Raphaëlle. 2017. "Le traitement médiatique du mouvement #AgressionNonDénoncée dans la presse écrite francophone." Master's thesis, Université du Québec à Montréal. https://archipel.uqam.ca/9675/.

Staggenborg, Susan, and Verta Taylor. 2005. "Whatever Happened to the Women's Movement?" *Mobilization: An International Quarterly* 10 (1): 37–52.

Szczepanik, Geneviève, Descarries Francine, Mélissa Blais, and Sandrine Ricci. 2010. "Penser le Nous féministe: le féminisme solidaire." *Nouveaux cahiers du socialisme* 4: 188–203.

Tourki, Dalia. 2017. "Le Québec et les droits LGBTQ, entre mensonge et réalité." *Je Suis Féministe*, January 18. https://jesuisfeministe.com/2017/01/18/le-quebec-et-les-droits-lgbtq-entre-mensonges-et-realites/.

Trudel, Flavie. 2009. "L'engagement des femmes en politique au Québec: histoire de la Fédération des femmes du Québec de 1966 à nos jours." PhD diss., Université du Québec à Montréal. https://archipel.uqam.ca/2212/.

White, Deena, Céline Mercier, Henri Dorvil, and Lili Jureau. 1992. "Les pratiques de concertation en santé mentale: trois modèles." *Nouvelles Pratiques Sociales* 5 (1): 77–93.

White, Deena, et al. 2008. *La gouvernance intersectorielle à l'épreuve: évaluation de la mise en œuvre et des premières retombées de la politique de reconnaissance et de soutien de l'action communautaire*. Montréal: Centre de recherche sur les politiques et le développement social. http://trocca.com/doc/2008DWhite EvaluationPRSACresume.pdf

FURTHER READING

Hamrouni, Naïma, and Chantal Maillé, eds. 2015. *Le sujet du féminisme est-il blanc? Femmes racisées et recherche féministe*. Montreal: Remue-ménage.

Lamoureux, Diane. 2001. *L'amère patrie: féminisme et nationalisme dans le Québec contemporain*. Montreal: Remue-ménage.

11

The Intersectional Politics of Black Lives Matter

Debra Thompson

Key terms: Black Lives Matter, criminal justice, inequality, race, racism

INTRODUCTION

The eruption of protests in 2014 and 2015 condemning the police killings of Michael Brown in Ferguson, Missouri; Freddie Gray in Baltimore; and far too many other African American men and women throughout the United States catalysed the emergence of the **Black Lives Matter** (BLM) social movement. Simultaneously a discourse, hashtag, rallying cry, and loose organizational structure, BLM is considered to be the "new" civil rights movement of the twenty-first century (Thompson and Thurston 2018). According to BLM co-founder Alicia Garza, "Black Lives Matter is an ideological and political intervention in a world where Black lives are systematically and intentionally targeted for demise. It is an affirmation of Black folks' contributions to this society, our humanity, and our resilience in the face of deadly oppression" (2014, n.p.). BLM challenges the proliferation of the American carceral state; the prison-industrial complex; the militarization of the police; the increased surveillance, disciplining, and criminalization of the poor; and the ways that public goods are unequally distributed along racial lines (Taylor 2016). In a relatively short period of time, BLM activism has changed the terrain of debate on issues of racial inequality, police violence, and the persistence of anti-Black **racism** in democratic societies. It is a contemporary and illustrative example of the transformative potential of social movements to challenge the societal ideas about **race**, gender, and class that simultaneously hide and solidify hierarchal relationships of political power.

Though the events that gave rise to BLM are widely understood both in and outside the United States as examples of a uniquely American "race problem," BLM is a global movement. In London, Paris, Palestine, Sydney, Toronto, and even Accra, Ghana, BLM's calls to bring awareness to issues of police brutality, mass incarceration, racial **inequality**, and anti-Black racism continue to resonate. When awarding its 2017 prize to the Global Black Lives Matter Network, the Sydney Peace Foundation recognized activists for "building a powerful movement for racial equality, courageously reigniting a global conversation around state violence and racism" (2017, n.p.). Though political mobilizations of Blackness are often tied to particular events, debates, or situations within a bounded territory or locality, Black solidarities have always been shaped by meanings that are transferrable across national boundaries, sometimes encompassed by the idea of "diaspora" (Hesse and Hooker 2017). This is true even in Canada, where the image of a multicultural nation and the celebration of diversity have at times masked the history and persistence of racism and racial inequality in the country (Thompson 2008; Banting and Thompson 2016). Satellite sites of BLM organizing, including those in Toronto, Vancouver, Edmonton, and Montreal have challenged Canadian police violence and practices of surveillance towards Black citizens, seeking to undo systemic racialized violence by centring Black voices, especially those who are queer, trans, women, differently-abled, poor, undocumented, immigrant, and otherwise marginalized (BLM-Vancouver, n.d.).

The purpose of this chapter is to examine the intersectional politics and gendered political strategies of BLM. I argue that significant elements of the movement include its creation by Black queer women (see also Weerawardhana in this volume), its unapologetic adoption and use of intersectional understandings of identity, and its advocacy for all people of African descent, including LGBTQ, immigrant, and incarcerated women. Secondly, this chapter details some of BLM's attempts to illuminate and challenge specifically Canadian manifestations of state violence towards Black communities by emphasizing the transnational nature of racial domination and the emancipatory potential of global alliances in anti-racism activism. In these and many other ways, BLM activism has already transformed the landscape of race politics in Canada and beyond.

BLACK LIVES MATTER: BACKGROUND/CONTEXT

The origins of the Black Lives Matter movement are fairly well known. Patrisse Cullors, Opal Tometi, and Alicia Garza created the hashtag #blacklivesmatter in the wake of the verdict that exonerated George Zimmerman for the murder of 17-year-old Trayvon Martin in July 2013. The movement crystallized after Michael Brown was shot and killed by police officer Darren Wilson in Ferguson, Missouri, in August 2014. Days of protest followed and spread across the United States. The movement spread as well, catalysed by the police killings of unarmed African Americans, some of which were captured on either bystander videos or police dash-cam footage that subsequently went viral: Eric Garner in July 2014, John Crawford III in August 2014, Laquan McDonald in November 2014, and 12-year-old Tamir Rice in November 2014. Police officers were not indicted in the deaths of Brown, Garner, Crawford, and Rice, and Chicago Police Department officer Jason Van Dyke was charged with murder only after the media exposed a year-long cover-up by both the Chicago Police Department and the City of Chicago (Harcourt 2015). BLM was further galvanized by the April 2015 death of Freddie Gray in Baltimore. Gray was injured by police while being placed under arrest and a post-mortem medical investigation revealed that he died of injuries sustained while being transported in police custody. Though Baltimore City State's Attorney Marilyn Mosby brought charges against each of the six officers involved, one trial ended in a mistrial, two officers were found not guilty, and by July 2016 the remaining charges against the officers were dropped. The list goes on; these are but a few examples of a much larger phenomenon of deadly, disproportionate police violence towards African Americans.

Broadly speaking, BLM protests have been highly effective at illuminating the pervasive nature and unjustifiable frequency of police brutality. Though there is no federal-level government database in the United States that tracks deadly police violence, the *Washington Post* (2019) estimates that nearly a thousand Americans are killed each year by "fatal force" exercised by police officers. Most of the victims of police shootings are white, but the police shoot and kill African Americans at a rate that is disproportionate to the size of the population. According to the United States Census Bureau, approximately 12.3 per cent of the population identifies as Black, though this population is around 25 per cent of police shooting victims. The data collected by the website Mapping Police Violence (www.mappingpoliceviolence .org) demonstrates that the rates of police killings of African Americans are higher in every state except six (all of which are notoriously racially homogenous): Idaho, Montana, North Dakota, New Hampshire, South Dakota, Vermont, and Wyoming. The organization's 2017 *Police Violence Report* (https:// policeviolencereport.org/) recorded a total of 1,147 deaths at the hands of the police (including shootings as well as the use of tasers, vehicles, and physical force), and in only 13 of these cases—roughly one per cent—were police officers charged with a crime. The online report notes that most killings began with the police responding to a suspected non-violent offence or a circumstance where no crime had been reported at all, and at least 89 people were killed after the police stopped them for a traffic violation.

Between 2014 and 2016, President Barack Obama's administration often responded to BLM protests and calls for action by initiating Department of Justice (DOJ) investigations of the police departments in question. DOJ reports in Ferguson, Baltimore, and Chicago reveal widespread unconstitutional policing practices and extensively detail how these police departments have disproportionately and often illegally targeted, detained, arrested, criminalized, exploited, assaulted, and killed African Americans (United States DOJ 2015, 2016, 2017). Since 2017, the administration of President Donald Trump has transformed the landscape of American **criminal justice** by instituting more stringent federal sentencing guidelines, increasing deportation orders, threatening the funding of sanctuary cities, reinvigorating the disastrous War on Drugs, backtracking on consent decrees that required police departments that have violated civil rights to reform their unconstitutional practices, and remaking the court system by stacking lower courts with conservative, white, male judicial nominees. These changes have disproportionately impacted Black, Latino, and immigrant communities (George 2018). Political mobilization, therefore, is an important strategy through which marginalized groups are able to make visible the often hidden but extraordinarily violent role of the state in their daily lives (Soss and Weaver 2017; Thurston 2018).

In recognition of the power and necessity of local, grassroots activism, BLM has a purposefully decentralized organizational structure. The Black Lives Matter Global Network "started out as a Black-centered political will and movement building project turned chapter-based, member-led organization whose mission is to build local power and to intervene when violence was inflicted on Black communities by the state and vigilantes" (BLM-GN 2017, 4). BLM chapters in American cities, such as Atlanta; the Bay Area; Washington, DC; Chicago; and Los Angeles, work alongside other grassroots organizations within and outside the coalition of groups that form the broader Movement for Black Lives. These include the Black Youth Project 100, Dream Defenders, Million Hoodies Movement for Justice, Mothers against Police Brutality, Campaign Zero, and the National Conference of Black Lawyers. Though it is often accused of being a "leaderless movement" with unclear policy aims, the platform developed for the Movement for Black Lives during its 2015 national convening in Cleveland is an unambiguous articulation of how policy changes at the local, state, and federal level can lead to substantive improvements in the lives of many African Americans (Movement for Black Lives 2016).

It is this decentralized, locally focused structure that enabled the emergence of BLM chapters in major Canadian cities such as Toronto, Montreal, Edmonton, and Vancouver. BLM-Toronto, the first international chapter of the movement, began with nine members in November of 2014. Its first demonstration was held outside the American consulate in Toronto when an estimated 3,000 people protested the failure to indict police officer Darren Wilson in the murder of Michael Brown (Onstad 2017). The message of these protests, according to BLM-Toronto co-founder Janaya Khan, was that "we unequivocally stand against the no indictment ruled in favour of Darren Wilson and that we completely support Mike Brown and Mike Brown's family. We support any kind of actions against state-sanctioned violence and police brutality and we want to draw parallels to what is happening here in Canada to black and African peoples" (cited in Russell 2014, n.p.).

The issues that the BLM chapters in Canada initially sought to bring to light were indeed quite similar to those that spurred the call to action in the United States. In September 2014, Jermaine Carby was shot and killed by Peel Regional Police after a traffic stop, which was precipitated by a "street check," a policy in which police officers can stop civilians—most of the time without anything akin to probable cause—and demand identification, which is then entered into a provincial database. The Special Investigations Unit (SIU), the provincial watchdog that investigates police-involved deaths and injuries, determined that the officer acted in self-defence, though the knife that the officer claimed Carby was wielding was not found until several hours after the shooting (Gillis 2016). In July 2015, Andrew Loku, a 45-year-old father of five originally from South Sudan, was shot and killed outside his Toronto apartment by Constable Andrew Doyle during an altercation that lasted just 20 seconds. The SIU again found that the officer was justified in his use of force and refused to release details of the investigation (including the officer's name), though a coroner's inquiry in June 2016 ruled Loku's death a homicide (Perkel 2017). In March 2016, members of BLM-Toronto created a "tent city" outside of police headquarters to protest these police-involved deaths as well as that of Alex Wettlaufer, a 21-year-old man who was shot and killed by police near the Leslie subway station just a few weeks earlier. After a two-week protest, organizers confronted Ontario Premier Kathleen Wynne, who conceded on the steps of the provincial legislature that systemic racism was a problem in Canadian society (Onstad 2017). Later that day, the tent city was dismantled, but organizers left a message for Toronto Police in the form of a banner: "You are on notice," it read. "We are not finished" (Onstad 2017).

The broad concerns of Canadian BLM chapters are not dissimilar from those articulated by activists in the United States. While it might be tempting to read these instances of deadly police violence as isolated, a recent study by the Canadian Broadcasting Centre (CBC) collected data on 461 fatal encounters between police and citizens between 2000 and 2017. The CBC's online database, Deadly Force, reveals that Black people across the country are overwhelmingly over-represented in police-involved deaths. For example: "Black people in Toronto made up on average 8.3 per cent of the population during the 17-year window, but represent nearly 37 per cent of the victims" (Marcoux and Nicholson 2018, n.p.). And much like circumstances in the United States, these deadly instances of police intervention rarely result in any criminal liability on the part of the police officer; the authors report that they could only identify 18 cases in which criminal charges were laid against an officer, and convictions in just two, though some cases are still before the courts.

Unlike the United States, however, BLM activists in Canada face the formidable obstacle of a national identity and societal consensus that seldom acknowledges the existence of racism (Thompson 2008). Canada often presents itself as a multicultural, tolerant, and egalitarian society, especially when compared to the overt racial discrimination in the United States (see Dobrowolsky in this volume). However, there is significant empirical evidence that demonstrates that Canadian racial inequality is both persistent and pervasive. As Keith Banting and Debra Thompson argue, the simultaneous existence of multicultural policies and a social safety net that many assume are far more robust, redistributive, and egalitarian than those that can be found in the United States makes the persistence of racial economic inequality all the more puzzling. Yet, in spite of the rhetoric of Canadian multiculturalism, "many racial minorities remain disadvantaged compared to white Canadians, and the picture is even more troubling for Aboriginal peoples, who face incredible disparities in terms of almost every socioeconomic indicator" (2016, 101).

For example, the Black unemployment rate is 73 per cent higher than for white Canadians (Block and Galabuzi 2011, 7), and Black workers earn just 75.6 cents for every dollar a non-racialized worker earns, contributing to an annual earnings gap of over $11,000 (13). Data from the 2016 census indicates that the unemployment rate for Black Canadians (12.5 per cent) is higher than for either the white population (7.3 per cent) or the visible minority population as a whole (9.2 per cent; Statistics Canada 2016). Though the Black population is just 3 per cent of the Canadian population, in 2017 Black inmates comprised 8.6 per cent of the total incarcerated population. While incarcerated, Black inmates are more likely to be classified as maximum security, are over-represented in admissions to prisoner segregation, are disproportionately involved in incidents of use of force, and are more likely to be gang affiliated (Canada 2017, 56). Census data shows slightly lower levels of educational attainment compared to other Canadians (Statistics Canada 2008) and research also indicates higher rates of poverty and poor living conditions among Black Canadians, which can negatively impact health (Rodney and Copeland 2009). The Black Experience Project, a multi-year study of the Black communities in the Greater Toronto Area, revealed that nearly two-thirds of survey participants say they frequently or occasionally experience anti-Black racism, and eight in ten report that they experience one or several forms of micro-aggressions on a daily basis, such as having their competency at work questioned or having their qualifications overlooked or not recognized (Black Experience Project 2017, 10).

These are Canadian problems, yet a predominant criticism of the Canadian chapters of BLM is that this kind of activism is not warranted because Canadian racism does not exist. *Globe and Mail* columnist Margaret Wente, for example, opined that BLM-TO is not needed, because of

> the obvious fact that Toronto is one of the most racially peaceable cities in all of North America ... we're not Ferguson, or anything like it. By pretending that Toronto is just another racist hellhole where police routinely gun down black kids, the Black Lives Matter folks do not create a useful forum for discussion. Nor do they pay attention to the black kids who are gunned down by other black kids. Don't those lives matter, too? (2016, n.p.)

She concludes by condemning BLM-TO as "the new bully on the block ... a tiny group of noisy activists who borrow their branding and belligerence from the United States" (2016, n.p.). Mike McCormack, the president of the union that represents 8,000 civilian and uniformed members of the Toronto Police Service, agreed with Wente's assessment, arguing that police brutality "is an issue for Black Lives Matter in the States. To say that we have the same issue in our Canadian policing model—I just totally reject that idea. The numbers don't back it up, the culture doesn't back it up" (quoted in Wang 2016).

Though many argue that BLM is not needed in Canada, BLM activists have catalysed important policy changes on several issues. Following the tent city protest, the Ontario government initiated a review of the province's three civilian police oversight bodies: (1) the SIU (discussed above); (2) the Office of the Independent Police Review Director, which oversees public complaints about the police; and (3) the Ontario Civilian Police Commission, which adjudicates appeals of police disciplinary hearings. In the final report, Justice Michael Tulloch (2017), a judge with the Ontario Court of Appeal appointed by the Ontario government to lead the review, made a number of recommendations, including the public release of reports on police-involved fatalities, the hiring and training of more investigators who do not have a policing background, initiating investigations any time a police officer fires a weapon, and collecting demographic data on complainants and victims of police violence, including race and religion. However, the report did not recommend that the identities of police officers involved in deaths or serious incidents be revealed unless they are charged, which disappointed BLM-TO activists (Rieti 2017). Following its release, Attorney General Yasir Naqvi committed to implementing several of the 129 recommendations from the review. In 2017, the Ontario government made important changes to the "carding" policy that allowed police officers to stop, question, and document individuals even when no offence was being investigated; passed the Anti-Racism Act in June; and created a provincial anti-Black racism strategy in December. The Ontario Human Rights Commission also launched a public inquiry into racial profiling by the Toronto police and the Toronto District School Board voted 18 to 3 to end the School Resource Officer Program, which placed armed police officers in schools that had high proportions of children from racialized backgrounds. The longevity of these policies remains to be seen, given that the Conservatives soundly defeated the Liberals in the 2018 election and other BLM chapters in Canada have been unable to make significant progress with their local or provincial governments. However, none of these policy developments would have occurred were it not for the sustained activism and campaigns of community organizers.

THE INTERSECTIONAL POLITICS OF BLM

The politics and activism of BLM are inherently intersectional. Originally developed by Black feminist theorist Kimberlé Crenshaw, the concept of intersectionality was introduced in critical race theory and legal theory in the late 1980s and early 1990s to dismantle the ways that law, academic disciplines, and social movements tend to rely on simplistic, unitary, or "additive" models of marginalization (Crenshaw 1989, 1991). Intersectionality is both a normative theoretical framework and an approach for conducting empirical research that emphasizes the interaction of various categories of difference (including, but not limited to, race, gender, class, sexual orientation, and nation) to produce both systems of domination and subjective identity positions (Hancock 2007; Nash 2008; Carbado et al. 2013; Cho, Crenshaw, and McCall 2013). Social movements that put intersectional theory into practice become living examples of how various identities can be "fostered within organizations that attend to a diverse array of issues and power differentials among members" (Cho, Crenshaw, and McCall 2013, 801). In particular, it is common for activists and social movements seeking social justice to struggle through complicated issues of identity and difference, themselves activated by and embedded within multiple, intersecting dynamics of power, oppression, and privilege.

BLM exhibits this grounded intersectionality in a number of ways. First, the movement is a twenty-first century corrective to the hierarchical and male-dominated model of leadership that characterized the civil rights movement. Though much of the literature that examines the emergence and dynamics of BLM underscores the long legacy of Black freedom struggles (Taylor 2016; Lebron 2017; Maynard 2017; Francis 2018), activists are quick to point out that "this is not your grandmamma's civil rights movement" (Harris 2015, n.p.). The charismatic leadership model, which dominated Black politics throughout the twentieth century, is often associated with Martin Luther King and the male-centred hierarchical structure of the organization he led, the Southern Christian Leadership Conference (Harris 2015). Though Black women played an important role in both the civil rights and Black Power movements (Collier-Thomas and Franklin 2001), their contributions are often overlooked in sanitized but dominant narratives of racial progress (Hall 2005). In contrast, BLM is much more akin to the intersectional approach established by the Black feminist Combahee River Collective, whose famous 1977 statement criticized Black liberation movements that refused to acknowledge sexism and white feminist movements that remained steeped in racism. It engages in a group-centred model of leadership, driven by ideas of participatory and deliberative democracy, which not only gives voice to those who were marginalized or silenced within the civil rights movement but is in fact driven by those voices. As Barbara Ransby argues, BLM is not only distinct in its radical inclusivity but is "defined by action—street protests, uprisings, and various forms of direct action—and is at its heart a visionary movement, calling not only for reforms but for systemic and fundamental change" (2018, 4).

Many of the prominent BLM activists in the United States and Canada are queer Black women or profess other marginalized identities. The policy platform of the Movement for Black Lives is also explicitly intersectional, intent on "elevating the experiences and leadership of the most marginalized Black people, including but not limited to those who are women, queer, trans, femmes, gender nonconforming, Muslim, formerly and currently incarcerated, cash poor and working class, disabled, undocumented, and immigrant" (Movement for Black Lives 2016). In order to recognize the full humanity and dignity of all Black people, BLM believes it is necessary to "amplify the particular experience of state and gendered violence that Black queer, trans, gender nonconforming, women and intersex people face" and to "center the voices and fight for those who have been marginalized."

For example, the same year that BLM protests erupted across the country, the African American Policy Forum (AAPF) began its #SayHerName campaign, which sought to bring attention to the specific forms of intimate partner and state violence that often destroy the lives of Black women. Though the public is familiar with the high-profile deaths of African American men, the similar experiences of Black women who are profiled, beaten, and killed by law enforcement officials are often ignored in popular understandings of police brutality. Further, "when [Black women's] experiences with police violence are distinct—uniquely informed by race, gender, gender identity, and sexual orientation—black women remain invisible" (AAPF 2015, 1). An important element of the work of the #SayHerName campaign is to highlight the forms of police violence that may not be legible given the current focus on police killings and excessive force (5). Many Black women who are abused and/or killed by the police are low-income and homeless people, targeted through the over-policing of poor communities of colour and the increasing criminalization of poverty, women without adequate health care that are in the midst of mental health crises, or women who associate with the "real" targets of police violence (Black men) and are perceived as collateral damage in the war on drugs and crime (12–20). Even in circumstances of domestic violence in which Black women seek help and protection from the police, they are still perceived as threatening: "Black women survivors of violence—and particularly poor, lesbian, gender-nonconforming, and transgender Black women—find that police responses to violence all too often result in further, and sometimes deadly, violence against them" (22; see also INCITE! 2008). To be clear, though the work of the African American Policy Forum is separate from BLM, the think-tank notes that its work on #SayHerName seeks to "honor the intention of the #BlackLivesMatter movement to lift up the intrinsic value of *all* Black lives by serving as a resource to answer the increasingly persistent call for attention to Black women killed by the police" (5).

Finally, and perhaps most consequentially, BLM is intersectional in, as they say, both word and deed. That is, BLM does not just claim that it represents Black people with various backgrounds, sexual orientations, gender identities, class positions, and access to power and resources; it actively works to force conversations about the myriad of ways that people within Black communities are vulnerable to state violence and other forms of political, economic, and social marginalization. For example, BLM chapters in Canada demand an end to the system of indefinite immigrant detention at the border, fight for the rights of migrant workers, and have staged protests and public awareness campaigns about the deportation of Black immigrants without due process (Jones 2017; BLM-TO, n.d.). In the United States, BLM chapters join forces with other organizations each spring to organize a national "Black mama's bail out day," which gives incarcerated mothers the chance to spend Mother's Day with their families instead of languishing in a jail cell because they could not afford bail (Alter 2017). An explicit component of BLM-TO's platform is to combat Islamophobia, especially at Canada's border with the United States.

The Canadian BLM chapters have also worked more conscientiously than their American counterparts to build solidarity with and support Indigenous communities and organizations in their efforts to challenge internal colonialism. Indigenous Peoples have faced many of the same racist and violent state practices faced by Black communities, but more consistently, intensely, and destructively, combined with the state-driven imperatives of cultural genocide and territorial dispossession that have shaped Aboriginal policy since the nineteenth century. For example, Indigenous people are also overwhelmingly over-represented in police-involved deaths. In Winnipeg, Indigenous people are approximately 10.6 per cent of the population but account for nearly two-thirds of victims of deadly police violence (Marcoux and Nicholson 2018). As Sherene Razack (2015) argues, even the numerous inquests and inquiries into Indigenous deaths in police custody often rely on pathologies of dysfunction that lay blame on Indigenous people's "inability to cope" with the demands of modern society, rather than the state's routine practices of racist and colonial violence. BLM chapters throughout Canada have made explicit efforts to be allies to Indigenous Peoples in their common efforts to dismantle systems of white supremacy. For example, BLM-Vancouver recognizes that the majority of BLM organizing work in Vancouver takes place on the "traditional, ancestral and unceded territory and homelands of the Musqueam, Tseil-Watuth, and Squamish First Nations" (BLM-Vancouver, n.d.). More concretely, BLM chapters across the country came out to support Indigenous organizations as they protested the non-indictments in the murder trials of Tina Fontaine and Colten Boushie, and have continued to work with Indigenous people to challenge the racism of the criminal justice system whenever possible.

Of course, one of the most prominent examples of the intersectional politics of BLM is its challenge to the police presence at Pride parades (see also DeGagne in this volume). In July 2016, BLM-TO activists staged a sit-in during the Pride parade, halting the procession for 30 minutes until Pride organizers responded to a list of demands. These demands included the hiring of more Indigenous and Black trans people in Pride leadership and, most controversially, that police floats be removed from future Pride parades. Within BLM-TO's protest was a broader argument about intersectionality; before the parade, BLM-TO activist Alexandria Williams said, "Folks are forgetting that we haven't all made it to the point of queer liberation. That not all communities who participate in Pride are actually able to be free in that celebration" (quoted in Battersby 2016). In announcing that it would not take part in its city's Pride parade, BLM-Vancouver elaborated on this point:

> We understand and support BLM-Toronto's reluctance towards having the police force, as it exists as an institution, involved as a permanent fixture in the parade. Having the Vancouver Police Department on the ground to perform a civil service is understandable. Having the institution participate on a float in the organized festivities of the actual parade is inappropriate and insulting to those who came before us to make Pride celebrations possible, some of us who even died for the cause. Embracing

the institution in an event that originates from protest against its actions makes us justifiably uncomfortable ... we ask the Vancouver Pride Society and the Vancouver Police Department to acknowledge and remedy our discomfort with the institutional representation of the police force as an instrument of structural violence, especially with a military vehicle in the parade, and we invite the Vancouver Police Department to voluntarily withdraw their float in the parade itself as a symbol of understanding and solidarity. This ... will serve to increase safety and inclusion for queer and trans POCs, black and Indigenous folks as per the ... Core Values listed on the Vancouver Pride Society's website. (2016, n.p.)

The Canadian BLM chapters in Toronto, Vancouver, and Edmonton did not seek the exclusion of the police as individuals from participating in the Parade but rather challenged the inclusion of the police as an institution that acts as an agent of state-sanctioned violence towards the most marginalized members of Canadian society. The criticism of the protests was swift and vehement; BLM was accused of hijacking a celebration to promote a political agenda that had no place in a tolerant, multicultural society like Canada (Wente 2016). The protest also launched a vicious debate within the queer community about the nature of inclusivity and intersectionality (Walcott 2017). Whether one agrees with the intersectional politics of BLM or not, it is clear that BLM is forcing conversations that centre marginalized voices.

CONCLUSION

Intersectionality is clearly both the philosophical basis and the practical reality of BLM activism in Canada, the United States, and beyond. The leadership of various BLM chapters, including those in Canada, is comprised of Black queer women and those with other identities that are often marginalized within discussions about racial inequality, including the poor and working class, LGBTQ people, immigrants, and the formerly incarcerated. The policy platforms and demands of BLM propose solutions that inscribe the value of all Black lives, paying particular attention to gender, sexual orientation, class position, and nationality, and call out the multiple systems of oppression that normatively order populations within Black communities by reinforcing power dynamics that privilege class positions and access to wealth, occupations that are legal and above-ground, legible and dichotomized gender identities, and "respectable" appearances and behaviours. Finally, the politics of BLM is inherently intersectional, in that it actively seeks to transform the interlocking systems of domination that bestow entitlement and status upon those who are able to obey heteronormative, middle-class, and/or patriarchal imperatives within societies that simultaneously privilege whiteness. Like older social justice movements, BLM demands the activation and protection of the civil and political rights of Black people, but also engages in a transformational politics that builds a broad-based resistance among various constituencies within Black communities that find common cause in concerns about criminalization, poverty, colonialism, and other forms of social, political, legal, and economic marginalization (Cohen 1997; Spade 2013).

This is not to say that BLM activism is without its problems. In "North American Necropolitics and Gender," Shatema Threadcraft (2017) urges caution in centring calls for racial justice around the metonym of a dead Black (male) body. Though BLM has done much to challenge, for example, the meaning of "thug" that is so often attached to the body of the Black slain, the very focus on a politics of death, Threadcraft argues, misses that the state is not the only dangerous force in the lives of Black women and that police brutality that does not result in death (e.g., sexual assault, rape, etc.) is *still* violent. However, the extent to which BLM has "moved the needle" on public awareness of anti-Black and systemic racism in a relatively short time frame is impressive; it is, undoubtedly, an excellent example of the transformational power of social movements to challenge racial and gendered orders in democratic societies. Though BLM was born in the United States, it has been bred as a transnational movement that challenges white supremacy in its various manifestations. Canadian chapters of BLM have brought to light those aspects of Canadian society that are too often minimalized or ignored because they contradict the national rhetoric of multiculturalism and diversity. Though structural racism is unlikely to become a distant memory in Canadian society any time soon, BLM has clearly challenged the status quo of twenty-first-century race politics in the United States, Canada, and around the globe.

DISCUSSION QUESTIONS

1. How are the politics of Black Lives Matter in Canada similar or different to the efforts of activists in the United States?

2. How does Black Lives Matter use intersectionality to centre marginalized voices?
3. What explains the backlash against Black Lives Matter in Canada and elsewhere?
4. Find out if there is a Black Lives Matter chapter in your city and/or on your university campus. What are its goals and priorities? What kinds of challenges does it face?

REFERENCES

African American Policy Forum. 2015. *Say Her Name: Resisting Police Brutality against Black Women*. New York: Center for Intersectionality and Policy Studies, Columbia University.

Alter, Charlotte. 2017. "Black Lives Matter Groups Are Bailing Black Women Out of Jail for Mother's Day." *Time*, May 12. http://time.com/4777976/black-lives-matter -mothers-day-bail/.

Banting, Keith, and Debra Thompson. 2016. "The Puzzling Persistence of Racial Inequality in Canada." In *The Double Bind: The Politics of Racial and Class Inequalities in the Americas*, edited by Juliet Hooker and Alvin Tillery, 101–22. Washington, DC: American Political Science Association.

Battersby, Sarah-Joyce. 2016. "Black Lives Matter Protest Scores Victory after Putting Pride Parade on Pause." *Toronto Star*, July 3. https://www.thestar.com/news/gta /2016/07/03/black-lives-matter-protest-scores-victory-after-putting-pride-parade -on-pause.html.

Black Experience Project. 2017. *The Black Experience Project in the GTA: Overview Report*. https://www.theblackexperienceproject.ca/wp-content/uploads/2017/07 /Black-Experience-Project-GTA-OVERVIEW-REPORT-4.pdf.

Black Lives Matter Global Network. 2017. *Celebrating Four Years of Organizing to Protect Black Lives*. https://static1.squarespace.com/static/5964e6c3db29d6fe8490b34e /t/59678445d482e97ec9c94ed5/1499956322766/BLM-4years-report.pdf.

Black Lives Matter Toronto. n.d. "Demands." https://blacklivesmatter.ca/demands/. Accessed December 10, 2019.

Black Lives Matter Vancouver. 2016. "Open Letter to the Vancouver Pride Society and the Vancouver Police Department from Black Lives Matter Vancouver." July 15. https://blacklivesmattervancouver.com/2016/07/15/open-letter-to-the -vancouver-pride-society-and-the-vancouver-police-department-from-black -lives-matter-vancouver/.

———. n.d. "About Us." https://blacklivesmattervancouver.com/about-us/. Accessed December 10, 2019.

Block, Sheila, and Grace-Edward Galabuzi. 2011. *Canada's Colour-Coded Labour Market: The Gap for Racialized Workers*. Ottawa: Canadian Centre for Policy Alternatives.

Carbado, Devon W., Kimberlé Williams Crenshaw, Vicki M. Mays, and Barbara Tomlinson. 2013. "Intersectionality: Mapping the Movement of a Theory." *Du Bois Review* 10 (2): 303–12.

Cho, Sumi, Kimberlé Williams Crenshaw, and Leslie McCall. 2013. "Toward a Field of Intersectionality Studies: Theory, Applications, and Praxis." *Signs* 38 (4): 785–810.

Cohen, Cathy J. 1997. "Punks, Bulldaggers, and Welfare Queens: The Radical Potential of Queer Politics?" *GLQ* 3 (4): 437–65.

Collier-Thomas, Bettye, and V.P. Franklin, eds. 2001. *Sisters in the Struggle: African American Women in the Civil Rights-Black Power Movement*. New York: New York University Press.

Crenshaw, Kimberlé Williams. 1989. "Demarginalizing the Intersection of Race and Sex: A Black Feminist Critique of Antidiscrimination Doctrine, Feminist Theory and Antiracist Politics." *University of Chicago Legal Forum* 1989: 139–67.

———. 1991. "Mapping the Margins: Intersectionality, Identity Politics, and Violence against Women of Color." *Stanford Law Review* 43 (6): 1241–99.

Francis, Megan Ming. 2018. "The Strange Fruit of American Political Development." *Politics, Groups, and Identities* 6 (1): 128–37.

Garza, Alicia. 2014. "A Herstory of the #BlackLivesMatter Movement." *Feminist Wire*, October 7. http://www.thefeministwire.com/2014/10/blacklivesmatter-2/.

George, Justin, 2018. "Trump Justice, Year One: The Demolition Derby." The Marshall Project, January 17. https://www.themarshallproject.org/2018/01/17/trump-justice-year-one-the-demolition-derby.

Gillis, Wendy. 2016. "Inquest into Jermaine Carby Sheds Light on Police Shooting." *Toronto Star*, May 10. https://www.thestar.com/news/crime/2016/05/10/inquest-into-jermaine-carby-sheds-light-on-police-shooting.html.

Hall, Jacquelyn Dowd. 2005. "The Long Civil Rights Movement and the Political Uses of the Past." *Journal of American History* 91 (4): 1233–63.

Hancock, Ange-Marie. 2007. "When Multiplication Doesn't Equal Quick Addition: Examining Intersectionality as a Research Paradigm." *Perspectives on Politics* 5 (1): 63–79.

Harcourt, Bernard. 2015. "Cover-Up in Chicago." *New York Times*, November 30. https://www.nytimes.com/2015/11/30/opinion/cover-up-in-chicago.html.

Harris, Fredrick C. 2015. "The Next Civil Rights Movement?" *Dissent Magazine*, Summer 2015. https://www.dissentmagazine.org/article/black-lives-matter-new-civil-rights-movement-fredrick-harris.

Hesse, Barnor, and Juliet Hooker. 2017. "Introduction: On Black Political Thought inside Global Black Protest." *South Atlantic Quarterly* 116 (3): 443–56.

INCITE! Women of Color Against Violence. 2008. *Law Enforcement Violence against Women of Color and Trans People of Color: A Critical Intersection of Gender Violence and State Violence*. Redmond, WA: INCITE!

Jones, Alexandra. 2017. "Black Lives Matter Shuts Down Yonge and Bloor Intersection to Protest Deportation of New Mother." *Toronto Star*, September 19. https://www.thestar.com/news/gta/2017/09/19/black-lives-matter-shuts-down-yonge-and-bloor-intersection-to-protest-deportation-of-new-mother.html.

Lebron, Christopher. 2017. *The Making of Black Lives Matter: A Brief History of an Idea*. New York: Oxford University Press.

Marcoux, Jacques, and Katie Nicholson. 2018. "Deadly Force: Fatal Encounters with Police in Canada: 2000–2017." *CBC News*. https://newsinteractives.cbc.ca/longform-custom/deadly-force.

Maynard, Robyn. 2017. *Policing Black Lives: State Violence in Canada from Slavery to the Present*. Halifax: Fernwood.

Movement for Black Lives. 2016. "Platform." https://policy.m4bl.org/platform/.

Nash, Jennifer C. 2008. "Re-thinking Intersectionality." *Feminist Review* 89: 1–15.

Onstad, Katrina. 2017. "Rebel Rebel." *Toronto Life*, February 27. https://torontolife.com/city/toronto-politics/rebel-rebel/.

Perkel, Colin. 2017. "Inquest Jury Rules Toronto Police Killing of Andrew Loku a Homicide." *Globe and Mail*, June 30. https://www.theglobeandmail.com/news/toronto/inquest-jury-rules-toronto-police-killing-of-andrew-loku-a-homicide/article35512946/.

Ransby, Barbara. 2018. *Making All Black Lives Matter: Reimagining Freedom in the 21st Century*. Oakland: University of California Press.

Razack, Sherene H. 2015. *Dying from Improvement: Inquests and Inquiries into Indigenous Deaths in Custody*. Toronto: University of Toronto Press.

Rieti, John. 2017. "Province Commits to Releasing All Past and Present SIU Reports as Recommended in Police Review." *CBC News*, April 6. http://www.cbc.ca/news/canada/toronto/Ontario-police-watchdog-report-1.4058601.

Rodney, Patricia, and Esker Copeland. 2009. "The Health Status of Black Canadians: Do Aggregated Racial and Ethnic Variables Hide Health Disparities?" *Journal of Health Care for the Poor and Underserved* 20 (3): 817–23.

Russell, Andrew. 2014. "Protesters Gather in Toronto and Ottawa in Wake of Ferguson Verdict." *Global News*, November 25. https://globalnews.ca/news/1692107/protest-planned-outside-of-u-s-consulate-in-wake-of-ferguson-verdict/.

Soss, Joe, and Vesla Weaver. 2017. "Police Are Our Government: Politics, Political Science, and the Policing of Race-Class Subjugated Communities." *Annual Review of Political Science* 20: 565–91.

Spade, Dean. 2013. "Intersectional Resistance and Law Reform." *Signs* 38 (4): 1031–55.

Statistics Canada. 2008. *Educational Portrait of Canada, 2006 Census*. Catalogue No. 97-560-X. http://www12.statcan.gc.ca/census-recensement/2006/as-sa/97-560/pdf/97-560-XIE2006001.pdf.

———. 2016. *2016 Census of the Population*. Data Tables. Catalogue No. 98-400-X2016286. https://www150.statcan.gc.ca/n1/en/catalogue/98-400-X2016286.

Sydney Peace Foundation. 2017. "2017 Black Lives Matter." http://sydneypeacefoundation.org.au/peace-prize-recipients/black-lives-matter/.

Taylor, Keeanga-Yamahtta. 2016. *From #BlackLivesMatter to Black Liberation*. Chicago: Haymarket Books.

Thompson, Debra. 2008. "Is Race Political?" *Canadian Journal of Political Science* 41 (3): 525–47.

Thompson, Debra, and Chloe Thurston. 2018. "American Political Development in the Era of Black Lives Matter." *Politics, Groups, and Identities* 6 (1): 116–19.

Threadcraft, Shatema. 2017. "North American Necropolitics and Gender: On #BlackLivesMatter and Black Femicide." *South Atlantic Quarterly* 116 (3): 553–79.

Thurston, Chloe. 2018. "Black Lives Matter, American Political Development, and the Politics of Visibility." *Politics, Groups, and Identities* 6 (1): 162–70.

Tulloch, Michael H. 2017. *Report of the Independent Police Oversight Review.* Toronto: Queen's Printer of Ontario.

United States Department of Justice, Civil Rights Division. 2015. *Investigation of the Ferguson Police Department.* March 4. https://www.justice.gov/sites/default/files /opa/press-releases/attachments/2015/03/04/ferguson_police_department _report.pdf.

———. 2016. *Investigation of the Baltimore City Police Department.* https://www .justice.gov/crt/file/883296/download.

———. 2017. *Investigation of the Chicago Police Department.* https://www.justice.gov /opa/file/925846/download.

Walcott, Rinaldo. 2017. "Black Lives Matter, Police, and Pride: Toronto Activists Spark a Movement." *The Conversation*, June 28. https://theconversation.com /black-lives-matter-police-and-pride-toronto-activists-spark-a-movement-79089.

Wang, Yanan. 2016. "The Controversy Surrounding Black Lives Matter in Canada." *Washington Post*, July 14. https://www.washingtonpost.com/news/worldviews /wp/2016/07/14/the-controversy-surrounding-black-lives-matter-in-canada /?noredirect=on&utm_ter m=.9403040bfe19.

Washington Post. 2019. Database. https://www.washingtonpost.com/graphics/2019 /national/police-shootings-2019/?utm_term=.e20182c70f59.

Wente, Margaret. 2016. "The Bullies of Black Lives Matter." *Globe and Mail*, July 4. https://www.theglobeandmail.com/opinion/the-bullies-of-black-lives-matter /article30746157/.

FURTHER READING

Khan-Cullors, Patrisse, and Asha Bandele. 2018. *When They Call You a Terrorist: A Black Lives Matter Memoir.* New York: St Martin's Press.

Maynard, Robyn. 2017. *Policing Black Lives: State Violence in Canada from Slavery to the Present.* Halifax: Fernwood.

Ransby, Barbara. 2018. *Making All Black Lives Matter: Reimagining Freedom in the 21st Century.* Oakland: University of California Press.

12

Pinkwashing Pride Parades: The Politics of Police in LGBTQ2S Spaces in Canada

Alexa DeGagne

Key terms: claims-making, criminalization, LGBTQ2S activists, pinkwash(ing), political protest, Pride parade, public spaces

INTRODUCTION

LGBTQ2S[1] **Pride parades** started as marches and riots against police surveillance, **criminalization**, and abuse, and are depicted as critical, galvanizing, and transformative moments in which queers and gender-non-conforming people fought back in collective ways against regulatory bodies of the state. Pride parades have served as a non-institutional means for LGBTQ2S people to carve out and claim **public spaces**[2] for forming identities, community building, challenging social and state homophobia and transphobia, and expressing their political demands to the state.

Since the 1990s, however, these once angry, politically radical protests and marches have increasingly become corporate-sponsored, "family-friendly," and pro-police celebrations. The meaning and political utility of Pride parades shifted, on the one hand, as states constrained and stifled public space in order to silence political engagement and **claims-making**.[3] Accordingly, Pride parade organizers toned down their political messaging and altered their protest tactics in order to adhere to the government's criteria for the appropriate use of public space such as the street. On the other hand, Pride parades were no longer cast as anti-police protests, as privileged LGBT community members and organizations argued that the criminal justice system was the best means to protect LGBT people against hate, discrimination, and violence. While privileged members of the LGBT community experience less violence at the hands of the police based on the intersections of their race, gender expression, and/or class, Indigenous, Black, gender-non-conforming, and poor people within LGBTQ2S populations continue to experience discrimination, surveillance, violence, and criminalization from Canadian police organizations. Police organizations, in turn, have tried to use Pride parades to pinkwash their image in relation to LGBT communities. **Pinkwashing** refers to governments' and corporations' attempts to appear pro-LGBT to distract from their violent and discriminatory actions and policies targeted at Indigenous people, POC (people of colour), and Black people. This has been epitomized by establishing LGBT police liaison committees, hiring LGBT officers, undergoing LGBT sensitivity training, and participating in Pride parades. These developments towards police protection, which have occurred over the last decade, distract from LGBTQ2S communities' fraught relationships with the police and the legal system, causing new moments of turbulence in a relationship understood to be violent and antagonistic, yet galvanizing.

This transforming relationship and the consequent effects on LGBTQ2S people and communities were articulated by Black Lives Matter Toronto (BLM-Toronto; see Thompson in this volume), who walked in Pride Toronto's 2016 parade as an honoured group. After initiating a sit-in, BLM-Toronto members presented a list of demands to Pride Toronto that included the removal of police floats from future Pride Toronto events. BLM-Toronto organizers argued that police organizations were colonial, racist, and anti-transgender institutions and, therefore, their presence in queer spaces was threatening to Indigenous, POC, and Black LGBTQ2S people. They also held that police should not be able to use Pride parades to deepen their regulation of LGBTQ2S communities, because the acceptance of police in the Pride parade legitimizes and normalizes increased police presence in and surveillance of LGBTQ2S communities and spaces. These actions sparked protests and discussions across Canadian LGBTQ2S communities about police organizations' presence in queer spaces.

This chapter considers the debates within LGBTQ2S communities pertaining to the inclusion of police organizations in Pride parades through the cases of Edmonton, Calgary, and Vancouver, as these three cities' LGBTQ2S communities came to different arrangements—ranging from banning police organizations to enabling police to determine the nature of their participation to cancelling the Pride parade. These debates caused turbulence within Canadian LGBTQ2S communities, as they elicited discussions on the political role and "appropriate" messaging of Pride parades; the meaning of intersectional solidarity across social justice communities; and whether police participation in Pride parades was a sign of progress or pinkwashing. This turbulence challenged and unsettled the assumption that police should be further integrated into LGBTQ2S spaces and communities and exposed fault lines and exclusions within LGBTQ2S community building and **political protest** in Canada. At this moment of turbulence, will LGBTQ2S communities transform their political goals and use their Pride parades to embrace an intersectional approach that acknowledges that LGBTQ2S people have different interactions with the police based on their race, sexuality, gender identity, and class?

THEORY, HISTORY, AND CONTEXT

The History and Meaning of Parades

Parades have been emblematic of changing relations between states and citizens and the parameters and function of public spaces. Initially, parades served as a means for performing and bolstering state power. The first iterations of state parades physically and publicly presented military members, arsenals, and vehicles to citizens to evoke reverence for and subservience to the state, to stimulate national pride and solidarity, and to call for public support of and sacrifice for military efforts and national values and interests (Borda 2002). They shifted to a site of community building, identity affirmation, political resistance, protest, and claims-making for marginalized people, as, for example, racialized and immigrant groups began holding parades to assert and bolster their identity and culture and claim a place of belonging within urban public space. The movement into heretofore restricted space, often characterized as civil disobedience, emphasized the urgency of the groups' claims, as they were willing to violate traffic laws for their causes and made it difficult for the public, government officials, and the press to ignore the presence and messages of the parades (Becerra 2014).

These transgressive claims to public space, recognition, and representation have evoked backlash, regulation, and punishment from audiences, the press, and the state. The inhabiting of public space can be uncomfortable, disorienting, and threatening to those whose power and positions are being challenged by groups who are systemically silenced and excluded from public forums and bodies. In order to limit **claims-making** on the state (see Dobrowolsky in this volume), governments have pursued several tactics for both shrinking public spaces in which people can gather and delegitimizing their claims, by establishing laws and bylaws that restrict the use of public spaces, especially roads, for political gatherings, parades, and protests; demonizing activist occupations of lands, travel ways, and public buildings as radical, violent, and unpatriotic; and requiring activists and advocates to either pay police organizations to marshal the parade and/or gather in a public space, or face police restriction of movement, violence, and arrests. Each of these tactics was carried out in the mass arrests of anti-G20 activists in Toronto in 2010 (Kennedy 2010), and later in reaction to Indigenous Peoples' and environmentalists' protests of the Kinder Morgan Trans Mountain Pipeline (see Wiebe in this volume). Thus, the police play an integral role in regulating and curtailing public space and engagements.

Police Regulation of LGBTQ2S Communities

To reproduce Western colonial power relations, police have long intervened in and regulated the lives of homosexual and gender-non-conforming people through various sodomy, obscenity, and gross indecency laws against sexual "deviance" and gender nonconformity (Alexander 2010; Everitt and Camp 2014; Lamble 2013; Maynard 2017; Monchalin 2016). The dominant myth and some advocates' rallying cry has been that white gay men were predominantly affected by these laws. Yet intersectional analysis reveals that Indigenous, Black, gender-non-conforming, and poor people within LGBTQ2S populations were more likely to be targeted by police and charged and convicted for such sex crimes, while Indigenous, Black, and poor queer, trans, and gender-non-conforming women[4] were most often targeted for gender-non-conforming violations (Mogul, Ritchie, and Whitlock 2011). Currently, Black, Indigenous, and LGBTQ2S people are more likely to experience harassment, violence, sexual assault, and death at the hands of the police; longer and stricter prison sentences; and harassment and violence in the prison system (Maynard 2017; Monchalin 2016). The 1970s and 1980s saw a series of large-scale police raids in cities across Canada, which activists believed were attempts to silence and delegitimize LGBT community-building, and activist efforts and to disrupt LGBT private and public safe spaces. Beginning in early 1975, police in

Montreal began raiding gay establishments in an attempt to "clean up" the city for the 1976 Olympic games (Kinsman and Gentile 2010). In 1981, during "Operation Soap," Toronto police targeted four bathhouses. Police officers inflicted violence, verbal abuse, and property damage and arrested 304 men (Guidotto 2011). The raids sparked anger and rebellion in Toronto's LGBT community, leading, in part, to the creation of new LGB organizations; marches demanding police accountability and gay rights; the building and expansion of gay neighbourhoods in Montreal, Toronto, and Vancouver; and the initiation of Toronto's first Pride parade in 1981 (Connor 2014; Hooper 2017; Warner 2002). As police raids of queer spaces continued—Edmonton's Pisces Health Spa in 1981; Toronto's Pussy Palace in 2000; Calgary's Goliath's Sauna in 2002—LGBTQ2S communities organized parades and marches to assert their place in the city, to have their voices heard, and to call out the injustices of police targeting and brutality (Bain and Nash 2007; Holota 2015).

Anti-racism **LGBTQ2S activists** have long stated that police target racialized and Indigenous LGBTQ2S people on a more insidious basis than the infamous bar raids. For example, critics and activists argue that police carding is based on systemic racist, colonial, anti-poverty, heteronormative, cisnormative, and anti-mentally ill profiling. Racialized, Indigenous, poor, LGBTQ2S, and mentally ill people are targeted, surveilled, and carded, as they are assumed to be (or to be always potentially) deviant and criminal. As a result, they are more likely to be charged and convicted of crimes. At the same time, marginalized LGBTQ2S people do not experience the same level of police protection as do white LGB people. For decades, members of Toronto's LGBTQ2S community warned Toronto police that someone was targeting, assaulting, and killing racialized men who have sex with men. LGBTQ2S community members felt that their pleas for police help were dismissed until a white gay man was murdered. In 2019, serial killer Bruce McArthur was charged with eight counts of first-degree murder against predominantly racialized men who have sex with men, thus demonstrating how marginalized LGBTQ2S people are over-policed and under-protected, and further stoking anger towards and distrust in the police (Hooper 2018).

Police and Pride Parades

Pride parades have changed in Canada over their near 40-year history. While initiated as protests and riots against state, police, and public homophobia and transphobia, Pride parades have always incorporated celebration, song, dance, drag, and exhibitionism. Debates often pit the politics against the party, but the two should not be seen as mutually exclusive. Rather, drag and sadomasochistic performance and displays of non-heterosexual and non-cisgender[5] nudity, sex, affection, and sexuality are political, as they push the boundaries of who is allowed in public spaces and how sexuality and gender can be expressed and liberated in public. Pride parades have therefore sought to bring what is relegated to the private, that which has been shamed and condemned, into the public in order to unsettle and then transform the heteronormativity of society (Enguix 2009; Hubbard 2001).

The ability for Pride parades to inhabit public space, and thereby transform both heteronormative society and LGBTQ2S communities' interactions with the state, has been constrained by push-back from within the LGBTQ2S community, heteronormative society, and government bodies, including the police. Increased public visibility was a goal of many Pride parades, but visibility can lead to vulnerability and regulation (Skeggs 1999). From within LGBTQ2S communities, public visibility has been pursued cautiously, as many hold that equality can be attained through a non-threatening homonormative politics of demonstrating sameness, particularly between white homosexuals and heterosexuals. To gain the support of white heterosexuals, and ascend to their positions of privilege, Pride parades have been changed to "family-friendly" events that promise not to demean "normal," loving homosexuals or offend heterosexual sensibilities. Racialized, low-income, and/or gender-non-conforming LGBTQ2S bodies and identities are consequently rendered unacceptable in Pride parade spaces (Enguix 2009; Mason and Lo 2009).

Pride parades have transformed in tandem with shifting relationships between the community and police. Police organizations across Canada reacted to the first Pride marches by attempting to constrain the movement of the participants to stifle anti-police sentiment. The role of the police in the Pride parades changed as police marshalled participants through the public streets, ostensibly to ensure that participants followed traffic laws and to protect the participants from counter-protesters. Pride parades then began working with police organizations to carve out space and displace people for the parades. The willingness of the state and police organizations to protect populations they have a history of targeting—pinkwashing—is celebrated as a "symbol of social inclusion and care for sexual diversity" (Lamble 2013, 230).

Asking for police protection legitimizes police engagement in LGBTQ2S communities. According to such anti-intersectional perspectives, the state is no longer seen as the perpetrator of homophobic violence (for some people) but is instead a "neutral arbiter of injury" and a protector against violence (Lamble 2013, 240). As Chandan Reddy (2011) argues, the expansion of freedom, protections, and rights for some often comes with reinforced and more severe violence for others. Police began marching in the parades in uniform and with their vehicles as representatives of their organizations and the state. This new incorporation of and dependence on the police for protection has led to deepened police presence in and regulation of LGBTQ2S spaces and communities, symbolized and normalized through police participation in Pride parades. There were reports, for example, of mass arrests of street-involved people, transgender people, sex workers, Black people, and Indigenous people before and during Toronto's hosting of World Pride 2014.

Pride parades have become turbulent and contested political moments in themselves as power, space, meaning, and representation are negotiated within the parades (Irvine and Irvine 2017), and as parades have been used as political, non-institutional tools for broader representation and claims-making to the state. In this current moment of turbulence, are Pride parades still effective as a non-institutional political tool for confronting and transforming the discrimination and regulation of LGBTQ2S communities? Should police be welcomed into LGBTQ2S spaces? Which members of the LGBTQ2S community are excluded when police are welcomed into LGBTQ2S spaces? Do police have a right to LGBTQ2S spaces equal to that of marginalized LGBTQ2S people?

Black Lives Matter Toronto brought these questions and contestations into sharp relief when they initiated a sit-in during Pride Toronto's 2016 parade. BLM-Toronto members, Indigenous Two-Spirit groups, Latinx groups, and allies sat down in the street, halting the parade, and began drumming, singing, chanting, and making speeches. A BLM-Toronto member pointed to the anti-intersectional nature of LGBTQ2S spaces, such as Pride:

> Are we proud? I don't think we have much to be proud about! I don't think this is a cause for celebration when there are Black people dying, when there are queer and trans people dying! We are constantly under attack. Our spaces are under attack. Pride Toronto: We are calling you out. For your anti-Blackness. Your anti-Indigeneity. Everyone in this space sit down. This is your space! (BLM-Toronto 2016)

BLM-Toronto carved out their own space by physically stopping their bodies and stopping the bodies of provincial and federal leaders, corporations, police and corrections organizations, and LGBT organizations. In that moment, the influential, powerful decision-making bodies could not ignore BLM-Toronto (Donato 2016). With the parade halted, BLM-Toronto presented a list of demands[6] to Pride Toronto's executive director, which included the "removal of police floats/booths in all Pride marches/parades/community spaces" (BLM-Toronto 2016). The BLM-Toronto group resumed marching in the parade, chanting in celebration, "We won," after Pride Toronto's executive director agreed to their demands[7] (CBC News 2016a).

Following BLM-Toronto's protest (see also Thompson in this volume), LGBTQ2S communities across Canada debated the role of police in Pride parades and LGBTQ2S spaces and communities, yielding a range of responses. This chapter focuses on the Vancouver, Edmonton, and Calgary cases. I analysed the public documents—press releases, public statements, blogs and publications, annual reports, meeting minutes, speeches, and videos—of each city's Pride organizations, police organizations, and LGBTQ2S community groups who were involved in the debates between July 2016 and June 2018. LGBTQ2S communities in each of these three cities engaged in prolonged, complex, and at times hostile debates about the meaning of Pride parades, who should be included in parades, and the role of police in the LGBTQ2S community more generally.

PRIDE PARADES IN VANCOUVER, EDMONTON, AND CALGARY

The Political Meaning and Role of Pride Parades

In reaction to BLM-Toronto's 2016 protest, members of LGBTQ2S communities in Toronto and across Canada flooded online comment boards, wrote op-eds, and sent hate mail to BLM-Toronto and Pride Toronto, claiming that it was inappropriate, disruptive, negative, and counter-productive to have a political protest during an event that was supposed to be a fun celebration of the community's progress and equality (Francis 2016). Pride organizations in Vancouver, Edmonton, and Calgary responded to this backlash by affirming that Pride parades have historically been both political and celebratory:

> Many people feel that Vancouver Pride Society events have become "one big party" that focuses too much on celebration without "political backbone" or recognition of queer history, the roots of the Vancouver Pride

Society, or current struggles faced by community members. There is a desire to have history acknowledged and represented at all Vancouver Pride Society events. (Vancouver Pride Society 2017b, 4)

Is Pride a Protest or is it a Party? Every year, Prides across Canada struggle with this single question and then they are challenged to find the magic balance between the two. The "party" lets us celebrate how far we have come and the "protest" reminds us of how far we still have to go. (Edmonton Pride Festival Society 2017a, 5)

Craig Sklenar, director of government affairs for Calgary Pride: "It really depends on why you're marching and that's really for individuality. It's changing over time, so what did start as a political rally is now morphing into both advocacy and celebration at the same time and that's a delicate balance we need to look at, to ensure that we continue to look toward equal rights here in Alberta." (Quoted in Dormer 2016, n.p.)

The three Pride organizations asserted that the Pride parade could be both political and celebratory by differentiating between celebrating past victories and fighting for present struggles. Activists in the three cities challenged these statements, arguing that they were vague and non-committal and offered few concrete plans for assuring that political protest would be welcomed and protected in Pride parades (BLM-Vancouver 2016).

An activist coalition of queer and trans people of colour stopped the 2018 Pride parade in Edmonton and presented a list of demands to the Edmonton Pride Festival Society, including un-inviting "the Edmonton Police Service, RCMP, and Military from marching in future parades" (Pride Action 2018, n.p.). Critiques of the 2016 BLM-Toronto sit-in and the 2018 Edmonton coalition of queer and trans people of colour argued that the protestors should have made use of the available channels of communication, including talking to and/or writing letters to the Pride boards. Such statements dismissed the years of engagement and work by Black, Indigenous, and trans people in Pride organizations and relegated appropriate political engagement to decidedly passive and routinely dismissed modes of communication. The Edmonton coalition of queer and trans people of colour argued that their decision to stop the parade was made after other means of formal communication and protest had been exhausted:

This year the Pride Society took positive steps forward to invite queer and trans folks of colour to Marshall the parade. It is unfortunate that

> when Marshalls brought up their concerns over Police presence in the parade to the Pride Board, they were ignored … The Pride Board had multiple opportunities to engage in dialogue with the queer and trans community of colour, after being ignored repeatedly, community members had no choice but to take action, by halting this year's Pride Parade. (Pride Action 2018, n.p.)

Shay Lewis, a protestor with the Edmonton coalition of queer and trans people of colour, stated that the protest was the only way to assure the Pride board listened to their community: "The protest happened because they were unwilling to talk with us without us having any type of leverage" (quoted in Muzyka 2018, n.p.).

LGBTQ2S communities have historically engaged in political parades, protests, and marches, as they were seen as the best means for making claims and effecting change. The politics of Pride waned, however, as mostly white members of the community began experiencing acceptance, equality, and protection from the police while the state suffocated political parades and protests. LGBTQ2S community organizations argued that Pride parades were started as political protests against the police and this work needed to continue. BLM-Vancouver stressed:

> The Pride Parade stems from the Stonewall Riots of 1969, led by trans and queer PoCs against police raids on the establishment … Embracing the institution [of the police] in an event that originates from protest against its actions makes us justifiably uncomfortable. (2016, n.p.)

Justifying the protest, a member of the Edmonton coalition of queer and trans people of colour stated: "What many don't know is that the first pride parade in Edmonton was also a protest. It began in response to a police raid on the Pisces Bathhouse" (Mohamed 2018, n.p.).

Some LGBT community members asserted that the parade should be a non-political celebration of equality, rendering invisible the current daily intersectional inequality, discrimination, and regulation of LGBTQ2S people on the basis of their race, gender identity, and class. By tying the parades to their historically political roots, the protestors attempted to take back the non-institutional political purpose of the parade. By stopping bodies in the parade, they attempted to re-establish political space within the community for those who continue to experience racist, colonial, and transphobic oppression and state violence. The Edmonton coalition of queer and trans people of colour stated:

> What we hope to accomplish today is that the voices of queer and trans people of colour and their allies are heard in the community and that this community reflects the voices of the many, not the few. By making pride spaces representative of our community, it will strengthen both pride and the broader community. (Pride Action 2018, n.p.)

Who Deserves to Be in a Public Queer Space?

Many within the LGBTQ2S communities assessed the appropriateness of politics in Pride parades based on who was speaking, believing that Black people, Indigenous people, and POC did not belong in Pride parades unless they were silent and passive. As discussed, particular homosexuals have attempted to gain equality by demonstrating the similarities between white, privileged, cisgender homosexuals and heterosexuals. Vocal and visible LGBTQ2S Indigenous people, Black people, and POC threaten to upset the relationship between privileged, predominantly white LGBT people and governments and the police. Some LGBT and straight people attempted to silence and condemn the protests and demands through racist hate mail, online comments, and threats of violence and death. This is an anti-intersectional tactic, which seeks to deny the existence and needs of LGBTQ2S Indigenous people, Black people, and POC. After Indigenous, Black, and POC LGBTQ2S community members spoke out against the racism, the Vancouver Pride Society issued an apology:

> These events, along with comments we have read on social media, news stories, and in correspondence we have received, make it clear that there is a significant amount of anti-Blackness and racism within our LGBTQ2+ community. This is not okay, and we must all do our part to speak out against it whenever we see it. The Vancouver Pride Society acknowledges we have not been quick to act in the past, and for this we are sorry. (2017a, n.p.)

Tokenism was a silencing tactic used by Pride organizations. For Edmonton's 2018 parade, dozens of influential community members, including people of colour, were asked to be parade marshals, but the Edmonton Pride Festival Society would not listen to their concerns about police participation, leading the Edmonton coalition of queer and trans people of colour to state: "The Edmonton Pride Festival Society views people of colour as decorations, to be seen and not heard" (quoted in Drinkwater 2018, n.p.). Similarly, BLM-Vancouver criticized Vancouver Pride for tokenism of Indigenous, POC, and Black LGBTQ2S people:

> Because there are relatively few queer Indigenous and POC folks (particularly those who identify or are read as Black) represented in Vancouver, it is imperative that Pride makes space to actively include these groups ... Tokenistic representation is different from intentional, self-motivated participation in an organization and an organization's events. (2016, n.p.)

In lieu of tokenism, BLM-Toronto, BLM-Vancouver, and the Edmonton coalition of queer and trans people of colour's demands also included stable annual funding, autonomy, and space for Indigenous, POC, and Black spaces and events at Pride festivals; the inclusion and hiring of Indigenous, POC, and Black people to Pride boards and staff; and town halls and consultations between Pride festival organizations and Indigenous, POC, and Black LGBTQ2S people. These demands called on the Pride festival organizations to be intentional in their inclusion of diverse LGBTQ2S people, to offer concrete support, and to amplify marginalized voices in the form of funding, space, and autonomy.

Pride festival organizations in Toronto, Vancouver, Edmonton, and Calgary did go through various modes of consultation within their respective LGBTQ2S communities. The consultations led to different arrangements for police inclusion and support for Indigenous, POC, and Black LGBTQ2S people, which will be discussed later in this chapter. These consultations—and the Pride festival organizers' support of the protestors' other demands—were criticized by members of the LGBTQ2S community for "giving in" to the demands of a small segment of the community and/or outsiders. In a "FAQs" section, Vancouver Pride answered the question, "Why are you letting one group make a decision for everyone else/push you around?" by responding, in part:

> This decision is based on the feedback of many members of our communities, while centering the experiences of those most marginalized. No one has "pushed" VPS into making a decision. This was an intentional decision made after listening to the community, considering all angles and carefully deliberating. (Vancouver Pride Society 2017c, n.p.)

After some consultation, which did not include BLM-Edmonton, Edmonton Pride stated that "queer people of colour generally view their relations with local police and military here positively and affirm that much progress has been made," and proceeded to announce that uniformed police officers would be welcome in the 2017 parade (Edmonton Pride Festival Society 2017a, 5). Edmonton Pride claimed that a minority of people were calling for police to be banned from the parade, and used that to justify the inclusion of police in uniform.

VOICES is "a coalition of people of colour, both trans & cis, queer and straight, committed to advocating for racialized and marginalized communities in the City of Calgary" (Voices, n.d., n.p.). In the Calgary case, VOICES supported Calgary Pride and the Calgary Police Services' decision to invite officers out of uniform. Yet Calgary Pride faced backlash from some members of the LGBTQ2S community for listening to the needs of a "minority" of the community. In both cases, minority voices were undermined from within the LGBTQ2S community: Edmonton Pride denied the needs of a minority of the community, while Calgary Pride was criticized for listening to "minority voices."

The marginalization of anti-racism activists persisted in online comments, op-eds, and news articles that argued it was exclusionary to ban the police from Pride parades (Mullin 2017). The inclusion arguments drew a false equivalency between the rights of police and marginalized people to be in the Pride parades' queer spaces. Anti-racism activists countered that such statements prioritized the inclusion of the police over the safety and inclusion of Indigenous, POC, and Black LGBTQ2S people. Imtiaz Popat, founder of the queer Muslim support group Salaam in Vancouver, stated:

> It's causing friction in the community, the rise of racism in the community. Things haven't gotten any better, they're actually getting worse ... The community loves the police more than they love queers of colour and trans folks. They don't feel welcome in the parade ... People want the police more than they want us ... They can have their white Pride parade then, that's what it's turning into and we don't want to be any part of that. (quoted in Bedry 2017a, n.p.)

Police organizations, as state institutions, hold immense power; therefore, how could a community Pride parade inflict any sort of injury or discrimination on this state body by excluding it from a carved-out queer space? While it could be argued that the Pride organizations were trying to mediate the two sides of the conflict, the prioritization of police inclusion was further seen as police organizations and anti-racism organizations being given equal importance in the Pride organizations' consultations with the LGBTQ2S communities. Moreover, police organizations in Edmonton and Vancouver were at times given the power to decide how they would participate in the parades; for example: "[The Edmonton Pride Society] will be asking these groups to reflect on how their entries can be respectful to the experiences of all attendees of the 2017 pride parade" (Edmonton Pride Festival Society 2017b, n.p.). BLM-Vancouver argued that the police should voluntarily withdraw from marching in the Pride parade "as a show of solidarity and understanding as to why participation in this particular manner perpetuates an unsafe atmosphere for the very same Indigenous, POC and Black communities the Vancouver Pride Society has committed to intentionally include" (Black Lives Matter Vancouver 2016, n.p.).

Anti-racism activists argued that the exclusion of police from the parade was a matter of safety for Indigenous, POC, and Black LGBTQ2S people who had experienced police harassment, violence, and criminalization. The potential danger of police participating in Pride parades was articulated by the Rainbow Refugee group in Vancouver, who decided not to march in the 2017 Pride parade because the Vancouver police would be marching. According to Rainbow Refugee, the Vancouver police collaborated with the Canada Border Services Agency's detentions and deportations of LGBTQ2S refugees (Bedry 2017b). Therefore, the physical presence of the Vancouver police in queer space posed a real threat to the safety of LGBTQ2S refugees. Pride organizations in the three cities each made statements acknowledging the historical oppression and institutionalized racism perpetrated by police organizations and decided that overt symbols of this oppression and violence—tanks, sirens, and vehicles—might intimidate and trigger Indigenous, POC, and Black LGBTQ2S people: "Community consultation participants told VPS to 'get rid of police,' have 'no police, no military,' have 'no cops, especially not with a fucking tank, ESPECIALLY not on motorcycles before the dykes on bikes'" (Vancouver Pride Society 2017b, 11).

While most Canadian Pride organizations agreed to remove these overt symbols of police oppression and violence, few organizations were willing to completely ban police from their parades except for Toronto 2016 and Edmonton 2018, where protestors stopped the parades and demanded police exclusion. In these cities and others, debates carried on about the appropriate role for police in Pride parades and all of the Pride organizations maintained that police organizations were needed to guard the parades in order to provide protection from counter-protesters and to assure that the parade could safely occupy public spaces (Vancouver Pride Society 2016).

Progress or Pinkwashing?

Pride organizations and many LGBT community members argued that including the police in Pride parades was a sign of progress for the communities' fraught relationships with the police. "Uniformed presence of the local police and military in the Edmonton Pride Parade," said the Edmonton Pride Festival Society in a statement, "is felt by our community to be, on balance, much more of a statement of progress than it is a statement of oppression and therefore should not be restricted" (2017a, 5). Calgary Pride argued that banning the police from the Pride parade "deters from engaging in meaningful discussions on how law enforcement agencies can best support Calgary's gender and sexually diverse (GSD) community" (2017a, n.p.), implying that the police need to be in the parade in order for progress to continue. Some LGBT activists, Pride organizations, and police organizations argued that the parade was an appropriate space in which to build relationships of trust and mutual respect (Calgary Pride 2017b; Edmonton Pride Festival Society 2017a, 53).

BLM-Vancouver member Jabari Cofer criticized police motivations in these instances as pinkwashing:

> Having the VPD and RCMP in the parade is pinkwashing these violent institutions and it seems like the whole purpose of having the cops in the parade in the first place seems to be a PR move to make it seem like they're so supportive of LGBT people, when in reality they just aren't. (quoted in Bedry 2017a, n.p.)

I argue that attempts to pinkwash—to legitimize and humanize the police in order to obscure their perpetuation of violence and discrimination—took two main forms: LGBT police officers and police uniforms.

In a swift reaction to BLM-Toronto's 2016 protest, several gay and lesbian police officers from across the country were featured in op-eds, letters to the editor, blog posts, and radio and television interviews as the victims of the decision to ban the police from the parade. They argued that they marched in

Pride parades to amplify their voices and to fight LGBT discrimination within their police organizations (CBC News 2016b). Pride organizations in Vancouver and Edmonton were also quick to assert their support for gay and lesbian police officers:

> We acknowledge that careers in law enforcement have been challenging due to historic and contemporary barriers for marginalized people. Police officers from marginalized groups have fought for the ability to be out and proud, and may feel disappointed by this decision. We invite LGBTQAI2S+ officers to continue participating in the Pride Parade out of uniform. (Vancouver Pride Society 2017c, n.p.)

> The LGBTQ2S+ community engagement meetings revealed 2 key areas that triggered individuals and made them uncomfortable: sirens and law enforcement vehicles. While uniforms were another area of issue, many LGBTQ2S+ law enforcement individuals felt that their uniform was as much a part of them as being LGBTQ2S+ was. (Edmonton Pride Festival Society 2017c, 18)

In the latter quote, police officers equated their sexual and gender identities and expressions with their police identities and uniforms, arguing that all should be freely presented in the Pride parade space. The same rhetoric has been seen with "Blue Lives Matter" statements in opposition to Black Lives Matter, which equated the occupational hazards of a profession to systemic racial oppression (CBC News 2016b).

While the Pride organizations made the decision not to have police vehicles, tanks, or sirens in the parades, the decision of whether or not police should wear their uniforms was more contentious within Pride organizations across Canada, causing changes to their policies between 2016 and 2018. Pride Vancouver's decision to ban police from wearing their uniforms and instead have them march as individuals with the City of Vancouver's entry in the 2018 parade was met with optimism from BLM-Vancouver, who called it a "huge victory" (Bedry 2017c, n.p.). Following the decision, Pride Vancouver publicly stated that the Vancouver Police Department actually protested their request to march without uniforms: "Not only did they not want to even consider the idea, they worked actively to change the position of other police forces who had previously said they were fine marching out of uniform" (Vancouver Pride Society 2017c, n.p.). Such push-back indicated a sense of entitlement on the part of the police to occupy Pride parade space on their terms. VOICES in Calgary said that the request for police to walk without uniforms "is a symbolic step which does not eliminate police violence and misconduct, but rather opens up a discussion and first steps towards creating a community that is safe for all and the one that truly honours the history of what Pride marches are meant to be" (2017, n.p.). In both Calgary and Vancouver, it seems, anti-racism advocates were reluctant to celebrate the banning of uniforms as an indication of deep shifts in the police organizations.

After consultations with Edmonton Pride, the Edmonton Police Service decided to humanize police officers by using "their entry in the Edmonton Pride Parade to look 'Beyond the Badge' and show the people behind the EPS uniform as individuals who are both members of and allies to the LGBTQ2S+ community" (Edmonton Pride Festival Society 2018, n.p.). This strategy marked a shift from earlier arguments that prioritized LGBT officers' police identities. Moreover, the strategy, while purporting to neutralize the police, did not nullify their power or status. Instead, it humanized and individualized the officers, obscuring their relationship to the institution they upheld and from which they benefited.

While Pride and police organizations negotiated the nuanced terms of police inclusion—whether vehicles, sirens, uniforms, and/or any identify-ing markers would be permitted—many within the LGBTQ2S communities grew frustrated with what they perceived as pinkwashing by the police. These pinkwashing efforts came at a moment when police, military, and RCMP organizations were embroiled in allegations of sexual harassment and assault of civilians and employees. For example, female employees with the RCMP launched a class-action lawsuit against the Canadian federal government over the sexual harassment that they experienced: "60 per cent of female RCMP members reported being the victim of sexual harassment in the workplace" (Janusz 2017, 23; see also chapters by Ashe, Paterson and Scala, and Eichler in this volume on related themes). Gaining favour in the LGBTQ2S com-munity, therefore, could serve to ease the public's criticism of systemic discrimination and harassment within the organizations. The three police organizations argued that they had changed their LGBT policies, were hiring LGBT officers, and were undergoing sensitivity training, and that the cul-tures of homophobia within their institutions were a thing of the past. At the same time, in the three western cities, police organizations were given equal (or more) consideration compared to the anti-racism protesters; many were asked, not forced, to change their parade entries; and still police organizations protested, stopped communication, or stated that they were "disappointed" with Pride parade organizers' decisions. Thus, the police reactions to the Pride organizations' requests led many LGBTQ2S activists to question whether the police merely saw the Pride parade as an opportunity to bolster their image and influence within LGBTQ2S communities and the general public without being held accountable to the most marginalized LGBTQ2S people.

CONCLUSION

In April 2019, the Edmonton Pride Festival announced that its 2019 parade would be cancelled. The festival organizers released a vague statement, saying that the "current political and social environment" led them to cancel the parade. The cancellation came as a result of a series of events following the coalition of queer and trans people of colour's halting of the 2018 Edmonton Pride parade. The Edmonton Pride Festival responded to the protest by undergoing several months of consultation with community members, consultations that were described as tense and non-productive by POC participants. In a meeting preceding the cancellation, the coalition of queer and trans people of colour attempted to re-present their demands to the Pride board, yet the Pride board was not willing to hear their request, and went so far as to call the police to intervene on the situation—a moment of true irony. Several days after, it was announced that the Pride parade was cancelled (Boissonneault 2019). On the 50th anniversary of the Stonewall riots, a grassroots, community-led march and vigil at the Alberta Legislature was organized by Indigenous, POC, and Black LGBTQ2S people, marking a reclamation of the meaning and power of Pride parades.

In light of these ongoing debates over police vehicles and uniforms and the safety and inclusion of LGBTQ2S people, we must ask why many police organizations are insisting on being in queer spaces—and Pride parades specifically—for the relationship between the two sides to change. By building trust among particular privileged LGBT people, police organizations used Pride parades to pinkwash their image; to deny the intersections of sexuality, gender, race, and class; and to erase their historic and ongoing perpetuation of racism and colonialism upon LGBTQ2S communities. The police sought to legitimize and deepen their presence in and ability to regulate the community. By physically participating in public queer space, the state challenged and obstructed the transformational politics of the Pride parades and the anti-racist LGBTQ2S protestors. Pride parades could not simultaneously include police organizations and remain spaces for anti-state protest. As states sought to constrain public space in order to undermine public engagement, LGBTQ2S communities reclaimed Pride parades as a powerful tool of political and community transformation. Activists in Toronto and Edmonton physically stopped their Pride parades—risking immediate physical harm and prolonged backlash from their LGBTQ2S community—because they believed that their Pride parade was both a public queer space that needed to be guarded against police infiltration and a means for voicing their needs and challenging the state.

DISCUSSION QUESTIONS

1. According to anti-racism activists, in what ways are marginalized LGBTQ2S community members excluded, silenced, and threatened when police are welcomed into LGBTQ2S spaces?
2. Do police organizations need to be welcomed into LGBTQ2S spaces and events in order to encourage the relationship between LGBTQ2S communities and police organizations to transform? Why/why not?
3. What are other examples of governments and/or corporations attempting to pinkwash their image? Do you think pinkwashing is effective? How should LGBTQ2S people and their allies react to pinkwashing?
4. In this current moment of turbulence, are Pride parades still effective as a political tool for confronting the discrimination and regulation of LGBTQ2S people?

NOTES

1 Throughout this chapter, I shift between using "LGB," "LGBT," "LGBTQ2S," etc., to refer to different organizations and communities. I have respected the identification organizations and communities use to describe themselves. When organizations and communities have not described themselves, I choose a description that seems to best suit their politics, location, and time period.
2 The meaning, need, and value of public spaces are contested, but I hold that public spaces are ideally spaces that are held by all people; accessible regardless of income,

gender, sexuality, race, ability, and citizenship status; freely occupied by individuals and groups; and used for social, political, and community-building needs.

3 Claims-making refers to the action—performed by individuals or groups—of asking the state for particular rights, protections, or social supports

4 While cisgender women were rarely involved in sodomy law cases, their sexuality has been regulated under marriage, adultery, sex work, and obscenity laws (Mogul, Ritchie, and Whitlock 2011, 17).

5 The term cisgender refers to people whose gender identity is congruent with the sex/gender that they were assigned at birth.

6 BLM-Toronto's demands included: increased funding and support for Black spaces and events during Pride Toronto; increased American Sign Language interpretation during Pride Toronto events; increased representation of Black trans women, Black queer people, and Indigenous folk among Pride Toronto's staff; and a public town-hall meeting between marginalized communities and Pride Toronto to discuss the implementation of the demands (Black Lives Matter 2016).

7 Pride Toronto's executive director rescinded his support of BLM-Toronto's demands the next day. Months later, Pride Toronto issued a statement in which it apologized for "its role in deepening the divisions in our community, for a history of anti-blackness and repeated marginalization of the marginalized within our community that our organization has continued" (Grief 2016, n.p.). At Pride Toronto's 2017 AGM, members voted to support all of BLM-Toronto's 2016 demands (BlogTO 2017).

REFERENCES

Alexander, Michelle. 2010. *The New Jim Crow: Mass Incarceration in the Age of Colorblindness.* New York: The New Press.

Bain, Alison L., and Catherine J. Nash. 2007. "The Toronto Women's Bathhouse Raid: Querying Queer Identities in the Courtroom." *Antipode* 39 (1): 17–34.

Becerra, M. Victoria Quiroz. 2014. "Performing Belonging in Public Space: Mexican Migrants in New York City." *Politics & Society* 42 (3): 331–57.

Bedry, Derek. 2017a. "Uniformed Police Will March in Vancouver's Pride Parade." *Daily Xtra News*, May 18. https://www.dailyxtra.com/uniformed-police-will -march-in-vancouvers-pride-parade-73525.

———. 2017b. "Refugee Support Group Pulls Out of Vancouver Pride Parade over Police and Border Guard Concerns." *Daily Xtra News*, July 31. https://www .dailyxtra.com/refugee-support-group-pulls-out-of-vancouver-pride-parade -over-police-and-border-guard-concerns-76947.

———. 2017c. "Vancouver Pride Bans Uniformed Police from 2018 Parade." *Daily Xtra News*, November 29. https://www.dailyxtra.com/vancouver-pride-bans -uniformed-police-from-2018-parade-81777.

Black Lives Matter Toronto. 2016. "Black Lives Matter—Toronto, along with Various Community Groups, Including BQY and Blackness Yes Have the Following Demands." Facebook, July 3. https://www.facebook.com/blacklivesmatterTO

/photos/a.319994704862693.1073741829.313499695512194/519230751605753
/?type=3&theater.

Black Lives Matter Vancouver. 2016. "Open Letter to the Vancouver Pride Society
and the Vancouver Police Department from Black Lives Matter Vancouver."
July 15. https://blacklivesmattervancouver.com/2016/07/15/open-letter-to-the
-vancouver-pride-society-and-the-vancouver-police-department-from-black
-lives-matter-vancouver/.

BlogTO. 2017. "Pride Toronto Says Yes to Black Lives Matter Demands." *BlogTO*,
January 18. https://www.blogto.com/city/2017/01/pride-toronto-says-yes-black
-lives-matter-demands/.

Boissonneault, Stephan. 2019. "Edmonton Pride Festival Faces Controversy—
Organizers Silencing Voices, Groups Say." *Daze Magazine*, April 7. https://dazemag
.ca/2019/04/07/edmonton-pride-festival-faces-controversy-organizers-silencing
-voices-groups-say/.

Borda, Jennifer. 2002. "The Woman Suffrage Parades of 1910–1913." *Western Journal
of Communication* 66 (1): 25–52.

Calgary Pride. 2017a. "Calgary Pride Parade and Law Enforcement Participation."
July 26. http://www.calgarypride.ca/press-releases/lea-participation-2017/.

———. 2017b. "Joint Statement Regarding Calgary Pride and Calgary Police Service."
August 25. http://www.calgarypride.ca/press-releases/joint-statement-regarding
-calgary-pride-and-calgary-police-service/

CBC News. 2016a. "Black Lives Matter Toronto Stalls Pride Parade." *CBC News*,
July 3. http://www.cbc.ca/news/canada/toronto/pride-parade-toronto
-1.3662823.

———. 2016b. "Black Lives, Blue Lives, All Lives: What Does It Mean When We Say
Certain Lives Matter?" *CBC News*, July 24. https://www.cbc.ca/news/world/black
-livespolice-1.3679595.

Connor, Kevin. 2014. "From Adversaries to Allies on Gay Rights in Toronto." *Toronto
Sun*, June 14. http://www.torontosun.com/2014/06/14/from-adversaries-to-allies
-on-gay-rights-in-toronto.

Donato, Al. 2016. "Black Lives Matter Held Pride Accountable—and Toronto Should
Too." *Torontoist*, July 6. http://torontoist.com/2016/07/black-lives-matter-held
-pride-accountable-toronto-should-too/.

Dormer, Dave. 2017. "United Conservative Party Application Rejected by Calgary
Pride Parade." *CBC News*, August 18. http://www.cbc.ca/beta/news/canada
/calgary/calgary-pride-parade-ucp-1.4254092.

Drinkwater, Rob. 2018. "Edmonton Pride Parade Blocked by Protesters Upset by Police
Participation." *CTV News*, June 9. https://www.ctvnews.ca/canada/edmonton-pride
-parade-blocked-by-protesters-upset-by-police-participation-1.3967000.

Edmonton Pride Festival Society. 2017a. *One Pride, Many Voices: Edmonton Pride
Festival 2017, Official Pride Program*. https://issuu.com/postvuepublishing/docs
/epfs-guide-2017.

———. 2017b. "2017 Pride Theme Statement." https://www.edmonton pride.ca/one
-pride-many-voices.

———. 2017c. *2017 Pride Festival Annual Report*. https://www.edmontonpride.ca /pride-society/annual-reports.

———. 2018. "Press Release: EPS and RCMP Entries in the 2018 Edmonton Pride Parade." Facebook, May 21. https://www.facebook.com/edmontonpride/posts /231769094044440.

Enguix, Begonya. 2009. "Identities, Sexualities and Commemorations: Pride Parades, Public Space and Sexual Dissidence." *Anthropological Notebooks* 15 (2): 15–33.

Everitt, Joanna, and Michael Camp. 2014. "In versus Out: LGBT Politicians in Canada." *Journal of Canadian Studies* 48 (1): 226–51.

Francis, Angelyn. 2016. "The Political Roots of LGBT Pride Parades." *Huffington Post*, July 8. http://www.huffingtonpost.ca/2016/07/08/political-history-of-pride_n _10831484.html.

Grief, Amy. 2016. "Pride Apologizes to Black Lives Matter Toronto." *BlogTO*, September 20. https://www.blogto.com/city/2016/09/pride_apologizes_to_black _lives_matter_toronto/.

Guidotto, Nadia. 2011. "Looking Back: The Bathhouse Raids in Toronto, 1981." In *Captive Genders: Trans Embodiment and the Prison Industrial Complex*, edited by Eric A. Stanley and Nat Smith, 69–81. Oakland, CA: AK Press.

Holota, Victoria. 2015. "The Pisces Bathhouse Raid—City Museum." Edmonton City as Museum Project, May 28. http://citymuseumedmonton.ca/2015/05/28/the -pisces-bathhouse-raid/.

Hooper, Tom. 2017. "Policing Gay Sex in Toronto Parks in the 1970s and Today." Activehistory.ca: History Matters, February 16. http://activehistory.ca/2017/02 /policing-gay-sex-in-toronto/.

———. 2018. "The Gay Community Has Long Been Over-Policed and Under-Protected. The Bruce McArthur Case Is the Final Straw." *CBC News*, April 16. https://www.cbc.ca/news/ opinion/pride-police-1.4618663.

Hubbard, Phil. 2001. "Sex Zones: Intimacy, Citizenship and Public Space." *Sexualities* 4 (1): 51–71.

Irvine, Janice M., and Jill A. Irvine. 2017. "The Queer Work of Militarized Prides." *Contexts: Understanding People in Their Social Worlds* 16 (4): 32–37.

Janusz, B. 2017. "Mounting Evidence: Discrimination and Sexual Harassment in the RCMP." *Herizons*, March 22, 21–23. https://www.thefreelibrary.com/Mounting +evidence%3A+discrimination+and+sexual+harassment+in+the+RCMP .-a0500824133.

Kennedy, Brendan. 2010. "Demonstrators Storm Police Pride Event." *Toronto Star*, June 29. https://www.thestar.com/news/gta/g20/2010/06/29/demonstrators _storm_police_pride_event.html.

Kinsman, Gary, and Patrizia Gentile. 2010. *The Canadian War on Queers: National Security as Sexual Regulation*. Vancouver: University of British Columbia Press.

Lamble, Sarah. 2013. "Queer Necropolitics and the Expanding Carceral State: Interrogating Sexual Investments in Punishment." *Law Critique* 24: 229–53.

Mason, Gail, and Gary Lo. 2009. "Sexual Tourism and the Excitement of the Strange: Heterosexuality and the Sydney Mardi Gras Parade." *Sexualities* 12 (1): 97–121.

Maynard, Robyn. 2017. *Policing Black Lives: State Violence in Canada from Slavery to the Present*. Halifax: Fernwood Publishing.

Mogul, Joey L., Andrea J. Ritchie, and Kay Whitlock. 2011. *Queer (In)justice: The Criminalization of LGBT People in the United States*. Boston: Beacon Press.

Mohamed, Bashir. 2018. "I've Been Very Disappointed at the Hostile & Defensive Reaction to the Protest at Today's #yegpride Parade." Twitter, June 9. https://mobile .twitter.com/BashirMohamed/Status/1005554790384918528.

Monchalin, Lisa. 2016. *The Colonial Problem: An Indigenous Perspective on Crime and Injustice in Canada*. Toronto: University of Toronto Press.

Mullin, Malone. 2017. "'You Take Away from Pride When You Exclude': First Responders Throw Their Own Party." *CBC News*, June 25. http://www.cbc.ca /news/canada/toronto/first-responders-pride-unity-festival-1.4177264.

Muzyka, Kyle. 2018. "Mid-Parade Protest Was Necessary to Be Heard, Pride Demonstrator Says." *CBC News*, June 11. http://www.cbc.ca/news/canada /edmonton/edmonton-pride-2018-shay-lewis-1.4701693.

Pride Action. 2018. "Pride Action Press Release." Document circulated by the Queer and Trans People of Colour coalition. In the author's possession.

Reddy, Chandan. 2011. *Freedom with Violence: Race, Sexuality, and the US State*. Durham, NC: Duke University Press.

Skeggs, Beverly. 1999. "Matter out of Place: Visibility and Sexualities in Leisure Spaces." *Leisure Studies* 18 (2): 213–32.

Vancouver Pride Society. 2016. "Vancouver Pride Statement on Black Lives Matter." Vancouver Pride, July 1. http://www.vancouverpride.ca/index.php?id=200810.

———. 2017a. "Facebook Statement." Facebook, February 22. https://www.facebook .com/VancouverPrideSociety/posts/1778189185540294.

———. 2017b. *2016–2017 Community Consultation Results*. Vancouver: Vancouver Pride Society, April 24. http://www.queeryme.com/display/viewpdf_applicationFile .php?id=127.

———. 2017c. "FAQ Regarding Police Decision." Vancouver Pride, December 1. http://www.vancouverpride.ca/news///252811/faq_regarding_police_decision.

VOICES. 2017. "Statement of Support to Calgary Pride on Police Participation." Facebook, July 26. https://www.facebook.com/yycvoices/posts/1722414567786283.

———. n.d. "Who Are YYC Voices." http://yycvoices.ca/about/. Accessed November 22, 2019.

Warner, Thomas E. 2002. *Never Going Back: A History of Queer Activism in Canada*. Toronto: University of Toronto Press.

FURTHER READING

Donato, Al. 2016. "Black Lives Matter Held Pride Accountable—and Toronto Should Too." *Torontoist*, July 6. https://torontoist.com/2016/07/black-lives -matterheldpride-accountable-toronto-should-too/.

Maynard, Robyn. 2017. *Policing Black Lives: State Violence in Canada from Slavery to the Present*. Halifax: Fernwood.

Mogul, Joey L., Andrea J. Ritchie, and Kay Whitlock. 2011. *Queer (In)justice: The Criminalization of LGBT People in the United States*. Boston: Beacon Press.

13

Refusing Extraction: Environmental Reproductive Justice across the Pacific[1]

Sarah Marie Wiebe

Key terms: 'āina, coastal protection, decolonial futures, environmental reproductive justice, felt knowledges, lived-experiences, more-than-human life, relationships, self-determination

INTRODUCTION

Across the Pacific Ocean, from British Columbia's (BC's) Burnaby Mountain in Coast Salish territory to Mauna a Wākea mountain in Hawai'i, Indigenous[2] communities are leading efforts to resist extraction and protect their territories. Women are frequently situated at the forefront of these movements. All too often, state-produced "jurisdictional nightmares" protect corporations conducting resource extraction and enable some Indigenous territories to operate as "sacrifice zones" (Million 2013, 37). Settler academic-activists like myself seeking to work in solidarity with communities encountering this bear responsibility for calling these uneven relations into question and holding decision-makers accountable. Critical Indigenous scholarship, including feminist Indigenous scholars, points out how collaboratively challenging settler colonialism and extraction in pursuit of more environmentally just futures requires a commitment to decentering the primacy of liberal knowledge production (Altamirano-Jiménez in this volume; Coulthard 2014; Driskill et al. 2011). A liberal orientation to natural resources assumes the primacy of (hu)man(s) over nature, which translates into treating territories as commodities for use and consumption. Focusing on the emergence of two social movements on Burnaby Mountain in BC (Canada) and Mauna a Wākea in Hawai'i, and the gendered dimensions of these movements, this chapter interrogates capitalist, extractivist liberal thought as an object of study, apparent in the state-sanctioned administrative procedures that enable the ease of each development. To do so, in this chapter I draw upon the voices of those advocating for a more relational approach to territory as emergent, alive, and imbued with animate meaning. From an **environmental reproductive justice** lens, I aim to reframe how we see, understand, and interpret human/more-than-human relations across the Pacific.

Ongoing efforts to defend Indigenous ways of life across Oceania in Coast Salish territory and Hawai'i are profoundly gendered. Young leaders, like Kayah George from the Tsleil-Waututh Nation, fight "with and for love" for her territory along the BC shoreline at the base of the Kinder Morgan pipeline terminus, slated for expansion enabled by the Government of Canada (Wikler 2018). Across the Pacific Ocean, protectors of Mauna a Wākea, one of the earth's highest mountains, articulate the importance of this sacred site as a *piko*, the core of one's being (Peralto 2014). These struggles reflect the importance of a regenerative and relational approach to the non-human or more-than-human world, often in Western terms referred to as local resource management. An extractivist approach to land and resources is premised on taking. In contrast, a relational approach is about emergence, regeneration, and relationship-building. With the encroachment of settler-state development marked by Kinder Morgan's request to the National Energy Board (NEB) for a pipeline permit in Canada and the Board of Land and Natural Resources' decision to uphold a permit issued to the University of Hawai'i for the construction of the Thirty Meter Telescope on Mauna a Wākea, Indigenous communities' livelihoods are on the line. Resistance at each site signals how the struggle is about much more than protesting development: it is about respecting Indigenous "body lands," **self-determination**, and protecting vital ecosystems for future generations (see Altamirano-Jiménez in this volume).

And so, in these "turbulent times," this chapter challenges a politics of extraction and consultation based on a settler-colonial governmentality and instead calls for an environmental reproductive justice approach informed by Indigenous feminist thought, ecofeminism, and queer theories, as well academic-activist sensibilities.[3] Because an environmental reproductive justice lens prioritizes the voices of those at the front-lines, **lived-experiences**, **felt knowledges**, human/more-than-human relations, and self-determination, it calls for decision-making based on robust and ongoing consent, which offers more promise for truly transformational politics and **decolonial futures**. The acts of resistance recounted in this chapter bring to light these possibilities. This chapter is motivated by the following central questions: How can settlers extract themselves from extractivist thinking? What can settlers learn from Indigenous feminist political thought to inform environmental policy and practice? When it comes to deliberative processes about industrial initiatives, whose voices count? Whose voices are missing and how can they be amplified in order to improve possibilities for transformative politics? To respond, I frame these deliberations in a context of environmental reproductive justice. In tune with tenets of ecofeminist thought, environmental reproductive justice aims to challenge dualisms associated with human dominance over nature, and in contrast centres **relationships**, embodied experiences and sensations, local experiential knowledge, storytelling, and an appreciation for the animacy of more-than-human environments. What is at stake here is not merely the in/ability to physically reproduce future generations, but the importance of cultural reproduction, related to Indigenous Peoples' embodied relationships to land (Altamirano-Jiménez in this volume; Hoover et al. 2012). This academic-activist approach moves from extraction to regeneration to promote community wellness and cultural knowledge for future generations (Klein 2014; Klein and Simpson 2013; Simpson 2017). Rather than treating the natural environment as a commodity or resource for extraction, numerous Indigenous voices articulate an animate, familial, loving relationship for the environments slated for industrial development.

ENVIRONMENTAL REPRODUCTIVE JUSTICE: ENGAGING MORE-THAN-HUMAN LIFE

Many Indigenous women's voices resonate in defence of their communities and territories, articulating a love and respect for their lands, waters, cultures, and ways of life (see Altamirano-Jiménez and Starblanket in this volume). These perspectives challenge dualistic thinking that categorically separates humans from their environments. Resisting a worldview that reinforces dualisms separating humans from nature, or more-than-human worlds, an environmental reproductive justice lens contributes to these conversations by emphasizing the reproduction of cultural knowledge (Hoover et al. 2012). In contention with a politics of extraction informed by neoliberalism—a form of governance that "involves practices, knowledge, and ways of inhabiting the world that emphasize the market, individual rationality and the responsibility of entrepreneurial subjects" (Altamirano-Jiménez 2013, 4)—where humans extract from the natural environment, a relational orientation to the environment centres Indigenous Peoples' senses of place (Altamirano-Jiménez in this volume; Native Youth Sexual Health Network, n.d.). Place-based arts and acts of resistance respond to ongoing politics of extraction. These struggles are "not only *for* land but also informed *by* land" (Flowers 2015, 42; emphasis in original). Natural resources are not merely commodities that exist outside of human subjectivity for consumption but are connected through relationships to the human self as (s)kin.

Turning to Indigenous theorists and activists, including Indigenous feminist perspectives, is a critical starting point to flesh this framework out (Altamirano-Jiménez in this volume; Casumbal-Salazar 2017; Hunt and Holmes 2015; Goodyear-Kaʻōpua 2013; Goodyear-Kaʻōpua, Hussey, and Wright 2014; Million 2013; Driskill et al. 2011; Starblanket in this volume). Following Leanne Betasamosake Simpson (2017), gender is central to the generative and affirmative refusal of extraction. A regenerative, relational, reproductive approach to human/environment relations is about "continuous rebirth," a "fertility of ideas," and alternatives (Klein and Simpson 2013, n.p.). Community voices, gender, women's leadership, and counter-narratives contribute to the discursive dimension of environmental justice. As Simpson has discussed, this relational orientation centres kinship and a deep connection between humans and their environments. When Indigenous Peoples stand up, speak out, and refuse industrial encroachment without "free, prior, and informed consent," the ways in which their lives are entangled within an assemblage of colonial institutions, discourses, and practices becomes apparent. Simpson articulates these settler-colonial tensions in her evocative words:

> Extraction and assimilation go together. Colonialism and capitalism are based on extracting and assimilating. My land is seen as a resource. My relatives in the plant and animal worlds are seen as resources. My culture and knowledge is a resource. My body is a resource and my children are a resource because they have the potential to grow, maintain, and uphold

> the extraction-assimilation system. The act of extraction removes all of
> the relationships that give whatever is being extracted meaning. (Klein
> and Simpson 2013, n.p.)

Indigenous feminist scholars discuss how lands cultivate life. Following Dian Million, "the nurturing inclusiveness that is often modeled as an ideal in kinship teaches us that we form one another and create social and spiritual relations that we extend and that are extended to us in radiating bursts of affective interrelations that also include nonhuman relations" (2013, 180).

This framing centres situated voices, deep reciprocity, relationships, and settler responsibilities to engage in the ongoing unfinished process of decolonization.

Environmental reproductive justice stems from the groundwork of environmental justice scholarship and extends the distributive, procedural, and discursive dimensions of justice (Schlosberg 2013; Wiebe 2016). This prismatic lens challenges linear thought and replaces it with a spectrum of perspectives and angles of vision; in doing so, it signals the necessary importance of including women and queer voices into meaningful processes about environmental futures. At the same time, inclusion is not enough. Hearing must translate into listening and witnessing with a genuine shift in authority and decision-making (Wiebe 2019). Doing so requires creative, collaborative, and innovative approaches to public engagement.[4] It requires continuous negotiation and deliberation. An application of these principles draws attention to the significance of designing policy processes that go from listening to those directly affected by a politics of extraction, to cultivating a politics of regeneration.

A PRISMATIC LENS: THE MULTIPLE ANGLES OF ENVIRONMENTAL REPRODUCTIVE JUSTICE

The environmental reproductive justice lens advanced here focuses on the following core features: lived-experience, felt knowledges, respect for **more-than-human life**, and self-determination. Procedurally, this approach can be applied to the management of and decision-making about natural resources through meaningful deliberation processes that engage communities in continuous and collaborative consent. First, by placing lived-experience at the centre of analysis, this lens troubles liberalism. Academic-activists play an interpretive role in translation efforts across different ways of knowing. Lived-experience gives expression to counter-discourses; for instance, challenging the overarching emphasis on extraction as a necessary means to progress. The counter-discourses of those affected by colonial policies are dialogic forces that can interrupt predominant narratives (Ahmed 2017; Million 2013). When non-Indigenous academic-activists bear witness to the situated discourses of those who express concern, they carry a responsibility to create space for, and amplify, the voices of those who have been marginalized by mainstream political processes.

Second, the articulations of concern for community health and wellness apparent in public statements and submitted evidence emphasize felt knowledges. Dian Million's "felt theory" approach to political thought entails an analytical focus that goes beyond discourse to centre affect, and how institutions and discourses affect the "lived sensory beingness" of peoples in their daily lives. This lived sensory beingness manifests in community stories. As "poetic knowledges," stories convey meaning (2013, 30). Stories emerge in complex and uneven relationships of power. According to Million: "Stories form bridges that other people might cross, to feel their way into another experience. That is the promise of witness. These feelings, these affects, are part of the power of transformation in politically charged arenas" (76). When non-Indigenous people hear Indigenous testimonies, they bear witness to them. An environmental reproductive justice lens aims to centre the stories that have been silenced and amplify them.

Third, expressions of love for lands and waters highlight a relational engagement with more-than-human life. Deliberative struggles over environmental management issues draw into focus contending narratives about how humans relate to the non-human or more-than-human world. As many Indigenous scholars and activists have voiced, this approach goes beyond considering land and water as resources to be managed, controlled, and extracted. Mauna a Wākea can be understood as an elder sibling or ancestor (Casumbal-Salazar 2017, 5). It is a source of life, celebrating water forms including mist, rains, clouds, the lake, and snow. In Casumbal-Salazar's words: "The spirits attached to these water forms are frequently women—the akua and kupua said to live on Mauna a Wākea." As a *mana wahine* (female power), she symbolizes a place of spiritual being and reflection, part of a "deeply held ethical positionality" that can be described as an "onto-genealogical ethos: that is, to care for the land, water and other natural beings" (6). Mauna a Wākea is more than a physical attribute; she is kin. This ethical way of being in relationship to the environment gives expression to what many Kanaka Maoli (Native Hawaiian) scholars and activists refer to as *aloha 'āina*, love and respect for that which feeds us. There exists a multiplicity of layered meanings to territories and senses of place across the Pacific that extend beyond liberal, extractivist, settler-colonial governmentality.

Fourth, environmental reproductive justice is not just about expanding the sphere of a discourse or including marginalized voices in deliberative process. It requires a serious interrogation of the systems and decision-making procedures that affect the livelihoods of the most directly affected citizens. This involves establishing administrative processes that go beyond consultation and accommodation to incorporate "free, prior, and informed consent." An approach based upon these principles extends further than a liberal politics of inclusion, participation, tolerance, and recognition. Noting a fundamental bind, Casumbal-Salazar cautions that "to participate in the laws of the state is to recognize its authority over us. Yet, we cannot not participate, because to do so would only encourage continued desecration and industrial development of our 'āina" (2017, 25). Participation presents a paradox. Moving away from settler colonialism involves self-determination. Those whose lives are poised to be most impacted by the encroachment of state-sanctioned industrial developments are entitled to play a key decision-making role in the determination of their futures. In Canada, Indigenous communities are beginning to partner with governments through a process of ongoing collaborative consent over the management of water resources (Simms et al. 2018). Public engagement on the governance and management of natural resources must go beyond "hearing" voices (Wiebe 2019; Levac and Wiebe, forthcoming). Moving from the politics of extraction to a politics of consent in the governance of natural resources requires that those who articulate deep-rooted and relational place-based connections must guide and inform the design of deliberative procedures that affect sacred places. Placing stories at the centre of public engagement and treating storytellers as experts of their own lived-experiences with insights to share into the design of deliberative processes regarding the administration of natural resources is crucial to ensure that "decolonization is not a metaphor" (Tuck and Yang 2012). These four features—lived-experience, felt knowledges, respect for more-than-human life, and self-determination—challenge settler-colonial governmentality and a politics of extraction and seek to replace it with a politics of relationships, care, and intimacy.

ENGENDERING COASTAL PROTECTION ACROSS THE PACIFIC

Contested Energy Futures: Pipeline Expansion in Western Canada

Located on the Burrard Inlet, along the Coast Salish shoreline outside of Vancouver, BC, on a body of water known as the Indian Arm, the terminus of the Kinder Morgan Trans Mountain Pipeline occupies Tsleil-Waututh territory. As an Indigenous community directly affected by the proposed expansion pipeline project, which would twin the pipeline and triple the amount of oil flowing from Alberta's tar sands, its members express deep concern about how the project would affect future generations. An increase in potential risks and susceptibility to accidents, incidents, and leaks would have devastating effects on the marine environment, affecting fishing and harvesting. Tsleil-Waututh, meaning "People of the Inlet," developed the Sacred Trust Initiative to stop the expansion of this project (Tsleil-Waututh Nation 2018). Their struggles to protect their coastline and their community reveal tensions over extraction and regeneration and the failure of a settler-colonial government to incorporate Indigenous law and jurisdiction in its decision.

The Canadian government approved the expansion of the Kinder Morgan Trans Mountain Pipeline project on November 29, 2016, after a 29-month review by the NEB, which determined the project to be in the public's interest (Prime Minister of Canada 2016). Numerous Indigenous leaders have expressed concern that this project did not properly consult affected Indigenous communities, thus calling the official approval of the expansion project a breach of Prime Minister Justin Trudeau's commitment to reconciliation (McCarthy 2018). Several Nations, including the Squamish, Tsleil-Waututh, and Neskonlith, challenged the federal government's decision in the Federal Court of Appeal. These Nations expressed frustration about the lack of meaningful consultation with Indigenous Peoples, which is a constitutionally protected commitment (McCarthy 2018). The decision to approve the project left Canadians and Indigenous Peoples questioning the federal government's commitment to reconciliation.

Canada's NEB reviewed the proposed pipeline expansion project in accordance with the National Energy Board Act and the 2012 Canadian Environmental Assessment Act. Public hearings took place between April 2014 and February 2016. In May 2016, the NEB recommended that the governor-in-council direct the board to issue the necessary Certificate of Public Convenience and Necessity with 157 conditions (City of Vancouver, n.d.; NEB 2016). The board was also charged with considering Aboriginal interests and ensuring that its process was "designed to be thorough and accessible to Aboriginal groups so that they may make their concerns known to the Board on potential impacts on their interests, and have those concerns considered and addressed" (NEB 2016, xii). The board's responsibilities under the NEB Act must be consistent with Canada's constitution, including section 35(1) of the Constitution Act, 1982, which recognizes and affirms the existing Aboriginal and treaty rights of Aboriginal Peoples.

The board's mandate included consideration of potential impacts of the project on directly affected parties and Aboriginal interests. This involved gathering oral evidence from Aboriginal people, described by the NEB as "typically non-technical information" about "the potential impacts of a project on Aboriginal communities' rights and interests" (2015, n.p.). The board established parameters for what constituted Aboriginal oral evidence during the public hearings. While the board accepted stories and knowledge orally, it would not consider scientific knowledge, opinions about the pipeline, or recommendations unless submitted in writing (NEB 2016; Scanlon 2014). This separation of Aboriginal oral evidence from scientific knowledge reproduces a binary between ways of knowing and marginalizes Indigenous expertise. Tsleil-Waututh Elder Carleen Thomas expressed concern about how the process impeded the meaningful participation of Indigenous communities and did not give them the space to be heard: "They should listen to communities and listen to people, and get a real understanding of our situation, and not rush the truth" (quoted in Scanlon 2014, n.p.). Her comments point to the need for careful consideration about how to engage Indigenous knowledge.

Many Indigenous women drew attention to these procedural constraints. Their responses to the pipeline project signal the importance of felt knowledge. In March 2018, as plans for Kinder Morgan to start construction pressed forward, Tsleil-Waututh Elder Amy George called on affected communities to "warrior up" and to "come with your drums and make a lot of noise and show that we really mean it" (quoted in Pynn 2018, n.p.). They refused to be idle. From unceded Secwepemc territory in south-central BC along the pipeline route, women like Kanahus Manuel of the Secwepemc Women's Warrior Society and Tiny House Warriors expressed grave concern about the lack of "free, prior and informed consent" and published the Women's Declaration against Kinder Morgan Man Camps (Secwepemcul'ecw Assembly 2018). Without consent, the pipeline expansion and the establishment of temporary housing or "man camps" along the route violate their rights. Supported by prominent Indigenous women and organizations including Idle No More, Indigenous Environmental Network, Families of Sisters in Spirit, No More Silence, Native Youth Sexual Health Network, Greenpeace, and Mi'kmaq Warrior Society, the declaration exposes the intersections of extraction and gender. Chiefs, Elders, women, and children assembled along the route, in ceremony, to assert their jurisdiction. Their website documents this felt knowledge with the stirring declaration "Not Over my Dead Body" as an enactment of the "Secwepemc Declaration on Protecting Our Land and Water against the Kinder Morgan Trans Mountain Pipeline" (Secwepemcul'ecw Assembly 2018).

With their bodies, homes, and lives on the pipeline route, community members built tiny homes to block access while asserting Secwepemc law and jurisdiction. The community-driven Tiny House Warriors initiative expresses a commitment to "upholding our collective and spiritual responsibility and jurisdiction to look after the land, the language and the culture of our people" and invites "anyone and everyone to join" (Secwepemcul'ecw Assembly 2018, n.p.). These homes speak back to a legacy of colonialism and housing shortages in the community while also envisioning sustainable alternative futures. They simultaneously serve to assert their jurisdiction, house community members, and function on solar energy. It is a model for Nations elsewhere.

The pipeline expansion project is poised to affect human and more-than-human life. "We're the voice for those who cannot speak," said Amy George at a Vancouver news conference in reference to the environmental impacts of an oil spill to fish and wildlife (quoted in Pynn 2018, n.p.). Rather than reinforce separations between humans, culture, and environments, these words centre connections through generations. According to Tsleil-Waututh councillor Charlene Aleck: "Our bloodline goes right back to the inlet, that's where our first grandmother came from, so what would happen to us is that culture—that lineage—would be severed once again. It's the sustenance of our traditions, our ceremonies, and who we are as a people would be damaged" (quoted in McSheffery 2016, n.p.). These remarks connect past, present, and future generations and articulate how increased industrial activity due to the pipeline expansion project would affect the cultural vitality of the Tsleil-Waututh and their ability to reproduce cultural knowledge. Women of all ages have expressed concern. At a Salish Sea bioregional gathering, youth leader Kayah George explained how the inlet is sacred to her people as the soil created the first woman: "That inlet is our oldest ancestor" (quoted in

Heidenreich 2017, n.p.). The pipeline expansion project also carries with it potential impacts to marine mammals.

A significant issue expressed by several Indigenous communities is how increased marine traffic would affect the southern resident killer whale populations. The Tsawwassen, Tsawout, T'Sou-ke, Tsartlip, and Pacheedaht Nations spoke before the board about the social and cultural affects (NEB 2016, 361). For Tsawwassen, their ocean-going canoe is adorned with a killer whale. Many Tsawout clans and families are connected to killer whales, and loss of whales in their territories would simultaneously be a loss to clans and families. Pacheedaht representatives mentioned how increased tanker traffic would further impede the recovery of killer whales. For T'Sou-ke, adverse effects on killer whales could have catastrophic ripple effects on their rights, title, and sense of identity. Killer whales bear cultural and spiritual significance. Tsartlip relationships to whales coincide with an obligation to protect them. These concerns challenge the human/more-than-human dualism.

Lack of meaningful engagement through the formal deliberative process prompted direct action across the province. On May 23, 2018, youth walked out of their classrooms to protest the pipeline in an event organized by Ta'Kaiya Blaney and Eden Reimer. Through a Facebook livestream, Blaney articulated the importance of the movement as a "chance to show our elected leaders and Kinder Morgan that our lands, livelihoods and future are more important than a pipeline" (quoted in Bellrichard 2018, n.p.). By walking out of their schools, young people showed the power of youth voices in raising awareness about the long-term impacts of environmental disasters and climate change. Their rally at the Vancouver Art Gallery, which brought together over 200 youth from Metro Vancouver, followed the inspiration from Ta'ah (Amy George) of the Tsleil-Waututh Nation, who called for people to come together protest the pipeline (Bellrichard 2018). It was a joyous assembly, featuring performers and poets, including JB the First Lady and Christie Charles, to generate momentum. Young peoples' voices resonated across the coast. In Bella Bella, Heiltsuk youth scheduled a solidarity walkout. A Twitter and video post from Band Councillor Jess Housty documented the walkout with support from hereditary and elected leadership and reiterated the importance of consent (Bellrichard 2018). Concerned citizens mobilized to stress the importance of intergenerational justice and articulate a politics of care for their human and more-than-human communities.

This youth-led mobilization followed a rally on March 10, 2018, when Indigenous Peoples, environmentalists, and local communities came together to stand up to the pipeline expansion project on Burnaby Mountain and express opposition to an injunction granted to Kinder Morgan that set a 50-metre "exclusion zone" (Waisman 2018). To protect their territories and engage Canadians in a wider dialogue about reconciliation, Tsleil-Waututh members built *Kwekwecnewtwx* (a place to watch from), a spiritual and ceremonial hub (Lambert 2018). Tsleil-Waututh continue to enact the defence of their territory as one of protection, not protest. In their written evidence, submitted as an intervention before the NEB, they explain their stewardship obligation to "act with respect for all beings, human and non-human, and for all elements of the natural and spirit worlds" (Tsleil-Waututh Nation 2015, 53). Their law highlights the centrality of *ʔaχwəstəl'* (reciprocal giving/reciprocity) and respect for the *snəwayəɬ* (the spirits of those who came before or the ancestors). Tsleil-Waututh stewardship centres upon an intimate connection between past, present, and future generations:

> Burrard Inlet is the "womb" of Tsleil-Waututh, where *Cicəɬ siʔem'*, with the help of the cedar tree, brought the first Tsleil-Watt woman to life from earth, rock, and sediment beneath the salt water. This intimate connection to Burrard Inlet gives rise to an obligation of stewardship and respect; we must care for it because our ancestors are part of the landscape. Through the centuries, we have returned our ancestors to the earth, where they have become part of the environment for the birds, fishes, and other species, contributing to the spiritual connection between us and to our stewardship obligation. Our *snəwayəɬ* tells us that if something is alive, it must be respected and that not just the animals but also the rivers, the sand bars, and the rocks are alive and are beings with spirits. (Tsleil-Waututh Nation 2015, 53)

Their stories elaborate how ancestral connections root the community to this territory. They are not simply of the territory, but they "*are* the places and beings of the territory" (Tsleil-Waututh Nation 2015, 53). Tsleil-Waututh stories articulate a cycle of knowledge that depends on a healthy ecosystem, which the pipeline expansion project is poised to threaten. Community health also requires an abundance of foods from their lands and waters. Their evidence notes the wisdom of their elders: "When the tide went out, the table was set" (54). Their lived-experience and felt knowledge underscore the importance of human/more-than-human relations for community health and environmental reproductive justice. Along the pipeline's path, from Secwepemc to Tsleil-Waututh territory, these struggles to resist extraction and centre relationships connect communities across the Pacific and Oceania.

Mauna a Wākea

In a similar vein, the struggle over Mauna a Wākea draws into focus ongoing conditions of settler colonialism and a continuing clash of cosmologies (Maile 2018; Casumbal-Salazar 2017). The Thirty Meter Telescope (TMT), poised to be the world's largest telescope, would be constructed and housed in a $1.4 billion observatory on one of the most sacred sites on the islands. Mauna a Wākea is part of the so-called "ceded lands" originally belonging to the Hawaiian Kingdom—illegally seized in 1893—and now administered by the state of Hawai'i to the "benefit" of Native Hawaiians (Goodyear-Ka'ōpua 2017, 1869; Overbye 2016). The jurisdiction of these lands became hotly contested when the TMT Observatory Corporation requested a permit to establish the world's largest telescope, in partnership with Canadian, Californian, Chinese, Indian, and Japanese astronomers, in 2010.[5] Resistance to this request drew into focus the global profile of Mauna a Wākea and the contentious terrain of cultural, scientific, and corporate interests in this sacred site. In 2014, 2015, and yet again in 2019, competing visions about what constitutes a better future for this mountain came into view when direct action tactics disrupted the TMT groundbreaking ceremony. The *kia'i mauna* or Guardians of the Mountain describe themselves as protectors, not protestors (Goodyear-Ka'ōpua 2017, 188). Their intervention at Mauna a Wākea has much to teach us about transforming the capitalist politics of extraction.

Development on the mountain advances rhetoric about economic prosperity, jobs, and scientific advancements, while marginalizing Native Hawaiian or Kanaka 'Ōiwi (Kanaka) kinship connections to this sacred place. The ways in which Kanaka have been "ruled ineligible as caretakers of land" coincides with how they have been "denied a meaningful voice in decisions about the future of Hawai'i" and take shape within gendered hierarchies of Western science and philosophy (Casumbal-Salazar 2017, 2) This is a place revered for worship and considered to be an ancestor and an elder sibling in the *mo'okū'auhau* (genealogical secession) of all Hawaiians (Casumbal-Salazar 2017). From the seafloor to its peak, Mauna a Wākea is one of the tallest mountains on earth. This dormant volcano reaches the highest point in the archipelago of Hawai'i. It is an "umbilical chord [*sic*]" or piko that connects Kanaka to the heavens: "It is the first to be touched by the rising sun's morning rays and the first to receive the highest clouds' life-giving waters" (Peralto 2014, 236). For many, the mountain is like a relative and a realm of the gods.

These struggles refuse systems of empire and settler-colonial governmentality. There are layered ways of understanding this resistance through Indigenous terms, national terms, and settler-state terms (Goodyear-Kaʻōpua 2017, 188). Direct action as a refusal of settler-colonial governmentality is an invitation for alternative relationships. The protectors created a "space of engagement" and an opening to join the efforts; they did not simply exclude others through the blockade (190). Leading up to and following the April 2, 2015, arrests of those whose bodies created a barrier against the machinery as it made its way up to the summit, an "Aloha Checkpoint" was established. This checkpoint was not a standard blockade to exclude anyone, or a "possessive, jurisdictional line"; instead, it served as a "porous boundary" intended to block construction vehicles and an invitation to "talk story" (190). Occupiers discussed how the TMT project would leave an impact on over five acres of the summit, including sites of worship, observation, and resting places for the "bones and umbilical chords [sic] of generations of some Hawaiian families" (190). The Aloha Checkpoint created space to learn and engage in dialogue. It was guided by kapu aloha, "a philosophy and practice of nonviolent engagement" ʻ(190). Kapu aloha asks people to carry themselves with compassion for ʻāina and empathy to others encountered.

Kapu aloha is a form of embodied, felt, relational conduct and knowledge. According to Kumu hula (hula master) Pua Case, it is grounded in teachings of kūpuna (elders). Kapu aloha manifested, and continues to manifest, at Mauna a Wākea during encounters between protectors and law enforcement officials. As they came to remove them from the mountain, protestors greeted them with lei lāʻī (garlands made from ti-leaf, known for its protective and healing qualities; Goodyear-Kaʻōpua 2017, 191). Kapu aloha at the Aloha Checkpoint created alternative terms of engagement. Though settler state officials passed regulations to target and remove protectors, the kiaʻi stewards invited the antagonists to "join them in reaching toward more expansive and sustainable futures" (191). Kanaka honour a corporeal connection to the Mauna. They are not simply fighting for the life of the Mauna but recognizing that "we are the Mauna" (192). As protectors renew connections, they invite others to join this regenerative renewal and engage in resurgent Indigenous futures.

Mauna a Wākea represents physical and spiritual connections to past, present, and future generations, like the piko of a human body. It is a place of transformation, renewal, and rebirth. In Hānau Ka Mauna, the Piko of our Ea, Leon

No'eau Peralto (2014) begins with a birth chant, which is infused with multiple layers of *kaona* (veiled meaning) to introduce the genealogy of Mauna a Wākea to present the direct familiar relationship between Kanaka 'Ōiwi and *Ka mauna a Wākea*, the mountain-child of Wākea. Since birth, the Mauna and Kanaka have been instilled with a particular *kuleana* (duty, responsibility) to each other. This reciprocal relationship requires ongoing maintenance to remain *pono* (balance, righteousness). As Peralto discusses, the birthing of the 'āina coincided with the birthing of Hawaiian consciousness and ancestral linkages between the genealogies of lands and peoples. Mauna a Wākea is considered to be a symbolic place for the highest potential of human consciousness.

A collective journey to *mālama* (care for) the kuleana to Mauna a Wākea has been an ongoing struggle since the settler state gained control of the 'āina. Peralto discusses the deep-rooted systems of governance that took place prior to US occupation within the Hawaiian Kingdom, which was seized in 1889 and became part of the Crown and Hawaiian Government Lands (2014, 236). In 1959, the US government transferred these 'āina to the state of Hawai'i, establishing the Public Land Trust. Returning to the piko or womb presents an opportunity for rebirth and transformation of these colonial relations. Consideration of Mauna a Wākea as a piko and an emphasis on felt experience challenges colonial knowledge systems that are apparent in formal deliberative spheres of engagement.

Many parties are implicated and invested in the management of Mauna a Wākea, including the University of Hawai'i, astronomers, the State of Hawai'i, and Kanaka. In 1968, for one dollar a year, the University of Hawai'i took out a 65-year lease on 11,000 acres of land (Overbye 2016). In 1970, the first telescope was established and many soon followed. In 1988, a state audit condemned the University of Hawai'i for not protecting the mountain's natural and cultural resources. In 2007, an environmental impact study led by NASA concluded that 30 years of astronomy development resulted in "significant, substantial and adverse harm" to Mauna a Wākea (Overbye 2016). The TMT corporation selected Mauna a Wākea for its operations in 2009. Two years later, after hearings in 2010 and 2011, the Department of Land and Natural Resources approved a permit for the telescope.

On September 2, 2010, the University of Hawai'i, Hilo requested approval from the Board of Land and Natural Resources (BLNR) for a Conservation District Use Application to construct the TMT on Mauna a Wākea on behalf of TMT Observatory Corporation. The board held public hearings in Hilo and Kailua-Kona, where 200 people attended and 84 people testified.[6] During the hearings, proponents of the TMT project asserted that this large, "next generation" telescope would facilitate cutting-edge scientific research that could not be undertaken elsewhere. Opponents of the project included Kanaka, who articulated that the summit was sacred and that the construction of the 18½-storey-high observatory would be a cultural devastation. When the board voted on the permit in February 2011 before a contested case hearing was held, it violated due process and denied the public the right to be heard "at a meaningful time, in a meaningful manner."[7]

On November 20, 2012, a contested case hearing began. The hearing officer issued a 124-page finding of fact, conclusion of law, and decision order, which granted the permit, subject to conditions. On April 12, 2013, the BLNR also approved the permit. A year later, on May 5, 2014, the Circuit Court's decision order affirmed the permit; however, this was vacated by the Hawai'i Supreme Court. On December 2, 2015, the Supreme Court of the State of Hawai'i found that the state's Board of Land and Natural Resources violated due process by approving the permit to construct an observatory in a conservation district before the results of the contested case hearing. Its decision noted that: "Quite simply, the Board put the cart before the horse when it issued the permit before the request for a contested case was resolved and the hearing was held."[8] This set the stage for another round of hearings in 2016.

Hearings provide an opportunity for public testimony and create space for proponents and opponents of industrial developments. During the 2011 contested case hearing, Kealoha Pisciotta expressed how according to Kanaka cosmology Mauna a Wākea is an origin place "where the heaven and the earth come together, where all life forms originated from."[9] Academics and community activists articulated their concerns. According to testimony given by Dr. J. Kēhaulani Kauanui, a professor of anthropology and American studies at Wesleyan University, the TMT could be read as a form of twenty-first-century colonialism, where observatories "literally supplant our indigenous temple of worship," and are thus a "desecration."[10] Marti Townsend, program director of KAHEA: The Hawaiian Environmental Alliance, also testified that TMT would negatively affect both cultural practices and the environment.

Protection of Mauna a Wākea emerges from respect for a relational and animate connection between human and more-than-human life. As Noelani Goodyear-Ka'ōpua explains, Indigenous communities are not simply stuck in time, holding on to the past, but "protecting ancestral connections to lands and waters" for the future (2017, 184). Resistance efforts at Mauna a Wākea give expression to a movement in order to protect ʻāina as well as relationships to ancestors, language, and culture. This movement reveals how Kanaka and settler allies can work together to "unmake relations of settler colonialism and imperialism, protecting Indigenous relationships between human and non-humans through direct action and compassionate engagement with settler-state law enforcement" (185). Such engagement serves as a generative form of decolonial and sustainable futures creation, where Indigenous Peoples and settlers respond to industrial projects that destroy or pollute territories as matters of concern to the health of all peoples. While this opportunity for alternatives is generative, we cannot eclipse the context of exploitation, imperialism, settler colonialism, and climate change, where islanders are "losing their ancestral homelands to the encroaching tides" (185). Mauna a Wākea protectors cultivate connections across generations. Though colonial discourses frame resistance as an obstruction to future progress, instead this grounded activism serves to protect "the possibilities of multiple futures" (186). It connects past, present, and future, which is essential for a transformative and regenerative approach that challenges a politics of extraction.

CONCLUDING REFLECTIONS: COASTAL CONNECTIONS, FLUID RELATIONS

Tsleil-Waututh Councillor Charlene Aleck spoke on behalf of her Nation when the Government of Canada announced its commitment to buy the Kinder Morgan pipeline expansion for $4.5 billion and turn it into a Crown corporation: "We remain dedicated to our sacred responsibility which is the stewardship of the Burrard Inlet" (quoted in McKeen and Li 2018, n.p.). The move to increase the flow of heavy bitumen from Alberta through to the lands and waters across British Columbia continued to face opposition from the Government of British Columbia, environmentalists, and many Indigenous communities. This was not lost on Indigenous leaders, who noted the lack of consent, as also affirmed in a 2018 Federal Court of Appeal decision (Phillip and Simon 2018). The decision to approve and fund the pipeline expansion raises serious questions about deliberative democracy, public engagement, climate change, and respect for Indigenous self-determination. In a time when state governments express a commitment to reconciliation, this executive decision to ease extraction leaves citizens questioning what it means for the future of Canadian-Indigenous relations and for the future of the health of the planet (Phillip and Simon 2018). An environmental reproductive justice lens contends that decision-making based on consent is crucial. It goes further than consultation to ensure that those directly affected by decisions over natural resource development have meaningful opportunities to design, deliberate, and decide the outcomes that respect their experiences, knowledges, and avenues to self-determine their futures.

Administrative procedures that include public hearings leave considerable room for creative visioning about how to create space for meaningful dialogue and engagement about how humans relate to more-than-human life. The environmental reproductive justice approach advanced in this chapter encourages policy-makers to enact a *sensing policy* orientation to public engagement that takes Indigenous voices, lived-experiences, knowledges, stories, and senses of place seriously (Wiebe 2016). As Noelani Goodyear-Kaʻōpua (2015) shared in a poem during an Aloha ʻĀina Unity March at Kapiʻolani Park in support for the protection of Mauna a Wākea, birth stories are inextricably connected to birthing flourishing decolonial futures. Environmental reproductive justice is a way of engaging the senses through stories and imagining alternatives to the settler-colonial status quo. This requires not simply a discursive reference to the United Declaration on the Rights of Indigenous Peoples and the principles of "free, prior and informed consent," but a substantive commitment to implement these principles into administrative procedures.

Through lived-experience, felt knowledge, human/more-than-human relations, and self-determination, this chapter has discussed four core components of an environmental reproductive justice lens. The implementation of these principles is crucial to move beyond a politics of extraction to a politics built upon relationships. This is a pivotal orientation to guide policy officials who embark on an unfinished and unsettling journey of reconciliation. Placing stories at the centre of public engagement and treating storytellers as experts of their own lived-experiences with insights to share in the design of deliberative processes regarding the administration of natural resources is crucial to ensure that "decolonization is not a metaphor" (Tuck and Yang 2012). Attempts to meaningfully restore relationships between humans and their environments requires creating space for re-storying knowledge, moving beyond hearing to listening, and envisioning alternatives to extraction across communities, Oceania, and generations.

DISCUSSION QUESTIONS

1. What is environmental reproductive justice and what can it offer the study of political science and policy?
2. Why is gender relevant to environmental justice?
3. Whose voices are included and excluded from public engagement on environmental justice issues and why?
4. How can decision-makers listen to the voices and stories of those experiencing environmental injustice?

NOTES

1 This chapter is enriched by the generosity of Uahikea Maile, who provided such a close and careful read of these emergent, always-in-progress ideas. Mahalo nui.

2 This chapter employs the term Indigenous in accordance with the United Nations Declaration on the Rights of Indigenous Peoples as a way of referring to peoples globally who have retained social, cultural, economic, and political practices, genealogies, and modes of relating to their environments in ways that are distinct from, yet in relation to, dominant settler-colonial societies. I will only use the term "Aboriginal" in the chapter when directly referencing the Canadian settler-colonial law and the language that derives from it within its affiliated policies and public engagement procedures.

3 As a non-Indigenous Canadian raised in Coast Salish territory living in Hawai'i, while considering my kuleana (duty, responsibility) as a settler seeking to work in solidarity for alternatives to the colonial status quo and envision decolonial, sustainable futures, I examine these sites of contestation and resistance from an environmental reproductive justice lens to "highlight the complex relationship that exists between the market, colonialism, Indigenous peoples, and gender" (Altamirano-Jiménez 2013, 2). I underscore how struggles to defend and protect sacred sites are gendered and I advocate for moving beyond a politics of extraction and circumscribed consultation to a politics of consent. Struggles over place are simultaneously struggles over "who controls how place is lived and imagined" as well as "represented, what stories are heard, in what forums they are told, and for what purposes" (7). Spaces that engage with stories and the lived-experiences of storytellers are not neutral: they are deeply politicized, gendered, and racialized.

4 It also requires a commitment to the implementation of the United Declaration on the Rights of Indigenous Peoples, which emphasizes principles of "free, prior, and informed consent" while respecting Indigenous self-determination. This cannot be a one-time event (Nosek 2017). For more, see Levac and Wiebe (forthcoming).

5 See Supreme Court of the State of Hawai'i, "Order Granting in Part Emergency Motion for Stay Upon Appeal," SCAP-14-0000873, November 17, 2015. http://www .courts.state.hi.us/docs/opin_ord/sct/2015/November/SCAP-14-0000873ord.pdf

6 Supreme Court of the State of Hawai'i, "Opinion of the Court," SCAP-14-0000873, December 2, 2015, 8. https://www.maunakeaandtmt.org/wp-content /uploads/2017/08/SCAP-14-00008731.pdf.

7 Ibid., 5.

8 Ibid., 5–6.

9 Ibid., 19.

10 Ibid., 20.

REFERENCES

Ahmed, Sara. 2017. *Living a Feminist Life*. Durham, NC: Duke University Press.

Altamarino-Jiménez, Isabel. 2013. *Indigenous Encounters with Neoliberalism: Place, Women and the Environment in Canada and Mexico*. Vancouver: UBC Press.

Bellrichard, Chantelle. 2018. "Youth Walk Out of Class to Protest Trans Mountain Pipeline." *CBC News*, May 23. https://www.cbc.ca/news/indigenous/youth-walk -out-of-class-to-protest-trans-mountain-pipeline-1.4675166.

Casumbal-Salazar, Iokepa. 2017. "A Fictive Kinship: Making 'Modernity,' 'Ancient Hawaiians,' and the Telescope on Mauna Kea." *Journal of the Native American and Indigenous Studies Association* 4 (2): 1–30.

City of Vancouver. n.d. "NEB Process and Timeline." http://vancouver.ca/green -vancouver/neb-process.aspx. Accesed November 22, 2019.

Coulthard, Glen. 2014. *Red Skin, White Masks: Rejecting the Colonial Politics of Recognition*. Minneapolis: University of Minnesota Press.

Driskill, Qwo-Li, Chris Finley, Brian Joseph Gilley, and Scott Lauria Morgensen, eds. 2011. *Queer Indigenous Studies: Critical Interventions in Theory, Politics and Literature*. Tuscon: Arizona University Press.

Flowers, Rachel. 2015. "Refusal to Forgive: Indigenous Women's Love and Rage." *Decolonization: Indigeneity, Education & Society* 4 (2): 32–49.

Goodyear-Ka'ōpua, Noelani. 2013. *The Seeds We Planted: Portraits of a Native Hawaiian Charter School*. Minneapolis: University of Minnesota Press.

———. 2015. "Aloha 'Āina Unity March | Noelani Goodyear-Ka'ōpua Poem." *'Ōiwi TV*, August 11. 00:05:24. https://oiwi.tv/maunakea/aaum-noelani-goodyear -kaopua-poem.

———. 2017. "Protectors of the Future, Not Protestors of the Past." *South Atlantic Quarterly* 116 (1): 184–94.

Goodyear-Ka'ōpua, Noelani, Ikaika Hussey, and Erin Kahunawaika'ala Wright, eds. 2014. *A Nation Rising: Hawaiian Movements for Land, Life and Sovereignty*. Durham, NC: Duke University Press.

Heidenreich, Sari. 2017. "A Three-Legged Stool: The Salish Sea Bioregional Gathering." United Religions Initiative, December 5. https://uri.org/uri -story/20171205-three-legged-stool-salish-sea-bioregional-gathering.

Hoover, Elizabeth, et al. 2012. "Indigenous Peoples of North America: Environmental Exposures and Reproductive Justice." *Environmental Health Perspectives* 120 (12): 1645–49.

Hunt, Sarah, and Cindy Holmes. 2015. "Everyday Decolonization: Living a Decolonizing Queer Politics." *Journal of Lesbian Studies* 19 (2): 154–72.

Klein, Naomi. 2014. *This Changes Everything*. New York: Simon & Schuster.

Klein, Naomi, and Leanne Betasamosake Simpson. 2013. "Dancing the World into Being: A Conversation with Idle No More's Leanne Simpson." *Yes! Magazine*, March 5. http://www.yesmagazine.org/peace-justice/dancing-the-world-into -being-a-conversation-with-idle-no-more-leanne-simpson.

Lambert, Shaena. 2018. "The Warriors and the Watch House." *National Observer*, March 25. https://www.nationalobserver.com/2018/03/25/opinion/warriors-and -watch-house.

Levac, Leah R.E., and Sarah Marie Wiebe, eds. 2020. *Creating Spaces of Engagement: Policy Justice and the Practical Craft of Deliberative Democracy*. Toronto: University of Toronto Press.

Maile, David Uahikeaikaleiʻohu. 2018. "Precarious Performances: The Thirty Meter Telescope and Settler State Policing of Kānaka Maoli." *Abolition*, September 9. https://abolitionjournal.org/precarious-performances/.

McCarthy, Shawn. 2018. "First Nations Leaders Claim Ottawa Did Not Properly Consult B.C. Communities on Trans Mountain Project." *Globe and Mail*, May 2. https://www.theglobeandmail.com/business/article-first-nations-leaders-claim -ottawa-did-not-properly-consult-bc/.

McKeen, Alex, and Wanyee Li. 2018. "'This Changes Nothing': Indigenous Leader Says Opposition Movement Will Only Grow as Federal Government Buys Kinder Morgan." *Star Vancouver*, May 29. https://www.thestar.com/vancouver/2018/05/29 /this-changes-nothing-indigenous-leader-says-opposition-movement-will-only -grow-as-federal-government-buys-trans-mountain.html.

McSheffrey, Elizabeth. 2016. "Tsleil-Waututh Blasts Kinder Morgan Expansion as Colonial Land Appropriation." *National Observer*, January 26. https://www .nationalobserver.com/2016/01/26/news/tsleil-waututh-blasts-kinder-morgan -expansion-colonial-land-appropriation.

Million, Dian. 2013. *Therapeutic Nations: Healing in an Age of Indigenous Human Rights*. Tuscon: University of Arizona Press.

National Energy Board. 2015. "National Energy Board Ministerial Briefing Binder – Status: NEB Review of the Proposed Kinder Morgan Trans Mountain Expansion Project." Government of Canada, November 4. https://www.neb-one.gc.ca/bts /whwr/gvrnnc/brfngbndr/dcmnt3-1-eng.html?=undefined&wbdisable=true.

———. 2016. *National Energy Board Report: Trans Mountain Expansion Project*. Catalogue no. OH-011-2014. Calgary: NEB.

Native Youth Sexual Health Network. n.d. "Environmental Violence & Reproductive Justice." Native Youth Sexual Heath Network. http://www.nativeyouth sexualhealth.com/environmentalviolenceandreproductivejustice.html. Accessed November 22, 2019.

Nosek, Grace. 2017. "Re-Imagining Indigenous Peoples' Role in Natural Resource Development Decision-Making: Implementing Free, Prior and Informed Consent in Canada through Indigenous Legal Traditions." *University of British Columbia Law Review* 50 (1): 95–160.

Overbye, Dennis. 2016. "Under Hawai'i's Starriest Skies, a Fight over Sacred Ground." *New York Times*, October 3. https://www.nytimes.com/2016/10/04 /science/hawaii-thirty-meter-telescope-mauna-kea.html.

Peralto, Leon No'eau. 2014. "Portrait: Mauna a Wākea. Hānau Ka Mauna, the Piko of Our Ea." In *A Nation Rising: Hawaiian Movements for Life, Land and Sovereignty*, edited by Noelani Goodyear-Ka'ōpua, Ikaika Hussey, and Erin Kahunawaika'ala Wright, 233–43. Durham, NC: Duke University Press.

Phillip, Stewart, and Serge Simon. 2018. "If Ottawa Rams through Trans Mountain, It Could Set Up an Oka-Like Crisis." *Globe and Mail*, April 12. https://www .theglobeandmail.com/opinion/article-if-ottawa-rams-through-trans-mountain -it-could-set-up-an-oka-like/.

Prime Minister of Canada. 2016. "Prime Minister Justin Trudeau's Pipeline Announcement." Justin Trudeau, Prime Minister of Canada, November 29. https://pm.gc.ca/eng/news/2016/11/29/prime-minister-justin-trudeaus-pipeline -announcement.

Pynn, Larry. 2018. "First Nations 'Warrior Up' for Kinder Morgan Protest Rally and March Saturday." *Vancouver Sun*, March 9. http://vancouversun.com/news/local -news/first-nations-warrior-up-for-kinder-morgan-protest-rally-and-march -saturday.

Scanlon, Liam. 2014. "Critics Blast 'Insensitive' Rules for Aboriginal Oral Evidence at Kinder Morgan Hearings." *Vancouver Observer*, May 13. https://www .vancouverobserver.com/news/critics-blast-insensitive-rules-aboriginal-oral -evidence-kinder-morgan-hearings.

Schlosberg, David. 2013. "Theorizing Environmental Justice: Expanding the Sphere of a Discourse." *Environmental Politics* 22 (1): 37–55.

Secwepemcul'ecw Assembly. 2018. "Tiny House Warriors Reclaim Land, Block Trans Mountain Expansion Pipeline Route." Secwepemcul'ecw Assembly, July 11. https://www.secwepemculecw.org/.

Simms, Rosie, Merrell-Ann Phare, Oliver M. Brandes, and Michael Miltenberger. 2018. "Collaborative Consent: Pathways towards Watershed Co-governance in B.C. and Beyond." *Water Canada* (March/April): 27–36. https://poliswaterproject .org/polis-research-publication/collaborative-consent-water-british-columbia -towards-watershed-co-governance/.

Simpson, Leanne Betasamosake. 2017. *As We Have Always Done: Indigenous Freedom through Radical Resistance*. Minneapolis: University of Minnesota Press.

Tsleil-Waututh Nation. 2015. *Assessment of the Trans Mountain Pipeline and Tanker Expansion Proposal*. North Vancouver: Tsleil-Waututh Nation, Treaty, Lands, and Resources Department. https://twnsacredtrust.ca/wp-content/uploads/TWN _assessment_final_med-res_v2.pdf File OF-Fac-Oil-T260-2013-03 02.

———. 2018. *Sacred Trust Initiative*. https://twnsacredtrust.ca/.

Tuck, Eve, and K. Wayne Yang. 2012. "Decolonization Is Not a Metaphor." *Decolonization: Indigeneity, Education & Society* 1 (1): 1–40.

Waisman, Dylan 2018. "B.C. Judge Protects 'Watch House' but Issues Permanent Injunction to Stop Disruptive Kinder Morgan Protests." *National Observer*, March 15. https://www.nationalobserver.com/2018/03/15/news/bc-judge-protects-watch -house-issues-permanent-injunction-stop-disruptive-kinder.

Wiebe, Sarah Marie. 2016. *Everyday Exposure: Indigenous Mobilization and Environmental Justice in Canada's Chemical Valley.* Vancouver: UBC Press.

———. 2019. "Hearing or Listening? Pipeline Politics and the Art of Engagement in British Columbia." In *The Palgrave Handbook of Intersectionality in Public Policy*, edited by Olena Hankivsky and Julia S. Jordan-Zachary, 579–99. London: Palgrave Macmillan.

Wikler, Maia. 2018. "Women Are at the Front Lines of the Fight against the Kinder Morgan Trans Mountain Pipeline." *Teen Vogue*, March 21. https://www.teenvogue .com/story/women-are-at-front-lines-of-ight-against-kinder-morgan-trans -mountain-pipeline.

FURTHER READING

Goodyear-Kaʻōpua, Noelani, Ikaika Hussey, and Erin Kahunawaikaʻala Wright, eds. 2014. *A Nation Rising: Hawaiian Movements for Land, Life, and Sovereignty.* Durham, NC: Duke University Press.

Hoover, Elizabeth, et al. 2012. "Indigenous Peoples of North America: Environmental Exposures and Reproductive Justice." *Environmental Health Perspectives* 120 (12): 1645–49.

Levac, Leah R.E., and Sarah Marie Wiebe, eds. Forthcoming. *Creating Spaces of Engagement: Policy Justice and the Practical Craft of Deliberative Democracy.* Toronto: University of Toronto Press.

Million, Dian. 2013. *Therapeutic Nations: Healing in an Age of Indigenous Human Rights.* Tuscon: University of Arizona Press.

Simpson, Leanne Betasamosake. 2017. *As We Have Always Done: Indigenous Freedom through Radical Resistance.* Minneapolis: University of Minnesota Press.

14

Erasure at the "Tipping Point"? Transfeminist Politics and Challenges for Representation: From Turtle Island to the Global South/s

Chamindra Kumari Weerawardhana

Key terms: Afrofeminism, Indigenous knowledges, movement-building, transfeminism, transfeminist-of-colour mobilization

On May 29th, 2014, *Time* magazine ran a cover story entitled "The Transgender Tipping Point" (Steinmetz 2014). It focused on the rise of several trans people in public life who had come to prominence through their artistic and other public engagements. This provides but one indication of how, today, there is a stronger dialogue than ever before on the importance of ensuring the rights of trans people and how many trans people are making hitherto unchartered inroads into public life, in Turtle Island as well as in other parts of the world.[1] However, these progressive developments do not necessarily imply an overall improvement in the treatment of trans people. In fact, in these "turbulent times," the rise of a handful of trans people in public life has also been accompanied by a considerable increase in anti-trans agitation, not only from the right but also from the left, including in certain so-called "feminist" milieux. For example, this anti-trans sentiment is upheld in socially conservative political circles, including US President Donald Trump's administration,[2] and even everyday practicalities, such as the use of public restrooms, have become topics of high controversy (Lopez 2017), giving way to campaigns that seek to "erase" trans people from public spaces. As incidents in several Western contexts have shown, such trans-exclusionary caucuses are also active in leftist feminist and LGBTQIA2S+[3] activist and advocacy lobbies.[4] In the sphere of what we know as worldwide LGBTQIA2S+ rights activism, trans people, if not all non-cisgender peoples, receive a lesser position of agency than cisgender people in the LGBTQIA2S+ panoply.[5]

It is in this broad context that the questions raised in this chapter become relevant, not only to the northerly territories of Turtle Island, which we know as Canada,[6] but also to the world at large. This chapter is an effort to examine the academic, activist, and advocacy challenges faced by intersectional transfeminist discourses and praxes in general and what I term **transfeminist-of-colour mobilization** in particular. In what follows, I first consider the sphere of transgender studies in the academy of Turtle Island, also dwelling upon **transfeminism** as discussed in academic circles. Secondly, I focus on transfeminist-of-colour mobilization, which has, to a large extent, been somewhat removed from the academic sphere of transgender studies. In this section, I especially discuss the reasons behind this divergence, also referring to recent attempts at bridging the gap between the academic and practitioner spheres. I then discuss how people-of-colour-led transfeminist activism operates in practice. In these ways, this chapter is an effort to bring a vital intersectional feminist discourse that has seldom, or very parsimoniously, made its way into academic discussions of feminist politics. Indeed, for this very reason, much of this chapter draws on primary research and the primary channels through which transfeminist-of-colour thought and activist praxes are documented: those of social media platforms (see Small and DeGagne in this volume) and the press.

In this chapter, I focus on transfeminist politics for a pertinent reason. In today's Western academy, increasing efforts are being taken to expand our understanding of feminist perspectives not only on politics and international relations (IR) but also with a specific praxis-centred focus, such as the growing emphasis on feminist foreign policy (Sjoberg 2012; see Eichler in this volume). In the international sector, the UN's Agenda 2030, for example, emphasizes "leaving no one behind," thereby implying a commitment to inclusion, especially vis-à-vis peoples who have been long sidelined on such platforms, such as Indigenous Peoples and LGBTQIA2S+ peoples. The UN Secretary General's 2016 decision to appoint an independent expert on Sexual Orientation, Gender Identity/Expression, and Sex Characteristics (SOGIESC) issues further signifies this growing emphasis on the accentuation of "inclusion." However, these discussions continue to take place in a highly polarized manner, thereby negatively affecting the very objectives they purport to reach. SOGIESC advocacy, for instance, is often distanced from a focus on feminist foreign policy or a discourse on feminist IR, where the sole concentration is best described by one word—cisnormativity. If feminist priorities in world politics are to be limited to a cisnormative approach centring exclusively on cisgender women, those priorities inevitably perpetuate the very exclusionary practices they purport to eradicate. This is evident, for example, in the work of research projects and centres focusing on feminist foreign policy, where the work centres 98 per cent on cisgender and socio-economically privileged white women from the Global North.[7] Some of their work may certainly include women of colour and migrant women, but that semblance of inclusion is always an accessory to the centrality of cis, and very often heteronormative, white women from the Global North. This way of functioning goes against the grain of the objectives of representation and inclusion. If there is to be an approach that well and truly centres marginalized women, Indigenous women, and women whose agency is often routinely denied in a racially hierarchized, ableist world order, there is a clear need to reflect upon critical approaches that differ from what is often understood and conceptualized as feminist IR, feminist foreign policy, or feminist politics in the Global North. The discussion that follows focuses on one such critical approach—transfeminist activist epistemologies, which are seldom evoked in politics and IR classrooms, or in national and supranational governance.

MAKING SENSE OF TRANS STUDIES: A BRIEF SYNTHESIS

The research field we know as transgender studies is an interdisciplinary area of academic inquiry that has been in the making for several decades (Joselow 2016). Key developments include Sandy Stone's 1987 essay "The Empire Strikes Back: A Posttranssexual Manifesto" (Stone 1992), which is generally considered as the major starting point of transgender studies in Turtle Island. Since its inception in 1993, the Centre for LGBT Studies at the University of Arizona has been among the first university institutions that pioneered in providing space for transgender studies. In 2013, Susan Stryker started the Transgender Studies Initiative within the institute. Stryker's work (see notably 2013, 2017) has been central to the popularization of trans studies as a field of academic inquiry in the academic sphere in Turtle Island as well as in Western Europe (see also Currah, Juang, and Price 2006; Carpenter and Currah 2011). In an unprecedented development, the world's first transgender studies chair was established at the University of Victoria (Canada), with a $2 million grant from Lieutenant Colonel Jennifer Pritzker. In terms of university teaching, trans studies has been taught as a subfield of LGBT+ studies or within women's studies departments, and is increasingly popular at the undergraduate level, as shown by the development of textbooks and learning resources specifically devoted to the subject (Haefele-Thomas 2019; Haefele-Thomas and Devor 2019).

Despite such developments in the academic sphere across Turtle Island (including both present-day Canada and the United States of America), very few trans academics make their way to tenure-track university teaching (see, for example, Baril 2017; see also Spade 2011). What is more, transgender studies continues to be an interdisciplinary field of academic inquiry where very little diversity exists. To begin with, transgender studies is a terrain marked by a preference for white transmasculinity. White transmasculine people hold a substantive monopoly in the trans studies academy. Very few trans women are represented in the academy, with rare exceptions such as Susan Stryker and Vivian Namaste (Namaste 2000, 2011). There is a severe, if not total, underrepresentation of all other aspects of diversity, including trans women of colour, disabled trans people, and Indigenous Peoples belonging to non-Western (and indeed, invariably non-cisnormative and non-heteronormative) gender identities. Even when space is provided to trans scholars of colour specializing in trans and queer racial politics, the representation is once again hierarchized, favouring trans men of colour. These inadequacies have been receiving increased attention in trans studies circles. For instance, recent issues of *Transgender Studies Quarterly* (*TSQ*), the first-ever academic journal that focuses on a non-pathological understanding of trans identities, experiences, and herstories, have been focused on highlighting the importance of intersectional inclusion in the sphere of trans studies. *TSQ*'s volume 4, issue 2 (May 2017) was devoted to "the issue of Blackness." This issue contains a range of contributions, mostly by Black trans and queer activists, highlighting the multiple levels of erasure of Black trans and queer activist work in white trans studies and advocacy circles, especially in Turtle Island. To provide but one example, Syrus Marcus Ware, a Canadian, Black, trans scholar-activist, examines the systemic erasure of trans people of colour (especially Black trans women) from the archives and historical records of LGBTQIA2S+ activism in Toronto (Ware 2017).

TRANSGENDER STUDIES AND TRANSFEMINISM: CONSTRAINTS AND OPPORTUNITIES

The term **transfeminism** stands for a form of feminism that is not limited to cisgender women, and takes into account the lived experiences of, and challenges confronted by, trans women and girls. Transfeminism has been described as a critique of second-wave feminism from third-wave perspectives (Koyama 2003, 2; also cited in Hines 2014, 85). The study of transfeminist approaches, epistemologies, and ontologies takes place within coursework focusing on trans studies, which occupies an ambivalent home in the sphere of gender and women's studies, enjoying a marginal position (Enke 2012). Degree programs often include trans studies as an add-on. In this state of affairs, discussions on transfeminism in gender and women's studies are largely focused on highlighting that "trans might be central and not marginal" to the gender and women's studies academy (Enke 2012, n.p.). This sums up the way in which "transfeminism" is generally approached in the Western academy—as an onerous effort to highlight the relevance of trans studies to the sphere of women's studies and feminist theory. In sum, the study of transfeminism in the academy is itself an add-on to the add-on, a means of strengthening the position of trans studies in the sphere of gender and women's studies.

The foundations of transfeminist epistemologies are rooted in the work of scholars such as Butler (1990, 1993), Koyama (2003), and Stone (1992). However, this brand of transfeminism has also focused near-exclusively on trans people of a specific demographic—Caucasian, coming from white settler backgrounds in Turtle Island. In the academic sphere, there is a growing interest in expanding the limits of transfeminist research and analyses, as attested, for example, in a 2016 special issue of *TSQ* devoted to transfeminism/s, bringing together a range of perspectives from ethno-racial minorities in Turtle Island and from non-English-speaking contexts. Despite these developments, transfeminist perspectives have seldom influenced the social sciences beyond the sphere of trans and queer studies. As one illustration, what we know as "feminist security studies" or "feminist politics" are highly cisnormative and considerably heteronormative spheres of research.[8] In university courses on feminist IR, "transfeminism" is typically not discussed.

TRANSFEMINISM-OF-COLOUR? A GRASSROOTS MOVEMENT IN TURBULENT TIMES?

A discussion on transfeminism is inadequate in the absence of a reference to a crucial caveat—the gap between transfeminist work in the academy and transfeminist activism at the grassroots. An important distinction needs to be made between the kind of transfeminism discussed in the academic sphere and the transfeminism I will focus on in the rest of this chapter: "transfeminism/s-of-colour" activism. The latter is not only inspired and influenced by Black feminist thought, while learning from all currents of non-whitestream feminisms, including Latina, Indigenous, and Global South feminisms, but it is also grounded in the struggles of people of colour, especially women of colour and very especially Black (cis and trans) women over many years. It is therefore very much a grassroots form of thought and action, which is yet to make substantive inroads into the academic sphere. Whenever space for analytical engagement on transfeminist perspectives has been provided in the academic sphere, transfeminist scholarship—especially produced by (trans and cis) women of colour, migrant women, and women at multiple intersections such as race, gender, and disability—has demonstrated strong potential to challenge modes of knowledge production in the Western academy and to advance decolonial epistemologies and approaches to teaching and critically question established practices of feminist advocacy and power relations in sectors such as the academy, politics, and international affairs (see, for example, Muñoz 2012; Weerawardhana 2017b, 2018b). However, transfeminist-of-colour thought is yet to occupy a position of significance in academic research and university teaching.

Transfeminist-of-colour activism has a long and eventful history of **movement-building** in turbulent times, under highly challenging socio-political circumstances. Indeed, the activist legacy of trans women of colour, such as the late Marsha P. Johnson, Sylvia Ray Rivera, and Miss Major Griffin-Gracy, was crucial to the coming to being of the LGBTQI2S+ rights movement in Turtle Island. Johnson and Riviera were pioneers in the struggles to secure the basic rights of non-cisnormative and non-heteronormative peoples. Their role as the founding pioneers of the LGBTQI2S+ rights movement in Turtle Island has long been overshadowed by powerful images of cis (and very often, white) gay men. Miss Major Griffin-Gracy, a Black trans woman, has devoted her life to developing support networks for younger Black women of trans experience. Griffin-Gracy's strong solidarity towards young trans people, irrespective of their gender identities, strongly echoes the above-mentioned Black feminist ethos of building solidarities, safe spaces, caring, and support networks beyond differences. This brand of transfeminist thought and activism has been and continues to be developed by women of colour and, significantly, by Black women working at the grassroots, quite often with limited resources. It is a body of work inspired by their day-to-day challenges of securing their most basic rights and fighting high levels of discrimination and violence. Black trans women face severe threats to their security, as one can observe in the ever-rising number of murders of Black trans women (see, for example, Orso 2018). Many transfeminist-of-colour activists in Turtle Island are also from migrant backgrounds and have personally experienced the challenges of border crossing, survival, and being confronted by structures of governance that are most often not in their favour. They share with Black women, Indigenous women, and gender-plural peoples of Turtle Island a closely relatable experience of facing multiple forms of marginalization. The intersectional strength of transfeminist-of-colour analyses, approaches, and epistemologies stems from the knowledge and insight gained from their lived experiences and efforts to challenge the multiple forms of oppression they face.

TRANSFORMATIONAL POSSIBILITIES: TRANSFEMINIST-OF-COLOUR ADVOCACY AS A LOCALLY GROUNDED DECOLONIAL DISCOURSE

"There can be no justice on stolen land."
—Shanice Nicole Yarde, poet, writer, and
Afrofeminist activist based in tio'tia:ke/Montreal, 2016

The focus on a locally grounded grassroots struggle is also extremely important in a settler-colonial context such as Turtle Island. Indeed, the cisnormative male/female gender binary was a founding principle of white settler colonialism. The gender binary was actively deployed as the guiding principle in the genocidal settler-colonial project of residential schools. To draw on Dr. Janice Acoose-Miswonigeesikokwe, a leading Nehiowe-Métis-Anishinaabe-kwe scholar, Elder, and residential school survivor, one of the rules that the children forcibly enrolled in residential schools were subjected to was the complete segregation of (cis) girls and (cis) boys (2016, 18). This segregation, based on the gender binary, is an Abrahamic concept alien to many of the socio-cultural traditions, knowledge systems, customs, and protocols of the local Peoples of Turtle Island. Debunking and dismantling colonially imposed cis-heteronormative gender politics thus forms a key component of ongoing dialogues on decolonizing across the Indigenous territories of Turtle Island. Transfeminist-of-colour activists from settler backgrounds accord the highest priority to the decolonial struggles of Indigenous Peoples and take pride in learning from **Indigenous knowledges** and epistemologies. Transfeminist-of-colour activism is therefore inextricably linked to ongoing progressive political advocacy initiatives in Turtle Island. As a result of this strong advocacy of Indigeneity and the rights of Indigenous Peoples worldwide (and especially of Indigenous women and gender-plural peoples), transfeminism-of-colour is very much a decolonial feminist discourse that is of special relevance to ongoing decolonial dialogues and advocacy initiatives in Turtle Island and elsewhere.[9]

MOVEMENT-BUILDING AND TRANSFORMING: THE BLACK FEMINIST LEGACY OF TRANSFEMINIST-OF-COLOUR THOUGHT

Transfeminist-of-colour thought in Turtle Island has primarily developed against the backdrop of the lived experiences of Black trans women and has therefore been strongly influenced and inspired by Black feminist activism. Indeed, Black feminism forms *the* primary source of knowledge and innovation for transfeminist-of-colour activism.

In Black- and people-of-colour-led transfeminist spaces in Turtle Island, there has been next to no space for the exclusive focus on cis women and the cisnormative outlook of white feminist circles. Whereas the inclusion of trans women in feminist circles and advocacy is often considered a relatively new development in white transfeminist circles (see, for example, Halberstam 2018), trans and cis women have a long history of working together in Black feminism in Turtle Island. This emphasis on solidarity and movement-building is a core component of transfeminist-of-colour thought, and its antecedents date back to the activist work of Marsha P. Johnson. In 1970, Johnson took part in a Gay Liberation Front protest held in front of Bellevue Hospital, holding a placard that read "Power to the

People." The reason for the protest concerned LGBT+ health care, with the objective of condemning the use of shock treatments in the hospital to "cure" homosexuality. When asked what Johnson implied by "the people," her response was "all people" (Ryan 2017, n.p.). This would invariably include queer people, street people, activists, artists, trans women, drag queens, sex workers, the poor, the homeless, and those who struggle with mental illness. The emphasis here is on widening the activist net beyond one's own specific group. Transfeminist-of-colour activism, in this sense, does not concern only trans women and is not in any way limited to trans womanhood. Instead, it is a discourse, an activist ethos, and an advocacy philosophy that constantly lays emphasis on developing transversal and intersectional feminist solidarities.

To illustrate further, some of the most important personalities in Black feminist advocacy, from Angela Davis to Robyn Maynard (Maynard 2017), have been and continue to be among the strongest voices for trans and queer liberation. Since the early years of her fearless activism, Davis has upheld a strongly trans-inclusive approach. For example, commenting at the beginning of the documentary film *MAJOR* (about the life of Miss Major), Davis clearly highlights the vital relevance of transfeminist advocacy for Black feminist and Black liberation initiatives, such as prison abolition. Davis notes that Black trans women have much to teach us about the prison-industrial complex, as trans women of colour are most often at multiple intersections of oppression all across Turtle Island, from transmisogyny and white supremacy to the War on Drugs.[10] Similarly, the rich body of work produced by Black feminist scholar-activist and poet Audre Lorde (see, for instance, Lorde 2009; see also Lorde 1982) repeatedly emphasizes concepts such as movement-building and Black women organizing in a sense of unity, beyond differences of life choices, lifestyles, and outlooks. A key component of transfeminist-of-colour thought precisely lies in developing such transformational intersectional feminist solidarities across the board and in inclusive movement-building, beyond differences and divergences.

Solidarity-building and movement-building thus form a core aspect of transfeminism-of-colour and its *discours-mère* (mother-discourse), Black feminism. In Black feminism, such inclusive activist perspectives have a long history. Writing in 1985, Audre Lorde, a Black lesbian cis woman, called for solidarity and collaborative action between Black lesbian and non-lesbian women. Given the climate of hostility and divisiveness in

Turtle Island in 2018, her words continue to be worth quoting at some length:

> Black women are not one great vat of homogenized chocolate milk. We have many different faces, and we do not have to become each other in order to work together ... It is not easy for me to speak here with you as a Black Lesbian feminist, recognizing that some of the ways in which I identify myself make it difficult for you to hear me. But meeting across difference always requires mutual stretching, and until you can hear me as a Black Lesbian feminist, our strengths will not be truly available to each other as Black women ... it is urgent that we not waste each other's resources, that we recognize each sister on her own terms so that we may better work together toward our mutual survival, I speak here about heterosexism and homophobia, two grave barriers to organizing among Black women ... I do not want you to ignore my identity, nor do I want you to make it an insurmountable barrier between our sharing of strengths. (1985, 3–4)

The underlying principle here is one of developing solidarities, support networks, and movements, beyond differences and celebrating such differences. An identical focus on inclusive movement and solidarity-building is embodied in a seminal document of Black feminist history in Turtle Island, the Statement of the Combahee River Collective (CRC). In this statement, CRC members, who were Black cis lesbian feminist activists, note that:

> The most general statement of our politics at the present time would be that we are actively committed to struggling against racial, sexual, heterosexual, and class oppression, and see as our particular task the development of integrated analysis and practice based upon the fact that the major systems of oppression are interlocking. The synthesis of these oppressions creates the conditions of our lives. As Black women we see Black feminism as the logical political movement to combat the manifold and simultaneous oppressions that all women of color face ... We believe that sexual politics under patriarchy is as pervasive in Black women's lives as are the politics of class and race. We also often find it difficult to separate race from class from sex oppression because in our lives they are most often experienced simultaneously. We know that there is such a thing as racial-sexual oppression which is neither solely racial nor

solely sexual, e.g., the history of rape of Black women by white men as a weapon of political repression.[11]

The CRC statement concludes with a sentence of vital importance: "As Black feminists and Lesbians we know that we have a very definite revolutionary task to perform and we are ready for the lifetime of work and struggle before us." Furthermore, the authors of the statement also reiterate that as Black women, they find any type of biological determinism a particularly dangerous and reactionary basis upon which to build a politic. As Jennifer Declue notes:

> The belief that black women are inherently valuable along with the absolute dismissal of biological determinism undergirds the Combahee River Collective's black feminist imperative around sexual politics, and this mode of analysis intended at addressing the multiplicity of black women's experiences of race, class, and sexuality can be expanded to include our contemporary understanding of gender as multiple, nonbinary, flexible, and transformative. (2017, 222)

TRANSFORMATIONAL POSSIBILITIES: TRANSFEMINIST-OF-COLOUR ADVOCACY IN THE ACTIVIST SPHERE

Today's Black feminist activism and advocacy are built upon historic documents of Black feminist theorizing, such as the above-mentioned CRC statement. The core underlying focus of these documents is a constant search for solidarities and working beyond differences. In today's context, with gender politics having been developed into stronger levels of analysis, especially by Black (trans and cis) women, Black feminist epistemologies provide the most insightful basis upon which transfeminist, and indeed other global intersectional feminist solidarities, can be developed. Work that falls under the transfeminist-of-colour advocacy umbrella, despite popular belief, is not done by trans women of colour alone. It is also constantly enriched by valuable input from cis women of colour, especially Black cis women. To provide a revealing example, Nigerian-American writer Chimamanda Ngozi Adichie, a cis woman, made a comment about trans women in a media interview on March 10, 2017, that to many gender justice advocates verged on the transphobic (Weerawardhana 2017a). Irrespective of Adichie's intent, this comment, aired on Channel 4, a popular mainstream (which, in transfeminist activist terms, is also "whitestream") media outlet, carried an unmistakable element of denying the agency of trans women, if not dehumanizing trans womanhood. Many commentators (including myself) reacted, explaining the problematic nature of Adichie's comment. In the northerly territories of Turtle Island, the most powerful and sharpest critiques and defences of trans women, however, came from Black queer women.

In her internationally acclaimed weekly radio broadcast, tio'tia:ke-based academic and journalist Jade Almeida, a black queer cis woman and decolonial activist from Guadeloupe, devoted a full program to Adichie's comments (Almeida 2017). Almeida deconstructed (and in so doing debunked) Adichie's comments, line by line, in a highly insightful commentary. Almeida's explanation carried special emphasis on the high levels of violence and systemic discrimination that target trans women and the fact that Black trans women are on the receiving end of the worst of systemic violence and discrimination. Almeida further highlighted the necessity of ensuring the agency of trans women, noting that Adichie, who is a cis woman and is consequently not a woman of trans experience, should have deployed her platform to highlight the marginalization and absence of trans women in the media. Almeida's sharp, detailed, and highly informative commentary was one that focused strongly on representation, agency, and the affirmation of womanhood of trans experience. In conclusion, Almeida notes:

> il y a une très grande différence entre dire ... "les femmes trans sont des femmes avec leur expérience spécifique qu'il faut mettre en avant parce que ce sont des violences qui au sein du féminisme ... et afroféminisme, doivent être combattues," et dire "les femmes trans ont leur expériences spécifiques de ce fait ne sont pas vraiment des femmes mais font partie de la cause féministe" ... vous voyez la différence?[12]

Almeida's response to Adichie represents a recent and pertinent example of how queer **Afrofeminist** activists develop intersectional transfeminist-of-colour solidarities. This response stands in line with strong support extended to trans women by Black feminist cis women of the earlier generation. Similarly, as the above-mentioned activist ethos of Marsha P. Johnson denotes, the work of Black trans women has always been inclusive of the multiple intersections that specifically concern Black cis women. This mutual affirmation and care extended to fellow women whose agency is diminished by systemic discrimination is a defining feature of contemporary transfeminist-of-colour activism.

In a similar spirit, Robyn Maynard's 2017 book *Policing Black Lives*—a seminal contribution to studies of racially motivated police violence in Canada—is an example of how Black feminism represents discourse where the keywords are solidarity and movement-building. Maynard, a Black cis woman, lays special emphasis on the policing of the lives of Black trans women and the trivialization of the murders of Black trans women in present-day Canada.[13] The global Black Lives Matter (BLM) movement, for its part, was founded by three cis queer women, Patrisse Khan-Cullors, Opal Tometi, and Alicia Garza, and is deeply grounded in Black feminist and transfeminist-of-colour thought (Khan-Cullors and Bandele 2018; see also Thompson in this volume). Since its inception, BLM has been primarily spearheaded by (cis and trans) queer women of colour, gender-non-conforming peoples, and people of colour in the broad LGBTQIA2S+ spectrum. Transfeminist-of-colour thought, activism, and knowledge production, inspired by Black feminist thought, are therefore bodies of work not limited to trans women alone. An intersectional feminist praxis of this nature is highly relevant to initiatives that seek to challenge cishetero-patriarchal forms of discrimination, which are highly common across many sectors, including the sphere of health care—or to be more precise, women's health care. A transfeminist-of-colour perspective on women's health is one that strongly emphasizes building solidarity and support networks. Here again, the transformational strength of transfeminist-of-colour advocacy comes from Afrofeminist thought, which strongly prioritizes intersectional solidarities among women. This is echoed in key Black feminist texts produced in Turtle Island, as exemplified in the following words of Audre Lorde:

> I am a lesbian woman of colour whose children eat regularly because I work in a university. If their full bellies make me fail to recognize my commonality with a woman of colour whose children do not eat because she cannot find work, or who has no children because her insides are rotted from home abortions and sterilization; if I fail to recognize the lesbian who chooses not to have children, the woman who remains closeted because her homophobic community is her only life support, the woman who chooses silence instead of another death, the woman who is terrified lest my anger trigger the explosion of hers; if I fail to recognize them as other faces of myself, then I am contributing not only to each of their oppressions but also to my own, and the anger which stands between us

then must be used for clarity and mutual empowerment, not for evasion by guilt or for further separation. I am not free while any woman is unfree, even when her shackles are very different from my own. (2017, 33–4)

The continuing relevance of these words can be clearly observed, for instance, if you apply Lorde's call for intersectional solidarity to campaigns for abortion rights based on bodily autonomy. As a woman of trans experience, I may not be brought to seek a termination. However, when following Lorde's above-mentioned words, the struggle of another woman (or for that matter, birth giver of any gender identity or expression) automatically becomes my own struggle. Equally, if the same principle is to be applied to abortion rights, if not reproductive justice advocacy by collectives led by cis women, it provides an opportunity to make activism more intersectional and inclusive by focusing on marginalized women, including trans women—a category of women whose reproductive rights have been (and in many cases, continue to be) severely restricted in many countries across the world.[14] Reproductive justice and health care advocacy developed in this spirit contains a strong force that can challenge the patriarchal practices of health care provisioning at its core, and a push for concrete changes to policies that result in systemic discrimination targeting women and disproportionately affecting women at multiple intersections of oppression—from race, ethnicity, Indigeneity, and disability to socio-economic circumstances and more.

The work of Kama la Mackerel, a tio'tia:ke (the island known as Montreal)-based performer, poet, storyteller, community arts facilitator, and multi disciplinary artist from Mauritius, is also strongly grounded in a similar emphasis on building support networks and opportunities for growth for trans and queer young people of colour.[15] In 2013, La Mackerel founded Gender Blender, which then happened to be the only queer open mic in tio'tia:ke. It developed as a platform that enabled large numbers of non-cis-heteronormative people, especially youth, to perform and develop new support networks. In its five years of existence, Gender Blender proved to be tio'tia:ke's foremost platform for young non-cis and non-heteronormative people of colour to develop their skills and, in some cases, emerge as successful artists.[16] La Mackerel subsequently provided leadership to a mentoring initiative, "Our Bodies, Our Stories," an arts mentorship program meant exclusively for queer and trans people of colour.[17] This body of work is quintessentially grounded in the long legacy of transfeminist-of-colour movement-building and, even more importantly, in Black feminist movement- and solidarity-building.

Transfeminist-of-colour activism in Turtle Island is marked by a range of critical input by women of colour artists and thinkers. In her work, multidisciplinary, performance-based, digital media artist Kim Ninkuru takes a highly critical-transfeminist approach.[18] Ninkuru, a Black trans woman, ensures that her critiques of oppressive and racially stratified structures we inhabit are razor-sharp, to the level of unsettling many people. Ninkuru's work

> is challenging and confrontational—and not in the way that those words are usually used to speak about, in particular, black women's work, which is challenging and confronting simply by existing. I use those words literally. Her work challenges and confronts us, members of her community, to examine our relationship to the black transfeminine experience ... Kim knows that we love to throw around buzz words like "feminism" and "allyship" as part of our queer political lexicon, and her art asks that we cut the shit. Her work explores misogyny and misogynoir, appropriation of and profiteering from Blackness, and the fallacy of a feminist agenda that violently, by the hands of cis-women, continues to push our trans sisters under and in front of any bus we can, just to name a few themes. Some of her work feels tongue-in-cheek and makes me LOL. Some of it is uncomfortably cutting. All of it is dope and necessary as a narrative thread in our queer cultural fabric. (Akimat 2018, n.p.)

This review of Ninkuru's work, written by a Black cis woman, encompasses the unsettling nature of Ninkuru's critical perspectives and the appreciation of such critical perspectives among Black feminist activists. In many other spheres of feminism—such as the highly divisive and cis-normative feminist discourses that are characteristic of white feminism—a critical perspective of this nature coming from a trans woman would be far from welcome. This openness to questioning established ways of working and, consequently, to engaging in a collective process of unlearning, re-learning, and reconceptualizing, is a core component of transfeminist-of-colour advocacy.

CONCLUDING REMARKS: TRANSFEMINIST-OF-COLOUR PERSPECTIVES AS DECISIVE IN TURBULENT TIMES?

In the context of the Trump administration's backlash on many aspects of fundamental rights, including, especially, trans rights, it can clearly be established that we live in highly turbulent times. In such a ferment, it is crucial to focus on movement-building and solidarity-building, in efforts to transform our societies and challenge the drift to socio-politically conservative if not extremist discourses. In the United Kingdom, an identically transphobic discourse gained popularity as a consequence of the British government's ongoing initiative intended at reforming the 2004 Gender Recognition Act. On either side of the Atlantic, these turbulent constraints have led to strong forms of resistance from trans and queer peoples, with even white feminist voices supportive of trans rights making it a priority to highlight why cis women must fight for transgender rights (Milano 2018). This chapter demonstrates that such transformational opportunities of solidarity-building have long been part and parcel of transfeminist-of-colour activism in Turtle Island. Black feminist discourses that developed in these Indigenous territories carry a long legacy of solidarity, caring, collaborative movement-building, and creating transformational opportunities among women across differences stemming from sexual orientation, gender identity, disability, and many other systemic factors. This brand of transfeminist activism, developed by women of colour, especially by Black women, remains one of the strongest intersectional feminist discourses focused on inclusive movement-building. Despite the richness of its concepts, epistemologies, and activist praxes, this brand of transfeminist activism is yet to make substantive inroads into the study of transfeminisms, gender studies, and women's studies in the academic sphere. Incorporating, and learning from transfeminist-of-colour activist work, developed at the grassroots by women of colour, is of special relevance to turbulent times marked by threats to basic human rights and an upsurge of extremist political ideologies. The intersectional movement-building-focused work of transfeminisms of colour and the ethos of working across differences and divergences carry transformational insights into any type of feminist and gender-justice-oriented work, in Turtle Island and beyond.

DISCUSSION QUESTIONS

1. What are your thoughts on the centrality of "intersectional feminist" perspectives to the study of politics/IR (and, for that matter, other cognate social sciences), especially in Turtle Island?
2. How can university teaching and research in feminist politics and IR be enriched by transfeminist-of-colour thought?
3. Discuss the two following statements:

a. "At the university, as we 'learn' from our coursework, we also need to engage in the processes of 'un-learning.'"

b. "In the academic sphere, we need not only to critically engage with what we are taught, but also to question what we are not taught."

4. How can transfeminist-of-colour activism and discourse help to create solidarity and movement-building in the current political climate?

NOTES

1 I use the Indigenous name for North America, Turtle Island.

2 A list of anti-trans actions taken by the Trump administration since 2017, compiled by the National Centre for Transgender Equality, is available at https://transequality.org/the-discrimination-administration. See also Khazan (2018); Meckler, Schmidt, and Sun (2018).

3 This abbreviation that refers to non-cisnormative and non-heteronormative people generally carries four letters, LGBT, standing for lesbian, gay, bisexual, and transgender; and in order to reflect the tremendous diversity and broad range of issues involved, the abbreviation is constantly being revised and extended. For the purposes of this chapter and in specifically addressing an audience in the northerly territories of Turtle Island, I use LGBTQIA2S+, incorporating queer, intersex, asexual, and two-spirited peoples. The plus sign is intended to ensure the broadest possible level of inclusivity.

4 In November 2017, the Fédération des femmes du Québec (FFQ) elected Gabrielle Bouchard, a trans woman, as its president (see Dufour and Pagé in this volume). This appointment raised eyebrows in conservative quarters, with some critiques upholding an exclusionary discourse targeting trans women. Bouchard and the FFQ responded to these critiques, deploying a strongly intersectional feminist discourse (Nelson 2017). In 2017–18, trans-exclusionary groups were active in anti-trans campaigning in British Labour Party circles as the British government expressed an interest in making the 2004 Gender Recognition Act more inclusive (see, for example, Weerawardhana 2018b). These campaigns specifically targeted trans women. Trans-exclusionary feminists have long been active in LGBT+ rights movements. The transmisogynist hate campaign of such a group at the 2018 London Pride parade is an example of their continued presence in Western LGBTQIA2S+ movements (see Necati 2018).

5 The term "cisgender" or "cis" refers to people whose gender identity is not in conflict with their gender assigned at birth. The term "transgender" broadly refers to people whose gender assigned at birth does not correspond to their true gender identity.

6 In this chapter, I use Jacques Derrida's deconstructive practice of placing certain terms deemed problematic and/or inadequate, yet necessary, *sous rature* (under erasure) for all colonially imposed terms, which carry substantive connotations of oppression to the Indigenous Peoples of Turtle Island. On the use of sous rature for this purpose in academic writing, see, for example, Nicholas and Agius (2018); Weerawardhana (2018a).

7 The Berlin-based Centre for Feminist Foreign Policy and its body of work provide an insightful example.

8 This is a reality in feminist research output in the spheres of American and Canadian politics. However, recent developments demonstrate a keenness to examine approaches, epistemologies, and ontologies that diverge from established research practices and priorities. This was highly evident in a special issue of the *Canadian Journal of Political Science/Revue canadienne de science politique* "showcasing contemporary feminist political research, theories, and practices in Canada" (Dobrowolsky et al. 2017, 403). This special issue contains a range of articles that demonstrate the growing diversity of feminist research in Canada. The review included one article on trans children and parents' advocacy of trans rights (Manning 2017), as well as articles that highlighted the importance of knocking down walls in political science in favour of an expansionist feminist agenda (MacDonald 2017), and a call for increased "research openness" (Johnson et al. 2017). The approaches and ideas discussed in this chapter are driven towards such a direction: expanding feminist epistemologies in the study of politics and IR.

9 For a discussion on the decolonial dimensions of transfeminist-of-colour thought, see Weerawardhana (2017b, 2018c).

10 *MAJOR*, a film by Annalise Ophelian (Floating Ophelia Productions, 2016). See https://www.missmajorfilm.com

11 Excerpt from the Combahee River Collective Statement. For the full statement, see http://circuitous.org/scraps/combahee.html.

12 My translation:

> There is a very big difference between saying "Trans women are women of specific experiences which should be emphasized because the violence [that disproportionately targets them] needs to be fought back in feminist and [especially] in Afrofeminist advocacy" and saying "trans women have different lived experiences and are therefore not really women but they can be accessories to the feminist cause." You see the difference?

13 For a discussion of police violence against Black (cis and trans) bodies, see Maynard (2017).

14 On the systemic denial of reproductive rights to trans women and related challenges, see, for example, Weerawardhana (2016).

15 See https://lamackerel.net.

16 Gender Blender, founded in 2013, ran consecutively until May 2018. The social media event page for the final "Good Bye Edition" is available at https://www

.facebook.com/events/160948818055570/. Insights into the founding of Gender Blender in 2013 and how it grew to become one of tio'tia:ke's most sought-after trans-led artistic events can be gleaned from a social media note by its founder, Kama La Mackerel, available at https://www.facebook.com/notes/kama-la -mackerel/gender-blender-time-to-say-goodbye/1217596138370490/.

17 See https://www.facebook.com/qtbipocmtlart/.

18 Apart from her live appearances, workshops, and other events in Turtle Island, Ninkuru's work can be glimpsed in her social media footprint, especially on Instagram (@sista_betina).

REFERENCES

Acoose-Miswonigeesikokwe, Janice. 2016. *Iskwewak Kah' Ki Yaw Ni Wahkomakanak, Neither Indian Princesses nor Easy Squaws*. Toronto: Women's Press.

Akimat, Tamika. 2018. "Gyal Dem Fiyah: Kim Ninkuru." Yohomo, October 17. https://yohomo.ca/blog/gyal-dem-fiyah-kim-ninkuru.

Almeida, Jade. 2017. "CHRONIQUE NQC / JADE ALMEIDA: Controverse sur les propos de CHIMAMMANDA NGOZI ADICHIE." *Radio NéoQuébec*, March 18. http://www.trocradio.com/podcasts/chronique-nqc-jade-almeida-controverse -sur-les-propos-de-chimammanda-ngozi-adichie-42.

Baril, Alexandre. 2017. "Trouble dans l'identité de genre: le transféminisme et la subversion de l'identité cisgenre, une analyse de la sous-représentation des personnes trans* professeur-es dans les universités canadiennes." *Philosophiques* 44 (2): 285–317.

Butler, Judith. 1990. *Gender Trouble: Feminism and the Subversion of Identity*. London: Routledge.

———. 1993. *Bodies That Matter: On the Discursive Limits of "Sex."* London: Routledge.

Carpenter, Monica J., and Paisley Currah, eds. 2011. *An Interdisciplinary Reader on Bodies and Knowledge*. Basingstoke, UK: Palgrave.

Currah, Paisley, Richard M. Juang, and Shannon Price, eds. 2006. *Transgender Rights*. Minneapolis: University of Minnesota Press.

Declue, Jennifer. 2017. "To Visualize the Queen Diva! Toward Black Feminist Trans Inclusivity in Beyoncé's 'Formation.'" *Transgender Studies Quarterly* 4 (2): 219–25.

Dobrowolsky, Alexandra, Fiona MacDonald, Tracey Raney, and Cheryl N. Collier. 2017. "Finding Feminism(s) in Canadian Political Science Scholarship: Diversity and Resistance in an Era of Global Uncertainty." *Canadian Journal of Political Science* 50 (2): 403–10.

Enke, Anne, ed. 2012. *Transfeminist Perspectives in and beyond Transgender and Gender Studies*. Philadelphia: Temple University Press.

Fernwood Publishing. 2017. "Robyn Maynard—Policing Black Lives." October 10. YouTube video, 3:28. https://www.youtube.com/watch?v=1-JpQjhVvlM

Haefele-Thomas, Ardel. 2019. *Introduction to Transgender Studies*. New York: Columbia University Press.

Haefele-Thomas, Ardel, and Aaron Devor. 2019. *Transgender: A Reference Text*. Santa Barbara, CA: ABC-CLIO Press.

Halberstam, Jack. 2018. "Towards a Trans* Feminism." *Boston Review*, January 18. http://bostonreview.net/gender-sexuality/jack-halberstam-towards-trans -feminism.

Hines, Sally. 2014. "Feminism." *Transgender Studies Quarterly* 1 (1): 84–86.

Johnson, Genevieve F., Mark Pickup, Eline A. de Rooij, and Rémi Léger. "Research Openness in Canadian Political Science: Toward an Inclusive and Differentiated Discussion." *Canadian Journal of Political Science* 50 (1): 311–28.

Joselow, Maxine. 2016. "A Push for Transgender Studies." *Inside Higher Ed*, June 22. https://www.insidehighered.com/news/2016/06/22/u-arizona-emphasizes -transgender-studies.

Khan-Cullors, Patrisse, and Asha Bandele, 2018. *When They Call You a Terrorist: A Black Lives Matter Memoir*. Edinburgh: Cannongate Books.

Khazan, Olga. 2018. "Why the Trump Administration's New Gender Definition Worries Doctors." *The Atlantic*, October 12. https://www.theatlantic.com/health /archive/2018/10/what-the-trump-eras-new-transgender-definition-means-for -patients/573694/.

Koyama, Emi. 2003. "Transfeminist Manifesto." In *Catching a Wave: Reclaiming Feminism for the Twenty-First Century*, edited by Rory Dicker and Alison Piepmeier, 1–15. Boston: Northeastern University Press.

Lopez, German. 2017. "Anti-transgender Bathroom Hysteria, Explained." *Vox*, February 22. https://www.vox.com/2016/5/5/11592908/transgender-bathroom -laws-rights.

Lorde, Audre. 1982. "Learning from the 60s." BlackPast.org. https://blackpast.org /1982-audre-lorde-learning-60s.

——. 1985. *I Am Your Sister: Black Women Organizing across Sexualities*. New York: Kitchen Table, Women of Colour Press.

——. 2009. *I Am Your Sister: Collected and Unpublished Writings of Audre Lorde*, edited by Rudolph B. Byrd, Johnetta Betsch Cole, and Beverly Guy-Sheftall. Oxford: Oxford University Press.

——. 2017. *The Master's Tools Will Never Dismantle the Master's House* (Kindle edition). New York: Penguin.

Manning, Kimberley E. 2017. "Attached Advocacy and the Rights of the Trans Child." *Canadian Journal of Political Science* 50 (2): 579–95.

Maynard, Robyn. 2017. *Policing Black Lives: State Violence in Canada from Slavery to the Present*. Black Point, NS: Fernwood.

MacDonald, Fiona. 2017. "Knocking Down Walls in Political Science: In Defence of an Expansionist Feminist Agenda." *Canadian Journal of Political Science* 50 (2): 411–26.

Meckler, Laura, Samatha Schmidt, and Lena H. Sun. 2018. "Trump Administration Considering 'Different Concepts' Regarding Transgender Rights, with Some Pushing Back Internally." *Washington Post*, October 24. https://www.washingtonpost.com /national/trump-administration-considering

-different-concepts-regarding-transgender-rights-with-some-pushing-back
-internally/2018/10/22/0668f4da-d624-11e8-83a2-d1c3da28d6b6_story
.html?utm_term=.c3707a490924.

Milano, Alyssa. 2018. "Alyssa Milano on Why Cis Women Must Fight for Transgender
Rights." *Vice: Broadly*, October 23. https://broadly.vice.com/en_us/article
/negpvm/alyssa-milano-transgender-rights-trump-memo-op-ed-essay.

Muñoz, Vic. 2012. "Gender/Sovereignty." In *Transfeminist Perspectives in and beyond
Transgender and Gender Studies*, edited by Anne Enke, 22–33. Philadelphia:
Temple University Press.

Namaste, Viviane. 2000. *Invisible Lives: The Erasure of Transsexual and Transgendered
People*. Chicago: University of Chicago Press.

———. 2011. *Sex Change: Social Change: Reflections on Identity, Institutions and
Imperialism*. Toronto: Canadian Scholars' Press.

Necati, Yas. 2018. "The Anti-trans Protests at Pride Were the Latest in a Long
History of Transphobia in the LGBTQ+ Community." *The Independent*, July 15.
https://www.independent.co.uk/voices/anti-trans-protests-london-pride
-transgender-transphobia-terf-lgbt-feminist-a8448521.html.

Nelson, Mélodie. 2017. "La première femme trans à la tête de la FFQ veut pousser le
féminisme au-delà de la tolérance." *Vice*, December 11. https://www.vice.com
/fr_ca/article/nededx/la-premiere-femme-trans-a-la-tete-de-la-ffq-veut-pousser
-le-feminisme-au-dela-de-la-tolerance.

Nicholas, Lucy, and Christine Agius. 2018. *The Persistence of Global Masculinism:
Discourse, Gender and Neo-colonial Re-articulations of Violence*. Basingstoke:
Palgrave Macmillan.

Orso, Anna. 2018. "Why 2018 Could Be the 'Deadliest' Year Yet for Transgender
Women of Color." *The Inquirer*, September 6. http://www2.philly.com/philly
/news/transgender-violence-women-of-color-shantee-tucker-20180906.html.

Ryan, Hugh. 2017. "Power to the People: Exploring Marsha P. Johnson's Queer
Liberation." *Out Magazine*, August 24. https://www.out.com/out-exclusives
/2017/8/24/power-people-exploring-marsha-p-johnsons-queer-liberation.

Sjoberg, Laura. 2012. "Towards Trans-Gendering International Relations?"
International Political Sociology 6: 337–54.

Spade, Dean. 2011. *Normal Life*. Boston: South End Press.

Steinmetz, Katy. 2014. "The Transgender Tipping-Point." *Time Magazine*, May 29.
http://time.com/135480/transgender-tipping-point/.

Stone, Sandy. 1992. "The Empire Strikes Back: A Posttranssexual Manifesto." *Camera
Obscura* 10 (29): 150–76.

Stryker, Susan. 2017. *Transgender History: The Roots of Today's Revolution*. New York:
Seal Press.

———, ed. 2013. *Transgender Studies Reader*. London and New York: Routledge.

Ware, Syrus Marcus. 2017. "All Power to All People? Black LGBTTI2QQ Activism,
Remembrance, and Archiving in Toronto." *Transgender Studies Quarterly* 4 (2):
170–80.

Weerawardhana, Chamindra. 2016. "Reproductive Rights and Trans Rights: Deeply Interconnected yet Too Often Misunderstood?" *Medium*, February 9. https://medium.com/@fremancourt/reproductive-rights-and-trans-rights-deeply -interconnected-yet-too-often-misunderstood-8b3261b1b0de.

———. 2017a. "CNA, Terfs and Whitefeminism." *Medium*, March 11. https://medium.com/@fremancourt/cna-terfs-and-whitefeminism-d60387cbeb3e.

———. 2017b. "Profoundly Decolonising? Reflections on a Transfeminist Perspective of International Relations." *Meridians* 18 (1): 184–213.

———. 2018a. *Decolonising Peacebuilding: Managing Conflict from Northern Ireland to Sri Lanka and Beyond*. Newcastle-upon-Tyne: Cambridge Scholars Publishing.

———. 2018b. "Transphobia in the UK Labour Party: A Peculiar Conflict?" *The Last Round* (blog), February 14. https://lastroundblog.wordpress.com/2018/02 /14/transphobia-in-the-uk-labour-party-a-peculiar-conflict/comment-page-1/.

———. 2018c. "A Transfeminist Perspective on Development Work." In *Routledge Handbook on Development Studies*, edited by Corinne L. Mason, 119–30. London: Routledge.

Yarde, Shanice Nicole. 2016. "On Black Lives Matter and Poetry as a Form of Healing and Social Justice." Dragonroot Media, July 19. https://soundcloud.com /dragonrootmedia/shanice-nicole-on-black-lives-matter-and-poetry-as-a-form -of-healing-and-social-justice.

FURTHER READING

Ahmed, Sara. 2016. "An Affinity of Hammers." *Transgender Studies Quarterly* 3 (1–2): 22–34.

———. 2018. *Living a Feminist Life*. Durham, NC: Duke University Press.

Davis, Angela. 2013. "Feminism and Abolition: Theories and Practices for the 21st Century." CSRPC UChicago, May 10. YouTube video, 01:06:00. https://www .youtube.com/watch?v=IKb99K3AEaA&fbclid=IwAR2i6slMZ7qX26BrRD djjVfn0k4PoB9bKAQ_LqnayNZGIWnlMq-qUMOuuDg.

Stanley, Eric A., and Nat Smith. 2015. *Captive Genders: Trans Embodiment and the Prison Industrial Complex*. Chico, CA: AK Press.

Weerawardhana, Chamindra. 2017. "Profoundly Decolonizing? Reflections on a Transfeminist Perspective of International Relations." *Meridians: Feminism, Race, Transnationalism* 16 (1): 184–213.

15

Rethinking Disability, Citizenship, and Intersectionality: New Directions for Political Science

Stacy Clifford Simplican

Key terms: composite model, compulsory capacity, crip theory, critical disability studies, medical model, social model, universal design

Why should political scientists care about disability? Disability studies emerged in the United States and Canada in the 1980s and 1990s, developing alongside political gains won by disability activists in both countries (Kelly 2013; Davis 2017). Yet, as Lennard Davis states, "while there has been much accomplished in the past 25 years, so much more remains" (2017, xiii). In both Canada and the United States, disability was regarded through the lens of "stigma, pity, and fear" (Prince 2010, 201). Though disability organizations had mobilized throughout the twentieth century (Zames Fleisher and Zames 2012; Vanhala 2009), disability rights groups gained momentum in the 1970s in the United States, bolstered by gains made by the civil rights and women's movements, and in Canada in the 1980s from early gains in public policy (Barnartt 2008). Landmark legislative victories ensued. In the United States, these included the Rehabilitation Act in 1973, the Individuals with Disabilities Education Act in 1975,[1] and the Americans with Disabilities Act in 1990. In Canada, the 1982 Charter of Rights and Freedoms recognized people with disabilities "as one of four disadvantaged groups" (Jongbloed 2003, 206), regarded by some as the pinnacle of success for disability rights (Kelly 2013, 2). In 1986, the Employment Equity Act included disabled people, and policy reforms in the 1980s and 1990s improved access to housing and transportation (Jongbloed 2003). Disability studies was forged in this history. As such, disability studies is an emancipatory discipline that aims to embrace alternative ways of being in the world, particularly at the intersection of multiple axes of oppression (Davis 2017).

But as Davis suggests, much more remains to be achieved—both in terms of addressing persistent inequalities around employment, housing, education, and poverty, and in regards to academic attention. Political scientists have good reason to study disability, yet few do so. This chapter builds on feminist scholarship to advance three reasons why political scientists should study disability: (1) to theorize how disability shapes conceptions of citizenship; (2) to improve intersectional analyses of how disability shapes the workings of race, class, and gender; and (3) to use disability as a lens to understand contemporary politics and behaviour. Research suggests that the "turbulent times" in which we live are making the lives of disabled people and their families even more precarious, as rates of poverty increase and state support remains contested. Thus, there are important academic and practical reasons to take up disability.

First, conceptions of citizenship tend to focus on intellectual capacities, such as abilities of reason, reflection, and deliberation. This not only excludes people with cognitive impairments but also ignores the creative and embodied expressions that disability activists have used to transform politics, both historically and today. Building on the work of feminist theorists, I show how political scientists can use disability to broaden conceptions of citizenship. Doing so can illuminate how disability activists respond to turbulent political times, and their relationship to other movement politics that have been examined in this volume, including feminist, Indigenous, environmental, and LGBTQ2I movements and Black Lives Matter.

Second, adding disability to intersectional analyses of gender, race, class, and nationality can improve both normative and empirical work. Disability rights and inequalities affect many people. According to a report by the US Census Bureau, about 27 per cent of people are disabled (Taylor 2018) and 25 per cent of households have at least one disabled family member (Altman and Blackwell 2016). In Canada, one in seven people aged 15 or older has a disability (Arim 2015). Women are more likely to have a disability, and all people are more likely to acquire disabilities as they age; hence, rather than understand disability as a "tragedy, deficit, or abnormality," we should see it as another "dimension of human diversity" (Arneil 2009, 237). Additionally, many people provide care (paid and unpaid) and supports to disabled people, and many of these caregivers are women who occupy marginalized positions around race, class, and nationality (Bauer and Crandford 2017). Disability is everywhere in our lives, and yet seldom appears in our scholarly explanations. I turn to work by Ange-Marie Hancock to show how adding disability strengthens intersectional scholarship in political science.

Third, I argue that political scientists should care about disability because it is a major component of contemporary politics, from health care and gun violence to immigration—to name just a few areas. For example, it is not well known that for every person killed by gun violence, three more are disabled (Ralph 2014). With respect to immigration in the United States, Douglas C. Baynton argues, "One of the driving forces behind early federal immigration law, beginning with the first major Immigration Act in 1882, was the exclusion of people with mental and physical defects" (2005, 32). As this chapter shows, concerns about disability continue to affect US immigration policy even today. Other disciplines, like sociology or anthropology, are more likely to offer explanations of how disability shapes contemporary politics than political science. I conclude by proposing new research agendas on disability for political scientists to stay relevant in our turbulent times.

Throughout the chapter, I draw comparisons between disability rights history and activism in the United States and Canada while highlighting differences. Sharon N. Barnartt analyses newspaper reports on disability protests in both countries to dispel the belief that US disability politics is simply diffused into the Canadian context. Instead, her analysis shows significant differences in the content and style of disability protests. Protests in Canada were more likely to target provincial governments and focus on services. In the United States, almost a third of protests were directed at the federal government and were far more likely to target rights. For Barnartt, differences across "the legislative situation, social structural patterns of disability service delivery, and patterns of organizational development" (2008, n.p.) impacted differently the history and aim of disability rights in the United States and Canada—important distinctions to keep in mind throughout this chapter.

In asking the question: Why should political science care about disability?, I imply that our discipline largely ignores disability. But why? According to Nancy Hirschmann, "Disability studies today is like women's studies in the 1970s and 1980s, when feminist scholars had to convince colleagues in 'mainstream' political science that gender was something worth attending to, that it was a serious enterprise, and that it should be part of the mainstream" (2012, 396). What explains the disregard for disability in political science? In my conclusion, I speculate on the reasoning behind this disinterest. As gender scholars have long argued, making scholarship gender inclusive involves more than "just add women and stir" (Harding 1995). Adding disability requires that we think critically about the meaning and history of disability, particularly as its meaning and significance intersect with gender, race, ethnicity, social class, nationality, and sexuality. What does it take to add an intersectional understanding of disability to political science, particularly in these turbulent times?

MODELS OF DISABILITY IN US AND CANADIAN HISTORIES

Before analysing how disability makes a difference to political science, this section reviews three models of disability—medical, social, and critical—and situates each within US and Canadian histories. These models circulate widely in disability studies, so it is important that political scientists and students understand them. Moreover, as Michael Prince argues: "Disability programs have developed as add-ons to other general programs, over the course of many decades, with the consequence that disability is inconsistently defined, and frequently ill-defined, in various areas of public policy" (2010, 201). New models of disability do not simply replace prior models. Instead, these models can co-exist, giving disability laws and policies multiple and even discordant messages.

Perhaps the most dominant model in the United States and Canada is the **medical model** of disability, which understands disability as an individual characteristic in need of intervention, rehabilitation, or cure, and has dominated policy and research (Donoghue 2003; Jongbloed 2003; Gabel et al. 2016). The medical model tends to pathologize disability (Grey, Lydon, and Healy 2016), and thereby treat disabled people as objects of pity, scorn, or fear (Shapiro 1994). Perhaps one of the most damaging permutations of the medical model was the one that influenced the eugenics era, which began to emerge in the United States in the 1890s and persisted up until the 1930s (McWhorter 2009). At this time, medical diagnoses of disability signalled a person's incompetence as a citizen, often intersecting with racial and gendered discourses that, at the time, constructed both women and non-whites as deviant and inferior (McWhorter 2009).

Others argue, however, that a medical model of disability is more nuanced and dynamic than critics allege, and that it can account for interactions between biology, environment, and a person's social and occupational activities (Frontera 2006). Additionally, for Allison Carey (2003), political disenfranchisement—although tied to medicalization during eugenics—was predicated also on the desire for social control, a desire that predates the medical model and will continue unabated if not addressed directly. For example, the medicalization of disability and desires for social control are evident in sterilization policies in both the United States and Canada, policies that drew upon neocolonial and racist discourses to target people with disabilities, Indigenous Peoples, and women of colour (Manning, Johnson, and Acker-Verney 2016).

In response to the pathologizing and depoliticizing thrust of the medical model, disability rights activists advocated for a **social model** of disability that distinguished between a person's impairment—a biological feature of an individual—and disability—how society constructs barriers and prejudice that foster ableism (Shakespeare 1996). The wheelchair user serves as an emblematic example of the social model. In this example, it is not the mobility that causes the impairment, but rather the built environment that disables a person. In the United States, the social model informs a minority model of disability, which emphasizes how ableism constitutes disabled people as a group with shared political interests (Sandahl and Auslander 2005).

Lisa Vanhala draws on disability rights groups' involvement in the Supreme Court in Canada to argue that the social model of disability led to three significant shifts in political discourse and activism. First, a social model enables people to develop a "citizenship-based disability identity and an understanding of disadvantage as discrimination instead of impairment associated." Second, the social model facilitated the creation of "cross-disability" organizations that mobilized people based on "the shared experience of exclusion" rather than "impairment-specific" identities. Finally, the social model helps create "the shared goal of removing barriers" (2009, 990). A definitional shift from the medical model to the social model thus enabled people to mobilize for disability rights.

Yet, the different political and historical contexts across the United States and Canada may also promote variations within the social model. For Barnartt, the minority model of disability is particularly salient in the United States, but in Canada, "disability is dealt with under 'human rights'" (2008, n.p.). For

Stienstra and Estey, "the so-called golden age of including disability in Canada's foreign and development policies was during the United Nations Year and Decade for Disabled Persons between 1981 and 1992" (2016, 382–83). During this time, Canada helped shift international discourse from a "biomedical model and charity approach to disability to one of human rights" (383). In 2010, Canada ratified the Convention on the Rights of Persons with Disabilities, a move that the United States has failed to make. Hence, adherents of the social model of disability might situate people with disabilities as a minority group in a context of identity politics in the United States, or as a human rights issue within an international context.

In addition, the social model and the medical model often coexist in political discourse and legislation. For example, in Stienstra and Estey's analysis of Canada's response to disability and global development, the medical model and social models compete, as the majority of projects funded by Canada adopt a "prevention or recovery approach" (2016, 389), rather than a human rights and inclusion approach. Despite the shifting terrain of disability in politics, the social model remains widely shared within disability studies, even as scholars criticize it.

Indeed, disability scholars and activists criticize the social model for ignoring aspects of disability that they cannot remedy through political change, such as the experience of chronic pain or depression (Crow 1996). Cripping actively resists "compliance with supposedly normal embodiment, behavior, and future desires" (Hamraie 2015, 307; see also Shildrick 2015). These criticisms have launched **critical disability studies**, which build on the politicizing thrust of the social model yet reject its attempt to create a dichotomy between the body (impairment) and society (disability) (Meekosha and Shuttleworth 2009). Robert McRuer built on work in queer theory and cultural studies to articulate **crip theory** as a way to "question the order of things, considering how and why [disability] is constructed and naturalized, how it is embedded in complex economic, social, and cultural relations; and how it might be changed" (2006, 2). In rejecting the social model's differentiation between impairment and disability, feminist disability scholar Alison Kafer (2013) theorizes disability as a relational model that "recognizes the imperative of working to eliminate 'disabling barriers' while also acknowledging the ways in which pain and fatigue within the disabled bodymind constrain daily life" (Carter 2015, n.p.). Likewise, Alexander Baril (2015) forwards a new **composite model** of disability by taking from the social model the politicization of experience while acknowledging the role of pain and suffering that attend some disabilities, to which the medical model may be more apt to attend. Yet, the embrace of "crip theory" is contested within disability studies, as some worry that it does little to actually change the lives of disabled people (Bone 2017).

Scholars have criticized the overt whiteness of disability studies, and have thus called for more intersectional and transnational approaches to the field (Bell 2006; Erevelles 2011; Schalk 2009; Ralph 2014; Kim 2017). Sami Schalk argues that claiming crip identity and crip theory are ways to build coalitional politics across minoritarian subjects, as it highlights the different ways that the "fat, black, queer, woman's body/mind/desire/behaviour is constantly read and reacted to as non-normative" (2009, n.p.). Just as Schalk criticizes disability studies for its omission and inattention to race, Nirmala Erevelles and Andrea Minear argue that critical race feminist theory often overlooks disability and disabled people, which can have "deadly consequences for disabled people of color caught at the violent interstices of multiple differences" (2010, 128).

Political scientists and political science students should familiarize themselves with these models, as each provides a different perspective on disability. Though quick summaries of each model are risky—as quick snapshots reduce their complexity and richness—we might say that the medical model aims to cure disabled people, the social model demands equal rights for disabled people, and the critical model aims to destabilize the meaning of disability.

As this overview should also convey, political science and disability studies have different epistemologies that may pose challenges that come with merging the two fields. Perhaps most significant is the way in which disability studies scholars imagine their intellectual responsibility as not only forwarding new knowledge but also improving the lives of people with disabilities (Bone 2017). Like other intersectional approaches used in this volume, disability studies share the normative and political commitments of intersectionality studies that "embody a motivation to go beyond mere comprehension of intersectional dynamics to transform them" (Cho, Crenshaw, and McCall 2013, 786).

This commitment to praxis makes it necessary for political scientists to understand the important role of language, as the words we use to describe disability shift and signal different motivations and epistemologies. In this chapter, I alternate between using the terms "people with disabilities" and "disabled people." These two terms capture differences between "people first" and "identity first" language. Importantly, scholars working within an intersectional and feminist approach to disability need to explain their language, whichever they choose. Moreover, it is important to pay close attention to and mirror the language that people use for themselves.

According to Tanya Titchkosky, people first language—that is, referring to persons with disability—is "*the* dominant linguistic formulation of disability in Canada" (2001, 126). "People first" language originated in the early 1970s, gained momentum in the 1980s, and was officially sanctioned in the Americans with Disabilities Act of 1990 (Haller, Dorries, and Rahn 2006, 63). For example, one of the first advocacy organizations for people with intellectual and developmental disabilities, People First, originated in 1974. According to its origin story, "in the course of planning the convention, the small group of planners decided they needed a name for themselves. A number of suggestions had been made when someone said, 'I'm tired of being called retarded—we are people first'" (People First of West Virginia, n.d.). Hence, for some, people first language signals a commitment to equal dignity and respect.

Yet, other disability activists and scholars contest this language. Instead, they prefer "identity first" language, such as the term "disabled people" (Andrews et al. 2019). Focusing on autistic people, Lydia Brown argues that "when we say 'Autistic person,' we recognize, affirm, and validate an individual's identity as an Autistic person."[2] Morton Ann Gernsbacher (2017) argues that person first language may increase, rather than decrease, stigma against disabled people, particularly children with disabilities.

Amid these differences in language, political scientists and students should remain mindful of the language they decide to use and aim to understand the significance that these different terms convey. In the next section, I explore three reasons why it is vital for political scientists to think about disability in the twenty-first century, and especially in these turbulent times.

Compulsory Capacity: Using Disability to Rethink Citizenship

Political scientists should take up disability as a way to make visible the invisible norms and values placed on democratic citizenship. By using the term democratic citizenship, I draw on feminist theorists' aim to broaden the scope of both politics and persons (Mouffe 2000). For Mary Dietz, democratic citizenship "takes politics to be the collective and participatory engagement of citizens in the determination of the affairs of their community" (1987, 14). Just as feminists and critical race scholars have drawn on histories and practices of women and people of colour to expand ideas of participation and communities, so too can disability studies reshape democratic citizenship. This aim aligns with the thrust of critical disability studies: to identify and challenge basic assumptions behind citizenship in order to make social change possible. But it also aligns with the social model of disability, which makes central issues of discrimination and exclusion.

Adding the lens of disability invites political scientists to question their assumptions about the requirements of citizenship. Idealizing the cognitive capacities of citizens, I argue, makes all humans subject to the demands of **compulsory capacity** (Simplican 2015).[3] The term "compulsory capacity" captures how, in theory, democratic citizens are often presumed to have a set of cognitive capacities—around reason, rationality, comprehension, and speech—that then safeguards democratic processes and governance. Compulsory capacity draws on the work of disability studies scholars who argue that myths about autonomous rational actors function, in part, through the stigmatization of people with disabilities. Just as importantly, compulsory capacity draws on a long history of feminist scholarship that destabilizes ideals of independence, autonomy, and rationality and instead imagines citizenship as the realm of interdependence and difference (Mouffe 2000; Pateman 1988; Young 2002). According to Hirschmann, "disability is configured as helplessness, weakness, and incapacity, all conceptually related to the ways that women have been seen throughout history" (2012, 397).

Compulsory capacity also draws on the work of feminist philosopher Eva Feder Kittay (1999; Kittay, Jennings, and Wasunna 2005), who argues that our belief in the myth of autonomy is made possible only by ignoring dependency and dependency care work. Care theorists criticized the ways in which liberal political theorists excluded issues of care from issues of justice (Gilligan 1982). Contemporary feminist care theorists like Joan Tronto argue that neoliberal beliefs and policies have continued to privatize issues of care, thus circumscribing democratic obligations. For Tronto (2013), revitalizing democracy requires that we first recognize that all people are vulnerable and, second, that the main task of democratic citizens is to ensure that all people receive and provide care equitably. Lorraine Krall McCrary argues that disability does more than just challenge liberal myths of autonomy and independence: "It points to the universal truth of our interdependence and need for community" (2017, 298).

Yet prominent accounts in the history of political theory evade the likelihood of vulnerability, particularly the mental and physical impairment of moral agents (Simplican 2015; Arneil 2009). Take, for example, deliberative democracy, which is "grounded in an ideal in which people come together, on the basis of equal status and mutual respect, to discuss the political issues they face and, on the basis of those discussions, decide on the policies that will then affect their lives" (Bächtiger et al. 2018, 2). Many accounts, whether John Rawls's idea of moral agents behind the veil of ignorance or Jürgen Habermas's communicative action, require unrealistic capacities of communication that thereby exclude and stigmatize people with disabilities (Rawls 1971; Habermas 1984; Clifford 2012; Swadley 2016).

There are political ramifications for assumptions about compulsory capacity. When we begin moral philosophy with assumptions about human life that evade disability, then we are less likely to understand dependency as a key issue for political communities. Yet we are all vulnerable, prone to illness and disability, and all of our capacities ebb and flow across our life-course (Kittay 2013, 79). This philosophical willingness to set aside disability shapes our contemporary political world. Take, for example, the fact that in-home care work is one of the fastest-growing occupations in the United States, and yet is also made up of workers who are generally underpaid and underinsured (Simplican 2017). Some people in Canada working in the field of in-home attendant services are excluded from employment policies that would raise or set their wages (Kelly 2016, 134). In the United States, a minority of people with intellectual and developmental disabilities still live in institutions (Conroy, Dale, and McCaffrey 2016), and supportive housing options for people with psychiatric disabilities tend to concentrate in communities "with more socioeconomic disadvantage, more residential instability, and a higher level of race/ethnic diversity" (Wong, Huangfu, and Hadley 2018, 115). Canada closed the last large-scale institutions for people with disabilities in 2009, yet institutionalized approaches "continue to structure the lives of many people living with intellectual impairments living in group homes and long-term care homes throughout Ontario and other parts of Canada" (Kelly 2016, 9). This invisibility in the philosophical world maps onto under-appreciation in the economic world. These ideals of compulsory capacity then seep into dominant political rhetoric. In the United States, the Department of Homeland Security (DHS) on August 14, 2019, published a final rule related to immigration and the issue of becoming a "public charge." Accordingly,

> the rule interprets a provision of the Immigration and National Act
> (INA) pertaining to inadmissibility. The inadmissibility ground at issue
> says a person is inadmissible if they are likely to become a public charge,
> which is a concept having to do with the likelihood that an immigrant

will be financially self-reliant or need publicly funded support. (Quinn
and Rodgers 2019, 1)

The new rule expands who can qualify as a public charge, encompassing anyone who may receive a range of public benefits. Additionally, the rule change
requires immigrants to attach a "Declaration of Self-Sufficiency" as part of
their green card application (Immigrant Legal Resource Center, n.d.). The
Trump administration's public charge rule reveals not only the ways in which
dependency and disability are stigmatized in US law but also how disability
intersects with national issues, including immigration.

This rhetoric of independence and control saturates even the disability
rights movement. According to Samuel Bagenstos, "achieving independence"
was central to the disability rights movement's political agenda (2009, 29).
This helps explain, for Bagenstos, why disability rights activists made gains in
the 1980s and 1990s, while other political movements around civil rights and
women's rights were waning in the United States. For Bagenstos, the disability
rights activists' emphasis on independence "resonated strongly with the ascen-
dant conservative ethic of individualism, self-reliance, and fiscal restraint"
(29; see also Simplican 2017). Christine Kelly investigates a similar synthesis
of neoliberal austerity and disability rights in the creation and continuance of
Ontario's Direct Funding Program. In this program, public funds are delivered
directly to disabled people, who can then hire and train paid attendants to
work in their homes for themselves. Though this model of service delivery fits
with the disability rights ethos of independent living, for Kelly it also means
that "disability organizations are often forced into service delivery under a continual threat of extinction," and thereby lose their radical edge (2016, 146; this
problem is also noted by Dufour and Pagé in this volume). This emphasis on
independence and consumer control in the Direct Funding Program has other
negative results, including the marginalization of attendant services as well as
the exclusion of people with intellectual disabilities from the program because
they are not considered sufficiently independent (147).

Rather than assuming that all humans pass a cognitive threshold of capacity
(and then rendering some humans invisible), we might instead centre personhood on vulnerability. Amber Knight argues that

a political appeal to shared human vulnerability can deconstruct the
able/disabled binary that continues to exist in the case of disability.
Specifically, the notion of a shared vulnerability is important because it

ultimately moves us beyond thinking about disability primarily as a discrimination issue facing a distinct group and instead approaches it as a shared matter of political planning and public welfare. (2014, 16)

Understanding all people as vulnerable could then bolster our commitment to **universal design**. Universal design is a principle that resonates disability activists' desire to create accessible built environments (Hamraie 2017).

How would our ideas of government, democracy, and citizenship change if we began *not* with foundational assumptions about human abilities but instead with a dedicated commitment to making political participation and democratic institutions accessible to all? Taking this universal approach requires that we expand our thinking about what democratic participation looks like, as people with disabilities and their allies have used embodied political action to make democratic demands (Clifford 2012; Simplican 2015). In including people with disabilities in democratic processes, Amber Knight argues, "nondisabled citizens may confront their own stigmatized ideas about impairment, learn to understand important aspects of disabled people's lives, and hopefully make better political decisions in the long run" (2015, 110). Disability can open up new transformational possibilities in rethinking democratic citizenship, particularly when we use an intersectional approach.

INTERSECTIONALITY AND DISABILITY

Feminist scholars within political science have encouraged political scientists to adopt intersectional approaches (Hancock 2007; Ackerly and True 2008), calling intersectionality one of the most important concepts to emerge from feminist theory in the twentieth century (Davis 2008; McCall 2005). At times, disability remains an under-theorized component of intersectional analysis; however, important work by feminist disability studies scholars show why disability can make a difference to our analyses (Hirschmann 2012).

For example, Erevelles and Minear chart how race and disability intersect both historically and structurally. These intersections include the over-representation of Black and Latino children among those labelled with intellectual disability, and that African Americans with disabilities face an unemployment rate of 75 per cent compared to 39 per cent of whites (2010, 131–32). In *Disability Incarcerated*, Chris Chapman, Alison C. Carey, and Liat Ben-Moshe chart the intersection of racism, colonialism, and ableism in residential schools in Canada and large-scale institutions in the United States. Accordingly, "a disproportionate number of persons incarcerated in the US prisons and jails are disabled, poor, and/or racialized" (Chapman, Carey, and Ben-Moshe 2014, 16). These intersectional analyses thus merge histories of the institutionalization of people based on race, nationality, gender, and disability to better understand contemporary patterns of diagnosis, schooling, and mass incarceration. Yet, as Erevelles and Minear argue, integrating a disability studies perspective requires that scholars wrestle with the complexity of disability, rather than interpreting it through a narrow medical lens (2010, 132).

Contemporary activists are integrating disability in an intersectional social justice lens, for example in the political platform of Black Lives Matter (BLM; see also Thompson in this volume). BLM's guiding principles take an intersectional approach, including emphasis on "actual or perceived sexual identity, gender identity, gender expression, economic status, ability, disability, religious beliefs or disbeliefs, immigration status, or location" (Matthews and Noor 2013, 7). Activists "demand a centering of the Black Disabled/Deaf," particularly as people with disabilities continue to experience adverse social outcomes such as higher rates of poverty and higher rates of entrance into the juvenile justice system, juvenile detention, and incarceration (Harriet Tubman Collective 2017, 17). For the Harriet Tubman Collective, it is "irresponsible to claim to seek justice for those who have died at the hands of police without naming victims' disabilities or advancing disability issues" (Harriet Tubman Collective 2017, 71).

Intersectional analyses that examine the connections of gender, class, and disability can also inform ongoing debates in the field of reproductive justice, for example politics around abortion. The Guttmacher Institute has tracked how policies in US states create either "hostile" or "supportive" landscapes for women seeking abortions (Nash 2019). Since 2010, more states have passed measures to restrict abortion: in 2019, 22 states were classified as "very hostile" or "hostile," an increase of 12 states since 2010. Some states have introduced restrictions based on a fetal diagnosis of disability (Smith 2019). North Dakota was the first state, in 2013, to ban abortions based solely on the diagnosis of genetic abnormality (McKinney 2016). Claire McKinney examines how these new restrictions are resurfacing debates within disability activism and scholarship that potentially pit the right to abortion against aims to affirm the value and dignity of disabled people. McKinney examines the work of Alison Piepmeier, who interviewed women facing the decision to abort: Piepmeier found that women struggled with the decision, writing, "'careful and agonizing thoughtfulness' defines the decision-making process" (2015, 13; quoted in McKinney 2016, n.p.). McKinney advocates preserving a robust defense of women's bodily autonomy. At the same time, she suggests that a "feminist disability agenda could focus instead on possible political interventions such as more informed health care professionals and better services for people with disabilities and their caregivers" (2016, n.p.). Thinking intersectionally requires that we pay attention to the particular locations and circumstances in which people live and make decisions.

How else might disability deepen intersectional analyses? Ange-Marie Hancock has raised the visibility of intersectionality in political science, and her work is illustrative of the ways in which disability can strengthen intersectional approaches. In *The Politics of Disgust: The Public Identity of the Welfare Queen* (2004), she analyses how public discourse around race, class, and gender drew upon stereotypes about Black women to legitimize the rollback of federal welfare policies. Importantly, in the United States, the 1996 welfare reform had a distinct impact on disabled people and the construction of disability. According to Hansen, Bourgois, and Drucker, "the dismantling of traditional welfare transfer payments has shifted indigent populations to a form of financial support that is increasingly medicalized—requiring a medical or psychiatric diagnosis to qualify a patient for disability payments" (2014, 76). Their analysis thus reveals new ways that people have begun to navigate government through a diagnosis of disability as a way out of poverty—a route that intersects with gender, race, and place. Karen Soldatic and Barbara Pini draw on Hancock's analysis of disgust to show how policy elites in Australia constructed people with disabilities as "historically shirking their civic responsibilities" to "disrupt the established normative notions of deserving tied to disability entitlements" (2009, 88, 89).

Adding disability to intersectional analyses also invites us to rethink the terms that we use to frame political science discourse, particularly as disability continues to signal democratic pathology. In Hancock's *Solidarity Politics for Millennials: A Guide to Ending the Oppression Olympics*, disability figures prominently in how she conceptualizes the five rings of the Oppression Olympics, including "Leapfrog Paranoia," "Willful Blindness," "Defiant Ignorance," and "Compassion Deficit Disorder" (2011, 4). Using the language of paranoia, blindness, ignorance, and deficit disorder reinforces a stigmatizing and pathologizing approach to disability. Hancock worries about how "Compassion Deficit Disorder" brands people as "hopelessly and irreparably dysfunctional," but does not consider how her choice of language may enact the same branding of disabled people (17).

Politicizing identity while pathologizing disability is also evident in contemporary politics and bears particular importance on our turbulent times. According to Bone, the original platform of the January 2017 Women's March on Washington failed to include disability as a social justice issue. Instead, it conceptualized people with disabilities as a "burden" that women, and especially women of colour, are tasked with carrying. This lack of attention was reflected in the overall inaccessibility of the march (2017, 1310).

Moving forward, political scientists who take up disability should think intersectionally—and notice ways that their language may reaffirm stereotypes that their commitment to intersectionality seeks to dismantle.

POLITICAL BEHAVIOUR, IDENTITY, AND THE QUESTION OF DISABILITY

Disability raises some puzzling and, at times, troubling findings. Though one in five people are estimated to experience disability in their lifetimes, far fewer identify as disabled (Kafer 2013, 14). Particularly as national attention to health care raises awareness about the importance of health coverage for "pre-existing conditions," why don't Americans identify as disabled? Surveys find that nondisabled people would rather be "dead than disabled," even though disabled people experience the same quality of life as nondisabled people (Disaboom 2008). Yet, when nondisabled people are informed of this fact, they simply disbelieve it (Scully 2008). As noted above, for every person in the United States killed by gun violence, three more are disabled; where are their stories? A major policy goal for disability rights activists and guiding research agenda within disability studies focuses on promoting the social inclusion of people with disabilities. But as several feminist scholars point out, calls for inclusion may require more than policy solutions—calling on communities, families, and individuals to challenge exclusion and adopt new modes of living together (McCrary 2017; Bumiller 2008). How might public policies invite these new forms of community and connection?

These questions and many more are questions that political scientists could aim to answer, explaining what contributes to people identifying as disabled and what difference this identification makes for politics. One method that political scientists might use to examine these questions is the comparative approach, particularly in analysing differences and similarities between the United States and Canada. For instance, recent work compares the United States and Canada on the level of social inclusion of people with disabilities (Wilson and McColl 2019) and different levels of disability insurance take-up (Milligan and Schirle 2019). Examining disability in a comparative approach might give political scientists new transformational possibilities in these turbulent times.

CONCLUSION: WHAT EXPLAINS DISINTEREST?

In many ways, disability seems an obvious concern for political scientists in North America: landmark legislation in both Canada and the United States has focused on people with disabilities, yet issues of underemployment, poverty, and access to political participation remain. Moreover, disability can add important insight to intersectional analyses on gender, race, class, nationality, and sexuality that align with cutting-edge work within the field. And because disability studies has its roots in the humanities, it seems that political scientists have ample room to contribute fresh insight drawing on their own disciplinary and methodological expertise.

As early as 1993, scholar and disability rights activist Harlan Hahn worried about the lack of institutional support for disability studies within political science. Hahn (1993) recommended that professional societies, like the American Political Science Association, create distinct separate groups to both support political scientists with disabilities and forward scholarship on disability policy. Over 20 years later, these suggestions remain unrealized.

Making disability a central component of our scholarship in these turbulent times requires a multi-faceted approach. First, following Hahn, we should look for ways we can institutionalize and thus support scholars with disabilities in our field and those scholars who pursue disability-related research. Second, we can add disability to intersectional analyses and think critically about how our language may reaffirm the kinds of stereotypes we aim to dismantle. Finally, disability invites us to rethink our basic assumptions about citizenship and democracy, thus injecting some turbulence into our disciplinary norms and practices.

DISCUSSION QUESTIONS

1. How do you think integrating disability into political science might forward new knowledge in each subfield, including American and Canadian politics, comparative politics, international relations, and political theory? Do you think political scientists might face different challenges integrating disability based on their subfield?
2. What do you think helps explain why disability remains a peripheral focus within political science? If Nancy Hirschmann is correct that the contemporary role of disability is similar to the peripheral role played by gender in political science in the 1980s, then are there specific actions that we can draw from feminist political scientists to help integrate disability more fully?
3. This chapter shows how diverse policies in Canada and the United States intersect with disability and thus impact disabled people, including immigration, social welfare, health care, policing, and abortion. Consider recent policy changes in your region. How do these policies impact people with disabilities? Do you think these policy changes are transforming the lives of disabled people in positive or negative ways?
4. What other issues at the intersection of political science and disability studies do you think scholars need to address in these turbulent times?

NOTES

1 Originally titled the EHA, Education for All Handicapped Children Act.
2 See http://autisticadvocacy.org/about-asan/identity-first-language/.
3 This section follows closely an argument I have made in *New Political Science* (Simplican 2017).

REFERENCES

Ackerly, Brooke, and Jacqui True. 2008. "An Intersectional Analysis of International Relations: Recasting the Discipline." *Politics & Gender* 4 (1): 156–73.

Altman, Barbara M., and Debra L. Blackwell. 2016. "Disability in U.S. Households, 2000–2010: Findings from the National Health Interview Survey." *Family Relations* 63 (1): 20–38.

Andrews, Erin E., Anjali Forber-Pratt, Linda R. Mona, Emily M. Lund, Carrie R. Pilarski, and Rochelle Balter. 2019. "#SaytheWord: A Disability Culture Commentary on the Erasure of 'Disability.'" *Rehabilitation Psychology.* Advance online publication. http://dx.doi.org/10.1037/rep0000258

Arim, Rubab. 2015. "A Profile of Persons with Disabilities among Canadians Aged 15 Years or Older, 2012." Canadian Survey on Disability. Statistics Canada. Catalogue no. 89-654-X. http://www150.statcan.gc.ca/n1/pub/89-654-x/89-654-x2015001 -eng.htm.

Arneil, Barbara. 2009. "Disability, Self-Image, and Modern Political Theory." *Political Theory* 37 (2): 218–42.

Bächtiger, André, John S. Dryzek, Jane Mansbridge, and Mark E. Warren. 2018. "Deliberative Democracy: An Introduction." In *The Oxford Handbook of Deliberative Democracy*, edited by André Bächtiger, John S. Dryzek, Jane Mansbridge, and Mark E. Warren, 1–32. Oxford: Oxford University Press.

Bagenstos, Samuel R. 2009. *Law and the Contradictions of the Disability Rights Movement.* New Haven, CT: Yale University Press.

Baril, Alexandre. 2015. "Transness as Debility: Rethinking Intersections between Trans and Disabled Embodiments." *Feminist Review* 111 (1): 59–74.

Barnartt, Sharon N. 2008. "Social Movement Diffusion? The Case of Disability Protests in the US and Canada." *Disability Studies Quarterly* 28 (1). http://dx.doi .org/10.18061/dsq.v28i1.70.

Bauer, Louise Birdsell, and Cynthia Cranford. 2017. "The Community Dimensions of Union Renewal: Racialized and Caring Relations in Personal Support Services." *Work, Employment and Society* 31 (2): 302–18.

Baynton, Douglas C. 2005. "Defectives in the Land: Disability and American Immigration Policy, 1882–1924." *Journal of American Ethnic History* 24 (3): 31–44.

Bell, Chris. 2006. "Introducing White Disability Studies: A Modest Proposal." In *The Disability Studies Reader*, edited by Lennard J. Davis, 275–82. New York: Routledge.

Bone, Kristen Marie. 2017. "Trapped behind the Glass: Crip Theory and Disability Identity." *Disability & Society* 32 (9): 1297–1314.

Bumiller, Kristin. 2008. "Quirky Citizens: Autism, Gender, and Reimagining Disability." *Signs: Journal of Women in Culture and Society* 33 (4): 967–91.

Carey, Allison C. 2003. "Beyond the Medical Model: A Reconsideration of 'Feeblemindedness,' Citizenship, and Eugenic Restrictions." *Disability and Society* 18 (4): 411–30.

Carter, A. 2015. "Teaching with Trauma: Trigger Warnings, Feminism, and Disability Pedagogy." *Disability Studies Quarterly* 35 (2). http://dx.doi.org/10.18061/dsq .v35i2.4652.

Chapman, Chris, Allison C. Carey, and Liat Ben-Moshe. 2014. "Reconsidering Confinement: Interlocking Locations and Logics of Incarceration." In *Disability*

Incarcerated: Imprisonment and Disability in the United States and Canada, edited by Liat Ben-Moshe, Chris Chapman, and Allison C. Carey, 3–24. New York: Palgrave Macmillan.

Cho, Sumi, Kimberlé Williams Crenshaw, and Leslie McCall. 2013. "Toward a Field of Intersectionality Studies: Theory, Applications, and Praxis." *Signs: Journal of Women in Culture and Society* 38 (4): 785–810.

Clifford, Stacy. 2012. "Making Disability Public in Deliberative Democracy." *Contemporary Political Theory* 11 (2): 211–28.

Conroy, James W., Steven J. Dale, and Robert P. McCaffrey. 2016. "Current and Emerging Trends for Residential Supports for Persons with Intellectual and Developmental Disabilities and the Impact of Managed Care Initiatives." In *Health Care for People with Intellectual and Developmental Disabilities across the Lifespan*, edited by I. Leslie Rubin, Joav Merrick, Donald E. Greydanus, and Dilip R. Patel, 255–63. Cham, Switzerland: Springer International Publishing.

Crow, Liz. 1996. "Including All of Our Lives: Renewing the Social Model of Disability." In *Exploring the Divide: Illness and Disability*, edited by C. Barnes and G. Mercer, 55–72. Leeds: The Disability Press.

Davis, Kathy. 2008. "Intersectional as Buzzword: A Sociology of Science Perspective on What Makes a Feminist Theory Successful." *Feminist Theory* 9 (1): 67–85.

Davis, Lennard. 2017. Preface to the Fifth Edition. In *Disability Studies Reader*, 5th ed., edited by Lennard Davis, xiii–xv. New York: Routledge.

Dietz, Mary G. 1987. "Context Is All: Feminism and Theories of Citizenship." *Daedelus* 116 (4): 1–24.

Disaboom. 2008. "Disaboom Survey Reveals 52 Percent of Americans Would Rather Be Dead Than Disabled." http://www.prweb.com/releases/Disaboom/Disability/prweb1082094.htm.

Donoghue, Christopher. 2003. "Challenging the Authority of the Medical Definition of Disability: An Analysis of the Resistance to the Social Constructionist Paradigm." *Disability & Society* 18 (2): 199–208.

Erevelles, Nirmala. 2011. *Disability and Difference in Global Contexts: Enabling a Transformative Body Politic*. New York: Palgrave Macmillan.

Erevelles, Nirmala, and Andrea Minear. 2010. "Unspeakable Offenses: Untangling Race and Disability in Discourses of Intersectionality." *Journal of Literary & Cultural Disability Studies* 4 (2): 127–46.

Frontera, Walter R. 2006. "Medicine." In *Encyclopaedia of Disability*, edited by G.L. Albrecht, 1067–74. New York: Sage. https://doi.org/10.4135/9781412950510.n529.

Gabel, Susan L., Denise Reid, Holly Pearson, Litzy Ruiz, and Rodney Hume-Dawson. 2016. "Disability and Diversity on CSU Websites: A Critical Discourse Study." *Journal of Diversity in Higher Education* 9 (1): 64–80.

Gernsbacher, Morton Ann. 2017. "Editorial Perspective: The Use of Person-First Language in Scholarly Writing May Accentuate Stigma." *The Journal of Child Psychology and Psychiatry* 58 (7): 859–61.

Gilligan, Carol. 1982. *In a Different Voice*. Cambridge, MA: Harvard University Press.

Grey, Ian, Helena Lydon, and Olive Healy. 2016. "Positive Behavior Support: What Model of Disability Does It Represent?" *Journal of Intellectual & Developmental Disability* 41 (3): 255–66.

Habermas, Jürgen. 1984. *The Theory of Communicative Action*. Boston: Beacon Press.

Hahn, Harlan. 1993. "The Potential Impact of Disability Studies on Political Science (as Well as Vice-Versa)." *Policy Studies Journal* 21 (4): 740–51.

Haller, Beth, Bruce Dorries, and Jessica Rahn. 2006. "Media Labeling *versus* the US Disability Community Identity: A Study of Shifting Cultural Language." *Disability & Society* 21 (1): 61–75.

Hamraie, Aimi. 2015. "Cripping Feminist Technoscience." *Hypatia* 30 (1): 307–13. https://doi.org/10.1111/hypa.12124.

———. 2017. *Building Access: Universal Design and the Politics of Disability*. Minneapolis: University of Minnesota Press.

Hancock, Ange-Marie. 2004. *The Politics of Disgust: The Public Identity of the Welfare Queen*. New York: New York University Press.

———. 2007. "Intersectionality as a Normative and Empirical Paradigm." *Politics & Gender* 3 (2): 248–54.

———. 2011. *Solidarity Politics for Millennials: A Guide to Ending the Oppression Olympics*. New York: Palgrave Macmillan.

Hansen, Helena, Philippe Bourgois, and Ernest Drucker. 2014. "Pathologizing Poverty: New Forms of Diagnosis, Disability, and Structural Stigma under Welfare Reform." *Social Science & Medicine* 103: 76–83.

Harding, Sandra. 1995. "Just Add Women and Stir?" In *Missing Links: Gender Equity in Science and Technology for Development*, edited by the Gender Working Group of the United Nations Commission on Science and Technology for Development, 295–307. Ottawa: International Development Research Centre.

Harriet Tubman Collective. 2017. "Disability Solidarity: Completing the 'Vision for Black Lives.'" *Harvard Journal of African American Public Policy*, January 1: 69–72.

Hirschmann, Nancy. 2012. "Disability as a New Frontier for Feminist Intersectionality Research." *Politics & Gender* 8 (3): 396–405.

Immigrant Legal Resource Center. n.d. "Public Charge." https://www.ilrc.org/public -charge. Accessed November 22, 2019.

Jongbloed, Lyn. 2003. "Disability Policy in Canada." *Journal of Disability Policy Studies* 13 (4): 203–09.

Kafer, Allison. 2013. *Feminist Queer Crip*. Bloomington: Indiana University Press.

Kelly, Christine. 2013. "Towards Renewed Descriptions of Canadian Disability Movements: Disability Activism outside of the Non-profit Sector." *Canadian Journal of Disability Studies* 2 (1): 1–27.

———. 2016. *Disability Politics and Care: The Challenge of Direct Funding*. Vancouver: University of British Columbia Press.

Kim, Eunjung. 2017. *Curative Violence: Rehabilitating Disability, Gender, and Sexuality in Modern Korea*. Durham, NC: Duke University Press.

Kittay, Eva Feder. 1999. *Love's Labor: Essays on Women, Equality, and Dependency.* New York: Routledge.

———. 2013. "Caring for the Long Haul: Long-Term Care Needs and the (Moral) Failure to Acknowledge Them." *International Journal of Feminist Approaches to Bioethics* 6 (2): 66–88.

Kittay, Eva Feder, Bruce Jennings, and Angela A. Wasunna. 2005. "Dependency, Difference and the Global Ethic of Longterm Care." *The Journal of Political Philosophy* 13 (4): 443–69.

Knight, Amber. 2014. "Disability as Vulnerability: Redistributing Precariousness in Democratic Ways." *The Journal of Politics* 76 (1): 15–26.

———. 2015. "Democratizing Disability: Achieving Inclusion (without Assimilation) through 'Participatory Parity.'" *Hypatia* 30 (1): 97–114.

Manning, Susan M., Pamela Johnson, and Julianne Acker-Verney. 2016. "Uneasy Intersections: Critical Understandings of Gender and Disability in Global Development." *Third World Thematics: A TWQ Journal* 1 (3): 292–306.

Matthews, Shanelle, and Miski Noor. 2013. "Celebrating Four Years of Organizing to Protect Black Lives." Black Lives Matter. https://blacklivesmatter.com/resource /4-year-anniversary-report/.

McCall, Leslie. 2005. "The Complexity of Intersectionality." *Signs: Journal of Women in Culture & Society* 30 (3): 1771–800.

McCrary, Lorraine Krall. 2017. "Geel's Family Care Tradition: Care, Communities, and the Social Inclusion of Persons with Disabilities." *Journal of Literary and Cultural Disability Studies* 11 (3): 285–301.

McKinney, Claire. 2016. "Selective Abortion as Moral Failure? Revaluation of the Feminist Case for Reproductive Rights in Disability Context." *Disability Studies Quarterly* 36 (1).

McRuer, Robert. 2006. *Crip Theory: Cultural Signs of Queerness and Disability.* New York: New York University Press.

McWhorter, Ladelle. 2009. *Racism and Sexual Oppression in Anglo-America.* Bloomington: Indiana University Press.

Meekosha, Helen, and Russell Shuttleworth. 2009. "What's So 'Critical' about Critical Disability Studies?" *Australian Journal of Human Rights* 1: 47–75.

Milligan, Kevin, and Tammy Schirle. 2019. "Push and Pull: Disability Insurance, Regional Labor Markets, and Benefit Generosity in Canada and the United States." *Journal of Labor Economics* 37 (S2): S289–S323.

Mouffe, Chantal. 2000. *The Democratic Paradox.* London: Verso.

Nash, Elizabeth. 2019. "State Abortion Policy Landscape: From Hostile to Supportive." Guttmacher Institute, August 29. https://www.guttmacher.org/ article/2019/08/state-abortion-policy-landscape-hostile-supportive.

Pateman, Carole. 1988. *The Sexual Contract.* Stanford, CA: Stanford University Press.

People First of West Virginia. n.d. "History of People First." http://peoplefirstwv.org /old-front/history-of-people-first/. Accessed November 22, 2019.

Piepmeier, Alison. 2015. "Would It Be Better for Her Not to Be Born? Down Syndrome, Prenatal Testing, and Reproductive Decision-Making." *Feminist Formations* 27 (1): 1–24.

Prince, Michael. 2010. "What about a Disability Rights Act for Canada? Practices and Lessons from America, Australia, and the United Kingdom." *Canadian Public Policy* 36 (2): 199–214.

Quinn, Erin, and Melissa Rodgers. 2019. "Public Charge and Naturalization." Immigration Legal Resource Center. https://www.ilrc.org/sites/default/files /resources/public_charge_and_natz_practice_advisory_092019.pdf

Ralph, Laurence. 2014. *Renegade Dreams: Living through Injury in Gangland Chicago*. Chicago: University of Chicago Press.

Rawls, John. 1971. *A Theory of Justice*. Cambridge: Cambridge University Press.

Sandahl, Carrie, and Philip Auslander, eds. 2005. *Bodies in Commotion: Disability and Performance*. Ann Arbor: University of Michigan Press.

Schalk, Sami. 2009. "Coming to Claim Crip: Disidentification with/in Disability Studies." *Disability Studies Quarterly* 33 (2). http://dx.doi.org/10.18061/dsq .v33i2.3705.

Scully, Jackie Leach. 2008. *Disability Bioethics: Moral Bodies, Moral Difference*. Lanham, MD: Rowman & Littlefield.

Shakespeare, Tom. 1996. "Disability, Identity and Difference." In *Exploring the Divide*, edited by Colin Barnes and Geof Mercer, 94–113. Leeds: The Disability Press.

Shapiro, Joseph P. 1994. *No Pity: People with Disabilities Forging a New Civil Rights Movement*. New York: Three Rivers Press.

Shildrick, Margrit. 2015. "Living On; Not Getting Better." *Feminist Review* 111 (1): 10–24. https://doi.org/10.1057/fr.2015.22.

Simplican, Stacy Clifford. 2015. *The Capacity Contract: Intellectual Disability and the Question of Citizenship*. Minneapolis: University of Minnesota Press.

———. 2017. "The 'Perverse Result' of Disability Rights: Deregulating Care Workers' Labor Unions in the Supreme Court." *New Political Science* 39 (1): 1–16.

Smith, S.E. 2019. "Disabled People Are Tired of Being a Talking Point in the Abortion Debate." https://www.vox.com/first-person/2019/5/29/18644320 /abortion-ban-2019-selective-abortion-ban-disability.

Soldatic, Karen, and Barbara Pini. 2009. "The Three Ds of Welfare Reform: Disability, Disgust and Deservingness." *Australian Journal of Human Rights* 15 (1): 77–95.

Stienstra, Deborah, and Steve Estey. 2016. "Canada's Responses to Disability and Global Development." *Third World Thematics: A TWQ Journal* 1 (3): 382–95.

Swadley, Heather. 2016. "Toward a Support-Based Theory of Democracy." *Res Philosophica* 93 (4): 971–97.

Taylor, Danielle M. 2018. "Americans with Disabilities: 2014. Household Economic Studies." Current Population Reports, United States Census Bureau.

Titchkosky, Tanya. 2001. "Disability: A Rose by Any Other Name? 'People-First' Language in Canadian Society." *Canadian Review of Sociology and Anthropology* 38 (2): 125–40.

Tronto, Joan. 2013. *Caring Democracy: Markets, Equality, and Justice*. New York: New York University Press.

Vanhala, Lisa. 2009. "Disability Rights Activists in the Supreme Court of Canada: Legal Mobilization Theory and Accommodating Social Movements." *Canadian Journal of Political Science* 42 (4): 981–1002.

Wilson, Clarke, and Mary Ann McColl. 2019. "Comparing Integration and Inclusion between Canadians and Americans with Disabilities: Evidence from National Surveys of Time Use." *Canadian Journal of Disability Studies* 8 (3): 18–40.

Wong, Yin-Ling Irene, Yiyue Huangfu, and Trevor Hadley. 2018. "Place and Community Inclusion: Locational Patterns of Supportive Housing for People with Intellectual Disability and People with Psychiatric Disorders." *Research in Developmental Disabilities* 83: 108–19.

Young, Iris Marion. 2002. *Inclusion and Democracy*. Oxford: Oxford University Press.

Zames Fleischer, Doris, and Frieda Zames. 2012. *The Disability Rights Movement: From Charity to Confrontation*. Philadelphia: Temple University Press.

FURTHER READING

Arneil, Barbara, and Nancy J. Hirschmann. 2016. *Disability and Political Theory*. Cambridge: Cambridge University Press.

Kelly, Christine. 2016. *Disability Politics and Care: The Challenge of Direct Funding*. Vancouver: University of British Columbia Press.

Simplican, Stacy Clifford. 2015. *The Capacity Contract: Intellectual Disability and the Question of Citizenship*. Minneapolis: University of Minnesota Press.

Vanhala, Lisa. 2013. *Making Rights a Reality? Disability Rights Activists and Legal Mobilization*. Cambridge: Cambridge University Press.

16

Engendering Fatness and "Obesity": Affect, Emotions, and the Governance of Weight in a Neoliberal Age[1]

Michael Orsini

Key terms: affects, body, fat activists, fat shaming, neoliberalism, obesity, responsibilization

So this fat bitch is at government health meetings literaly [*sic*] stuffing her food hole with pies and no one is allowed to say shit?

Also fuck those betas for apologizing. If you call a bitch fat press the attack. Yea I called her obese she is 300 pounds. This is a medical fact. No im [*sic*] not apologizing. Yes she does drink mapple [*sic*] syrup out of the bottle.
> —Reddit user commenting on Alberta Health
> Minister Sarah Hoffman

Fat people are the cancer of modern society. The more of them there are, the worse off we will be. The damage they are causing has only just begun.
> —VOAT user DelusionalHominid,
> "Fat People Hate" message board

INTRODUCTION

In 2015, Alberta's minister of health and seniors, Sarah Hoffman, was fat-shamed by a Progressive Conservative Party operative in a Facebook post. "Our morbidly obese Health Minister Sarah Hoffman is going to ban the sale of menthol tobacco products in Alberta as of September," Jordan Lien wrote. "I would assume then that if health is the chief concern, that all sodas, candy, processed sugar products ... and fast foods ... should then follow?" (Urback 2015, n.p.). The party brass was quick to denounce the comment and apologized to Minister Hoffman. And if that was not enough, just a year later, the *Calgary Sun* ran an article with the headline "Wait Watchers" next to an image of Hoffman and a story about the government's efforts to reduce wait times in health procedures. The newspaper's editor later apologized for any offence taken, suggesting it was simply a "poor attempt at a pun" (Butterfield 2017). If you believe media pundits such as *National Post* columnist Robyn Urback, while the Hoffman attack was odious, it is "utter nonsense" to suggest that this incident was somehow gendered or misogynist because, well, Quebec's health minister, Gaétan Barrette,[2] was also the target of **fat shaming**, as was late Toronto mayor Rob Ford (Urback 2015). Seeing as male politicians are being fat-shamed too, should we simply put down our gender-based-analysis lens?

This chapter considers the gendered constructions of fatness and **obesity** that circulate in policy discourse and how these discourses are structured by emotions and **affects** that are difficult to dislodge from, or even understand, without a keen attention to their gendered effects or components. Individuals marked as "obese" are pitied for their "careless" lifestyles, treated with compassion for their seeming inability to make better choices, or framed as objects of disgust. Policies reflect our own deep-seated feelings about fat.[3] Moreover, as a societal "problem," obesity is difficult to dislodge from the multi-billion-dollar diet industry and corporations that specialize in producing addictive junk food. In our neoliberal age, paradoxically, individuals are exhorted to consume more and eat less (see Guthman 2009). And there is increasing debate among feminist and political economy scholars about some of the fat-phobic undercurrents embedded in perspectives advanced by otherwise progressive thinkers (Guthman 2011). There is evidence that our own thinking about fatness and obesity is affected by anxieties about our own health in these "turbulent times." Just as we are growing increasingly aware that our health is not necessarily the direct product of individual decisions we make in our day-to-day lives, there is a recourse to simplistic ideas about complex problems. Moreover, despite decades of research on the pernicious effects of the weight-loss industry, there is a stubborn acceptance that if we manage our weight, not only can we gain personal transformation but also broader social transformation.

I begin with a discussion of the contentious policy narratives that circulate around fatness and explore how these are structured by intersections of race, class, disability, and gender. These narratives are not, of course, mutually exclusive, but in the context of the contradictions embedded in neoliberal forms of rule (which I address later in the chapter) they are worth exploring for their, perhaps, unintended effects and affects. Scholars often distinguish affects from emotions by clarifying that affects include non-conscious sensations, intensities, and feelings that might be difficult to capture or read as specific expressions of emotion such as anger, fear, or disgust. Second, I turn to the affective terrain on which fat/obesity politics is grounded. Individuals might have particular feelings vis-à-vis their own weight, but these affects are themselves structured by complex sets of relations among race, gender, class, and disability (see Clifford-Simplican in this volume). In the US context, for instance, the Black **body** continues to be a site of hyper-surveillance (see Thompson in this volume), so it is perhaps not surprising that the Black bodies of fat women are potent signifiers in North American culture (for more on the cultural representation of fatness and Blackness, see Mobley 2014). In the third part of the chapter, I discuss the intersection of **neoliberalism** and the governance of weight, focusing on some of the contradictions embedded in an approach to weight as a public "problem" that needs to be managed.

THE CONTENTIOUS POLITICS OF FATNESS AND OBESITY

What is contentious about obesity? What is political about fatness? Apart from identity struggles around self-naming that are common to social movements— is it more appropriate to say "person living with obesity," "obese person," or "fat person"?—there are competing claims with regard to the nature of the "problem" itself and whether public intervention is required in the first place to deal with the so-called obesity epidemic.

In this chapter, I use the term "obesity" in quotation marks when discussing policy interventions that actually employ this language (see Ellison,

McPhail, and Mitchinson 2016). The language of obesity is viewed as problematic because it frames weight in excess of the norm as a medical problem that needs to be fixed or managed. It is common for anti-obesity advocates, for instance, to warn of impending crises and epidemics if societies or governments fail to act. A recent Senate report on "obesity" is a good example of this type of thinking (see Senate of Canada 2016; see Orsini 2016 for a critique).[4] Importantly, and in contrast, those who are interested in exploring the social, cultural, and political understandings we attach to weight generally use the terms "fatness" or "fat." **Fat activists** vehemently reject the medical term "obesity" as pathologizing, arguing that it is unreasonable to assume that all fat people need to be fixed or should fixate on their weight. As one activist describes it: "Over whose weight? I'm not over my own weight, after all. So what weight am I over? A standard I'm expected to live up to? A standard which I'm not defined by my failure to attain? Obese is what we 'officially' are ... Obese medicalizes our bodies. It defines us as diseased. It has a powerfully dehumanizing effect" ("More to Love" 2007).[5]

In the Canadian context, a number of researchers and scientists who have adopted the anti-stigma messages associated with fat activism use the term "living with obesity," arguing that society and government need to focus on obesity as a problem that requires public attention, rather than on strategies of victim-blaming. Framing obesity as a chronic disease, they argue, can help to command the necessary public resources for individuals who might need help (Nutter et al. 2018). These obesity researchers and activists, many of whom are connected to Obesity Canada (formerly known as the Canadian Obesity Network), draw on evidence and emotions to drive home the message that we need broad, sweeping changes in government approaches to and funding of obesity "treatment" and interventions. Their approach, while loudly criticized by fat activists, purports to find a middle ground between pathological views of obesity and one that is respectful of the lived experience of people who seek medical support to deal with their weight and the stigma they encounter in daily life.

Individuals who identify as fat or living with "obesity" challenge dominant ways of thinking about them by engaging in acts of self-naming and identity building, which are crucial to social movements and broader struggles associated with transformational politics. Fat activists insist on using and reclaiming the term "fat" to describe their embodied form of politics, while others, often more closely aligned with obesity researchers, prefer the person-first term "people living with obesity." In each case, these actors are working to rethink how we understand our own relationship with our bodies. Feelings and emotions are central to these understandings. Later in this chapter, I will discuss the unsettled distinction between these two identities: those who identify as fat versus obese or overweight.

Fatness and obesity open a window into how a series of complex moral emotions, such as shame and disgust, can structure how we think about policy problems. The social science literature on obesity and fatness has expanded in recent years, with scholars examining the links between obesity as a pressing policy issue and the broader neoliberal project of **responsibilization** (Campos et al. 2006; Saguy and Riley 2005; Townend 2009). Responsibilization refers to strategies that seek to download or off-load responsibility for problems onto individuals as a way to relieve the state's role. It is often associated with the so-called retrenchment of the welfare state and cuts to government spending in fields such as health care or social policy (see Dobrowolsky in this volume). While there has been prolonged attention to the presumed health effects of obesity, especially as they relate to children, there has also been concern about how policies purported to "help" fat people actually compound their stigmatized status (Puhl and Heuer 2009). While Canada has yet to invoke incendiary language likening fat to "a form of domestic terrorism," as the US Surgeon General has done in the past, governments at both the federal and provincial levels have stepped up their anti-obesity efforts (Rail, Holmes, and Murray 2010). Fat-acceptance activists challenge the epidemic language summoned to justify policy interventions to deal with obesity and how it reinforces gendered constructions of idealized bodies (Kirkland 2008). These activists denounce "obesity epidemic" talk and images of ticking time bombs, preferring to rescue the term "fat" from its stigmatized status in much the same way the LGBTQ+ movement has reclaimed the term "queer."

Despite a growing body of research challenging the ubiquity of weight-based discrimination, there is a nagging tendency to frame "obesity" and fatness in stark terms: either it is seen as a problem of individuals who are consciously making poor choices, or it is viewed as a societal problem for which we must assume collective responsibility. Fat people are either shameful sloths who lack the fortitude to tackle their problems head-on or they are pitiful characters deserving of our compassion for reaching a difficult point in their lives in which they cannot resist the many temptations that surround them daily. On the latter point, proponents of the food addiction model suggest that individuals who have a problematic relationship to certain foods need to avoid those foods at all costs. Curiously, the growing chorus of public health interest in harm reduction has not had an effect on those "experts" who cling to the addiction model. For instance, a harm reduction model in the area of drug use recognizes that abstinence-based approaches do not necessarily make sound public health sense. Providing support for individuals to engage in safe consumption of drugs, by contrast, reduces the harms associated with drug use. A model of food consumption rooted in addiction promotes the view that certain foods must be avoided at all costs, rather than embracing an approach that recognizes our own complex relationship to food. Moreover, it leaves little room for individual agency and the autonomy to engage in decisions that affect our lives.

So, what exactly is the "problem" of obesity? Is obesity even a problem? Some have criticized the use of Body Mass Index (or BMI) as *the* standard measure of obesity, even if it is generally accepted in the medical community. Nicholls has shown how measures, such as BMI, need to be understood as more than simply evidence-based tools for tackling obesity. The classification of individuals into categories of underweight, normal weight, overweight, or obese "serves to minimize the differences within these weight categories and introduce perceptions of significant differences between classes." Moreover, processes of classification are not benign: "Grouping does not just classify weight, it classifies people. An often-neglected effect of classification is that it can affect how we see those so classified in ways that are more substantial" (2013, 10).

Boswell's (2014) analysis of UK and Australian discourse identified six dominant narrative accounts of obesity as a policy problem: facilitated agency; regulatory reform; individual intervention; nanny state; social dislocation; and moral panic. Each narrative has a particular construction of the problem in question and the range of possible actions that are required to address the problem as defined. It is beyond the scope of this chapter to discuss each in detail, so I will focus on facilitated agency, individual intervention, and social dislocation, which have explicitly gendered dimensions and resonate in the Canadian context. First, "facilitated agency"—with its focus on the speed of social changes and the attendant uncertainty of individuals about how to live a healthy life—is attuned to a politically strategic way of framing obesity. If people are confused or uneducated, then surely educating them or clearing up their muddled thoughts or feelings is socially and politically desirable since it conveniently sidesteps questions of moral culpability. This information-deficit model of thinking is concerned with enhancing health literacy, a laudable goal indeed, but it can be rightly challenged for implicit race, gender, and class bias.

The "individual intervention" narrative frames obesity as a problem that has created a veritable industry to help individuals cope with the effects of obesity, including medical intervention, self-help, and the dieting industry. This is a deeply gendered phenomenon, with the majority of attention focused on women, for whom there is great social pressure to lose weight and fulfil unrealistic body expectations. The diet industry, for instance, heralds itself as empowering individuals to take control of their lives and promises physical transformation when the only thing that is actually transformed is the diet and weight loss industry's profit margins. Finally, the idea of "social disloca-tion" frames obesity in the context of deeper social problems related to socio-economic inequality. In such a formulation, obesity is a mere symptom of wider social ills or one of the manifestations of social unrest. Not surprisingly, simple policy solutions are not available to address the problem. What is clear, however, is that individuals are seen as unhappy, disconnected, and almost pitiful from the perspective of able-bodied, healthy citizens who can only look upon them with a mixture of empathy and derision.

Fatness and obesity are also gendered in the ways in which they regu-late motherhood and children. Bethan Evans discusses a process by which obesity is discursively produced and managed through "extraction from the individual body to establish fatness as threat (through population-level cor-relations." When "explaining the threat of obesity," she adds, "the body is often reduced to biological matter (fat cells) seen to universally determine future health" (2010, 23). This "pre-emptive obesity biopolitics" relies upon the "fleshy materiality of the body," which vacillates between a present and future state, as well as an embodied individual self and an abstracted body. In both instances, the fat body is characterized, paradoxically, by its looming present and distant but frightful future. Childhood, in such a formulation, is a site of anxiety and dread; a future that must be acted upon, in the present, by actors who are exhorted to stand in for the vulnerable, the defenceless (see also Rollo in this volume). Evans argues that these types of interventions rely on "affective entanglements," in which individual anxieties about fat futures co-mingle with hopes for leaner, vital selves. In the context of welfare state retrenchment, mothers are expected to "perform the fine balancing act of protecting their children from insidious market forces, indulging them, and teaching them how to make disciplined, wise choices—to consume properly and responsibly—in the name of health" (Power 2016, 61).

As noted earlier, the much-publicized Senate committee report on obe-sity devoted little energy to the messy policy challenges that straddle social, environmental, gender, and economic policy realms. Rather, it reiterated some familiar tropes, including that we should care about obesity in pregnancy because obese moms tend to raise obese children:

> Committee members were told that larger infants are more likely than healthy weight babies to become overweight children, who grow into overweight and obese adolescents. The cycle continues when these overweight young women become pregnant. The problem is further compounded when women do not get down to a healthy weight before the next pregnancy. (Senate of Canada 2016, 18)

While reference is made to social determinants of health, the women who are presumably perpetuating this "cycle" are portrayed as helpless and hopeless, incapable of getting down to a healthy weight! The only hope, it seems, is medical interventions to ensure that these "high risk" pregnancies are managed through (increasingly intrusive) technologies of surveillance. This type of approach fits well within the frame of welfare state intervention as "social investment" (see Dobrowolsky in this volume).

Fatness intersects with other forms of oppression, such as race, in complicated ways. In discussing how race, poverty, and fatness intersect in contemporary America, noted feminist and cultural theorist Lauren Berlant uses the term "slow death" to refer to "a condition of being worn out by the activity of reproducing life" (2007, 759). As she notes:

> To the extent that emaciation in the U.S. remains coded as white and weight excess coded as black, the so-called crisis of obesity continues to juggle the symbolic burden of class signified through the elision of whiteness from the racial marking of poverty; these markings, at minimum, shape not only particular aversions to people of excess (already negated as both too much and too little for ordinary social membership) but also the topic of excess as a general issue of public health. (773)

Berlant's work has been criticized by fat activists, however, as advancing a problematic "obesogenic" account of fatness. As one critic argued, "Obesogenic accounts open the door for interventionist, paternalistic policies targeted at curbing consumption, always with an eye toward poor communities and communities of color, and often yoked to nationalist discourses of security and progress" (Ward 2010, n.p.). For Sanders, the public face of obesity as the obese Black woman fuses the stigma of fatness with the most deplored traits of the welfare queen. By personifying the typical obese American as black and female and by invoking tropes of black women as indulgent, undisciplined bad mothers who exploit state funds and deplete the economy, even well-meaning and left-leaning raced and gendered anti-obesity discourses invite and justify the systematic practices of discrimination and exclusion that sustain status quo racial inequality. (2017, 4)

FEELING FATNESS: ON THE ROLE OF EMOTIONS AND AFFECT

I begin from the premise that emotions are not necessarily irrational, but instead critical features of sense-making in politics. They should not be bracketed from our attempts to grapple with the messy world of public policy or collective action, but they can be difficult to pin down. As Fraser, Maher, and Wright explain: "Emotions do not 'cross' boundaries of subjects and collectivities (moving outwards or inwards). Rather, they actually work to define the boundaries of subjects, and of collectivities—it is in this sense that they are performative" (2010, 204). While I am interested in integrating emotions in our respective analytical tool kits, I oppose an approach that privileges "good" emotions and banishes "bad" ones. Political actors seek to make us *feel* something. Complex moral emotions such as compassion, disgust, fear, and anger "express explicit principles that we hold, or mere intuitions that we have never fully articulated." Moreover, they reveal that we attach certain moral ideas to our ability to express certain emotions (Jasper 2006, 17). We might feel shameful, for instance, about expressing anger.

While a turn to emotions is not entirely new for critical race, feminist (Dobrowolsky 2014), and gender studies scholars, it challenges us to think about how seemingly rational behaviours and actions operate within emotional scripts. In previous work (Orsini and Wiebe 2014), I have used the term "emotional landscape" to refer to an environment that includes affect and emotions, sensory experiences, the conscious and the unconscious. Embedded in these landscapes is a series of "feeling rules" or norms that communicate the boundaries, albeit shifting, of appropriate expressions of emotion. The concept of feeling rules was first coined by Hochschild (1979) to reveal some of the ways in which rituals and conventions captured, documented, and codified felt experience, especially in the workplace (see also Gould 2009).

Feeling rules require "emotion work" or labour. For instance, learning how to "read" a workplace environment and respond appropriately requires a certain level of skill or emotional intelligence.

Unlike other rules, feeling rules "do not apply to action but to what is often taken as a precursor to action" (Hochschild 1979, 566). What might be appropriately felt in one context may not be in another. Hochschild usefully distinguishes between a feeling rule "as it is known by our sense of what we can expect to feel in a given situation and a rule as it is known by our sense of what we should feel in that situation" (1979, 564). One might, for instance, feel something even when one is aware that they should be feeling something else. As I discuss later, the notion of stigma—fighting and countering it—has mobilized movement actors associated with fat activism as well as those who adopt the language of obesity. While fiercely opposed to one another, both groups frame their political interventions in the language of opposing and resisting weight and fat stigma. In a recent blog post, a Canadian obesity researcher took fat activists to task for attacking those who identify obesity as a chronic disease:

> Never mind that in my view (and that of an increasing number of obesity experts) obesity needs to be diagnosed and treated as a chronic disease only when weight affects a person's health. Never mind that as a life-long feminist, I am a strong believer in promoting body diversity and inclusivity. Never mind that my own engagement and research is entirely dedicated to fighting weight bias and discrimination … None of this seemed relevant—there was simply no room for respectful discussion or thoughtful exchange of perspectives. (Ramos Salas 2018, n.p.)

Fat stigma and bias, it seems, is the final frontier. Why is it socially acceptable to discriminate against fat people? Does it reflect a general agreement that they are lazy, unmotivated, and just need to work harder at trimming the fat? Racism, sexism, and homo- and transphobia are rampant, but they are socially and culturally proscribed. Stigma and bias have effects on the lives of people who identify as fat or obese; many are discriminated against in the workplace and avoid the health care system for fear of being lectured by well-meaning health care professionals about their weight. In 2018, one case that gained national attention concerned a BC woman, Ellen Maud Bennett, whose obituary decried the **fat shaming** she experienced in the health care system: "Over the past few years of feeling unwell she sought out medical intervention and no one offered any support or suggestions beyond weight loss ... Ellen's dying wish was that women of size make her death matter by advocating strongly for their health and not accepting that fat is the only relevant health issue" (Canadian Press 2018, n.p.). In Manitoba in 2016, activists led a campaign with help from opposition Liberal MLA Jon Gerrard to pressure the provincial government to introduce human rights protections for people discriminated against because of their size, but their efforts were unsuccessful.

As Farrell discusses, fat people experience different forms of stigma and, of course, stigma is experienced differently depending upon an individual's social location, gender, and racial identity, among other factors. Beyond the physical stigma of being visibly fat to others, Farrell discusses the notion of character stigma, in which meanings are assigned to fatness that purportedly speak to an individual's character, for instance "that a person is gluttonous, or filling a deeply disturbed psychological need, or irresponsible and unable to control primitive urges" (2011, 6). More importantly, she adds, cultural beliefs about fatness are "deeply rooted in the development of ideas about race, gender, and civilization" (8). Fatness, Farrell adds, has been used to identify "inferior bodies," citing the high-profile case of a US sorority at DePauw University in Indiana that expelled 22 "overweight" and non-white women for failing to be fully committed to the sorority.

Interestingly, while there is a growing chorus of support for anti-stigma messages in public health campaigns, there are others who suggest, drawing on the case of anti-smoking policy, that a little stigma—"stigmatization lite"— might be a good thing: "There has to be a popular uprising when so many aspects of our common lives, individually and institutionally, must be changed more or less simultaneously. Safe and slow incrementalism that strives never to stigmatize obesity has not and cannot do the necessary work" (Callahan 2013, 37–38). So, while there is greater policy recognition that punitive measures do not work, there is a feeling that it would be dangerous to send a message that it is okay to be fat.

ON THE WEIGHT OF NEOLIBERALISM

By now, there has been much discussion of the impact of neoliberalism and neoliberal forms of rule on politics and policy-making. Neoliberalism is summoned to signal the creeping conservatism of the New Right and is the preferred punching bag of progressives. It is critical, however, to avoid the tendency to employ neoliberalism sloppily as an explanation for everything. It is useful here to recall Larner's distinction between neoliberalism as policy, as ideology, or as governmentality. I will focus for the sake of space on the idea of neoliberalism as governmentality. While the first and second are self-evident, denoting neoliberalism as either a policy response to the exigencies of the global economy, or the capturing of the policy agenda by the New Right, Larner suggests that viewing neoliberalism solely in the first two senses runs "the risk of underestimating the significance of contemporary transformations in governance." Neoliberalism, she counters, "is both a political discourse about the nature of rule and a set of practices that facilitate the governing of individuals from a distance" (2000, 6). It is a mode of governing that exhorts "people to see themselves as individualized and active subjects responsible for enhancing their own well-being. This conception of the 'active society' can also be linked to a particular politics of self in which we are all encouraged to 'work on ourselves' in a range of domains" (13). Individuals are expected to be enterprising and working towards bettering themselves through forms of active citizenship. While there are important examples of policies and programs to combat obesity that appear to be draconian and focus on blaming the victim, there are many examples of so-called "healthy living" or "active living" programs that seek to mobilize individuals to take charge of their health (and their weight). The growth of the "quantified" self and the Fitbit explosion is another example of how technologies enable as well as constrain (Lupton 2016).

What does it mean to think about weight and fatness through the lens of neoliberalism? Following disability studies and fat studies scholars Anna Mollow and Robert McRuer (2015), I suggest that we need to "fatten" our accounts of neoliberalism and austerity politics. Fattening austerity is an invitation to draw greater feminist attention to the link between so-called progressive politics and the persistence of fatphobia. In this regard, there are important contrasts between the feminist- and queer-inspired roots of radical fat activism centred on the celebration of different embodiments, and efforts by other actors associated mainly with a public health approach who respond to "obesity" in ways that seek to reduce stigma and bias as well as those features of our environments that seem to encourage "unhealthy" behaviours. This seemingly progressive current of advocacy to tackle "obesity" purports to favour more holistic understandings of health and wellness that tackle social determinants such as income, gender, and race. In addition, anti-obesity activists and advocates seek to downplay a shaming discourse of personal responsibility, arguing instead that fat people are structured to be that way as a result of our "obesogenic" environment, which encourages poor eating and limited physical activity.

A focus on fattening austerity has important implications for feminist activism, as well as for broader progressive struggles in these neoliberal times (for a critical disability studies perspective on austerity politics, see McRuer 2018). What does it mean to suggest that feminists need to get fat? It means those who study different forms of contentious politics, including feminist and other forms of progressive activism, need to think about the "fleshy materiality" of fatness, both for the sake of thinking through how bodily difference is deeply political but also how activist struggle, in general, tends to neglect the ableist assumptions that undergird contentious politics. The sheer physical effort involved in struggle can act as a physical barrier to involvement, in much the same way as the notion of able-bodiedness that disability activists have alerted us to, which normalizes certain kinds of bodies and shuns others. The "social model" of disability emphasizes how disability is produced by environments that inhibit access to and participation by people with disabilities (see also Clifford-Simplican in this volume). Like their predecessors in the disability rights movement, fat activists seek to disrupt and "queer" these accounts and reveal some of the problematic assumptions of otherwise progressive political projects.

Drawing interesting parallels between the fight against neoliberalism and the fat justice movement, Mollow and McRuer argue that struggles against austerity must engage with critiques grounded in fat justice: "In place of neoliberalism's valorization of personal agency (as in 'losing the weight and keeping it off'), fat justice calls forth a conceptualization of fat agency as a collective mode of acting in the world" (2015, 41). The authors use the term "fattening austerity" in two ways:

> First, like other fat scholars, we employ the word "fattening" in ways that resemble the terms "cripping" (in disability studies) and "queering" (in queer theory); fattening a concept means examining it through the lenses of fat studies and the fat justice movement … Second, since a language of dieting, leanness, and self-sacrifice is frequently invoked in the service of austerity politics—and since, as we shall see, austerity literally makes people go hungry—our phrase "fattening austerity" calls for an end to punitive austerity measures. (25)

Taking fat justice seriously

> not only honors our commitment to seeking justice for oppressed groups;
> it also strengthens our critiques of neoliberalism. At the heart of both fat-
> phobia and neoliberalism is a fantasy of infinite corporeal malleability.
> According to this fantasy, one can be or become whatever one wants, as
> long as one is willing to keep trying, or keep buying. (Mollow 2016, n.p.)

Greater engagement is needed with important intersections—and schisms—between fat activism and feminist and LGBTQ+ activism. In one recent history of fat activism, Charlotte Cooper (2016) discusses some of the feminist movement's historic engagement with fat issues, including a normative preference for certain kinds of feminist bodies. To contend that fat is a feminist issue (see Orbach 2017) is insufficient, Cooper suggests, if overt forms of fat hatred are replaced with kinder, gentler forms of fatpho-bia. Indeed, consumer and capitalist interest in feel-good messaging around body positivity sidesteps important political questions about the structural features of our economies and our polity that privilege particular kinds of bodies.

CONCLUSION

The act of engendering fatness and obesity politics is, admittedly, unfinished and messy. Fatness and obesity are not only gendered, of course; discourses about what constitutes "obesity" operate in a highly medicalized environment that pathologizes deviations from the normatively "healthy" body. Fatness is also tethered to state efforts that seek to regulate unruly bodies and minds, including those of disabled people, racialized individuals, or others who pre-sumably violate the boundaries of acceptable bodily representation. And, of course, excess weight is linked to poor health outcomes, so it is not surpris-ing that in an age of "healthism"—where being healthy and performing the healthy body is a moral imperative— weight management has become a way in which citizens can flex their class-based privilege. After all, the "business" of weight loss demands that individuals have the necessary financial resources to expend in pursuit of a leaner, fitter body.

Narratives that swirl around obesity and fatness are inextricably linked to the affects and emotions they engender and produce. While there are very real and painful experiences of stigma and hatred that are deeply felt by individuals, emotions also defy our attempts to pin them down, to localize and contain them somewhere. Bringing emotions in then requires us to ask what it might mean if we departed from thinking about emotions as always residing either in individuals or collectivities. As Fraser, Maher, and Wright argue, drawing on feminist theorist Sara Ahmed, while there is no shortage of attempts to isolate emotions using an individual calculus or to think about emotions in aggregate terms, we need to shift the focus to a consideration of how emotions are always already present on an ever-shifting landscape or terrain: "Emotion emerges between subjects, and between subjects and society: ... it is in this 'in-between' space that these emotions occur and have their effect" (2010, 204–05).

If we are to challenge the social norms that circulate in these spaces, it will require "having a different affective relation to those norms," not simply replacing bad feeling with good feeling (Ahmed 2004, 196). Shame, for instance, "has a resonance well beyond its homophobic generation, enabling queer subjects both to identify the bodily resonances of a heterosexual status quo, and to create community through empathy and shared experience" (Hemmings 2005, 549–50). One lesson we can draw from this might be to resist the tendency to try to banish certain emotions but instead work to overturn their meanings in ways that challenge the dominance or taken-for-grantedness of knowledge and expertise framed by expert-driven discourses. We can also resist the urgency to replace bad feelings with good feelings. As Ahmed reminds us,

> Feeling better, whatever form it might take, is not about the overcoming of bad feeling, which are effects of histories of violence, but of finding a different relationship to them. It is in the face of all that endures of the past in the present, the pain, the suffering and the rage, that we can open ourselves up, and keep alive the hope that things can be different. (2005, 84)

DISCUSSION QUESTIONS

1. We talk in the popular media about "corporate fat cats," "lean government," or "trimming the fat." How would you describe our cultural fascination with ridding the world of fat? Are these harmless terms or do they tell us something about

how our politics are infused with morally loaded, fatphobic language?

2. Feminists have long struggled for control of their bodies. How does fat discrimination or weight stigma fit into this broader struggle? How do struggles for bodily autonomy intersect with other progressive struggles related to class, race, or disability status?

3. How do you understand the role of emotions in these "turbulent times"? Feminist movements have long struggled for the right to express particular emotions such as anger, especially in the context of current struggles around sexual violence such as the #MeToo movement. In this current context, how do you understand the relationship between gender and emotion?

4. The self-help movement has been a key site of struggle for feminists, urging women to centre their own care in a world in which patriarchal structures position women's needs as peripheral or marginal. How do you understand the diet industry and its insistent focus on weight loss as a sign of success in this regard?

NOTES

1 This chapter was generously supported by an Insight Grant from the Social Sciences and Humanities Research Council of Canada.

2 Barrette was the subject of an online petition demanding a "healthy health minister." Like other victims of fat shaming, Barrette responded to allegations that he was unfit for the job by explaining that he had tried to lose weight, albeit unsuccessfully.

3 For an important historical (and intersectional) discussion of post–World War II obesity discourse, see McPhail (2017).

4 The cover of the Senate report features a large image of a bathroom scale with an arrow pointing past 280 pounds. The report contains several recommendations, including those related to imposing new taxes on sugary drinks and revamping Canada's food guide. The report is silent, however, on issues related to weight stigma or fat bias.

5 I use the term "obesity" because it is how some scientists, advocates, and researchers think about fatness and fat bodies; my use of the term is not meant to suggest that I support the pathologization of fat bodies.

REFERENCES

Ahmed, Sara. 2004. *The Cultural Politics of Emotion*. London: Routledge.
———. 2005. "The Politics of Bad Feeling." *Australasian Journal of Critical Race and Whiteness Studies* 1: 72–85.
Berlant, Lauren. 2007. "Slow Death (Sovereignty, Obesity, Lateral Agency)." *Critical Inquiry* 33 (4): 754–80.
Boswell, John. 2014. "'Hoisted with Our Own Petard': Evidence and Democratic Deliberation on Obesity." *Policy Sciences* 47 (4): 1–14.
Butterfield, Michelle. 2017. "Sarah Hoffman Fat-Shamed by Postmedia Headline." *Huffington Post Alberta*, January 5. https://www.huffingtonpost.ca/2017/01/05/sarah-hoffman-headline_n_13978040.html.
Callahan, Dan. 2013. "Obesity: Chasing an Elusive Epidemic." *Hastings Center Report* 43 (1): 34–40.
Campos, Paul, Abigail Saguy, Paul Ernsberger, Eric Oliver, and Glenn Gaesser. 2006. "The Epidemiology of Overweight and Obesity: Public Health Crisis or Moral Panic?" *International Journal of Epidemiology* 35 (1): 55–60.
Canadian Press. 2018. "Woman Uses Obituary to Advocate against Fat Shaming in Medical Profession." *CBC News*, July 30. https://www.cbc.ca/news/canada/newfoundland-labrador/fat-shaming-medical-1.4766676.
Cooper, Charlotte. 2016. *Fat Activism: A Radical Social Movement*. Bristol: HammerOn Press.
Dobrowolsky, Alexandra. 2008. "The Women's Movement in Flux: Feminism and Framing, Passion, and Politics." In *Group Politics and Social Movements in Canada*, edited by Miriam Smith, 159–80. Toronto: University of Toronto Press.
Ellison, Jenny, Deborah McPhail, and Wendy Mitchinson, eds. 2016. *Obesity in Canada: Critical Perspectives*. Toronto: University of Toronto Press.
Evans, Bethan. 2010. "Anticipating Fatness: Childhood, Affect, and the Pre-Emptive 'War on Obesity.'" *Transactions of the Institute of British Geographers* 35 (1): 21–38.
Farrell, Amy E. 2011. *Fat Shame: Stigma and the Fat Body in American Culture*. New York: New York University Press.
Fraser, Suzanne, JaneMaree Maher, and Jan Wright. 2010. "Between Bodies and Collectivities: Articulating the Action of Emotion in Obesity Epidemic Discourse." *Social Theory and Health* 8 (2): 192–209.
Gould, Deborah. 2009. *Moving Politics: Emotion and ACT UP's Fight against AIDS*. Chicago: University of Chicago Press.
Guthman, Julie. 2009. "Teaching the Politics of Obesity: Insights into Neoliberal Embodiment and Contemporary Biopolitics." *Antipode* 41 (5): 1110–33.
———. 2011. *Weighing In: Obesity, Food Justice, and the Limits of Capitalism*. Berkeley: University of California Press.
Hemmings, Clare. 2005. "Invoking Affect: Cultural Theory and the Ontological Turn." *Cultural Studies* 19 (5): 548–67.

Hochschild, Arlie. 1979. "Emotion Work, Feeling Rules, and Social Structure." *American Journal of Sociology* 85 (3): 551–75.

Jasper, James M. 2006. "Emotions and the Microfoundations of Politics: Rethinking Ends and Means." In *Emotion, Politics and Society,* edited by Simon Clarke, Paul Hoggett, and Simon Thompson, 14–30. London: Palgrave-Macmillan.

Kirkland, Anna. 2008. *Fat Rights: Dilemmas of Difference and Personhood.* New York: New York University Press.

Larner, Wendy. 2000. "Neo-liberalism: Policy, Ideology, Governmentality." *Studies in Political Economy* 63 (1): 5–25.

Lupton, Deborah. 2016. *The Quantified Self: A Sociology of Self-Tracking.* Cambridge: Polity Press.

McPhail, Deborah. 2017. *Contours of the Nation: Making Obesity and Imagining Canada, 1945–1970.* Toronto: University of Toronto Press.

McRuer, Robert. 2018. *Crip Times: Disability, Globalization, and Resistance.* New York: New York University Press.

Mobley, Jennifer-Scott. 2014. "Fat Black Miscegenation." In *Female Bodies on the American Stage,* 97–111. New York: Palgrave Macmillan.

Mollow, Anna. 2016. "The Ninety-Five Percent: Fighting Neoliberalism and Fatphobia Together." *Food, Fatness, and Fitness* (blog), February 2. http://foodfatnessfitness.com/2016/02/02/fighting-neoliberalism-and-fatphobia-together.

Mollow, Anna, and Robert McRuer. 2015. "Fattening Austerity." *Body Politics* 3 (5): 25–49.

"More to Love: Fat Semantics." 2007. *Red No. 3* (blog), August 23. http://red3.blogspot.com/2007/08/more-to-love-fat-semantics.html.

Nicholls, Stuart. 2013. "Standards and Classification: A Perspective on the 'Obesity Epidemic.'" *Social Science and Medicine* 87: 9–15.

Nutter, Sarah, Angela S. Alberga, Cara MacInnis, John H. Ellard, and Shelly Russell-Mayhew. 2018. "Framing Obesity a Disease: Indirect Effects of Affect and Controllability Beliefs on Weight Bias." *International Journal of Obesity* 42: 1804–11. https://doi.org/10.1038/s41366-018-0110-5.

Orbach, Susie. 2017. *Fat Is a Feminist Issue.* Random House/Penguin Books.

Orsini, Michael. 2016. "You Can't Fight Obesity without Tackling Fat Shaming." *Globe and Mail,* March 17.

Orsini, Michael, and Sarah Wiebe. 2014. "Between Hope and Fear: Comparing the Emotional Landscapes of the Autism Movement in Canada and the United States." In *Comparing Canada,* edited by Luc Turgeon, Jennifer Wallner, Martin Papillon, and Stephen White, 147–67. Vancouver: UBC Press.

Power, Elaine. 2016. "Fat Children, Failed (Future) Consumer-Citizens, and Mothers' Duties in Neoliberal Consumer Society." In *Neoliberal Governance and Health: Duties, Risks, and Vulnerabilities,* edited by Jessica Polzer and Elaine Power, 43–65. Montreal: McGill-Queen's University Press.

Puhl, Rebecca, and Chelsea A. Heuer. 2009. "The Stigma of Obesity: A Review and Update." *Obesity* 17: 941–64.

Rail, Genevieve, Dave Holmes, and Stuart J. Murray. 2010. "The Politics of Evidence on 'Domestic Terrorists': Obesity Discourses and Their Effects." *Social Theory and Health* 8 (3): 259–79.

Ramos Salas, Ximena. 2018. "The Dichotomy of Obesity and Fat Acceptance Narratives." *Weighty Matters* (blog), July 5. http://www.weightymatters.ca /2018/07/guest-post-highlighting-how-fat.html.

Saguy, Abigail C., and Kevin W. Riley. 2005. "Weighing Both Sides: Morality, Mortality, and Framing Contests over Obesity." *Journal of Health Politics, Policy and Law* 30 (5): 869–921.

Sanders, Rachel. 2017. "The Color of Fat: Racializing Obesity, Recuperating Whiteness, and Reproducing Injustice." *Politics, Groups, and Identities* 7 (2): 287–304. https://doi.org/10.1080/21565503.2017.1354039.

Senate of Canada. 2016. "Obesity in Canada: A Whole-of-Society Approach for a Healthier Canada." March. Senate Standing Committee on Social Affairs, Science, and Technology. https://sencanada.ca/content/sen/committee/421/SOCI /Reports/2016-02-25_Revised_report_Obesity_in_Canada_e.pdf.

Townend, Louise. 2009. "The Moralizing of Obesity: A New Name for an Old Sin?" *Critical Social Policy* 29 (2): 171–90.

Urback, Robyn. 2015. "The Cheap, Lazy Attack on Alberta Health Minister Sarah Hoffman's Weight." *National Post*, June 5. http://nationalpost.com/opinion/robyn -urback-the-cheap-lazy-attack-on-alberta-health-minister-sarah-hoffmans-weight.

Ward, Anna E. 2013. "Fat Bodies/Thin Critique: Animating and Absorbing Fat Embodiments." *Scholar and Feminist Online* 11 (3). http://sfonline.barnard.edu /life-un-ltd-feminism-bioscience-race/fat-bodiesthin-critique-animating-and -absorbing-fat-embodiments.

FURTHER READING

Farrell, Amy E. 2011. *Fat Shame: Stigma and the Fat Body in American Culture*. New York: New York University Press.

Guthman, Julie. 2009. "Teaching the Politics of Obesity: Insights into Neoliberal Embodiment and Contemporary Biopolitics." *Antipode* 41 (5): 1110–33.

Mollow, Anna. 2014. "Disability Studies Gets Fat." *Hypatia: Journal of Feminist Philosophy* 30 (1): 199–216.

———. 2016. "The Ninety-Five Percent: Fighting Neoliberalism and Fatphobia Together." *Food, Fatness, and Fitness* (blog), February 2. http:// foodfatnessfitness.com/2016/02/02/fighting-neoliberalism-and-fatphobia -together.

17

The "Alt" Right, Toxic Masculinity, and Violence

John Grant and Fiona MacDonald

Key terms: alternative right, ethno-state, hegemonic masculinity, manosphere, populism

The politics of masculinity are now front and centre in mainstream society. The Toronto "incel" attack in 2018, the Halifax Proud Boys protest of an Indigenous ceremony in 2017, and Donald Trump's US presidential campaign and election victory in 2016 were key events in positioning the topic of masculinity publicly in new and unprecedented ways. All of these actors and events reflect a similar kind of toxic masculinity often associated with traditional notions of being a man— that is, a narrow and constraining understanding of masculinity primarily characterized by dominance, aggression, strength, sexual conquest, and the rejection of any traits or behaviours associated with femininity. At the same time, we are witnessing a kind of turbulence as some men in politics challenge traditional notions of masculinity. Prime Minister Justin Trudeau and his unapologetic (if largely symbolic) feminism have been lauded internationally for promoting a new kind of masculine strength on the world stage. Trudeau's gender presentation is also central in the discourse of his political opponents. As Sabin argues: "The Conservative attack ads with taglines like 'nice hair though' and 'he's in way over his head' were designed to make Trudeau the butt of a masculine joke" by making "both implicit and explicit connections between Trudeau's masculinity and his fitness for government" (2016, n.p). A similar tactic was employed by Trump following the 2018 G7 meetings in tweets describing the Canadian prime minister as "meek," "mild," and "weak" (Tasker 2018, n.p.).

Clearly, masculinity matters in politics. Yet, while sociologists (Connell 2005; Kimmel 2013; Hearn 2014) have been researching the societal impact(s) of various masculinities over the last two decades, the discipline of political science has been relatively silent on the complex ways that masculinities impact the political sphere (MacDonald 2017). This omission is a significant gap in the political science scholarship and is particularly problematic for feminist political scientists and feminist political praxis. As Hebert argues: "Empowering individual women through building a sense of personal efficacy and independence may be possible in the absence of attention to men, but transforming the social structures that sanction and sustain masculinism and its damaging manifestations is not" (2007, 41). Hebert's position highlights a harsh reality for contemporary feminists: feminism(s) will be limited in both reach and impact if feminist theory and praxis fail to engage with the complexities of men and masculinities.

This chapter explores the politics of masculinity and masculinism by considering and reflecting on the complex interplay between dominant notions of "being a man" and far-right political movements, most notably those associated with the **alternative right**.[1] While it is important to recognize that there are women involved in alt-right organizations, this does not undermine the foundational role masculinism plays in alt-right ideology. As Childs and Webb argue, there is a big difference between a "feminized" (i.e., includes women) and a "feminist" (i.e., actively pursues feminist projects) political party or organization (2012, 6). While many alternative right women would eschew a feminist identity in most contexts, those who do publicly identify as conservative feminists typically advocate a politics based on some kind of return to a traditional socio-political order founded on a masculine public sphere and a feminized private sphere. Thus, the participation of women in the alt-right demonstrates feminization that is, in many ways, at odds with feminism.

As we explain below, we regard far-right or alternative right movements as deeply and regressively populist. Our depiction of **populism** reveals it to be the predominant political vehicle for masculinity, while masculinity stands as a quotidian expression of populism. It follows that masculinity is central to understanding how men become involved in alternative right movements and it is equally central to understanding how they might get out of them. In particular, we focus on the dominant and protest masculinities that coalesce in the alt-right, as revealed by the 2016 US presidential election and related events both in Canada and abroad. Providing a convincing counter-narrative to these masculinities is central to diminishing the popularity of the alt-right. Doing so contributes to an immediate political goal of reducing two kinds of violence: the multiple forms of violence that members of the alternative right commit upon others, especially racialized, Indigenous, and LGBTQIA2S+ persons, as well as cisgender male allies; and the violence they commit upon themselves to keep their version of masculinity intact.

WHAT IS THE ALT-RIGHT?

The alternative right is reshaping much of our current political landscape and discourse. Defining the alternative right is a complex task both epistemologically and ethically because the foundation of contemporary alt-right movements is racism. It is possible that by using the innocent-sounding term "alt-right" rather than a more politically explicit term like "white supremacist movement," we inadvertently grant legitimacy to the innocuous framing of the movement's politics. The alt-right is indeed a movement founded on racism. In using the term "alt-right" we do not want to diminish its white supremacist nature. However, in using the term we are trying to highlight important distinctions between the alt-right and other right-wing political movements. Hawley discusses these and other complexities in his book *Making Sense of the Alt-Right*. Hawley argues:

> At this point the racist nature of the Alt-Right is well known, and ... I am not using the term to downplay this element of the movement. Relying exclusively on the umbrella term "white supremacist" would furthermore mask the ways the Alt-Right differs from other manifestations of the racial right. The Alt-Right is unlike any racist movement we have ever seen. It is atomized, amorphous, predominantly online, and mostly anonymous. Although it remains small, it is growing. And it was energized by Donald Trump's presidential campaign. (2017, 3)

Like Hawley, we claim that there is good reason to study the alternative right as a distinct entity in contemporary politics. At the same time, it is important to underline that the alt-right arises out of a particular context, in "turbulent times," and is neither monolithic nor static. There is no reliable survey data available on membership or affiliation and, given the alt-right's use of anonymity, irony, vicious online attacks, trolling, and misinformation, it is difficult to truly know the size, demographics, or the full landscape of alt-right political positions.

Despite the absence of membership numbers, the significance of the alt-right is evidenced not only by the Trump presidency but also in other political events both domestic and international. For example, the violence in Charlottesville, Virginia, between alt-right groups and anti-fascist protestors in August 2017; the UK's 2016 Brexit referendum and the racist contributions of the United Kingdom Independence Party (UKIP); the increasing electoral success of Marine Le Pen in France in 2017; the continued rise of media personalities associated with the alt-right such as Ann Coulter in the United States and Rebel Media's Katie Hopkins and Ezra Levant in Canada (Houpt 2017); and the increasing publicity of "incels" or involuntarily celibate men who respond with an intense misogyny towards all women and especially those who have relationships with men who are regarded as strong or powerful.

These developments cannot simply be understood as more extreme versions of conservatism. In fact, the rejection of mainstream or "establishment" conservatism is a central tenet of the alternative right: "Whereas earlier right-wing critics of the conservative movement wanted a seat at the conservative table, the alt-right wants to displace conservatism entirely and bring a new brand of right-wing politics into the mainstream" (Hawley 2017, 7). Nagle also argues for the newness of the alternative right, particularly its online "culture war" tactics:

> Those who argue that the new right-wing sensibility online today is just more of the same old right are wrong. Although it is constantly changing, in this important early stage of its appeal, its ability to assume the aesthetics of counterculture, transgression and nonconformity tell us many things about the nature of its appeal and about the liberal establishment it defines itself against. It has more in common with the 1968 left's slogan "It is forbidden to forbid!" than it does with anything most recognize as part of any traditionalist right" (2017, 28). Thus, the alternative right is indeed new in many ways. Still, while there is much that is distinct about today's alt-right politics, these movements also draw on a sense of threat to status and belonging that is consistent with older white supremacist movements. At the core of this anxiety and perception of threat is a kind

of "American identitarianism" defined by the Southern Poverty Law
Center as "a version of an ideology popular in Europe that emphasizes
cultural and racial homogeneity within different countries. (n.d., n.p.)

The alt-right has also given new energy to long-standing conflicts between
nostalgic nationalism and decolonization and/or reconciliation in settler
societies. Again, the Proud Boys' disruption of an Indigenous ceremony at a
statue of Governor Cornwallis is an important Canadian example. Cornwallis
is known both for founding the city of Halifax and for having done so in part
through his 1749 "Scalping Proclamation," which paid a bounty to anyone who
killed a Mi'kmaq child or adult. As Pam Palmater argues, while the alt-right
is the latest popular vehicle for this kind of nationalism, the racism itself is
not new but rather "an unveiling of the white nationalist thought upon which
both Canadian and American governments and societies were built" (2017,
n.p.). Certain reactions to the City of Victoria's decision to remove a statue
of Sir John A. Macdonald also fit Palmater's argument, along with some in
the American South regarding the removal of statues of Confederate soldiers
from the Civil War (Shakeri 2018; Wilson 2017).

One way that the alt-right's white nationalism is different from older white
supremacist groups such as the Ku Klux Klan is that its racism can be made to
seem less overt, for example, by having its advocates assume the look of white-
collar professionals who use academic and scientific language (Neiwert 2017,
220–23). KKK-style lynching has largely disappeared, though the number of
Black and Indigenous men who are involved in attacks by police and subject
to incarceration is highly disproportionate (see Thompson in this volume).
Such violence relies on arguments about the racial and cultural superiority of
whites. The immediate implication—which is often made explicit anyway—is
that the inferiority of non-whites is the leading cause of everything from social
and moral decay to economic struggles. Much of the alt-right identifies the
only permanent solution as an **ethno-state** populated exclusively by whites
of a particular cultural background, hence its opposition to any immigrants
who do not fit a very narrow profile, to virtually all refugees, and to non-
Christians (especially Muslims and Jews), and its desire to "secure its borders" by methods such as building walls. In addition to its xenophobia, other
prominent alt-right political positions include strong support for free-market
capitalism domestically, tempered by scepticism towards free trade and dislike
for multinational corporations, especially foreign ones; unwavering nationalism; antipathy towards supporting international organizations like the United

Nations or NATO; and a strong law and order agenda including harsh prison sentences and the death penalty. Unlike previous versions of the far-right, the alt-right has established institutional footholds through electoral politics (e.g., Trump, Doug Ford's culture-war politics in Ontario, and UKIP). Collectively, these positions, in addition to the at times explicit or implicit racism, amount to a muscular, bullying politics that is highly masculine.

CONCEPTUALIZING HEGEMONIC MASCULINITY

Masculinity is often referred to as a singular thing despite the many variations of masculinities that exist. Analytically, we treat masculinity and femininity as the same: sets of practices and norms that involve our bodies and what is done with and to them, without those practices and norms being reducible to our bodies and especially not to biology. As Connell rightly puts it: "Gender exists precisely to the extent that biology does *not* determine the social" (2005, 71). What distinguishes masculinities and femininities is how they fit into our overall system of gender and its ordering of our social practices. Complex gender hierarchies exist that are historically durable, on the one hand, while being open to contestation and change thanks to shifting ideas and material circumstances on the other. Thus, it is correct to say that systems of male privilege have dominated in the West for hundreds of years *and* that struggles to rewrite the gender system are destabilizing the straightforward reproduction of those privileges. But what does this general historical reality mean for contemporary masculinities and the alt-right?

One of the ongoing controversies in gender studies is whether something called **hegemonic masculinity** is a useful concept and, indeed, whether it exists in the real world at all. Hegemony refers to the dominant social position occupied by a specific group of people, a position that is enjoyed thanks to a significant, though not unlimited, degree of cultural legitimacy. To possess hegemonic power means being able to rely largely on non-coercive means to sustain that power. Connell describes hegemonic masculinity as "the configuration of gender practice which embodies the currently accepted answer to the problem of the legitimacy of patriarchy, which guarantees (or is taken to guarantee) the dominant position of men and the subordination of women" (2005, 77). In Connell's view, hegemony combines cultural dominance with institutional power so that the top echelons of business, government, and the military are most likely to house hegemonic masculinity (see Eichler in this volume). Elsewhere, she takes "transnational business masculinity" (defined by egocentrism, conditional loyalties, limited responsibilities to others, and libertarian sexuality) as the hegemonic form in the late-twentieth and twenty-first centuries (2000, 51–52).

The concept of hegemonic masculinity has benefits. By offering analytical specificity regarding what version of masculinity is most dominant, it allows for a focused challenge to hegemonic assumptions. However, the potential drawbacks are considerable. Connell admits that we risk turning hegemonic masculinity into an inflexible stereotype that resists investigating how every man's masculinity involves compromises and tensions between different masculinities (2000, 23, 219; Garlick 2016, 35–39). Moreover, hegemonic masculinity should not be conflated with patriarchal rule or "masculinism," generally speaking. The latter refers to the dominance of men over women in general, whereas the former involves a very specific group of men that are dominant not only in comparison to women but to all other men and their subordinate masculinities as well. In our view, if the concept of hegemonic masculinity is to be helpful, it should be used more loosely than Connell would like. Beyond acknowledging that multiple masculinities will contribute to every man's identity, this involves seeing masculinity as a hybrid product that is context dependent: the dominant form of masculinity can and will change depending on the setting, which means that there is no one dominant version.

Our loosening of the strict boundaries that accompany the concept of hegemonic masculinity is not meant to downplay the existence of the "patriarchal dividend" that most men enjoy to one degree or another. For example, the typical benefits that men enjoy simply thanks to being men rather than women include higher wages and lower unemployment rates, increased chances of reaching positions of institutional power (government, economy, military, media), the ability to rely on women's labour in the home, superior cultural regard, and the expectation of sexual access to women (see Craig in this volume), any and all of which can rely on the threat of violence. The patriarchal dividend is distributed unevenly, however, and groups like gay or non-white men (in North America) receive fewer benefits. This is particularly interesting in the context of the alt-right because it views the patriarchal dividend as having disappeared, and it would say the same thing about what we can call the "cultural dividend," namely the intrinsic benefits to being white. It is essential, then, to investigate how real material and cultural changes in people's lives are combined with perceptions of such changes, along with their implications for masculinities and the alt-right.

MASCULINITIES AND THE ALT-RIGHT

In addition to hegemonic masculinities, other categories include subordinate, marginalized, complicit, and protest masculinities. None of these masculinities exists independently of the others; rather, they are products of the interaction between different men. For example, gay men will often be regarded (by others and themselves) as possessing a subordinate masculinity, one that does not measure up to the stereotypical masculinity of a heterosexual man (Connell 2000, 30). In a white-dominant context, non-white men will often possess marginalized masculinities—ones that are not palpably different from those that are more dominant, except that a clear social marker (in this case, race) symbolizes why such men are not worthy of the same status. Woodhams, Lupton, and Cowling's findings are illustrative here. Their research shows that men who work in female-dominated areas of employment are disproportionately drawn from disadvantaged groups of men, "specifically in relation to minority ethnicity and disability" (2015, 277). Their research clearly demonstrates that ethnic minority men and men with disabilities are far less likely than other men to "ride the glass escalator to higher-level work" (425).

Complicit masculinities are those that are non- or subdominant, yet still benefit from the existing gender system without being inclined to offer significant vocal support for it or resistance to it. Often these are "average" men who are non-violent, assist their wives with housework and contribute to parenting, and enjoy "manly" activities (e.g., sports) without being particularly good at them (Connell 2005, 79–80). Finally, recall the importance of context: within the gay community there will be dominant and marginalized masculinities, just as there will be in various racial communities and within different economic classes.

The masculinities we find in the alt-right are better understood if we consider some of the long-term social trends that have changed Western societies in the post–World War II era. They include the following: (1) the evolution of the family structure; (2) women's increased participation in higher education (both as students and teachers) and in the workforce; (3) the growing commitment by government (still very much a work in progress) to treat people equally, which takes a variety of forms, from rights legislation and multiculturalism to affirmative action plans, anti-discrimination laws, and official reconciliation with Indigenous Peoples; (4) increasing acceptance of the idea that women's sexuality is active rather than passive; (5) increasing acceptance of gay, lesbian, queer, and transgender individuals; (6) growing influence of women and non-whites in cultural fields or activities, such as the media, sports, and music industries; and (7) movement towards a post-industrial economy.

Whether individually or collectively, none of these changes have put an end to male dominance. What has happened is that the taken-for-granted legitimacy of white male domination and privilege is questioned more often. This is confirmed by the very existence of the alt-right and its growing resistance towards what it sees as the illegitimate loss of white male privilege. We can turn to the 2016 US presidential election voter behaviour literature to see this impact. As Schaffner, MacWilliams, and Nteta (2017) demonstrate, voter behaviour was strongly influenced by attitudes of sexism and racism. Despite much political rhetoric and media framing to the contrary, the gap in voting behaviour between whites with college education and whites without college education is not well explained by economic differences or anxieties (i.e., the "left behind" thesis) but rather best understood as the outcome of sexism and racism. The left behind thesis is also debunked by Mutz, who documents overwhelming evidence that the central motivation behind Trump support was a perception of status threat among dominant or "high-status" groups, which in her research includes those who fall into one or more of the following categories: white, Christian, and male (2018, 1). Similarly, Bartels and Cramer (2018) document a longer-term trend (1965–97) showing how white Americans become more conservative as their economic well-being increases rather than when it decreases. The perception of a status threat fuels a politics of "aggrieved entitlement," a reactionary perspective Kimmel describes as "that sense that those benefits to which you believed yourself entitled have been snatched away from you by unforeseen forces larger and more powerful" (2013, 18). Women can also be drawn towards this view. More than 40 per cent of women who voted in the 2016 election supported Trump. Analysis from Setzler and Yanus reveals that sexism and racial bias had a "virtually identical" influence on voters of both genders (2018, 525).

These insights about the significance of social status compared to economic well-being mean that the alt-right cuts across economic class. As Kimmel puts it, white anger "knows no class nor originates in a specific class" (2013, 13).

Consequently, the alt-right stands as an uncommon example of protest masculinities overlapping from multiple class locations, especially middle- and upper-class positions, where men are much more likely to possess dominant or hegemonic masculinities. In other words, dominant masculinities and protest masculinities can not only co-exist, they can be one in the same thing depending on the circumstance. In this instance, there is no choice but to depart from Connell's description of the political contradictions that define protest masculinity: "It builds on a working-class masculine ethic of solidarity. But this is a solidarity that divides the group from the rest of the working class. The loss of the economic basis of masculine authority leads to a divided consciousness—egalitarianism *and* misogyny—not to a new political direction" (2005, 117–18). We assert two important differences: the declining economic basis of masculine authority is not a dominant explanatory factor; and, contrary to Connell's view about protest masculinity in general, the alt-right *does* lead to a new political direction, one that arrived most obviously with Donald Trump's electoral success and aspects of his political agenda. The alt-right's masculinist outlook is fundamentally one of emasculation and loss. The following quotation from *National Vanguard*, an American neo-Nazi magazine, captures the extent to which emasculation is thought to have occurred:

> As Northern males have continued to become more wimpish, the result of the media-created image of the "new male"—more pacifist, less authoritarian, more "sensitive," less competitive, more androgynous, less possessive—the controlled media, the homosexual lobby and the feminist movement have cheered ... The number of effeminate males has increased greatly ... legions of sissies and weaklings, of flabby, limp-wristed, non-aggressive, non-physical, indecisive, slack-jawed, fearful males who, while still heterosexual in theory and practice, have not even a vestige of the old macho spirit, so deprecated today, left in them. (quoted in Kimmel 2013, 256–57)

We contend that these sentiments are widely shared within the alt-right and among wider conservative circles; what matters is the degree to which they are held, which goes some way to determining how militant one's political response will be. Additionally, those responses can be both aspirational (restoring what has been lost) and aggressively protective (guarding what remains). Nothing prevents either of those sentiments from including economic concerns, though cultural grievances play a greater role. The passage from *National Vanguard* does not mention immigrants (and particularly non-white and illegal immigrants) or increased cultural diversity, but they too are central to the alt-right's story of cultural antagonism and loss across anglophone democracies. In the case of the United States, we can add America's defeat in the Vietnam War, the terrorist attacks on American soil against the World Trade Center on September 1, 2001, and Amerca's long-running difficulties in the Middle East and Afghanistan (both pre- and post-9/11) to explain a more general sense that America's masculine traits of power and control are in decline.

The alt-right's narrative is powerful on its own. What makes it a movement is its ability to offer solidarity and a sense of belonging to those who are open to alt-right views. It brings people together (more often virtually and in their own heads rather than physically) for a common cause. Aggrieved entitlement underpins that cause and it is easy to imagine that the result is a very simplistic and nasty kind of politics. The reality may not be far from this, but it is also more complex. Consider Kimmel's insight: "Masculinity is not ... the experience of power; it is the experience of entitlement to power" (2000, 241). Deep down, some members of the alt-right know that not every man can achieve their masculine ideal; but they feel entitled to have the opportunity to do so and that the lack of opportunity constitutes widespread emasculation. Members of the alt-right can even defend egalitarian views—an equal playing field for everyone with no special treatment for women, minorities, or foreigners—that in turn are used to justify hatred towards those same groups. For example, the problem is not necessarily with women or Blacks or immigrants per se (though it is for some), but with feminists, advocates of affirmative action, and immigrant and Indigenous activists. They are the ones who have challenged the status quo and traditional masculinity along with it. This alt-right view is why we think the connection between the alt-right and populism is such a strong one.

THE ALT-RIGHT AND POPULISM

For members of the alt-right, one of the functions that its toxic masculinism serves is to disguise or cover up the fact that these men are, variously, *unsure* of their own masculine qualities, *uncertain* about what masculinity requires of them, and *insecure* about their present social standing and future hopes. Toxic masculinity is thus itself split between its outward presentation of uniform strength and dominance and its motivating (and hence, unresolved) core of uncertainty, doubt, suspicion, and resentment.

What forms of politics are associated with alt-right masculinity? We think that the alt-right has encouraged a toxic form of authoritarian populism that in turn has supported the alt-right's growth. Some scholars have associated populism with progressive movements (Grattan 2016) but the dominant position, which we support, is that populism—especially the more successful versions recently—more often breeds regressive and even authoritarian politics (Urbinati 1998). The literature on populism is vast and cannot be summarized here. The most basic feature of populism is that it privileges "the people" and their will as the most authentic features of politics. Populists wish to reassert the primacy of that will, which they believe has been thwarted by a variety of other actors, such as political and economic elites, minority groups, international political organizations, and multinational corporations. Consequently, populists happily include those people who are devoted to their vision of the people, the culture, and the nation to which they belong, while readily seeking to exclude those who fail such a test. Authoritarian populist movements and the alt-right are both adept, then, at recruiting members from a variety of social backgrounds, although this should not be mistaken as intersectional in a feminist sense: the latter is devoted to social justice, while the former oppose it. For us, populism is also symptomatic: in times when its strength is on the rise, we should be able to identify trends associated with increased narratives of social stress.

The alt-right and authoritarian populism share affinities regarding their views of the past and the present, along with how to secure their desired future. The past is recalled with great reverence as a time of natural social order when success was available to all who would work for it. Whether such a time ever existed scarcely matters—it is the *perception* of an uncorrupted past that does the work. Present-day nostalgia stems from the loss of that past, and from the disappointment and hurt that it is no longer available. Populist and alt-right politics are reclamation projects: they aim to restore a past that has been lost.

Authoritarian populism offers a natural political vehicle for toxic masculinity, while toxic masculinity provides an everyday home for populist sentiments. More specifically, the dominant populist vision of the people (Grant 2020) and the alt-right's conception of masculinity and the gender system mirror one another in three explicitly political ways. First, the idea of the people as an organic and homogenous body mirrors the alt-right view, not just of masculinity, but of gender itself as a set of natural features that must be kept intact. Second, the idea of an authentic people generates populism's moralism, which is what it uses to decide who counts as the people and who does not. The gendered reality of populism and the alt-right is especially noticeable here. Certain individuals (white, non-elite, non-immigrant) who would normally belong to the people can end up being excluded if they are regarded by populists as being too liberal, too inclusive, and too tolerant of people's identity choices. In short, they are too feminine to qualify as defenders of the people and their culture.

Finally, populists wish to establish an "identity-lock" between themselves and the state. The aims of the people and the actions of the state should be identical. In contrast, there are those who think it is politically attractive (and potentially unavoidable) for a tension to exist between the state and the people who live in it. Any large population is a heterogeneous collection of people who give authority to the state to act in their interests. Just like the people themselves, political interests are diverse. Thus, different groups present the state with contrasting political demands that cannot be brought together into a cohesive, singular political program that suits everyone. What exists is a dialectic where the people and the state engage in a relationship of mutual support *and* opposition. These contrasting outlooks map onto two competing views of gender. The essentialism inherent in populist identity-lock (there is but one legitimate, true, natural position to occupy) is the same lens that leads to the alt-right's unbending views on gender, whereas the dialectic of indeterminacy that ensures distance is maintained between the people and the state can be aligned with understandings of gender that accommodate aspects of social construction. In other words, gender, like the people–state relationship, changes according to circumstances and resists being reduced to a singular essence that persists throughout time.

TOXIC MASCULINITY AND VIOLENCE

The masculinist politics of aggrieved entitlement, exemplified by contemporary alt-right politics, is deeply violent on multiple levels, both physically and psychologically. As Aoláin, Cahn, and Haynes observe: "Violence may literally 'make the man' in many societies" (2013, 131). While a comprehensive overview of toxic masculinities and violence is beyond the scope of this chapter, the complex connections between the two are well evidenced by the hypermasculine role of the military in many contexts (see Eichler in this volume).

The underlying philosophy and actions of the military are fundamentally constituted by an ideology of male toughness and the establishment and maintenance of manhood through dominance and/or conquest: "Violence on the largest possible scale is the purpose of the military; and no arena has been more important for the definition of hegemonic masculinity in European/American culture" (Connell 2005, 213). The impact of this ideology goes far beyond the military per se as the violent enactment of masculinity does not end with the completion of one's military duty, whether at home or abroad: "Once the official conflict ends, men who have acted militarily and the (generally) male political elite are deeply enmeshed in this cultural vision of manhood" (Aoláin, Cahn, and Haynes 2013, 130). While it is difficult to confirm claims (Kimmel 2013, 243) that a significant portion of the alt-right is made up of military veterans, we know that the number of armed far-right militia chapters is on the rise, up by as much as 65 per cent (from 165 to 273) in 2017 (Beirich and Buchanan 2018). As Johnson explains, far-right movements specifically target both military and law enforcement personnel for a variety of reasons, including their combat, weapons, and surveillance training; their disciplined way of life; leadership skills; and access to weapons, equipment, and sensitive and/or classified information (2012, 9).

This militant reactionary politics is evidenced not just by alt-right rallies, marches, and other political events but also in the popularization of its discourse, public displays of racist imagery, and various acts of violence that transgress the public-private divide, including gay bashing, domestic violence, and rape. As Connell argues, men involved in these acts of targeted violence often perceive themselves as "avengers on behalf of society" who are "punishing betrayers of manhood" and, in so doing, working to return society to its proper order (2005, 213). Central to understanding these phenomena is the relational nature of gender. From this perspective, the crux of gender injustice lies in the relations between various gendered agents who are asymmetrically constrained and/or enabled by their gender. Change in any one dimension creates tensions that impact other dimensions. This relationality explains why women and marginalized men "often bear the brunt of the flux in masculine roles" (Connell 2005, 132; Connell 2012, 1677).

Threats of physical violence, sexual violence, and psychological violence via tactics such as online trolling and cyberbullying (see Small in this volume) also dominate the so-called **manosphere**. This term is used quite broadly in popular discourse and refers to a variety of groups and organizations, including men's rights activists focused on issues of fathers' rights or men's health, and blatantly misogynistic groupings of "pick up artists," "incels," and "red pill" revolutionaries (Nagle 2017; Nicholas and Agius 2018). These groups may or may not be directly linked to alt-right organizations but they share the same roots and much of the same anti-feminist and misogynist worldviews.

Some of the most high-profile actions taken up by various manosphere actors were the events of #GamerGate in 2014. These events started with a blog post by Eron Gjoni in which he accused his ex-girlfriend and game developer, Zoe Quinn, of cheating on him. This post resulted in intense cyberbullying and abuse against Quinn and her family, including threats of rape and death. Quinn was also "doxxed"—her personal information was shared widely online (Nagle 2017, 22). The attacks soon went beyond Quinn to include other feminist gamers and scholars, including game developer Brianna Wu and feminist cultural critic Anita Sarkeesian. Both Wu and Sarkeesian received numerous rape and death threats and were also doxxed. In October 2014, Sarkeesian made international headlines after she cancelled a speaking engagement at Utah State University due to an anonymous threat of a mass shooting unless the event was cancelled (Todd 2015, 64).

In many ways, these events foreshadowed the 2016 US election. Proponents of #GamerGate framed their actions as "a defense of free speech and journalistic ethics and against political correctness" (Lyons, quoted in Nicholas and Aguis 2018, 48). The same discourses, tactics, and public figures also came to dominate in Trump's campaign and provided much of the foundation for his alt-right support. Thus, the manosphere is a central space for the development of toxic masculinist ideology and the practice of symbolic and physical violence, both of which have become central in the growth of the alternative right. As such, the manosphere has proven a significant site for contemporary politics.

It is important to acknowledge that toxic masculinity is also a key factor in understanding men's violence(s) directed at the self. Men suffer psychological harm when they continually fail to live up to the expectations of masculinism and the narrow masculinities that remain dominant in society. Masculinity is increasingly recognized as an important factor in understanding many contemporary social issues that reflect a kind of violation of the self. In British Columbia, for example, men accounted for 80 per cent of the 935 fatal opioid overdoses in 2016 (Kassam 2017, n.p.). Men also have a high rate of reported death by suicide when compared with women in almost all parts of the world. The male suicide rate is about three times that of women, with the suicide rate for Canadian men peaking in the 40–50 age range (Bilsker and White 2011). These statistics suggest that men's expectations for themselves to be strong, unemotional risk takers have many social and political costs that have yet to be fully explored or understood.

These findings also support the notion that many men will benefit from a decentring of masculinism. From this perspective, the evolution and broadening of women's social roles need not contribute to increased anxiety and anger among men. Instead, it offers a shared opportunity to contest hegemonic breadwinner or "strong silent type" understandings of manhood and boyhood; that is, "boys will be boys" (see Rollo in this volume). In their place, alternative understandings and practices of masculinities can accommodate a greater focus on care work and service to others.[2]

CONCLUSION

In this chapter, we have highlighted some of the most significant impacts masculinism and the various competing and contradictory masculinities are having on contemporary politics. While our primary focus has been on the complex interactions between the alt-right, toxic masculinity, and violence, we hope to have offered some insight into how the politics of masculinity is also central to challenging these current political developments. Political science is only just beginning to engage with these topics and we hope to have demonstrated the need for more work on men as gendered subjects in our discipline, particularly feminist work that is centred on the relational and intersectional nature of gender. This work is crucial for those interested in challenging the alt-right and transforming the current political terrain. Instead of seeing feminism as a threat to male privilege, a transformative approach emphasizes how it relieves men from the burden of living up to stereotypes of traditional masculinity. Rather than regarding immigration as an attack on the status quo, a transformative politics articulates its economic, social, and political benefits and emphasizes the diversity of all cultures. Rather than viewing free speech as an opportunity to say anything about anybody, a transformative politics draws on free speech debates to discuss the role that words play in civic life. Thus, while contemporary politics is indeed turbulent, this instability also brings many opportunities to further develop and articulate transformative feminisms.

DISCUSSION QUESTIONS

1. Is there any point at which democracies can legitimately exclude certain kinds of politics? If so, what is the justification?
2. Can men and women be more than just allies in combating the alt-right? Can men be just as feminist as women?
3. In what ways do traditional and social media reinforce or challenge the political views associated with the alt-right and hegemonic masculinities?
4. What strategies are best to pursue the transformation of hegemonic masculinities?

NOTES

1 Arthur Brittan (1989) provides a useful distinction between masculinism and masculinities that is consistent with our approach: "While 'masculinity ... is always local and subject to change ... what does not easily change is the justification of and naturalization of male power; that is, what remains relatively constant is the masculine ideology'" (quoted in Nicholas and Aguis 2018, 5).
2 It is worth noting recent scholarship that challenges the widely accepted premise that social spending in care services, welfare, and social development is a "drain" on the economy. Cohen's analysis suggests the opposite. In the Canadian case, it is the reduction in government social spending as a proportion to GDP that puts a drag on the economy (2017, 309).

REFERENCES

Aoláin, Fionnuala Ni, Naomi Cahn, and Dina Haynes. 2013. "Gender, Masculinities and Transition in Conflicted Societies." In *Exploring Masculinities: Feminist Legal Theory Reflections*, edited by Martha Albertson Fineman and David Thomson, 127–43. Surrey, UK: Ashgate.
Bartels, Larry, and Katherine Cramer. 2018. "White People Get More Conservative When They Move Up—Not Down—Economically." *Washington Post*, May 14. https://www.washingtonpost.com/news/monkey-cage/wp/2018/05/14/heres -the-evidence-white-people-grew-more-conservative-when-they-moved-up-not -down-economically.
Beirich, Heidi, and Susy Buchanan. 2018. "2017: The Year in Hate and Extremism." Southern Poverty Law Center, February 11. https://www.splcenter.org/fighting -hate/intelligence-report/2018/2017-year-hate-and-extremism.
Bilsker, Dan, and Jennifer White. 2011. "The Silent Epidemic of Male Suicide." *British Columbia Medical Journal* 53 (10): 529–34.

Childs, Sarah, and Paul Webb. 2012. *Sex, Gender, and the Conservative Party: From Iron Lady to Kitten Heels*. New York: Palgrave Macmillan.

Cohen, Marjorie Griffen. 2017. "Using Information about Gender and Climate Change to Inform Green Economic Policies." In *Climate Change and Gender in Rich Countries: Work, Public Policy and Action*, edited by Marjorie Griffen Cohen, 297–314. New York: Routledge.

Connell, R.W. 2000. *The Men and the Boys*. Berkeley: University of California Press.

———. 2005. *Masculinities*. 2nd ed. Berkeley: University of California Press.

———. 2012. "Gender, Health, and Theory: Conceptualizing the Issue, in Local and World Perspective." *Social Science & Medicine* 74 (11): 1675–83.

Garlick, Steve. 2016. *The Nature of Masculinity*. Vancouver: UBC Press.

Grant, John. 2020. "Justifying Constituent Power in an Age of Populism." *Polity* 52 (1): 3–34.

Grattan, Laura. 2016. *Populism's Power: Radical Grassroots Democracy in America*. New York: Oxford University Press.

Hawley, George. 2017. *Making Sense of the Alt-Right*. New York: Columbia University Press.

Hearn, Jeff. 2014. "On Men, Organizations, and Intersectionality: Personal, Working, Political, and Theoretical Reflections (or How Organization Studies Met Profeminism)." *Equality, Diversity, and Inclusion: An International Journal* 33 (5): 414–28.

Houpt, Simon. 2017. "Rebel Media Co-founder Quits over Company's Ties to Right-Wing Groups." *Globe and Mail*, August 14. https://www.theglobeandmail.com /life/rebel-media-co-founder-quits-over-companys-perceived-white-supremacist -ties/article35988984.

Johnson, Daryl. 2012. *Right-Wing Resurgence: How a Domestic Terrorist Threat Is Being Ignored*. Lanham: Rowman & Littlefield Publishers.

Kassam, Ashifa. 2017. "Is North America's Opioid Epidemic a Crisis of Masculinity?" The *Guardian*, July 12. https://www.theguardian.com/world/2017/jul/12/opioids -crisis-men-overdoses-psychology.

Kimmel, Michael. 2000. "Reducing Men's Violence: The Personal Meets the Political." In *Male Roles, Masculinities and Violence: A Culture of Peace and Perspective*, edited by Ingeborg Breines, Robert Connell, and Ingrid Eide, 239–47. Paris: UNESCO.

———. 2013. *Angry White Men: American Masculinity at the End of an Era*. New York: Nation Books.

MacDonald, Fiona. 2017. "Knocking Down Walls in Political Science: In Defense of an Expansionist Feminist Agenda." *Canadian Journal of Political Science* 50 (2): 411–26.

Mutz, Diana C. 2018. "Status Threat, Not Economic Hardship, Explains the 2016 Presidential Vote." *Proceedings of the National Academy of Sciences* 115 (19). https://doi.org/10.1073/pnas.1718155115.

Nagle, Angela. 2017. *Kill All Normies: Online Culture Wars from 4chan and Tumblr to Trump and the Alt-Right*. London: Zero Books.

Neiwert, David. 2017. *Alt-America: The Rise of the Radical Right in the Age of Trump*. New York: Verso.

Nicholas, Lucy, and Christine Agius. 2018. *The Persistence of Global Masculinism: Discourse, Gender, and Neo-colonial Re-articulations of Violence*. Cham, Switzerland: Palgrave MacMillan.

Palmater, Pam. 2017. "Resurgence or Revelation? White Nationalist Legacies in Canada." *Canadian Dimension* 51 (4). https://canadiandimension.com/articles /view/resurgence-or-revelation-white-nationalist-legacies-in-canada

Sabin, Jerald. 2016. "Are You 'Man Enough'? Masculinity in the 2015 Federal Election." *Policy Options*, May 26. http://policyoptions.irpp.org/2016/05/26/man -enough-masculinity-2015-federal-election.

Schaffner, Brian F., Matthew MacWilliams, and Tatishe Nteta. 2017. "Understanding White Polarization in the 2016 Vote for President: The Sobering Role of Racism and Sexism." *Political Science Quarterly* 133 (1): 9–34.

Setzler, Mark, and Alixandra B. Yanus. 2018. "Why Did Women Vote for Donald Trump?" *PS: Political Science & Politics* 51 (3): 523–27. https://doi.org/10.1017 /S1049096518000355.

Shakeri, Sima. 2018. "Brock University to Vote on Stripping Garth Stevenson of Title after Racist Tweets. *Huffington Post*, August 12. https://www.huffingtonpost .ca/2018/08/12/ brock-university-professor-garth-stevenson-tweets-indigenous _a_23500869.

Southern Poverty Law Center. n.d. "Alt-Right." Accessed July 15, 2018.

Tasker, John Paul. 2018. "G7 Unity Torpedoed by Angry Trump Tweets Dismissing Trudeau as 'Dishonest & Weak.'" *CBC News*, June 9. https://www.cbc.ca/news /politics/g7-leaders-final-communique-1.4699658.

Todd, Cherie. 2015. "GamerGate and Resistance to the Diversification of Gaming Culture." *Women's Studies Journal* 29 (1): 64–67.

Urbinati, Nadia. 1998. "Democracy and Populism." *Constellations* 5 (1): 110–24.

Wilson, Jason. 2017. "Why Is the US Still Fighting the Civil War?" *The Guardian*, August 16. https://www.theguardian.com/world/2017/aug/16/why-is-the-us-still-fighting-the -civil-war.

Woodhams, Carol, Ben Lupton, and Marc Cowling. 2015. "The Presence of Ethnic Minority and Disabled Men in Feminised Work: Intersectionality, Vertical Segregation, and the Glass Escalator." *Sex Roles* 72 (7–8): 277–93.

FURTHER READING

Childs, Sarah, and Melanie Hughes. 2018. "'Which Men?' How an Intersectional Perspective on Men and Masculinities Helps Explain Women's Political Underrepresentation." *Politics & Gender* 14 (2): 282–87. https://doi.org/10.1017 /S1743923X1800017X.

Cohn, Carol, and Cynthia Enloe. 2003. "A Conversation with Cynthia Enloe: Feminists Look at Masculinity and the Men Who Wage War." *Signs* 28 (4): 1187–207.

Johnson, Allan G. 2014. *The Gender Knot: Unraveling Our Patriarchal Legacy.* 3rd ed. Philadelphia: Temple University Press.

Messner, Michael A., Max A. Greenberg, and Tal Peretz. 2015. *Some Men: Feminist Allies and the Movement to End Violence against Women.* Oxford: Oxford University Press.

Wendling, Mike. 2018. *Alt-Right: From 4chan to the White House.* London: Pluto Press.

About the Authors

Dr. Isabel Altamirano-Jiménez is Zapotec from the Isthmus of Tehuantepec, Mexico and Associate Professor of Political Science at the University of Alberta. As Canada Research Chair in Comparative Indigenous Feminist Studies, she examines the connections between body land, water, resource extraction, and Indigenous refusal in both Canada and Mexico. She has published numerous journal and book chapters and among her recent books are: *Living on the Land: Indigenous Women's Understandings of Place* (co-edited with Nathalie Kermoal; Athabasca University Press, 2016) and *Indigenous Encounters with Neoliberalism: Place, Women, and the Environment* (UBC Press, 2013).

Dr. Jeanette Ashe is Chair of the Political Science Department at Douglas College. Her research interests include political recruitment, political parties, representation, and gender and politics. She is the author of *Political Candidate Selection: Explaining Who Wins, Who Loses, and Underrepresentation in the UK* (Routledge, 2020) and has been published in the *Canadian Journal of Political Science, Party Politics, British Politics*, and the *Journal of Women, Politics and Policy*. Jeanette is part of the international Gender Equality Policy in Practice project. She has advised MPs in drafting legislation on electronic petitioning and gender equity.

Dr. Elaine Craig is Associate Professor at Schulich School of Law, Dalhousie University. She is the author of two books, *Troubling Sex: Towards* *a Legal Theory of Sexuality* (UBC Press, 2012) and *Putting Trials on Trial: Sexual Assault and the Failure of the Legal Profession* (McGill-Queen's University Press, 2018), as well as numerous articles on issues related to sexual assault law, criminal law ethics, feminist legal theory, and sexual minority rights.

Dr. Alexa DeGagne is Assistant Professor in Women's and Gender Studies at Athabasca University. Her research and teaching are focused on LGBTQ social justice movements and activisms in Canada and the United States. Her current SSHRC-funded research project examines the changing relationships between LGBTQ communities and police organizations across Canada. She has published widely and has forthcoming works on LGBTQ politics, specifically on the following topics: same-sex marriage activism in California; the history of LGBTQ politics in Alberta; LGBTQ refugees in the Canadian refugee system; homonationalism and the Canadian criminal justice system; policing and public sex; and the uses of anger as a tool in LGBTQ activism. Alexa's activism is based in her Edmonton queer community, where she has worked with several social justice projects as a community organizer and agitator, public educator, columnist, queer arts festival co-chair, and radio producer and host.

Dr. Alexandra Dobrowolsky is Full Professor of Political Science at Saint Mary's University and Adjunct Professor in the Faculty of Graduate Studies at Dalhousie University. She teaches in the areas of Canadian politics, comparative politics, and women/gender and politics. She has published in a range of national and international journals and written, edited, and co-edited six books on issues related to representation and citizenship broadly conceived, including *Women and Public Policy in Canada: Neo-liberalism and After?* (Oxford University Press, 2009). She is a contributor to, and the co-editor of, a special issue of the *Canadian Journal of Political Science* on "Finding Feminisms" (2017).

Dr. Pascale Dufour is Full Professor of Political Science at the University of Montreal. She specializes in issues related to collective action and representative democracy and does so from a comparative perspective. Her research projects include work on individual informal participation as a political action; the institutional foundations of struggles in housing and education in Spain, France, and Quebec; food sovereignty; and the World March of

Women. She is in charge of the undergraduate program in feminist studies, genders, and sexualities at the University of Montreal and heads the doctoral program in Political Science.

Dr. Maya Eichler is Canada Research Chair in Social Innovation and Community Engagement and Assistant Professor in the Department of Political and Canadian Studies and the Department of Women's Studies at Mount Saint Vincent University (Halifax). Her research interests lie in the transition from military to civilian life, gender and the armed forces, military families, and the privatization of military security. She has written the book *Militarizing Men: Gender, Conscription, and War in Post-Soviet Russia* (Stanford University Press, 2012) and edited the volume *Gender and Private Security in Global Politics* (Oxford University Press, 2015). Her recent articles have appeared in *Critical Military Studies, Armed Forces and Society, Critical Studies on Security, Citizenship Studies, International Journal, Military Behavioral Health*, and the *Journal of Military, Veteran and Family Health*. She co-chairs the 5th Canadian Division (5 CDN DIV) and Mount Saint Vincent University (MSVU) Operation Honour Community Working Group and serves as associate editor for the *International Feminist Journal of Politics*.

Dr. John Grant is Associate Professor in Political Science at King's University College at Western University. He is the author of *Dialectics and Contemporary Politics: Critique and Transformation from Hegel through Post-Marxism* (Routledge, 2011) and *Lived Fictions: Unity and Exclusion in Canadian Politics* (University of British Columbia Press, 2018), as well as articles on topics such as populism and constituent power, political imaginaries, riots, and citizens' assemblies. He is also a co-editor of the journal *Contemporary Political Theory*.

Dr. Fiona MacDonald is Associate Professor specializing in contemporary political theory at the University of the Fraser Valley. Prior to her current appointment, she was Assistant Professor in Canadian Politics at the University of Manitoba. Dr. MacDonald co-edited the "Finding Feminisms" special issue of the *Canadian Journal of Political Science* (June 2017). Her other publications can be found in the journals *Hypatia, Citizenship Studies, Constellations*, and *Canadian Public Administration*. Her article "Indigenous Peoples and Neoliberal 'Privatization' in Canada: Opportunities, Cautions and Constraints" won the 2012 John McMenemy Prize for the best article published in volume 44 of the *Canadian Journal of Political Science*.

Dr. Michael Orsini is Full Professor in the Institute of Feminist and Gender Studies and the School of Political Studies and previously served as Vice-Dean, Graduate Studies in the Faculty of Social Sciences at the University of Ottawa. He is in the process of completing a SSHRC-funded study exploring the role of emotions and stigma in a range of contested policy fields. Michael is interested in critical approaches to policy and politics, and specifically approaches that highlight the role of marginalized communities in policy-making. He is co-editor of *Seeing Red: HIV/AIDS and Public Policy in Canada* (University of Toronto Press, 2018), as well as *Mobilizing Metaphor: Art, Culture and Disability Activism in Canada* (UBC Press, 2016), and the *Handbook of Critical Policy Studies* (Edward Elgar, 2016).

Dr. Geneviève Pagé is Associate Professor of Political Science at the Université du Québec à Montréal. She teaches political theory and specializes in the development, transformation, and movement of feminist theory across linguistic and cultural barriers, with a focus on the Quebec women's movement as a social movement and its difficulty translating its commitment to an intersectional approach into concrete practices. Her research interests also include feminist and decolonial pedagogies and the (co-)construction of knowledge.

Dr. Stephanie Paterson is Full Professor in the Department of Political Science at Concordia University. She specializes in feminist and critical policy studies, with particular focus on state feminism, gender mainstreaming, and feminist policy theory. Her work has been featured in outlets such as *Critical Policy Studies*; *Gender, Work and Organizations*; *Administrative Theory & Praxis*; and the *Canadian Journal of Political Science*. She is currently working on several projects, including an exploration of Canadian gender mainstreaming at federal and provincial levels; an investigation of the transition to motherhood; and the role of emotions, care, and empathy in policy processes.

Dr. Toby Rollo is Assistant Professor of Political Science at Lakehead University. He specializes in Western political thought and his research explores the history of ideas related to political agency, how these ideas came to shape modern democratic institutions, and the unexpected exclusions they can produce. His published work on political exclusion as it relates to children can be found in *Political Theory, Settler Colonial Studies, Journal of Black Studies*, and in a number of book chapters.

Dr. Francesca Scala is Full Professor in the Department of Political Science at Concordia University. Her general research interests include gender and public policy, gender mainstreaming, the politics of reproductive technologies, and the politics of knowledge and expertise in policy-making. Her current research includes a study on gender mainstreaming in Canada and a project on gender and street-level bureaucracies in work-care reconciliation policy. Her research appears in *Policy and Society, Policy Sciences, Canadian Journal of Political Science,* and *Gender, Work and Organization.*

Dr. Stacy Clifford Simplican is Senior Lecturer in the Women's and Gender Studies Program at Vanderbilt University. She is the author of *The Capacity Contract: Intellectual Disability and the Question of Citizenship* (University of Minnesota Press, 2015); her book analyses the role of intellectual and developmental disabilities in the history of political thought and the disability rights movement. Stacy received her PhD in political science and a Graduate Certificate in women's and gender studies from Vanderbilt University in 2011. In 2013–15, she was a postdoctoral fellow at Michigan State University and the National University of Ireland Galway. Some of Stacy's articles appear in *Disability & Society; Contemporary Political Theory; Politics, Groups & Identities;* and *Hypatia: A Journal of Feminist Philosophy.* Her research interests include disability studies, democratic theory, feminist care theory, and the social inclusion of people with intellectual and developmental disabilities.

Dr. Tamara A. Small (PhD, Queen's University) is Associate Professor in the Department of Political Science at the University of Guelph. Her research interest is digital politics: the use and impact of the internet by Canadian political actors. She is the co-author of *Fighting for Votes: Parties, the Media and Voters in an Ontario Election* (UBC Press, 2015) and the co-editor of *Mind the Gaps: Canadian Perspectives on Gender and Politics* (Fernwood, 2013) and *Political Communication in Canada: Meet the Press, Tweet the Rest* (UBC Press, 2014).

Dr. Gina Starblanket is a Canada Research Chair in the Politics of Decolonization and Assistant Professor in the Department of Political Science at the University of Calgary. Gina is Cree/Saulteaux and a member of the Star Blanket Cree Nation in Treaty 4 territory. She is co-author of *Storying Violence: Unravelling Colonial Narratives in the Stanley Trial* and co-editor of the fifth edition of *Visions of the Heart: Issues Involving Indigenous People in Canada.* Gina has also published critical work in the *Canadian Journal of*

Political Science, The American Indian Culture and Research Journal, and *Constitutional Forum.* Her work is centred in Indigenous and Canadian politics and takes up issues surrounding treaty implementation, gender, feminism, decolonization, resurgence, and relationality.

Dr. Debra Thompson is Associate Professor of Political Science at McGill University, specializing in race and ethnic politics. A leading scholar of the study of race politics in comparative context, Debra has teaching and research interests in the relationships among race, the state, and public policy in advanced industrialized democracies. She has taught at the University of Oregon and Northwestern University and held a SSHRC postdoctoral fellowship with the Center for American Political Studies at Harvard University in 2010. Her award-winning book *The Schematic State: Race, Transnationalism, and the Politics of the Census* (Cambridge University Press, 2016) is a study of the political development of racial classifications on the national censuses of the United States, Canada, and Great Britain.

Dr. Chamindra Kumari Weerawardhana is a political analyst and an international gender justice activist working in the areas of inclusive reproductive justice and intersectional feminist advocacy. She is Research Affiliate at the Centre for Gender, Feminisms and Sexualities at University College Dublin. She currently serves as the Secretary to the Regional Steering Committee of the Asia-Pacific Transgender Network. She is also the founder and Executive Director of the Consortium for Intersectional Justice, a policy dialogue and human rights advocacy body based in Sri Lanka. In 2017 she was the recipient of a Transgender Studies Chair fellowship from the University of Victoria. Her ongoing research carries a three-pronged focus on gender politics, intersectional feminist international relations, and the politics of deeply divided places. She has held elected office as the LGBTQIA+ Officer and an Executive Committee Member of the Labour Party in Northern Ireland. Dr. Weerawardhana is the author of *Decolonising Peacebuilding: Managing Conflict from Northern Ireland to Sri Lanka and Beyond* (2018). She is a graduate of Université François Rabelais in Tours (France) and of Queen's University Belfast and has taught in the French public university system. A Marie Sklodowska-Curie fellowship alumna, Dr. Weerawardhana has had her writing published in peer-reviewed journals and media outlets in several countries.

Dr. Sarah Marie Wiebe is Assistant Professor in the Department of Political Science at the University of Hawai'i, Manoa, where she focuses on environmental sustainability. She grew up on Coast Salish territory in British Columbia, BC, and now lives in Honolulu, Hawaiʻi. She has published in journals including *Citizenship Studies* and *Studies in Social Justice*. Her book *Everyday Exposure: Indigenous Mobilization and Environmental Justice in Canada's Chemical Valley* (UBC Press, 2016) won the Charles Taylor Book Award (2017) and examines policy responses to the impact of pollution on the Aamjiwnaang First Nation's environmental health. Alongside Dr. Jennifer Lawrence (Virginia Tech), she is the co-editor of *Biopolitical Disaster* (Routledge, 2017). At the intersections of environmental justice and citizen engagement, her teaching and research interests emphasize political ecology, participatory policy-making, and deliberative dialogue. As a collaborative researcher and film-maker, she worked with Indigenous communities on sustainability-themed films including *Indian Givers* (2012) and *To Fish as Formerly* (2014). She is currently collaborating with artists from Attawapiskat on a project entitled Reimagining Attawapiskat, funded through a SSHRC Insight Development Grant. Sarah is also Project Co-director for the Seascape Indigenous Storytelling Studio, funded through a SSHRC Insight Grant with research partners from the University of Victoria, University of British Columbia, and coastal Indigenous communities.

Index

Page numbers with *t* indicate tables. Page numbers with *f* indicate figures.

transformations
  gender equality, 58
  and Indigenous Peoples' resistance,
    1–2
  military culture, 145–46, 154–55
  Quebec women's movement, 235
  using feminism for, 383
transgender people
  and Black feminist activism, 309,
    311–15
  defined, 320n5
  as elected, 92n1, 320n4
  in military, 155
  and police, 250, 261, 264
  and Pride parades, 266–67
  progressive developments, 304
  and Quebec women's movement, 231
transgender studies, 306–08
Transgender Studies Initiative, 306–07
Transgender Studies Quarterly (TSQ)
  (journal), 307, 308
"The Transgender Tipping Point"
  (Steinmetz), 304
transphobia, 5, 319, 320n4
Tremblay, Manon, 70
trolls, 188–89, 382. *See also* alt-right
Tronto, Joan, 334
Trudeau, Justin/Liberal government
  and Canada's relations with
    Indigenous Peoples, 3, 288
  dates of government, 92n4
  and Facebook feminism, 69, 86
  as feminist, 23, 30–31, 41
  Feminist G7, 24
  feminist government, 49, 52–53, 58,
    61–62 (*see also* GBA+; GRF)
  vs Harper, 23, 24, 30, 86–87, 91, 92n5,
    93n14, 94n33
  and immigration, 24, 36–40, 37
  infrastructure of parliament, 75–80, 76t
  and masculinity, 368–69
  and military/defence policy, 153–54
  and neoliberal feminism, 31–33
  policies and legislation, 80–90, 81t, 87t

  representations in parliament,
    72–75, 72t, 73, 87t, 92–93nn5–9,
    93nn11–15, 94n31
Trudeau, Pierre Elliot, 23, 25–26
Trump, Donald, 33, 243, 336, 369, 370,
  376–77, 382
Trump, Ivanka, 33
Truth, Sojourner, 8
Tsartlip Nation, 291
Tsawwassen Nation, 291
Tsleil-Waututh Nation, 282, 288–92, 297
T'Sou-ke Nation, 291
Tulloch, Michael, 247
Tungohan, Ethel, 7–8, 11
Twitter, 177, 180–81, 185–86, 188–92,
  193n2

unemployment, 246, 337
unions, 168
United Declaration on the Rights of
  Indigenous Peoples, 299n4
United Nations Agenda 2030, 305
United Nations Year and Decade for
  Disabled Persons, 331
universal design, 337
University of Arizona, 306
University of Hawai'i, 295–96
University of Victoria, 307
UNSCR 1325, 145, 149–50
Urback, Robyn, 350
US Surgeon General, 353

Vahabi, Mandana, 38
Vancouver Pride, 265–66, 268–69,
  270–73
Vandenbeld, Anita, 86
Vanhala, Lisa, 330
#victimblaming, 181, 187
Vindication of the Rights of Women
  (Wollstonecraft), 202–03
violence. *See also* sexual violence
  of alt-right, 370
  against Black people (*see* Black
    Lives Matter)

against children, 213n1
and data, 59
domestic violence, 186
and toxic masculinity, 380–83
VOICES, 270, 274
vulnerability, 334–35, 336–37

wage disparity, 31, 39, 60–61, 63n4, 246
Wager (court case), 105–06
Wängnerud, Lena, 70
war, 142, 144, 149
Ware, Syrus Marcus, 307–08
warriors, 145, 148, 154
washrooms, 79
water, 169, 170, 286
Watson, Emma, 28
As We Have Always Done
      (Simpson), 135
Weir, Erin, 82
#WelcomeToCanada, 36–37
welfare policies, 339
Wente, Margaret, 246–47
Wettlaufer, Alex, 245
whales, 291
white collar crimes, 39–40
white privilege, 262, 265–66, 267, 268
white supremacy, 370, 371–72
white transmasculine people, 307
white women
   and Black feminists, 209
   and Combahee River Collective, 249
   feminist foreign policy, 306
   gender mainstreaming, 4
   and hashtag feminism, 189–90
   in labour market, 63n4
   and Quebec feminists, 227, 231–32

Royal Commission on the Status of
   Women, 52
and Steubenville rape case, 185
#WhyIStayed, 186
Wilde-Blavatsky, Adele, 189
Williams, Alexandria, 251
Williams, Sherri, 186
Wilson-Raybould, Jody, 41, 92n5
Wollstonecraft, Mary, 202
"On Women" (Schopenhauer), 202
Women, Peace and Security (UN
   resolution), 145, 149–50
#WomenAgainstFeminism (WAF), 190–91
Women's Declaration against Kinder
   Morgan Man Camps, 289–90
Women's March on Washington, 2,
   180, 340
Women's Marches, 2, 180, 228, 234, 340
Women's Warrior Society, 289–90
Wong, Josephine Pui-Hing, 38
Woodhams, Carol, 375
Woodward, Rachel, 145
work-family balance, 29
World March of Women, 228, 234
World Pride 2014, 264
Wright, Jan, 357, 363
Wu, Brianna, 382
Wynne, Kathleen, 245

xenophobia, 372

Yanus, Alixandra B., 376

Zapotec peoples, 162, 167–71
Zero Tolerance for Barbaric Cultural
   Practices Act, 28